THE DEVELOPMENT OF
MORAL THEOLOGY

Selected Titles from the MORAL TRADITIONS SERIES
James F. Keenan, SJ, *Editor*

THE DEVELOPMENT OF
MORAL
THEOLOGY

FIVE STRANDS

Charles E. Curran

Georgetown University Press
Washington, DC

Library of Congress Cataloging-in-Publication Data

Curran, Charles E.
    The development of moral theology : five strands / Charles E. Curran.
        pages cm. — (Moral Traditions)
    Includes bibliographical references and index.
    ISBN 978-1-62616-019-4 (pbk. : alk. paper)
    1. Christian ethics—Catholic authors.   I. Title.
BJ1249.C815   2013
241'.042—dc23

2013002330

15   14   13   9 8 7 6 5 4 3 2   First printing

Printed in the United States of America

To my friends in Dallas, especially
The Gus Melito Group
Members of Community
The Sunday Night Supper Group
Gianna and John
Leroy
Milam

CONTENTS

PREFACE

THIS BOOK TRACES the historical development of five strands in the shaping of moral theology: (1) sin, reconciliation, and the manuals of moral theology; (2) Thomas Aquinas and the Thomistic tradition; (3) natural law; (4) the papal teaching office; and (5) the Second Vatican Council. These five strands are what differentiate Catholic moral theology from other forms of Christian ethics coming out of other Christian traditions and approaches.

To properly evaluate, analyze, and criticize these strands in moral theology today, it is most helpful to know how they developed historically. In light of this, the book studies the historical development of each of these strands down through the years. Many studies over the years have examined each of these strands and their historical development. However, no one has attempted to bring together in one volume a critical study of the historical development of these five significant strands in the weaving of moral theology today.

Moral theologians by definition are not historians. I am not a historian and make no pretense to be one. My historical knowledge is dependent on the many works that are explicitly mentioned in the course of this volume. However, since these strands are theological and ethical in nature, the moral theologian brings these theological and ethical perspectives to the historical development of these aspects. My own approach to and understanding of moral theology have obviously influenced how I have put together, interpreted, and analyzed the historical data. After analyzing the historical development of these strands, a final concluding chapter shows how moral theology today stands with regard to each of these strands and their influence on the contemporary scene.

I am most grateful to all those who have helped me in the research and writing of this book. My students, faculty colleagues, the librarians of Bridwell Library, and the administration of the university have made

Southern Methodist University (SMU) a very congenial and challenging academic home. Since coming to SMU in 1991, I have been privileged to hold the Elizabeth Scurlock University Professorship of Human Values, established by Jack and Laura Lee Blanton in memory of Laura Lee Blanton's mother. Although Laura Lee Blanton died in 1999, she continues to influence the life of SMU thanks to the major and significant benefactions of the Blantons. Richard Brown, the director of Georgetown University Press, and James F. Keenan, the editor of its Moral Traditions series—together with the most cooperative and competent staff of the press—have been most supportive in publishing my research. The critical reading of the manuscript and suggestions by Julia Fleming, John Gargan, Kenneth Himes, and Richard Sparks were most helpful. This manuscript would never have seen the light of day without all the work of my administrative and graduate assistant, Christopher Dowdy, who, in addition to professionally preparing this manuscript for publication, has assisted in many ways with his efficient and friendly help.

CHAPTER 1

STRAND ONE

Sin, Reconciliation, and the Manuals of Moral Theology

Sin, CONVERSION, AND FORGIVENESS constitute significant aspects in the moral life of the Christian. Moral theology as a thematic, critical, and systematic reflection on the Christian moral life must pay serious attention to these realities. These realities have also exerted a significant influence on how moral theology has conceived its own purpose and function. This chapter discusses the historical development of these important realities and how they shaped the discipline of moral theology.

BIBLICAL UNDERSTANDING OF SIN AND CONVERSION

The nature of sin is central to understanding the message of Jesus and of the Church. Jesus came to redeem us through his gracious love from the power of sin. The paschal mystery involving the life, death, and resurrection of Jesus constitutes the victory of Jesus over sin and death. In a very true sense, sin brings about the death of Jesus, but through redeeming love Jesus triumphs over sin and death.

Perhaps the best theological understanding of sin is found in the book of Genesis. In the popular mind, Genesis tells us the story of Creation. Genesis, after all, is the first book of the Bible, and it begins with the Creation story or really two different versions of the Creation story. But I think that Genesis has a much different purpose. Genesis was never meant to be an eyewitness account of the beginning of life in this world through the creative activity of God. Genesis is a very mythical account written centuries into human history. The authors and redactors of Genesis were dealing with the problem that has always faced religious believers—how can you believe in a good and gracious God in the midst of all the evil, sorrow, and suffering that exists in our world? Genesis responds to this existential question by pointing out that God does not cause evil because God created all things good. Evil comes from the devil and human beings.

There are two different Creation narratives at the beginning of Genesis. Genesis 1–2:4a comes from the priestly source and follows the trajectory of the six days of Creation, ending with the creation of human beings with the frequent repetition that God saw that the work of Creation was good. Genesis 2:4b–3:24 comes from the Yawhist source. Here there is a different version of the Creation narrative. The creation of human beings does not come at the end of Creation, as in the first version. Adam is created and, after Adam, God creates the beasts of the field and birds of the air. But even with these, Adam was still lonely and had no one to share love and life with him. So God took a rib from Adam and made the woman. But then came the story of the "Fall." Only good comes from God. Sin and evil come from the serpent and from the free will of human beings. The whole thrust of the story is to show that evil does not come from God.

In describing the Fall, there is an insightful description of sin. The popular understanding of the sin of Adam and Eve is that they disobeyed God's command and ate of the fruit of the tree. Their sin was thus an act of disobedience against the command of God. But the understanding of sin portrayed here is much deeper. Sin affects our multiple relationships with God, neighbor, world, and self. Sin ruptures the relationship with God. Adam and Eve refused to accept their relationship of loving dependence on God; they wanted to be like God. In a very anthropomorphic way, the story narrates that God comes down in the cool of the evening to walk with them in the garden. What happened after their sin? They hid themselves because they had broken their relationship with God. At the end of the story of the Fall, God expels them from the garden. This expulsion is not an extrinsic penalty thought up by an angry God. Their expulsion from the garden constitutes the logical consequence of their own action. They had broken their relationship with God and could no longer live in the garden.

Sin also affects the relationship with the neighbor. This section of Genesis provides a lyrical account of the love union between Adam and Eve. Despite all of creation, Adam was lonely and yearned for a helpmate. So God made Eve. She was bone of his bone and flesh of his flesh. Genesis describes their relationship as leaving all else and becoming two in one flesh. This relationship is greatly affected by their sin. When God confronts Adam about what he did, Adam points the accusing finger at Eve—she did it, not me. Instead of defending her and giving his life for her, he accused her. Genesis 4 tells the mythical story of the children of Adam and Eve—Cain and Abel. Cain became angry that God had no regard for his offering, but God did accept the offering of his brother Abel. Cain was jealous of Abel, and then killed him. The following chapters of Genesis show how sin spread throughout the world, so that by the time of Noah, there were very few just people.

According to Genesis, sin also affects human beings in their relationship to the world. Before the Fall, Adam had dominion over all the animals and plants that God had made. There was a perfect harmony with all other things serving the man and the woman. Recall that Adam had given a name to all the cattle, the beasts, and the wild birds. But sin brought discord into this harmonious world. In accord with the understanding of the time, the man's life was primarily working to provide food and sustenance. But as a result of sin, the earth was now cursed, and the man suffered and sweat in his toil and efforts to till the soil. The earth was no longer like putty in his hand that he could easily work with; instead he knew sweat, toil, tears, and pain in his working. Also in accord with the prevailing understanding, the primary role of the woman was that of child bearer. As a result of sin, she now experienced the pains of childbirth and brought forth her children in pain and suffering. The muscles and tissues of her body would resist the process of birth. Childbearing should have been a joyful bringing of new life into the world, but now it was accompanied by pain and sorrow.

Sin also affects the relationship of human beings to themselves. Genesis 2:25 notes that the man and the woman were both naked but they felt no shame. After the Fall, their eyes were opened and they realized they were naked, so they made themselves loincloths. As created by God, the individual human person lived in perfect harmony with oneself. But after the Fall, they experienced the lack of harmony in their own selves. Genesis gives a most insightful understanding of the reality of sin in light of these fourfold relationships. Since the fundamental role of Jesus involves redeeming us from the power of sin and making us sharers in God's love and life through the power of the Spirit, the new life must be seen in terms of the same four relationships.

In the Hebrew Bible, "covenant" is the primary way of understanding the relationship of God to God's people. God's loving-kindness moves God to choose a people as his own, and in return the people promise to be God's people. God is faithful to the covenant promise, but the people often fall and do not live in accord with the covenant. The covenantal relationship thus describes the basic relationship of the individual with God. The initiative here is on God's part—the free gift of grace. The people are called to respond to this gift. But the covenant does not just involve individuals. God made a covenant with a people. The individuals are called to be members of this community.[1]

The New Testament retains the concept of covenant, but especially the Synoptic Gospels see the relationship to God in light of the twofold command of loving God and neighbor (Mt 22:34–40; Mk 12:28–34; Lk 10:25–28). Thus, God's love for us also involves our relationship to other human beings. This raises the obvious question: who is my neighbor? The answer in Luke 10:25–37 is the person in need. Therefore, the new life in Christ Jesus also involves our relationship with neighbors far and near.

The twofold love command in the Synoptic Gospels also speaks about self-love.[2] We are to love our neighbor as ourselves. The Catholic tradition has always recognized the role for a proper love of self while also appreciating the danger of our inordinate self-love. The Christian scriptures heavily emphasize the kingdom or the reign of God. This is to be a reign of justice and peace, so the Christian must work for justice and peace in our world. Just as sin involves the fourfold relationships with God, neighbor, world, and self, so too the new life in Christ Jesus embraces the same relationships.

In light of such an understanding of sin and the new life we have in Christ Jesus through the power of the Spirit, we can understand better how Mark's Gospel describes the preaching of Jesus. Jesus came into Galilee proclaiming the good news. The time has come; the reign of God is at hand; repent (change your heart) and believe in the good news (Mk 1:15). The Greek word "*metanoia*" means a change of heart and is perhaps best translated as a true conversion—moving from sin to grace, from enmity to friendship with God. Logically, such conversion must involve the same fourfold relationships.

In this general understanding, sin is not seen as a particular act but as the state or basic orientation of the person that has to be changed. Sin in this case is always in the singular. The Pauline writings emphasize this concept of sin. Sin refers to the ontological state of the person. Paul often refers to this state as slavery or estrangement from God. The person is either under sin or under grace. In Christ Jesus we are freed from sin and brought into the true freedom of the children of God—free to be at the service of God and others. According to the letter to the Romans, the Christian is freed from sin, death, and the law and now enjoys this true freedom of the children of God. Paul in 1 Corinthians 6:20 and 7:23 insists that the Christian is no longer a slave to sin because the Christian has been bought and paid for by Christ. Paul also describes sin as a state of enmity with God. We were enemies, but now we have been reconciled through the death of Jesus (Rom 5:10–11). For Paul there is this struggle between Christ and sin, so that redemption brings about reconciliation. Christians are no longer under sin and the law but now live under the power of the Spirit. The Christian is a new spiritual being who is dead to sin.[3]

The Johannine writings likewise stress the notion of sin in the singular, mentioning it thirteen times in the singular while the plural appears only three times. John's notion of sin is that of separation from God and being in hatred of God and servitude to the devil.[4]

The New Testament also speaks of sin in the plural, which refers to sinful actions. The Greek word "hamartia," which is often used in the New Testament, basically signifies missing the mark and thus refers primarily to acts. In Matthew's Gospel, Mary's son is to be called Jesus because he will save his people from their sins (Mt 1:21). The Synoptic Gospels frequently use the plural. The Lord's Prayer has two different versions in the Synoptic Gospels. The Matthean version (6:9–13) prays for God to forgive our debts as we also have forgiven our debtors. The Lucan version (11:2–4) asks forgiveness for our sins as we ourselves forgive everyone who is in debt to us. Most English translations today speak of "our trespasses."

The New Testament frequently contains catalogues of sins. In the Synoptic Gospels, for example, Matthew 15:19 and the parallel verse in Mark 7:21 mention fornication, theft, murder, adultery, avarice, malice, deceit, indecency, envy, slander, pride, and folly. The Pauline writings likewise contain such catalogues. As an illustration, Galatians 5:20 lists fornication, gross indecency and sexual irresponsibility, idolatry and sorcery, feuds and wrangling, jealousy, bad temper and quarrels, disagreements, factions, envy, drunkenness, avarice, and similar things. The pastoral epistles and the catholic epistles likewise contain such lists. For example, 2 Timothy 3:2–5 recognizes that some people are self-centered and grasping, boastful, arrogant and rude, disobedient to their parents, ungrateful, irreligious, heartless, and implacable, slanderous, profligates, savages and enemies of everything that is good.

Sins in the plural are the concrete manifestation in the New Testament of sin in the singular, which I have understood in terms of affecting my relationships with God, neighbor, world, and self.

This role of the forgiveness of sin should have a significant place in the ongoing life of the community of the disciples of Jesus. The New Testament itself testifies to the role of the Church in the forgiveness of sin. Luke's Gospel ends with the admonition that repentance and forgiveness of sins should be preached in Jesus's name to all the nations beginning from Jerusalem. Matthew 18 speaks of forgiveness in terms of the sin of a brother against you. First you should go to the brother in private. If that does not work, bring in two or three witnesses; if that does not work, go to the Church. If the sinner refuses to listen to the Church, let him be to you as a Gentile and a tax collector. Matthew then has Jesus telling the disciples that whatever you bind on earth shall be bound in heaven, and whatever you loose on earth shall be loosed in heaven.

Karl Rahner and others maintain that binding and loosing are two distinct and successive acts in the total reaction of the Church to sin. To bind means to put under the ban in the sense that the sinner by her actions separates herself from the love that joins together the members of the Church into one community, so that the Church must react in a visible way to the sin of the member. Loosing, then, is the reconciliation of the penitent sinner with the Church community. Such an understanding fits with the context of Matthew 18 and with some older Israelitic traditions. This process of excluding and then reconciling the sinner with the community is not the same as the contemporary canonical practice of excommunication, which comes from a different source. Such an approach was more visible in the practice of canonical penance in the early church but is still present in a recognition that the person in mortal sin cannot fully participate in Eucharistic communion. Reconciliation with the Church constitutes the sign of the reality of reconciliation with God.[5]

This interpretation of binding and loosing has been rediscovered only recently and is not accepted by all. The more common opinion, especially in the pre–Vatican II Church, sees binding and loosing as two distinct and alternate powers that can be exercised by the priest in the sacrament of penance. The priest has to choose between the two powers of loosing and remitting sin or binding and retaining sin—in other words, between the judgment to give absolution and remit sin or not to give absolution and thus retain sin.[6] The current practice of penance obviously influenced this understanding. No matter how this passage is interpreted, it serves as a scriptural basis for the important role of the Church in continuing the mission of Jesus to forgive sin.

The other main Gospel reference to the role of the Church in continuing the mission of forgiving sins is found in John 20:21–23. On the evening of the Resurrection, Jesus appeared to the disciples with the gift of peace and sent them out as the Father had sent him: through the gift of the Holy Spirit, "whose sins you shall forgive, they are forgiven them; and whose sins you shall retain, they are retained" (23).

In biblical times, the followers of Jesus recognized that the Church was a community of salvation with authority over sin. The sins of individuals affect the community of the blessed, and the community's prayers and decisions about sinners had consequences in the eyes of God for the future fate of the sinner.[7] The passages from Matthew 18 and John 20 that recognize the Church's power to forgive sin have already been mentioned. Paul was somewhat optimistic about the likelihood of sinners being reconciled with the Church and God after they had been separated from the community because of their sin. The first letter of John 5:14–17 is hesitant to admit that all sins can be forgiven. Hebrews 6:4–8 explicitly says that those who have fallen away after receiving the Spirit and being cleansed cannot be restored again to repentance. The Synoptics report Jesus's saying that the sin against the Holy Spirit cannot be forgiven (Mk 3:29; Mt 12:32; Lk 12:10).

The Church, in fidelity to the invitation of Jesus, has continued to carry out the work of reconciliation and the forgiveness of sin. So central is this mission that in the Catholic tradition the two sacraments of baptism and penance concentrate on this aspect of the encounter of a loving God with the sinner. But other sacraments such as the Eucharist also share the same dimension.

This comparatively short development of sin, conversion, and forgiveness in the New Testament is sufficient to show the central theological importance of sin and reconciliation in the Christian life in general and the Roman Catholic Church in particular. In the Catholic tradition the

understanding of sin is intrinsically connected with the sacrament of penance, but the theory and practice of the sacrament of penance have
changed dramatically in the course of history.

RECONCILIATION AND SIN
IN THE EARLY CHURCH

Despite some possible limitations, the New Testament testifies to sinners
being reconciled with the blessed community. In the first century of its
existence, the community of the disciples of Jesus recognized the possibility that one who had sinned against the holiness of the community could
at least in some circumstances undergo conversion, repentance, and be
reconciled with the community, which is indicative of one's reconciliation
with God. But there is no description of the nature of this process, the
ritual used, or any possible limitations.[8]

The understanding of the reconciliation of sinners with the Church
and thus with God was obviously influenced by many factors in the developing life of the Church. In the very early postapostolic times, the
churches were very small Christian communities scattered about the
world. They often saw themselves as very different from and separate
from the world around them. Members joined these small communities
in the beginning especially through adult baptism. Christians were very
committed to living out fully the life of this holy and blessed community.
To sin grievously was not only a betrayal of one's own commitment but
also a sin against this holy community. This understanding logically could
lead to some limitations on the possibility of forgiveness and reconciliation. Throughout the whole history of the sacrament of penance there is
a tension between what has often been called rigorism and the mercy of
God. Perhaps it should better be seen in terms of the tension between
the holiness of the community and the mercy and forgiveness of God
manifested in the community. Later, when the vast majority of Christians
were baptized as infants, the community of the Church had a very different ethos and feeling. The Church had many more members and often
they were not as committed as those who had been baptized as adults.
The original small and scattered communities were also greatly affected
by persecutions and then later by their own growth and acceptance within
the broader society. Different practices developed within the individual

communities, and for a comparatively long time there was nothing like a universally accepted practice of penance.[9]

Even in the second century these intense and even radical small Christian communities consisting of many who were baptized as adults recognized the reality of sins committed by their members. Recall that the Acts of the Apostles 5:1–12 recounts the story of Ananias and Sapphira, who lied to Peter about the money they received from the sale of their property. Cyrille Vogel provides a catalogue of sins found in the writings of the Apostolic Fathers and the Apologetes. Often these lists are somewhat similar, which indicates there could very well have been a common ethical catechesis at this time. Vogel reduces these lists to twelve categories— impurity including adultery, fornication, pederasty, concupiscence; murder; idolatry; magic; avarice; stealing; envy; lying in all its forms; wickedness, including anger, perversity, and injustice; pride; inconstancy; and drunkenness and intemperance.[10]

The most significant document from the second century is the *Shepherd of Hermas*, which was even considered by many as canonical and belonging to scripture. This work was entirely devoted to penance. However, it is very allegorical and often difficult to understand. Hermas emphasizes both the necessity and the possibility of forgiveness and reconciliation through genuine conversion. God recognizes human frailty and offers the possibility of conversion. But this possibility of conversion is offered only once. This characteristic of penance as being nonrepeatable became a significant part of the subsequent practice. Hermas, however, set forth no process by which this conversion takes place or what reconciliation with the Church involves in practice.

We know more about the understanding and practice of conversion and reconciliation at the end of the second and the beginning of the third centuries, especially from the writings of Tertullian (c. 160–c. 225), who devoted a number of works to penance. Tertullian himself in later life embraced the rigid Montanist approach, which today we call a heresy.

Tertullian distinguished grave sins from the daily sins that we all commit. The penitential process for grave sins involved a long and severe time of probation ending with reconciliation to the community given by the bishop, which is the sign of forgiveness and reconciliation with God. The process begins with internal acts of conversion expressed in external signs such as penitential garb and practices. After a long and very difficult time of probation and works of satisfaction, reconciliation could take place. Tertullian insisted that the offering of reconciliation could be had only once in a lifetime. Like the first forgiveness of baptism, the second penance could not be repeated.

Tertullian the Montanist insisted that some sins could never be forgiven through this process leading to reconciliation. They were unforgivable. Some claim that the sins that could not be forgiven were the famous triad of idolatry, murder, and adultery, but Tertullian also included blasphemy, fornication, false witness, cheating, and involvement with the spectacles of the circus and stadium.

Tertullian employed the Greek word "*exomologesis*" to describe the public process of repentance and reconciliation. The word basically means confession, but it is different from our modern understanding of confession. According to James Dallen, *exomologesis* acknowledges God's greatness, a greatness shown through mercy leading sinners to repentance. It is not primarily the acknowledgment of sins but rather a confession of faith, the praise of God, and an appeal for the community's prayerful support.[11]

Controversy arose in the third century, especially in Carthage and Rome, about reconciliation for those Christians who in the midst of persecution had given up their faith. Cyprian, bishop of Carthage, ultimately solved this problem created by the Christians who had given up their faith (the *lapsi*, or lapsed) during the Decian persecution in the middle of the third century. A synod of North African bishops in 251 accepted Cyprian's policy. Those who through bribery received false documents saying they had apostatized even though they had not done so could be reconciled if they had done penance. But those who actually offered pagan sacrifices had to do lifelong penance and could be reconciled only on their deathbeds. But a year later, faced with a threat of a new persecution (which never occurred), Cyprian changed his policy. The bishop of Carthage was afraid that the penitent *lapsi* would again apostatize during the persecution if they were without full Eucharistic participation. He maintained their situation now was analogous to a deathbed emergency and declared they could be reconciled immediately. Thus Cyprian adopted a quite lenient approach.

During the third century Rome also had a division over reconciling those who had lapsed at the time of persecution. After a long and somewhat bitter controversy, the more lenient approach was adopted, which showed that the Church and the bishop had authority over sin. Cyprian also gives us more information about the process of *exomologesis*. This process began with the laying on of hands by the bishop and ended with the laying on of hands. The laying on of hands appears to be both an exorcism and a granting of peace with the Church community and the gift of the Holy Spirit.

CANONICAL AND TARIFF PENANCE

From the fourth to the sixth centuries in the post-Constantinian era, there emerged what has most accurately been called "canonical penance" since it was governed by canons or Church laws. Some have called this public penance, but such terminology is not accurate and can be very misleading since it never involved the public confession of sins. This canonical penance grew out of the previous practices. It could be done only once and never repeated. Interior conversion was the starting point that led sinners into the canonical penance that involved a long and extremely severe period of expiation before reconciliation. The object of this penance was grave or capital sins. From various sources, Cyrille Vogel catalogues these grave sins as sins against the Decalogue, the capital sins themselves—avarice, hatred, envy, anger, pride, and habitual drunkenness—and diverse faults such as grave civil crimes. Reconciliation for these sins requires canonical penance. Venial sins include lesser faults involving one's relationship to God, to neighbor, and to oneself. Private works of penance, prayer, fasting, and almsgiving could bring about the forgiveness of these sins.[12]

The penitential process for grave sins involved three stages. The entry into this order of penance was a public act done by the imposition of the hands of the bishop in the presence of the Christian community, but there was no public confession of sins as such. The public entry into the order of penitence was not meant to be a form of humiliation but rather a solemn call for the intercessory prayer of the community for the sinner. The second stage was the long and severe period of expiation, which intended to show the sincerity of the change of heart. For example, during the long time of the process, the sinner could not have conjugal relations and often could not be involved in public or business affairs. Even after reconciliation some of these prohibitions, including no marital relations, continued. The third stage involved the reconciliation with the Christian community by the imposition of the hands of the bishop, often on Holy Thursday. Note here the important role played by the community in all of this penitential rite. Ultimate reconciliation with the community was recognized as reconciliation with God.

The whole penitential process was most severe and could be done only once and never repeated. However, as in earlier times, people on their deathbeds could be reconciled without going through the long, severe process. But if they recovered, they had to enter the order of penance. In light of the fact that this penance could be done only once, and in light of the severity of the expiation that even continued after reconciliation, bishops counseled that the young and the married should not enter into the order of penitents. As a result, the process was not really used, and deathbed reconciliation became the only possibility. People were urged to do their own expiation for their sins so they could avail themselves of the reconciliation offered on their deathbeds. Vogel concludes that it is infinitely probable that the faithful, following the exhortation of their pastors to sincerely repent of their sins and try by their good works to merit reconciliation on their deathbeds, were admitted without reconciliation to the Eucharist.[13]

It was obvious that this whole process could not continue. From the sixth century on, a new form of penance came into practice—tariff penance, which emphasized more the aspect of the mercy and forgiveness of God. The general outline of this process is clear, but there are doubts and disagreements about some details. First of all, this penance could be repeated as often as one experienced the need for it. The community itself, unlike in the older canonical penance, now played a much reduced role. What today we would call the minister of penance changed from the bishop to the individual monk or presbyter. The role of the confession of sins took on a much greater significance. The word "tariff" comes from the penances that were assigned for each sin. There were penitential books that contained lists of sins and the appropriate penances that should be assigned for each sin. These books also indicated the ways in which the presbyter should question the person about the sins committed. The process no longer ended with a rite of reconciliation with the community through the hands of the bishop. For the first time in history, the word "absolution" began to appear to describe what the presbyter did, although the term "reconciliation" also continued to be used.

There is general agreement that the Celtic and Anglo-Saxon Churches played a very prominent role in the development of this new form of penance. Some scholars maintain that the Celtic and Anglo-Saxon

Churches never knew the older canonical penance that had been practiced on the Continent, but others disagree.[14] The Celtic Church in Ireland, England, and Scotland was organized with the abbots perhaps having even a greater role than bishops. The monks then began to extend to the laity a practice that had originated with the process of spiritual direction in the monasteries. The practice of tariff penance as described earlier thus came into existence in these countries. The idea of tariff was also familiar to the Irish people because of the civil laws that gave a tariff or retribution for particular civil transgressions.

The Irish missionaries began working on the Continent at the end of the sixth century and brought their system of tariff penance with them. There is some debate about whether such a practice had already been taking place in parts of the Continent even before the coming of the Irish missionaries, but there is no doubt that the missionaries played a significant role in the growth and development of this new form of penance. As was to be expected, there was initial opposition to this new form of penance. Canon 11 of the Council of Toledo in 589 strongly condemned this practice based on an appalling presumption that one could be reconciled as often as one sins. However, a half century later the Council of Chalon-sur-Saône in Gaul (644–56) gave ecclesiastical approval to this new penitential practice.[15]

There were numerous penitential books (*Libri poenitentiales*) that provided the instruction for the presbyters about how to deal with the sins that were brought up. In 1938, the Protestant historian John T. McNeill and Helen M. Gamer translated most of the known penitentials into English in a very large volume.[16] These books go into great detail about the sins of thought, word, and deed and the tariffs for them. For example, the *Penitential of Finnian* (c. 525–550) maintains that swearing a false oath is a great crime, such that one should "do penance for seven years, and for the rest of one's life to do right, not to take oaths, and to set free one's maidservant or manservant or to give the value of one [servant] to the poor or needy."[17]

The *Penitential of Columban*, composed on the Continent about 600, was well known and frequently used. This penitential, like many others, explains the role of the presbyter as a physician of souls who, like the physician of bodies, prepares and gives different medicines depending on the different diseases. The physician of souls must know how to treat all the different spiritual ills and sins. The tariff penances are given as a help to the presbyter in carrying out this function. More severe penances or satisfactions are given to clerics than to lay people. If a lay person commits homicide, he shall "do penance on bread and water for three years unarmed, in exile, and after three years shall come back to his own, rendering to the parents of the dead man filial piety and service in his stead, and so the satisfaction being completed, he shall, at the judgment of the priest, be joined to the altar."[18]

There were abuses associated with the practice of tariff penance. By the second half of the eighth century, a proliferation of penitential books existed with many different and even contradictory penances assigned for the same sin. Some of the penances were still quite severe, and this led to the practice of commutation—the person or one's substitute could be given shorter but more severe penances. Also, a sum of money could be given rather than penitential works themselves. Donations were also often given to the presbyter on the occasion of penance, and this led to abuses.[19]

The Carolingian reform in the ninth century tried to deal with some of the abuses. Attempts were made to put together more authoritative penitential books, and this ultimately led to the famous *Decretum Gratiani* (1140), which brought together into a consistent whole all the existing canons or Church laws. The Carolingian reform proposed a formula of canonical or solemn penance for public grave sins and tariff penance for private grave sin, but in reality such canonical penance seldom if ever took place.[20] At this time there were also other penitential realities, such as pilgrimages, and some instances of general absolutions often connected with Lent or the Eucharistic liturgy. Commentators are divided about the exact nature, status, and meaning of these forms of penance.[21]

As mentioned earlier, as the tariff penance developed over time, confession and absolution took on primary importance. The original word *"exomologesis"* used to describe the rite of canonical penance referred primarily to the praise of the mercy and forgiveness of God and not to the confession of one's sins. Tariff penance by its very nature gave much greater importance to the confession of one's sins. In canonical penance, and even in tariff penance at the beginning, the primary work of the penitent was satisfaction or expiation through long and severe penance. However, as tariff penance was frequently repeated, the works of penance and satisfaction were shortened, sometimes through commutations and through frequent regular practice. Often there was no formal reconciliation after the satisfaction was done in tariff penance. By the end of the twelfth century, satisfaction had for all practical purposes been absorbed into confession. The shame and humiliation inherent in the act of confessing sins constituted the expiation done by the penitent.[22]

The changing role of confession meant that the confessor now gave absolution in the same rite after the confession of sins. Recall that the original terminology was being reconciled with the community. "Reconciliation" was also the word used with regard to tariff penance, but then the word "absolution" also began to be used. Since there was no community involvement and one's confession became the primary act of the penitent, absolution by the presbyter was given immediately. Absolution originally referred to the concluding blessing in any liturgy. From the Carolingian reform onward, absolution began to take on the meaning of an official Church declaration of forgiveness through the power of the keys. Consistent with this change is a development in the literary formulas themselves. The early formula was in the form of an intercessory prayer. The absolution became the supplicatory prayer with the priest addressing God directly and asking for forgiveness for the sinner or the optative prayer addressed to the penitent speaking of God in the third person and expressing the desire for the penitent's forgiveness ("May God absolve you"). From the eleventh century the indicative formula ("I absolve you") came into use, and by the late twelfth century it was the common form.[23]

THE COUNCILS OF LATERAN IV AND TRENT

These developments with the emphasis on the role of the confession of sins and absolution by the presbyter led to the modern understanding and practice of the sacrament of penance in the Catholic Church. The Fourth Lateran Council in 1215 obliged all who had reached the age of discretion to make an aural annual confession of sins to their priest and to receive communion at Easter. The Council further required the confessor to inquire diligently about the circumstances of the sins and thus reinforced the need for a complete confession.[24] H. C. Lea, the Protestant historian of penance, calls this "perhaps the most important legislative act in the history of the Church."[25]

To implement this new universal law of the Church, a new genre of literature—the *Summae confessorum*—came into existence to help priests carry out their role in the sacrament of penance. These *summae* were intended to describe all possible sins and gave great attention to the distinction between mortal and venial sin. These books were not as systematic as the later manuals of moral theology, which often followed the schema of the Ten Commandments. Some later *summae*, such as the *Summa angelica*, simply followed an alphabetical order. However, their description of the many possible sins was quite detailed. The confessor was also required to inquire of the penitent distinctly and methodically to determine the nature and number of sins. These *summae* are unique because they try to be complete, concise, simple, and usable.[26]

The purpose of the *summae* was to educate the clergy in their care of souls. The ordinary priest at this time did not have a university education. These books strove to provide the necessary knowledge so that priests could carry out their role in penance. The *summae* provided the clergy with the decrees of popes and councils, the teachings of theologians and canonists, and considered all aspects of personal, social, and economic life.[27]

Between the decree of Lateran IV in 1215 and 1520, from twelve to twenty-five such *summae* (depending on how one classifies them) came into existence. One of the earliest and most influential was the *Summa Raymundiana* written by Raymond of Peñaforte. This book aimed to train priests in the fledgling Dominican Order (the Order of Preachers) to carry out the task assigned to them by Pope Honorius III in 1221, who made hearing confessions a part of the order's mandate. Raymond was a significant figure in Church history—a master general of the Dominican Order and a renowned canonist who later became the patron saint of canon lawyers. As a canonist, Raymond saw the moral life primarily in terms of law—ecclesiastical law, human law, divine and natural law—which he then applied to concrete human situations. The work is divided into four books—book 1 treats sins against God; book 2 discusses sins against neighbor; book 3 concerns Holy Orders and penance; and book 4 considers matrimony. Book 1, in treating sins against God, discusses problems and issues dealing with simony, Jews, Saracens, pagans, heretics, apostates, schismatics, vows, oaths, lying, sorcery, sacrilege, ecclesiastical immunities, titles, and burial.[28]

At the same time as Lateran IV, Scholastic theologians were developing sacramental moral theology in general and were writing about penance, especially how to put together the work of the penitent and the efficacy of the sacrament. Expiation and satisfaction had been the primary work of the penitent earlier, but now confession was the primary work.

The work of the Church was no longer reconciliation but absolution by the priest in the sacrament. Since our focus is on the meaning and understanding of sin, this important discussion warrants a brief summary. Thomas Aquinas (d. 1274) put together the acts of the penitent and the absolution of the priest as the matter and form of the sacrament, which come together as a single cause, bringing about the forgiveness of sins and justification with God. However, Thomas also recognized that because of the penitent's own sorrow and contrition, sins were often forgiven and justification occurred before the sacrament was celebrated.[29]

The Protestant Reformers had problems with the sacrament of penance. It smacks of a works righteousness that forgets we are saved by faith in a gracious God. Forgiveness comes from the proclamation of the good news of forgiveness, and not from the sacramental absolution of the priest. Luther and Calvin passionately opposed the call for integral confession of sins according to number and species. The Council of Trent formulated its thinking on penance as a response to its understanding of Luther and the Reformation.[30] Especially in the light of basic agreement between Lutherans and Catholics today on justification and the continuing ecumenical dialogue, more careful analyses of the differences between Trent and Luther have been recognized.[31] In light of our focus on the Catholic understanding of moral theology and sin, two aspects of the Tridentine teaching on penance are important—absolution as a judicial act and integral confession of sins.

The Council of Trent declared, "If anyone says that the sacramental absolution of the priest is not a judicial act, but the mere ministry of announcing and declaring that sins are forgiven through the one confessing providing only he believes he is absolved . . . let him be anathema." This is canon nine of Trent's teaching on penance at its fourteenth session in November 1551.[32] This session of Trent devoted nine short sections to an exposition of its teaching on penance and fifteen corresponding canons condemning the opposing positions. The Council also made other references to the judicial nature of penance. In the expository section, Trent compared absolution to a judicial act in which the sentence is proposed by a judge.[33] Since the nature of a judgment requires that it be carried out only on subjects, the priest needs jurisdiction in order to absolve his penitents.[34] Priests are like rulers and judges to whom all mortal crime should be brought so that through the power of the keys they might pronounce the sentence of forgiveness or retention of sins. Priests cannot exercise this judgment unless they know the case, so the penitent must confess sins not in a general way but according to their species and number.[35] On the basis of this teaching of Trent, one pre–Vatican II textbook on the theology of the sacraments describes the judicial nature of the power of absolving or forgiving sin. The penitent is a true culprit who accuses himself before the priest. The priest or minister is a true judge who authoritatively declares the sentence of granting or refusing absolution. The forgiveness itself is a judicial act that is authoritatively given according to the governing norms.[36]

The same session of Trent insisted on the integral confession of sins as necessary for the priest to carry out his role as judge. It condemned those who (like Luther) said that such a confession of all of one's sins is impossible. The Council maintained that by divine law, it is necessary to confess all and every mortal sin, even occult sins and those against the last two precepts of the Decalogue, and the circumstances that change the species of sin insofar as one can recall these with due and diligent examination.[37]

Subsequent theologians and canonists discuss this integrity in some detail.[38] Formal integrity is always required. Material integrity involving the enumeration of all mortal sins since the last confession is not always required. Material integrity might sometimes be impossible or difficult; for example, the penitent is dying, the confessor and the penitent do not speak the same language, the penitent could not confess without being overheard by others. Even Church law allowed general absolution without auricular confession when there exists an altogether grave and urgent necessity proportionate to the gravity of the divine principle of the integrity of confession; for example, if penitents would be forced to lack for a long time sacramental grace and Holy Communion.[39] One example of such general absolution involves wartime circumstances. However, in these circumstances the penitent has to confess one's sins at the next regular confession. (I have previously maintained that there could and even should be forms of penance that do not involve integral confession of sins, but further discussion of this issue lies beyond the scope of this chapter.[40])

The Council of Trent strongly emphasized the judicial nature of penance and the need for the integral confession of sins. Before Vatican II theologians still made occasional reference to the fourfold office of the confessor as father, teacher, physician, and judge, but the manuals put almost total emphasis and treatment on the role as judge.[41] The acts of the penitent according to Trent are three—contrition, confession, and satisfaction. After Trent, satisfaction meant only the willingness of the penitent to accept the rather light or token penance assigned by the confessor. Contrition as sorrow for sin was required, but in the sacrament of penance, one needed only a lesser form of contrition called attrition. The most emphasis was on the confession of sins. This confession required an examination of conscience, imperfect contrition, and a firm purpose of amendment. Imperfect contrition does not require the motive of sorrow for having offended God, but an inferior motive such as the fear of hell suffices.[42] Confession became the popular and generally accepted term for the sacrament of penance in the post-Tridentine Church.

Trent also stressed the importance of penance (confession) for Christian life. One cannot reacquire the state of grace lost after baptism by faith alone without in reality or in intention confessing one's sins in accord with the understanding and practice of the Church.[43] Theologians recognized that one can acquire God's grace and have the forgiveness of sins by perfect contrition (which by its very nature involves the intention of going to confession), but it is very difficult to determine if one has perfect contrition. Trent also taught that one in a state of mortal sin, even if the person seems to have perfect contrition, ordinarily needs to go to sacramental confession before partaking of the Eucharist.[44]

The last paragraphs have briefly outlined the teaching of the Council of Trent on aspects of penance. Trent, however, was intended to do more than teach. Trent was the primary instrument for carrying out the Catholic Counter-Reformation. In response to the Reformation, the Catholic Church realized it needed its own reform, and stressed especially greater participation in the sacramental life of the Church. Penance was to play an important role in this renewal.[45]

Trent brought about another important reform that was to have important ramifications on the development of what became the manuals of moral theology. The twenty-third session in 1563 called for the establishment of seminaries in every diocese (or a group of dioceses, if they were comparatively small) to prepare, form, and educate the local clergy. "Seminary" comes from the Latin word "*seminarium*," which describes the place where young seedlings grow and mature so they can later be transplanted elsewhere. The seminary should be under the direct supervision of the local bishop and located if possible near the cathedral. The student "shall be instructed in sacred scripture, ecclesiastical books, the homilies of the saints, the manner of administering the sacraments, especially those things that seem adapted to the hearing of confessions, and the rites and ceremonies."[46]

Trent responded to the vital need for an intellectually trained and spiritually grounded clergy. In an earlier period of history future priests were trained in cathedral schools, but with the passing of feudalism these schools on the whole ceased to exist. Some clerics, especially those who came from a more wealthy background, pursued the long and rigorous course of university studies where they studied under the masters in theology and canon law. Most of the local clergy did not have such an education. Their intellectual knowledge was abysmally limited. Often they knew little beyond how to administer the sacraments of the Church. Any real reform in the Church required well-trained priests whose spiritual formation and theological knowledge enabled them to carry out a fruitful ministry.[47]

The establishment of seminaries began immediately after Trent and developed in the subsequent years. One year after the Council of Trent came to a close, Pope Pius IV, as bishop of Rome, opened the Roman Seminary under the direction of the recently founded Jesuit Order. The pope's nephew, Cardinal Charles Borromeo, the archbishop of Milan, became a model of the post-Tridentine reform bishop, who even opened several seminaries in his diocese. In the latter part of the sixteenth century seminaries were founded in a good number of German dioceses. The seminary movement developed somewhat more slowly in France, but in the seventeenth century the seminary movement in France became a significant instrument of Church reform. The "French school" of spirituality under the influence of Pierre de Bérulle, who was later made a cardinal, developed a priestly spirituality that was then promoted in seminaries. Religious congregations such as the Oratorians, the Eudists, the Vincentians, and the Sulpicians took a special interest in seminary work. The latter two religious groups founded many of the early diocesan seminaries in the United States.[48]

THE MANUALS OF MORAL THEOLOGY

One can safely assume that the participants in the Council of Trent had no idea about bringing about a new theological genre and discipline, which came to be called moral theology. In retrospect one clearly recognizes the important role played by Trent with regard to moral theology. This Council emphasized the sacrament of penance as an integral part of reform in the Church. However, priests had to be trained to serve as ministers in the sacrament of penance, especially to carry out their primary function as judge. Diocesan seminaries came into existence to train the local clergy. Then there must be the professors and textbooks to carry out the training of future priests for their work.

The *Institutiones morales*, a new genre of theological texts that later became the manuals of moral theology, came into existence soon after Trent. The Jesuits had made the administration of the sacrament of penance a primary aspect of their apostolate. The *Ratio studiorum* (the curriculum of study) of the Jesuits, proposed a two-year course to train seminarians for their role as confessors. The first-year course covered human acts, conscience, law, sins, and the Decalogue, except for the seventh commandment. The second year treated the seventh commandment, sacraments, censures, and the different conditions and duties of particular states in life. This course included not only moral matters but also canonical and disciplinary concerns. Juan Azor, a Spanish Jesuit (d. 1603) who taught this course, published his *Institutiones morales* following this outline.[49] So practical and helpful were the outline and approach that subsequent authors even to the time of Vatican II followed the same basic approach.

However, even in the sixteenth and seventeenth centuries these *Institutiones* were not the only examples of what could be called moral theology. In the European university world, Jesuits, Dominicans, Franciscans, and other priest scholars continued to write commentaries on the *Secunda pars* of Aquinas's *Summa theologiae*, which treats the basic principles of the moral life of the Christian in general, with emphasis on the virtues in discussing particular spheres of life and actions. Other scholars dealt with particular issues, often in the area of justice such as trade, finance, and the treatment of the Native Americans by the Spanish colonizers.[50]

By the middle of the twentieth century, it was easy to understand how moral theology could be totally identified with the manuals. The manuals of moral theology were the textbooks used in the seminary classes. Moral theology was taught primarily in seminaries. The purpose of this course was to prepare future priests to "administer" the sacrament of penance. (Note the word "administer." A more accurate word commonly used in the post–Vatican II period is to "celebrate" the sacrament of penance. "Administer" has legalistic and institutional connotations, whereas "celebration" reminds us that the sacraments themselves always involve praise and thanks to God for gifts and mercy that have been received.)

Devotional practices prepared Catholics to go to confession. In the United States and elsewhere, parishes often had a yearly mission, which gave the most importance to sin, the fear of hell, and the need to go to confession. Popular piety thus reinforced the importance given to confession. Long lines of penitents waiting to go to confession were familiar sights in Catholic churches on Saturday afternoons and evenings. Looking back from today's experience, perhaps the role of confession in the life of Catholics has changed as much if not more than any other aspect of change in Catholic life in this country.

The manuals were basically monolithic in their approach in service of the purpose of teaching what acts are sinful and the degree of sinfulness. The manuals of moral theology usually consisted of three volumes or three parts—fundamental moral theology, the specific acts that are morally wrong, and the sacraments. The treatises in fundamental moral theology basically followed the same outline in keeping with the pragmatic purpose of the manuals. A very brief discussion of the ultimate end of human beings was followed by a consideration of human acts and how to determine their morality. The objective norm of morality is law in all its different forms, with great emphasis on the natural law. Law received the most attention in these treatises. In the popular manual of Marcellinus Zalba more than 250 pages were devoted to law.[51] The authors considered conscience as the subjective norm of morality. Such an approach stressed the legal model of morality as obedience to law. There followed a discussion of sin with attention given to the important distinction between mortal and venial sin. Many also contained a shorter section on virtues, which focused primarily on sinful acts against the virtues.

There was some variation in the second volume or second part of these manuals. The primary authors of the manuals were priests from religious orders who generally followed the approach characteristic of their religious community. The Jesuit and Redemptorist authors who constituted the vast majority of the writers of the manuals used the schema of the Ten Commandments in spelling out what were sinful acts. Dominican authors, claiming to follow in the footsteps of Thomas Aquinas, employed the schema of the theological and moral virtues rather than the commandments. However, their primary emphasis was not on the virtues as ways of growing in the Christian life but on the sinful acts against the virtues.

The third volume of the manuals dealt with the sacraments. Here the focus was not on the sacraments as transforming the moral life of Christians but on the canonical requirements that were necessary to make sure the sacraments were performed in such a way that their grace was truly conferred and the rituals were faithfully carried out. One sees here the very close connection between moral theology and canon law. In fact, in many seminaries the same professor taught the courses in moral theology, which in its treatment of the sacraments was basically canonical, and the other courses in canon law. When I started teaching moral theology at St. Bernard's Seminary in Rochester, New York, in 1961, I taught three courses in moral theology and two courses in canon law on a three-year or two-year cycle.

Creativity, initiative, and originality were not desirable characteristics in these manuals. They were written in Latin and used throughout the world, sometimes with accommodations to other countries and cultures, but not always. According to a 1935 doctoral dissertation, the most popular manual of moral theology in diocesan seminaries in the United States was originally written by the Austrian Jesuit Hieronymus Noldin as a three-volume Latin textbook in 1902. Fourteen diocesan seminaries used this textbook in the United States at that time. This manual went through sixteen editions in Noldin's lifetime, and subsequent editions were published by the Jesuits who succeeded him at the Jesuit theologate at Innsbruck. G. Heinzel published a thirty-third edition in 1961. The manual was never modified to the different culture and situation in the United States.[52]

Aloysius Sabetti, an Italian Jesuit teaching at the Jesuit Theologate in Woodstock, Maryland, published his manual in 1884, which he then updated, and his successors as professors of moral theology at Woodstock updated through more than thirty editions before Vatican II. In 1935, ten diocesan seminaries in the United States used this textbook.[53]

If originality and creativity were not desirable qualities, why were all these new editions needed? They were needed to incorporate new developments, especially in canon law. The new Code of Canon Law, which came into effect in 1918, called for substantial revisions in these manuals. There was also the need to incorporate the ever-increasing number of authoritative documents coming from the hierarchical magisterium of the pope and Roman Curia dealing with moral and canonical issues. These manuals never engaged in any dialogue or gave any mention in the footnotes to contemporary secular writings. The most numerous citations were to other moral theologians, especially those who had written in the past, and to Church documents.[54]

With their very limited scope, these manuals could correctly be described as minimalistic. Their only concern was what acts were sinful and the degree of sinfulness. There was no consideration of growth in the Christian life, the call to live out the baptismal commitment, or the virtues as perfecting the person and disposing the person to good actions in this life. Many people familiar with Catholic moral theologians were amazed that Vatican II could insist on the call of all Christians to perfection.

These manuals appealed to scripture only to supply proof texts that certain actions such as lying or stealing were wrong. The liturgy was not a dynamic force transforming the believer to live out the Christian life in daily existence. The only concern with the liturgy was to make sure that the rubrics or directions were followed and that the sacraments themselves were truly valid and licit. The technical word "valid" refers to the fact that the sacrament was a true sacrament. For instance, in the Eucharist if you used rice and not bread, the sacrament was not valid or truly in existence. Liceity meant that the sacrament was valid, but it was done in a way that involved some guilt on the part of the sacramental minister for doing something that was against the rubrics. These moral textbooks were totally cut off from the concerns of dogmatic theology and spiritual theology. The Christian moral life was reduced to the basic schema of obedience to law.

In light of the biblical understanding of sin, forgiveness, and conversion developed earlier, the teaching of the manuals was shockingly different and insufficient. Not only did the manuals of moral theology not discuss the full reality of sin and conversion, but they also distorted the meaning of sins as sinful actions. These textbooks put the emphasis on sin, especially mortal sin, only in terms of the objective act alone. Thus, murder is a mortal sin, stealing a large amount of money is a mortal sin, adultery is a mortal sin. In fairness, the comparatively short description of mortal sin in fundamental moral theology was more nuanced. The manuals in theory discussed three conditions necessary for a mortal sin—grave matter, full advertence or knowledge, and full consent of the will. This threefold criterion recognizes that not only the objective act but also the subjective involvement of the person is necessary to have a mortally sinful act. As psychology grew in the nineteenth and twentieth centuries, theologians recognized the fact that these subjective factors often reduce the culpability for the action so that it was not a mortal sin.[55]

Despite this very short theoretical recognition of the need for subjective involvement of the person in order to have mortal sin, once these textbooks started talking about particular mortal sins and sins against the Decalogue, they never again referred to this subjective involvement. They assumed that the subjective aspect was present and considered only the objective act itself as being a mortal sin. At the very least the moral theology textbooks should have recognized that in all of these descriptions they were dealing only with the aspect of grave matter and not with mortal sin as such. But often the moral theology textbooks themselves referred to the objective acts themselves as mortal sin. If the matter itself was grave, it was presupposed that there was mortal sin. This view of mortal sin as the objective act itself made the confessor's role as judge much easier and simple. It was easy to judge what was a mortal sin and what was not. In reality, no confessor or other outside observer can ever know for sure the subjective reality of the person who did the act. There is a generally accepted axiom that we should never judge another person simply on the basis of one act. Thus, the manuals themselves distorted to a great degree the reality of mortal sin.

If we see mortal sin as the breaking of our fourfold relationships with God, neighbor, world, and self, then it is evident that one can never judge or determine the existence of mortal sin simply on the basis of the objective or external act itself. This also furnishes a very significant reason why the Catholic understanding of penance today should no longer emphasize as much the judicial nature of confession.

However, some criticism of the approach of the manuals began with the Tübingen School in Germany in the nineteenth century. Johann Michael Sailer (1751–1832) in 1817 published his handbook of moral theology. He emphasized the fullness of the Christian life and a theology of the heart. John Baptist Von Hirscher (1788–1865) based his moral theology on the biblical concept of the reign of God. These were fledgling attempts that did not gain much traction but still had some effect on the future development of moral theology. Some succeeding theologians tried to follow in their footsteps and develop their approaches. A century later, Fritz Tillmann (1874–1953) wrote his famous book on moral theology with a theme of the imitation of Christ. Tillmann had been trained as a scripture scholar but then wrote in moral theology while leaning heavily on his scriptural knowledge.[56]

Odon Lottin (1880–1965), a Belgian Benedictine, also criticized the manuals of moral theology. He published extensively on the history of morality in the twelfth and thirteenth centuries and called for writing a contemporary moral theology in the spirit of Thomas Aquinas. Gérard Gilleman wrote a book on the primacy of charity in moral theology, which was published in 1952 but was actually written as a dissertation in 1947. Other scholars in Europe calling for a different approach to moral theology included Arthur Vermeersch, O. Schilling, Émile Mersch, and Gustav Ermecke.[57] Thus, there was a growing number of criticisms of the manuals of moral theology and a call for a different approach to the discipline even before 1950.

In 1954, Bernard Häring, a German Redemptorist, published his monumental *Das Gesetz Christi* (*The Law of Christ*), which was ultimately translated into fifteen languages.[58] The subtitle, *Moral Theology for Priests and Laity*, shows his different approach. In this book Häring proposed a biblical, liturgical, Christological, and life-centered moral theology. Häring's moral theology was based on the covenant—the good news of God's loving gift for us and our grateful response. Christians are called to growth and continual conversion in their moral life and in their multiple relationships with God, neighbor, world, and self. He staunchly opposed any legalism that made God into a controller rather than a gracious savior. Häring also discussed the morality of particular actions, but he inserted these considerations into a broader understanding of the total Christian moral life.[59]

A very important article written by Häring in 1961 well exemplifies the deep theological reality of sin and conversion in contrast to the approach of the manuals.[60] The article deals with conversion in two main parts. The first part develops the centrality and importance of conversion in the Christian life and its essential characteristics in light of scripture and the liturgy. Conversion as the basic change of heart goes from opposition to God to the loving union with God, and takes place in the eschatological reality that has begun with the coming of Jesus and his redeeming work. Conversion is a gift of the grace of the reign or kingdom of God, and our actions acknowledge or participate in this reign of God. Conversion is not primarily a legal or even a moral obligation for the Christian but is the response to the joyful proclamation of the good news of returning to the house of the Father. The sacramental celebration of conversion in the liturgies of baptism and penance underscores and makes visible these essential characteristics of conversion.

The second part of Häring's article deals with the process of conversion by which the sinner passes from separation and alienation from God to participation in the love of God and the community of salvation. Since sin has both individual and communitarian dimensions, so too repentance brings us to the reign of love and participation in the solidarity of redemption. Sin is properly described as darkness and a lie, but the work of confession of sins brings us to the light and the truth. Sin is a supreme injustice against God, but the works of satisfaction of the penitent sinner unite us with divine justice. Sin is our refusal of God's law but conversion brings us to the new law of the Spirit, which gives us life in Christ Jesus. Häring strongly emphasizes the importance of continual conversion in the Christian life as the believer grows in wisdom, age, and grace after having been reconciled and forgiven. This very significant article shows in great detail and depth the theology of the reality of sin and conversion in the Christian and Catholic understanding.

This criticism of the manualistic approach to moral theology appeared even before Vatican II, but it was Vatican II's call for a life-centered moral theology that sounded the death knell for the manualistic approach. The penultimate chapter in this volume discusses in detail the role of Vatican II with regard to moral theology.

NOTES

1. Roland J. Faley, *Bonding with God: A Reflective Study of Biblical Covenant* (New York: Paulist, 1997).

2. See, for example, Darlene Fozard Weaver, *Self Love and Christian Ethics* (Cambridge: Cambridge University Press, 2002).

3. In this and in subsequent paragraphs, unless otherwise indicated, I am following A. Deschamps, "La péché dans le Nouveau Testament," in *Théologie du péché*, ed. Ph. Delhaye et al. (Tournai, Belgium: Desclée, 1960), 49–124.

4. J. Lachowski, "Sin in the Bible," in *New Catholic Encyclopedia*, 13 vols. (New York: McGraw-Hill, 1967), 13:239.

5. Karl Rahner, "Forgotten Truths about the Sacrament of Penance," in *Theological Investigations*, vol. 2 (Baltimore: Helicon, 1963), 135–74. For an Italian collection of Rahner's studies on penance, see Karl Rahner, *La penitenza della Chiesa* (Rome: Edizioni Paoline, 1964).

6. Eduardus F. Regatillo, *Theologiae moralis summa*, vol. 3, *De sacramentis, de delictis et poenis* (Madrid: Biblioteca de autores Cristianos, 1954), 263.

7. James Dallen, *The Reconciling Community: The Rite of Penance* (New York: Pueblo, 1986), 17–24.

8. Ibid., 19.

9. In describing sin and the reconciliation of sinners in the second and third centuries, I am heavily dependent on Dallen, *Reconciling Community*, 25–55; Cyrille

Vogel, *Le pécher et la pénitence dans l'église ancienne* (Paris: Cerf, 1966), 13–26; and Bernard Poschmann, *Penance and the Anointing of the Sick* (New York: Herder and Herder 1964), 19–80. I do not pretend to present a full history of penance but only those aspects that cast light on the development of moral theology.

10. Cyrille Vogel, "Le péché et la pénitence," in *Pastorale du péché*, ed. Ph. Delhaye et al. (Tournai, Belgium: Desclée, 1961), 150–58.

11. Dallen, *Reconciling Community*, 32.

12. In this section I am again dependent upon Dallen, *Reconciling Community*, 56–138; Vogel, *Le pécher*, 27–50; and Poschmann, *Penance and the Anointing of the Sick*, 81–154. For tariff penance, see a second volume by Vogel, Cyrille Vogel, *Le pécheur et la pénitence au Moyen-âge* (Paris: Cerf, 1969, 2007).

13. Vogel, *Le pécheur et la pénitence au Moyen-âge*, 48.

14. Kate Dooley, "From Penance to Confession: The Celtic Contribution," *Bijdragen: Tijdschrift voor filsofie en thelogie* 43 (1982): 391–97.

15. Ibid., 398–409.

16. John T. McNeill and Helena Gamer, *Medieval Handbooks of Penance: A Translation of the Principal Libri poenitentiales and Selections from Related Documents* (New York: Columbia University Press, 1938, 1990). For Vogel's discussion of these books, see Cyrille Vogel, *Les "Libri poenitentiales"* (Turnhout, Belgium: Brepois, 1978).

17. McNeill and Gamer, *Medieval Handbooks*, 91.

18. Ibid., 254.

19. Dooley, "From Penance to Confession," 404–6.

20. Ibid., 407–8.

21. Dallen, *Reconciling Community*, 124–28.

22. Vogel, *Le pécheur et la pénitence au Moyen-âge*, 31.

23. Dallen, *Reconciling Community*, 141–42.

24. Henricus Denzinger and Adolfus Schönmetzer, eds. *Enchiridion symbolorum definitionum et declarationum de rebus fidei et morum*, 33rd ed. (Barcelona: Herder, 1963): no. 812–14. See also Dallen, *Reconciling Community*, 149–50.

25. Henry Charles Lea, *A History of Auricular Confession and Indulgences in the Latin Church* (Philadelphia: Lea Brothers, 1896), 1:230.

26. Thomas N. Tentler, *Sin and Confession on the Eve of the Reformation* (Princeton, NJ: Princeton University Press, 1977), 31–39.

27. Leonard E. Boyle, "The *Summa* for Confessors as a Genre and Its Religious Intent," in *The Pursuit of Holiness in Late Medieval and Renaissance Religion*, ed. Charles Trinkaus and Heiko A. Oberman (Leiden: E. J. Brill, 1974), 128.

28. Thomas N. Tentler, "The *Summa* for Confessors as an Instrument of Social Control," in *The Pursuit of Holiness in Late Medieval and Renaissance Religion*, ed. Charles Trinkaus and Heiko A. Oberman (Leiden: E. J. Brill, 1974), 105–7.

29. Poschmann, *Penance and the Anointing of the Sick*, 168–79.

30. Tentler, *Sin and Confession*, 349–63.

31. Kilian McDonnell, "The *Summa Confessorum* on the Integrity of Confession as Prologomena for Luther and Trent," *Theological Studies* 54 (1993): 405–26; and McDonnell, "Luther and Trent on Penance," *Lutheran Quarterly* 7 (1993): 261–76.

32. Denzinger and Schönmetzer, *Enchiridion symbolorum*, 1709.

33. Ibid., 1685.

34. Ibid., 1686.

35. Ibid., 1679.

36. Severianus González Rivas, "De paenitentia," in *Sacrae theologiae summa IV: De sacramentis, de novissimus,* ed. Josephus de Aldama et al. (Madrid: Biblioteca de autores Cristianos, 1956), 405–6.

37. Denzinger and Schönmetzer, *Enchiridion symbolorum,* 1679–83.

38. Marcellinus Zalba, *Theologiae moralis specialis,* vol. 3, *De sacramentis, de delictis et poenis* (Madrid: Biblioteca de autores Cristianos, 1958), 372–81.

39. "Instruction of the Sacred Penitentiary," March 25 1944, in Denzinger and Schönmetzer, *Enchiridion symbolorum definitionum,* 3834.

40. Charles E. Curran, *Contemporary Problems in Moral Theology* (Notre Dame, IN: Fides, 1970), 67–68.

41. Gerald A. Kelly, *The Good Confessor* (New York: Sentinel, 1951), 53–59.

42. Zalba, *Theologiae moralis summa,* 3:333–55.

43. Denzinger and Schönmetzer, *Enchiridion symbolorum,* 1579, 1527.

44. Ibid., 1647.

45. John W. O'Malley, *Trent and All That: Renaming Catholicism in the Early Modern Era* (Cambridge, MA: Harvard University Press, 2000).

46. Joseph M. White, *The Diocesan Seminary in the United States: A History from the 1780s to the Present* (Notre Dame, IN: University of Notre Dame Press, 1989), 6. For an in-depth study of Trent on seminaries, see James A. O'Donohoe, *Tridentine Seminary Legislation: Its Sources and Its Formation* (Louvain, Belgium: Publications Universitaires Louvain, 1957).

47. Louis Vereecke, "Le concile de Trent et l'enseignement de la théologie morale," in *De Guillaume d'Ockham à Saint Alphonse de Liguori: Études d'histoire de la théologie morale moderne 1300—1787* (Rome: Collegium S. Alfonsi de Urbe, 1986), 497–500.

48. White, *Diocesan Seminary,* 9–19.

49. Vereecke, *De Guillaume d'Ockham,* 505–8. For the early Jesuit approach to confession, see John W. O'Malley, *The First Jesuits* (Cambridge, MA: Harvard University Press, 1993), 136–52.

50. Bernard Häring, *The Law of Christ: Moral Theology for Priests and Laity,* vol. 1, *General Moral Theology* (Westminster, MD: Newman, 1961), 18–19.

51. Marcellinus Zalba, *Theologiae moralis summa,* vol. 1, *Theologia moralis fundamentalis* (Madrid: Biblioteca de autores Cristianos, 1952), 331–595.

52. Theodore H. Heck, *The Curriculum of the Major Seminary in Relation to Contemporary Conditions* (Washington, DC: National Catholic Welfare Conference, 1935), 46–47.

53. Francis J. Connell, "The Theological School in America," in *Essays on Catholic Education in the United States,* ed. Roy J. Deferrari (Washington, DC: Catholic University of America Press, 1942), 234; Paul E. McKeever, "Seventy-Five Years of Moral Theology in America," *American Ecclesiastical Review* 152 (1965): 19–20; and John P. Boyle, "The American Experience in Moral Theology," *Proceedings of the Catholic Theological Society of America* 41 (1986): 26.

54. For an analysis and criticism of the manuals, see James F. Keenan, *A History of Catholic Moral Theology in the Twentieth Century: From Confessing Sins to Liberating Consciences* (New York: Continuum, 2012), 9–34.

55. Zalba, *Theologiae moralis summa*, 1:618–23.

56. Häring, *Law of Christ*, 1:24–33.

57. Keenan, *History of Catholic Moral Theology*, 35–75.

58. Bernhard Häring, *Das Gesetz Christi* (Freiburg: Verlag Wevel, 1954).

59. Bernard Häring, *The Law of Christ*, 3 vols. (Westminster, MD: Newman, 1961–66).

60. Bernard Häring, "La conversion," in *Pastorale du péché*, ed. Ph. Delhaye et al. (Tournai, Belgium: Desclée, 1961), 65–145.

CHAPTER 2

STRAND TWO

Thomas Aquinas and the Thomistic Tradition

WITHOUT DOUBT, Thomas Aquinas is the most significant figure in the history of Catholic theology in general and Catholic moral theology in particular. Aquinas (1225–74) was a Dominican friar who was recognized not only as the foremost Catholic theologian but also as the most influential Catholic philosopher. The genius of Aquinas was to bring together the metaphysics and thought of Aristotle with the Christian understanding as found in scripture and in the fathers of the Church, especially Augustine. His most famous theological work is the *Summa theologiae*, which he never actually finished before his death. Thomas spent much time at the University of Paris and in various teaching roles in Dominican houses. The *Summa* shows very much the influence of the university world and was often thought to have been written for university students. However, many now agree with Leonard Boyle that the *Summa* was written at the Dominican House of St. Sabina in Rome and was composed for Dominican students preparing for their future ministries.[1]

Since this book deals with moral theology, it must discuss Aquinas in some detail. How did Thomas see the nature of moral theology? What has been the influence of Aquinas through the centuries? How have subsequent Catholic scholars understood and interpreted his work?

THE *SUMMA* OF AQUINAS

Over time, Aquinas has been understood both as a theologian and as a philosopher. In reaction to a modern emphasis on Aquinas as primarily a philosopher, many contemporary theologians have insisted that Aquinas, especially in the *Summa*, was primarily a theologian.[2] In my judgment there is no doubt that the *Summa* is primarily a work of theology, but there is a heavy dependence on philosophy even here.

The very title of the work shows its theological nature. In the prologue, Aquinas explains its purpose: to treat what belongs to the Christian religion in a scientific way for the instruction of beginners in the field.[3] Thomas himself refers to what he is doing not as theology but as Sacred Doctrine. Also, he does not use the term or concept of moral theology. The term "moral theology" appeared for the first time in the writings of Alan of Lille in the twelfth century.[4] Nor, for that matter, does Aquinas use the terms "spiritual" or "mystical theology." In fact, for Aquinas all theology is one. Only later did Catholic theologians begin to treat as separate realities the different species of theology.

Basic Structure

The basic structure of the *Summa* is that of *exitus* (going out) and *reditus* (return). In creation, a human being comes from God and then journeys back to God. Such an approach with its neo-Platonic overtones had been used by Augustine and Pseudo-Dionysius as well as Bonaventure and others.[5] This organizing principle serves as a backbone and structure of the work, which is divided into three parts. The first part (in Latin, *Prima pars*, often abbreviated as *Ia*) discusses God and Creation, especially the creation of human beings who come forth from God's love. The second part (*Secunda pars*, *IIa*) treats the return or the journey of the human being back to God. The third part (*Tertia pars*, *IIIa*), which was never finished, considers Jesus Christ the Savior, who has freed us from sin and provided us with all the blessings that we have received, and is the way back to the Father. Aquinas conceived of the third part as discussing three different realities—Jesus the Savior, the sacraments by which we share in our friendship with God, and the future of everlasting life in heaven.

The *Secunda pars* treats the material that is today called moral theology but also includes what today is called spiritual theology. The fundamental organizing principle for this part within the general framework of the *exitus–reditus* is the principle of finality—the journey of human beings to God as the ultimate end. The first five questions of the *Prima secundae* (the first part of the second part) deal with the ultimate end. This discussion shows how Aquinas uses an Aristotelian metaphysics and approach to understand the Christian reality and life. The citations in this discussion well illustrate this approach. These pages cite scripture sixty times, Church fathers sixty-one times, and Aristotle sixty-six times. According to Aquinas, the ultimate end of human beings is beatitude. The Latin word "*beatitudo*" is usually translated into English as happiness, which is certainly accurate, but beatitude has a much closer connection to the Gospel message with its emphasis on the beatitudes as the way of life for the disciples of Jesus.[6]

Happiness is the ultimate end for which we strive. But what is happiness and in what does it consist? Happiness is not found in wealth, honor, fame, power, or in any created good. For Aquinas, the two primary and fundamental powers of the human person are intellect and will. The intellect seeks the truth and the will seeks the good. No created good could ever satisfy these fundamental basic drives. Thus, final and perfect happiness can consist in nothing else than the vision of the divine essence. This vision alone can satisfy the thrust of the intellect and the will. Happiness consists essentially in an act of the intellect but it also involves the act of the will.

How does one obtain this happiness or beatitude? Perfect and true happiness cannot be achieved in this life. In this life the seeking of the intellect for perfect truth and the will for perfect good cannot be attained. A certain participation of happiness can be experienced in this life, but not its fullness. A perfect happiness consists in the vision of the divine essence, but attaining this vision is beyond merely human powers. Perfect happiness can come about only through the gift of God; humans on their own can never achieve it. This section of the *Summa* puts the emphasis on the fact that human powers by themselves can never achieve this perfect happiness, but it says very little about the way God ultimately brings this about. However, much more will be said about God's gracious gift later in the *Summa*.

The principle of finality organizes the whole of the *Secunda pars*, which involves the journey of the Christian to God who is our ultimate end and the source of our happiness. The *Prima secundae* considers this journey back to God in general; that is, in what is true of all human acts. The person comes to God through one's acts. The intrinsic principle of human acts consists in the virtues that inhere in the human powers and incline us to do good actions. The extrinsic principle—that is, reality outside the human person as such—is God, who instructs by his law and enables us by grace. The *Secunda secundae* then discusses the particular actions of human beings and first considers the acts that pertain to people living in all the different states or conditions of life. In keeping with the emphasis on the virtues that are good habits, Aquinas discusses acts in light of the virtues. The theological virtues are the traditional three—faith inheres in the intellect and hope and charity inhere in the will. The *Secunda secundae* adopts the traditional understanding of the four cardinal virtues—prudence inheres in the intellect, justice in the will, fortitude in the irascible appetites whose object is what is hard and arduous, and temperance in the concupiscible appetites whose object is the sensitive good. Then there is a much shorter consideration of the acts that pertain to the different states and roles in life. The basic structure of the *Summa* in general and the organization of the *Secunda pars* shows how theology has shaped the whole work.

Explicitly Theological Aspects

To accentuate the theological basis of the *Summa*, I will briefly describe how the *Prima secundae* treats the specifically theological aspects that are found there.[7] In the treatment of the virtues, for example, Aquinas insists on the need for virtues infused by God. Effects are proportionate to their principle and causes. Natural virtues come from natural causes. God bestows on us the theological virtues whereby we are directed to our supernatural end. But we need other virtues infused by God that are to the theological virtues what the moral and intellectual virtues are to the natural principle of virtue (q.63 a.3c). For Aquinas, only the infused virtues are perfect and deserve to be called virtues simply because they direct us to the ultimate supernatural end. The acquired moral virtues are virtues in a restricted sense precisely because they cannot direct us to our ultimate end (q.65 a.2c). All these moral virtues are infused together with charity. Scripture itself in Romans 8:8 reminds us that the whole law is fulfilled through charity, for whoever loves his neighbor has fulfilled the law (q.65 a.3c). In other words, God's loving gift of grace uses the theological virtues and the moral virtues to provide what we need to journey to our ultimate supernatural end, which we could never achieve on our own.

Aquinas devotes a very important question (q.68) to the gifts of the Holy Spirit—understanding, counsel, wisdom, knowledge, piety, fortitude, and fear of the Lord. These gifts are found in Isaiah 11. These gifts are habits that are perduring within us. They are not passing, occasional bursts of the Spirit, but thanks to God's gift they are habitually in us. These gifts dispose us to be amenable to the promptings of the Holy Spirit. God's Spirit works in us in and through these gifts. For Aquinas these gifts are therefore necessary for salvation. The gifts are superior to the virtues insofar as by the gifts we are moved by the higher principle of the Holy Spirit.

Immediately after discussing the gifts of the Holy Spirit, the *Prima secundae* considers in question 69 the beatitudes, which traditionally were related to the virtues and the gifts. Aquinas distinguishes the beatitudes from the virtues and gifts because the beatitudes refer to acts, whereas the virtues and gifts are habits. Through the virtues and gifts we are now enabled to act in this perfect way.

In this discussion Aquinas shows how the virtues, the gifts, and the beatitudes interact. Happiness or beatitude has been described as consisting in either the sensual life, the active life, or the contemplative life. Sensual happiness is opposed to true happiness; the happiness of the active life disposes one positively to the future life and imperfect contemplative happiness is possible in this life and is the beginning of future happiness here and now. But contemplative happiness is the fullness of happiness that comes only in the afterlife.

A life of sensual pleasure rests on external goods such as riches or honors. The virtue of temperance disposes us to enjoy these external goods in moderation, whereas the gift in a more excellent way moves us to despise such external goods. Hence, the first beatitude "blessed are the poor in spirit" refers to the contempt of these goods, which comes from humility. The sensual life consists in giving in to our appetites. We are withdrawn from following the irascible appetites by virtue that keeps the appetites under the control of reason and by the gift that makes us undisturbed by them. Hence, the second beatitude is "blessed are the meek." In a similar manner Aquinas shows how virtue and the corresponding gift result in all the other beatitudes that deal with other aspects of sensual pleasure, then with the active life (justice and mercy), and finally with the contemplative life (clean of heart and peacemakers). In my judgment, there is a bit of a stretch in some of these relationships, but the presentation shows how the habits of virtues and gifts bring about actions related to our ultimate happiness. This discussion provides the groundwork for how Aquinas structures the *Secunda secundae*. To each virtue he relates a gift and indicates the corresponding beatitude.[8] Granted, only one question is devoted to the gifts and one to the beatitudes, but these realities affect all the good actions of the Christian.

Thomas O'Meara uses the word "crescendo" to deal with the way Aquinas develops the explicitly Christian and theological aspects of morality.[9] These aspects, as already noted, are found throughout the *Prima secundae*, but they reach their apex and culmination at the end of the discussion. This is in keeping with Aquinas's characteristic understanding that grace brings the human to its fulfillment and perfection. One first considers the human and only then how grace brings it to its fullness. The last section of the *Prima secundae* considers the extrinsic principles of human acts. The extrinsic principle moving to good is God, who instructs us by means of God's law (qq.90–108) and assists us by grace (qq.109–14). Law and grace are extrinsic insofar as they come from God, who is outside us. But they become intrinsic because they modify and make the human being and the Christian who she is.

Under law, the *Prima secundae* considers the eternal law, the natural law, human law, the Old Law, and the New Law. The natural law is discussed in a subsequent chapter, but for now it suffices to say that the natural law has a theological basis in the eternal law of God. Because human law is closely related to natural law either by simply repeating the natural law or by determining what it leaves undetermined, human law relates back to God's eternal law.

The Old Law as found in the Old Testament, especially in the Ten Commandments, comes from God and is good. But goodness admits of various degrees. In light of the organizing principle of finality, the perfect good is such that it brings one to the end. The imperfect good is of some assistance in attaining the end but is incapable of realizing it. The perfection of the divine law requires that the human being partake of eternal happiness. The Old Law cannot confer this grace and, hence, while good, it is imperfect.

Aquinas distinguishes and explains the three different types of precepts found in the Old Law—the moral, the ceremonial, and the juridical. His first consideration of the moral precepts proves that these precepts belong to the natural law. The moral precepts are about good morals, but good morals are those that are in accord with reason. Thus, all the moral precepts of the Old Law belong to the law of nature but not all in the same way. There are certain things, such as honoring parents or not killing, that the natural reason of every human being judges to be done or not done. There are certain things that require a more careful consideration such as wise people do—for example, honoring the aged person. There are other things where human reason needs divine instruction, such as keeping holy the Sabbath or not taking God's name in vain. By contrast, the ceremonial and juridical precepts are good, but as such they lose their binding force with the coming of Christ (qq.98–105).

The three questions (qq.106–8) on the New Law are remarkable in their theological depth and creativity. The New Law is the law of the Gospel, but that raises the question of whether it is a written law. Aquinas begins his answer with a citation from Aristotle, to whom he always refers as the Philosopher. A thing appears to be what preponderates in it. What is preponderant in the law of the New Testament, and in which all its efficacy is found, is the grace of the Holy Spirit given through faith in Christ. As a result, the New Law is primarily the Holy Spirit. Aquinas here cites two passages from the Letter to the Romans, including the beginning of chapter 8—the Law of the Spirit of life in Christ Jesus has delivered us from the law of sin and death. The New Law is primarily the law inscribed in our hearts, and secondarily it is a written law. The written law in the Gospel has a twofold purpose—to dispose us to receive the gift of the Holy Spirit and to direct us on how we should act as a result of having the grace of the Holy Spirit. Insofar as the New Law consists in the grace of the Holy Spirit, it justifies us. But the secondary written aspects do not justify us. Here Aquinas appeals to the famous distinction between the spirit of the law and the letter of the law. The letter of the law would kill if it were not for the inward presence of the grace of the Holy Spirit.

The relationship between the Old Law and the New Law is that of the imperfect to the perfect. This difference involves both the end of the law (note again the principle of finality at work) and the precepts of the law. The end of every law is to make human beings righteous and virtuous. The end of the Old Law was the justification of human beings, but it could not accomplish this end. All it could do was to foreshadow this end by certain ceremonial actions and to promise it in words. Christ fulfilled the precepts of the Old Law both in his works (e.g., he was circumcised and obeyed the legal proscriptions of the Old Law) and in his teaching. This teaching fulfilled the Old Law in three ways: first, by explaining the true sense of the Law with emphasis on the interior aspect of it and not just the external act; second, by showing the safest way to comply with the Old Testament precepts; and third, by adding counsels of perfection, such as giving up all of one's possessions to follow Jesus. Note here the famous and somewhat contested distinction between precepts that are obliging on all and counsels that go beyond such requirements and are often referred to as works of supererogation.

What are the acts proscribed or prohibited by the New Law? Grace that comes to us from the Incarnate Word should fittingly come to us through certain visible objects, and this grace should become flesh in external works. The New Law thus deals with acts that are essential for the reception and the right use of grace. The New Law recognizes the need for both external and interior acts.

The last treatise in the *Prima secundae* considers grace under three headings—its necessity, its cause, and its effects (qq.109–14). Here Aquinas tries to bring together the various aspects of his anthropology—by creation the human being is good but limited and unable to do anything with regard to the supernatural. Sin affects human beings in this world, but sin does not totally corrupt the human. Grace alone provides that the human being can act on the supernatural level. Thus, in a state of perfect nature, the human creature could know truth and do good in accord with that nature but not with regard to the supernatural. Fallen human beings are not totally corrupt, so they can know some truth and do some particular human goods. However, grace is absolutely necessary to bring about justification. Only grace can save human beings from their sin. Human beings on their own without the help of grace cannot even prepare themselves to receive grace. Even with grace in their souls, Christians will never eliminate all venial sin because of the corruption of the lower appetites. In keeping with his Aristotelian anthropology, Aquinas sees grace as an infused habit dwelling in the soul. But to do good and avoid sin even after justification and the habitual presence of grace, the Christian needs further grace (often called actual grace) to be moved to act righteously. The Christian possessed of grace does not need another habitual grace but needs divine assistance to persevere in grace precisely because of the passions that can so easily get out of control.

Aquinas recognizes that the gift of grace must cause some effect and good in created human beings. Grace is a habitual gift infused by God into the essence of the soul. In creation God gives to human beings certain forces and powers that cause human acts to come somewhat readily and easily. So, too, grace involves certain forms and qualities that help the individual to do good on the supernatural level. This habitual grace resides in the essence of the soul and not in one of the powers of the soul. The habitual grace that resides in the soul is called sanctifying grace. This section then goes on to talk about other kinds of grace, for example, prevenient and subsequent. Grace also differs from virtue. The infused virtues presuppose sanctifying grace. You might say that grace is the supernatural nature that the infused virtues then assist in acting. Just as acquired virtues enable a person to walk and act in accord with the natural light of reason, likewise the infused virtues allow a person in sanctifying grace to walk as befits the light of grace.

Philosophical and Ethical Aspects

This overview of the *Prima secundae* clearly shows that what is today called general moral theology as found in Aquinas is truly theological. The whole *Summa* and all its parts are a work of theology. However, there can be no doubt that philosophy, especially the thought of Aristotle, plays a very significant role here. Even within the *Summa* itself one can see Aquinas's philosophy at work.

Recall Thomas O'Meara's metaphor, that the theological aspect comes to a crescendo. This is very true of the *Prima secundae*, with its treatment of human action in general. It is only at the end that the explicit theological aspects are developed in depth with the understanding of God as the extrinsic principle of morality instructing us by God's law and assisting us by God's grace.

By its very nature, Aquinas's theology sees grace as bringing the human to its fulfillment and perfect happiness. Logically, such a perspective must begin with the human as Aquinas does in the *Prima secundae*. He introduces this whole treatise with a prologue stating that he will now consider the human being who is an image of God because, precisely like God, the human being has intellect, free will, and the power of self-determination. The human being desires and seeks happiness, but the human on one's own can never attain such happiness. God's grace does not destroy the human but brings it to its perfect happiness in the vision of the divine essence where the intellect achieves its end of knowing the perfect truth and the will attains the end of loving the perfect good. Some Christian theologians insist that theology should begin with Christ and not the human person. Note that Aquinas only treats Jesus Christ in the third part of the *Summa* after having already considered creation and humans coming forth from God, and then the return journey of the human being to God.

Aquinas's theological approach by its very nature builds on the human and on the understanding that philosophy gives to the human. Granted, there are theological aspects throughout the *Prima secundae*, but the primary consideration begins with the human and develops it in some length and depth. The treatise on human acts (qq.6–21) is primarily philosophical. The further discussion of human acts considers both the passions and acts that are common to humans and the animals with emphasis on the passions of the concupiscible and the irascible appetites (qq.22–48). Aquinas considers the intrinsic principles of human action that are habits in general, and then considers the virtues, with discussions of the intellectual virtues and the moral virtues, and then the theological virtues. It is at the end of this discussion of virtues that Aquinas treats in individual questions the gifts of the Holy Spirit, the beatitudes, and the fruits of the Holy Spirit (qq.55–70). Questions 71–89 deal with vice, especially sin, which obviously is a theological subject. Questions 90–97 treat law in general, natural law, and human law. Questions 100–108 consider the Old Law and the New Law followed by the treatment of grace (qq.109–14). Theology appears in its most concentrated form at the end of the *Prima secundae*, but it is present throughout. Nevertheless, the philosophical aspects are substantial and can be studied and considered apart from the theological aspects.

The integration of the theological within the philosophical also meant that the philosophical understandings colored and influenced how the theological was understood. A number of examples illustrate this philosophical influence on the theological. The basic structure of the *Prima secundae* in terms of finality means that God is primarily seen as the ultimate end. Such an approach certainly has room for other understandings of God but gives primacy to God as the ultimate end. One coming from a more biblical perspective would not understand God primarily as the ultimate end. There are many other understandings of God, such as the loving parent, that are more primary in scripture.

Thomistic philosophy also colors the understanding of grace. The treatment of grace in the *Prima secundae* is very short and quite metaphysical, to the detriment of the broader understanding of grace as a participation in the life of God through Jesus in the Holy Spirit. Through grace we become friends of God. Elsewhere, Aquinas does see our relationship with God primarily in terms of friendship, but this does not come across in the discussion of grace as such.[10] What is grace? It is a quality inhering in the soul (*Ia IIae*, q.110). Yes, Aquinas says more about grace than that, but still such a metaphysical understanding somewhat distorts the meaning of grace.

Aquinas also follows a classic philosophical notion of the cardinal virtues of prudence, justice, fortitude, and temperance. "Cardinal" does not necessarily mean the most important but comes from the Latin word "*cardo*" meaning "hinge." The cardinal virtues inhere in the four powers in the Thomistic metaphysical psychology—prudence in the intellect, justice in the will, fortitude in the irascible appetites, and temperance in the concupiscible appetites (*Ia IIae*, q.61). In the *Secunda secundae*, there is no separate treatment of humility, but from the Christian perspective humility is a most important virtue. The first Beatitude in Matthew concerns the poor in spirit. Being poor in spirit is the basic dependence of the Christian before the gift of God's love. We must be open and ready to receive the gift that God gives to us. This is the true meaning of humility and the reason for its fundamental and basic theological importance. Aquinas mentions humility in places but does not give a systematic treatment of humility as such.

Aquinas's use of the four cardinal virtues means that religion is categorized as a virtue adnexed to justice. A virtue adnexed to a principal virtue has something in common with a principal virtue but in some respects falls short of the perfection of that virtue. All the virtues that are involved in relationship to other persons have a common aspect with justice that involves giving an equal one's due. A virtue falls short of the perfection of justice (perfection here does not mean that it is more important existentially) either in terms of the equality or in terms of what is due. Religion involves our relationship to God, but obviously we are not equals to God and we can never give God all that is due to God. Here Aquinas cites Psalm 115:12—what shall I return to the Lord for all the Lord has given me? (*IIa IIae*, q.80c) Again, from a biblical perspective our rendering to God should have primacy of place and not merely be considered as a virtue adnexed to justice.

Thus far in this section we have considered the philosophical nature of the *Summa*, but something must be said about its ethical nature.[11] First, the method of the *Summa* is teleological. Ethicists today often speak of a difference between a teleological approach and a deontological approach. Teleology comes from the Greek word "*telos*," meaning end or goal; deontology comes from the Greek word basically meaning duty or obligation. Deontology understands the moral life as obedience to duty, obligation, or law. One who sees the Christian moral life in terms of the Ten Commandments is employing a deontological model. In philosophical ethics, Immanuel Kant well illustrates a deontological approach with his categorical imperative. In ethics today, consequentialism and utilitarianism exemplify a teleological approach. The act producing better consequences (ends) should be done.

Thomistic ethics is a teleological approach but in a different sense. Consequentialism is an extrinsic teleology—consequences come after and outside the act. Aquinas proposes an intrinsic finality. The human person has the basic inclination to happiness as the ultimate end, and in securing this ultimate end one brings oneself to happiness. All the human powers have a built-in inclination toward an intrinsic end. The intellect seeks the truth, and the will seeks the good. Thomistic sexual ethics is based on the purpose and finality of the sexual organs. An intrinsic teleology is based on the finality of the God-given inclinations that bring about human flourishing.

The second important aspect of Thomistic "moral theology" is its intrinsic character. This characteristic follows from its intrinsic teleology. Morality is what is good for the person. An intrinsic approach seeks what contributes to true human flourishing. In an intrinsic morality, something is commanded because it is good. What is good forms the basis of obligation. A deontological approach maintains something is good because it is commanded. Notice the important difference here on how obligation is understood. For Aquinas, morality consists in striving for one's good, one's fulfillment, and one's happiness. His is not an ethic of obligation. As is developed in the following chapter dealing with natural law, Aquinas gives priority to the ordering of the intellect both in God and in us and not to the will.

Broader Contexts and Controversies

The Thomism of Aquinas is only one part of the broader movement that goes by the name of Scholasticism, although in our day Scholasticism has often been equated with Thomism. Scholasticism refers to the common method of teaching and learning in the schools of the Middle Ages after 1200. The Franciscan school in what is called the "high Scholasticism" of the thirteenth century differed from the Thomistic approach. This school included such figures as Saint Bonaventure (d. 1274), Alexander of Hales (d. 1245), and John Duns Scotus (d. 1308). The Franciscans emphasized the importance of wisdom, the centrality of love, and the primacy of the will over the intellect, and they did not give that much importance to Aristotle.[12]

Controversies came to the fore immediately after the death of Aquinas in 1274. The University of Paris witnessed a struggle between neo-Augustinian conservatives in the theology faculty and the radical Aristotelians in the arts faculty. On March 7, 1277 (ironically the Catholic Church until recently celebrated the feast of Thomas Aquinas on that day), Stephen Tempier, the archbishop of Paris, condemned 209 heterodox propositions. Actually, none of these propositions explicitly came from Aquinas, but Aquinas certainly was implicated in the condemnation. A few days after the action of the archbishop of Paris, the Dominican archbishop of Canterbury, Robert Kilwardby, issued a similar condemnation that specifically included the Thomistic position about the unicity of the substantial form of the human person—there is only one substantial form in the human person—namely, the intellectual soul. Notice that these condemnations dealt primarily with philosophy and not theology. Aquinas himself was canonized as a saint in 1323. Jean-Pierre Torrell describes the time after Thomas's death in a chapter titled, "Difficult Sequels: Cult, Process, Disputes."[13]

For Thomists, the most influential opposition to Aquinas in the fourteenth century came from the English Franciscan William of Ockham (d. 1350). Ockham was a nominalist who denied the possibility of universals. Reality is a collection of singulars with no necessary connection between them. Everything depends on the free will of God. The good is not determined by ontological reality but only by God's free will. The good is what God orders, and precisely because God has ordered it. But God is not bound by God's own decrees, and is free at any time to change these decrees. Consequently, morality exists in obedience to the will of God and the law. The emphasis on singulars encouraged a casuistic approach to moral theology.[14]

Such an approach to moral theology is diametrically opposed to the intrinsic morality proposed by Aquinas. Thomists then and now strongly oppose Ockhamism because it disagrees with the fundamental tenets of Thomism.[15] However, other philosophers strongly support Ockhamism.[16] Ockhamism played a significant role in the university life of the fourteenth and fifteenth centuries. The University of Paris was a strong center of Ockhamist thought, and it influenced many of the new universities in Germany. Ockhamism was called the *via moderna* (the modern way) in comparison to the *via antiqua* (the old way) of the early Scholastics, including Aquinas.[17]

SECOND THOMISM

What has been called "Second Thomism" began in the sixteenth century after the Protestant Reformation and was part of the Catholic reform movement. The movement started in Germany but then spread to Paris and had its greatest vitality in Spain and Italy. Until this time the *Sentences* of Peter Lombard remained the textbook of theology in the schools and universities. Now the *Summa* of Aquinas began to be used in the places associated with Second Thomism. The custom of writing commentaries on the *Summa* became an important literary genre. Between 1507 and 1520, the Italian Dominican Tommaso di Vio, Cardinal Cajetan, wrote what is still reputed to be one of the outstanding commentaries on the *Summa*.[18]

The Thomistic revival flourished at the University of Salamanca, especially in the area of what we call moral theology. Between 1470 and 1570, twenty universities were founded in Spain.[19] The renewal of Thomism in the fifteenth century came especially from the Dominican professors who were teaching there. Francisco de Vitoria had the first chair of theology at the University of Salamanca from 1526 to 1542. Vitoria introduced the *Summa* as the textbook for theology in the university in place of the *Sentences* of Peter Lombard, although this was contrary to the statutes of the university, which were finally changed in 1561. The school of Salamanca was above all a school of moral theology, and the *Secunda pars* of the *Summa* was the center of interest. Vitoria addressed many of the important social, political, and moral issues of the day. He is best known today for his political teachings and is often called the father of international law. Vitoria developed the just war theory and defended the rights of the Native Americans in opposition to some of the actions of the Spanish conquistadors. He placed a heavy emphasis on the more philosophical aspects of Thomism.

The Dominican successors to Vitoria in the first chair of theology at Salamanca, especially Melchior Cano, Domingo de Soto, and Bartolomé de Medina, continued to defend and develop Thomism, again often using the *Secunda secundae* of the *Summa*. The professors of the Society of Jesus, the Jesuits, which was founded by Ignatius Loyola in 1539, were basically committed to Thomism but with some of their own interpretations. The Roman College, which is today called the Gregorian University, was the center of Jesuit theological and philosophical activity with outstanding scholars such as Gabriel Vazquez and Francisco Suárez. Recall that in the late sixteenth century the Jesuits pioneered a new genre of moral theology, the *Institutiones morales*, to train confessors to know what is sinful and the degree of sinfulness. These textbooks soon became identified with all of moral theology and were not really Thomistic in their approach. To some degree moral theology continued to be taught in a more speculative approach in the universities, but a vast majority of those training to be priests went to seminaries and theologates and did not have the speculative approach to moral theology that was taught in the university.

The Second Thomism was enervated by internal controversies and by many attempts of Catholic theologians and philosophers to dialogue with recent and contemporary thought. By the middle of the eighteenth century Thomism was not a vital part of Catholic intellectual life. James A. Weisheipl, OP, a biographer of Aquinas and the author of the major long articles on Thomism and Scholasticism in the *New Catholic Encyclopedia*, pointed out that the Catholic textbooks of Christian philosophy produced during the eighteenth and early nineteenth centuries frequently cited the Bible, modern science, and post-Cartesian philosophers, but Aristotle and the Scholastics were barely mentioned.[20]

THIRD THOMISM

Third Thomism began in the nineteenth century and was championed by Pope Leo XIII, who was bishop of Rome from 1878 to 1903. To appreciate the rise of and support for Thomism at this time, it is necessary to see the historical context.

Historical Context

The Catholic Church in the nineteenth century was quite defensive about what was occurring in the modern world. The famous *Syllabus of Errors* of Pius IX in 1864 brought together in one document the errors that had been mentioned in earlier Church documents. The topics include rationalism, errors about the rights of the Church, civil society and its relationship to the Church, errors in ethics, and errors concerning marriage. It closed with a section on errors connected with contemporary liberalism. The last error maintained that the pope can and should reconcile with and accept progress, liberalism, and modern civilization.[21]

There is no accepted definition or even description of liberalism, but there is a general agreement on its insistence on individual human reason and human freedom.[22] Liberalism in the Catholic understanding showed itself in a wide variety of different areas—religious liberalism, philosophical liberalism, political liberalism, and economic liberalism. Religious liberalism with its emphasis on freedom and reason denied the existence of God and the role of the Church in faith and morals. For many Catholics of the time, the problem began with Martin Luther and his insistence on freedom, especially from the teaching and discipline of the Catholic Church. Later, the Enlightenment, with its extolling of human reason as supreme, denied the very existence of God. Extreme and even moderate rationalism gave no role whatsoever to faith. Philosophical liberalism opposed the very idea of a law of God. Reason alone is supreme. God's law and the natural law, which is ultimately related to God but found in human reason, were no longer recognized.

Political liberalism was unwilling to accept the old order with its hereditary monarchical rule, stratified class society, and the union of church and state. Liberty, equality, and freedom was associated with the French Revolution. Such an approach denied any public role to the Church in trying to teach and work for a better human society. France was not the only problem for the Church in this area. The Catholic Austrian emperor Joseph II tried to subordinate the Church to the state. In the late nineteenth century Otto von Bismarck's Kulturkampf sought to deprive the Church of any public role. Even closer to home for the papacy, liberalism spurred the ultimately successful efforts to take away the temporal power of the pope as the ruler of the Papal States.

Undoubtedly, there were problems and abuses in these movements, especially with regard to the French Revolution. However, in the nineteenth century some French Catholics tried to move the Church to make peace with political liberalism. Felicité Robert de Lamennais was a leader of this movement. He published books on the subject and a newspaper, *L'Avenir*, to support his cause. Others such as Jean-Baptiste Lacordaire and Charles de Montalembert collaborated with him. He urged the Church to accept freedom and democracy and support the separation of Church and state, which meant that episcopal nominations belong to the Church and not the state, and that clergy should not be paid by the state. Lamennais and his collaborators went to Rome in 1831 to submit their proposals to Pope Gregory XVI. Lamennais also strongly supported the role of the pope in the Church. However, the papal encyclical *Mirari vos* in 1832 warned against the spirit of the age and implicitly censured Lamennais and his followers. In the end, Lamennais left the Church and died without any reconciliation with it. At that time there was to be no reconciliation of the Church with political liberalism.

Economic liberalism emphasized the freedom of the employer or owner and opposed the rights of workers and unions and the interference by the state to regulate the economic order. The Catholic Church, in keeping with its consistent opposition to liberalism, also condemned economic liberalism as illustrated above all in Leo XIII's 1891 encyclical *Rerum novarum*.[23]

The nineteenth century also witnessed the triumph of ultramontanism, with its support of a centralized and very authoritative papacy. The term "ultramontanism" literally means "beyond the mountains," and refers to the perspective of northern Europe looking south to Rome and strengthening the papacy. This approach wanted to free the Church from any outside control by secular rulers and also wanted to elevate the power of the papacy at the expense of national and local bishops. Ironically, as the papacy lost its temporal power, it increased its spiritual power in the life of the Church. In the nineteenth century, the teaching role of the papacy greatly expanded as illustrated by the growing role of papal encyclicals in the life of the Church. The declaration of Vatican I in 1870 on papal infallibility marked the crowning achievement of ultramontanism in the nineteenth century.[24]

Rationalism and modern philosophy also occasioned disputes within the Church. How should faith and reason relate to one another? The transcendentalists, especially in France, took the radical position maintaining that human reason was absolutely incapable of reaching true and certain conclusions not only about religion but also about morals. A less radical way to refute the claims of the rationalists was to adapt one of the contemporary philosophical approaches in explaining Catholic apologetics and theology. Such a modern theology based on contemporary philosophical tenets would provide a rigorous theological system that would appeal to many contemporary thinkers. Georg Hermes, Anton Günther, and some Tübingen theologians and ontologists in dialogue with aspects of contemporary thought adopted such an approach. However, the papacy intervened to condemn all these different approaches. These condemnations came from the fear that all the modern philosophies were vitiated by the effect of individualistic rationalism that insisted on the separation of reason from the faith of the Church and its tradition.[25]

The preceding paragraphs explain the context for the renewal of Thomism, which alone could show how the Church should teach the contemporary world about a better human society and at the same time solve the faith/reason problem.

Pope Leo XIII and Thomism

The renewal of Thomism in the nineteenth century occurred especially in Italy.[26] After the middle of the century, the Jesuits associated with the journal *Civiltà Cattolica* and the Gregorian University were dedicated Thomists. It was in Italy that Gioacchino Pecci became converted to Thomism. After serving as archbishop of Perugia for more than twenty years, he became Pope Leo XIII in 1877, serving until his death in 1903. In 1879, he issued the famous encyclical *Aeterni Patris*, calling on the whole Church to accept and follow Scholasticism and especially Thomism.

The triumph of Thomism in the nineteenth century in Italy is fascinating, especially in light of the strong opposition to Thomas in the first part of the nineteenth century. A small number of people were most influential in the spread of Thomism in Italy at this time. Canon Vincenzo Buzzetti (d. 1824) taught Thomistic philosophy and theology in the diocesan seminary at Piacenza. Among his students were the Sordi brothers, who later became Jesuits, and Giuseppe Pecci, the brother of the future Leo XIII. The Jesuit general wanted Serafino Sordi (d. 1865) to teach at the Gregorian University, but he was dissuaded because of the strong opposition from the professors at the Gregorian to Sordi's Thomism. Domenico Sordi (d. 1880) taught Thomism to Luigi Taparelli, who then became the Jesuit provincial in Naples and brought in Sordi to teach at the Jesuit College there. Sordi formed a small, somewhat secret group that met in his room to study Thomism. But in 1833 the Jesuit visitator dissolved this small group, sent Sordi into pastoral work, and sent Taparelli to Palermo as a teacher of French and music. Gaetano Sanseverino (d. 1865), a diocesan priest of Naples, had a major role in renewing Thomism, especially with his five-volume work on Christian philosophy. Jesuits Matteo Liberatore (d. 1891) and Luigi Taparelli (d. 1891) were leading forces behind the influential Jesuit journal *Civiltà Cattolica* and its support for Thomism. German Jesuit Joseph Kleutgen, who taught at the Gregorian University, also played a major role in the spread of Thomism. The movement spread beyond Italy, especially in Germany, and made inroads in Belgium, Spain, and elsewhere.

Gioacchino Pecci, as a student of Taparelli's at the Roman College, became a convinced Thomist. As archbishop of Perugia, he worked with his brother Joseph to transform the diocesan seminary into a center of Thomistic studies. He also was in contact with the Jesuit neo-Thomists on *Civiltà Cattolica*.[27]

Gioacchino Pecci was elected as Pope Leo XIII in 1878. In his first encyclical, *Inscrutabili Dei consilio*, Leo lamented the evils that oppressed the human race on every side. The primary problem was subversion of primary truths and an obstinacy of mind that will not brook any authority, which resulted in civil strife, ruthless war, bloodshed, the contempt of law, the insatiable craving for things perishable, recklessness, mismanagement, waste, and misappropriation of public funds. In summary, these developments have caused a deadly kind of plague that infects society in its inmost recesses, foreboding ever-fresh disturbances and final disaster. A solution to these problems lay with true philosophy.[28]

In 1879, Leo XIII issued his famous encyclical *Aeterni Patris*. The encyclical as such is not given a title but is often called "The Restoration of Christian Philosophy."[29] In a document written a year later, Leo himself gave a title to *Aeterni Patris*—"The Restoration in Catholic Schools of Christian Philosophy According to the Mind of St. Thomas Aquinas, the Angelic Doctor."[30]

What is the role that Leo gives to philosophy? The encyclical begins by lamenting the bitter strife of these days and the great troubles that vex public and private life. False conclusions based on false philosophies have caused these great problems. God's grace is absolutely necessary here, but true philosophy plays a significant role in overcoming these problems (no. 2). True philosophy is of great help to the Church by showing the errors of false philosophy and combating all the problems that come from it. True philosophy also has a positive apologetic function because it can prove by natural reason the existence of God and the qualities of God, such as divine wisdom and justice. Reason can establish what later scholars call the credibility of the Gospel and credibility of the Church on the basis of the signs that all can see (no. 5). But philosophy also enables theology to have the nature of a true science, bringing together in one body the many and various parts of the theological doctrines to form a unified and synthetic whole (no. 6). Philosophy can also help to defend the truths of revelation from attacks against faith and the Church, and to refute those who make these attacks (no. 7).

Some maintain that philosophy means that the human intellect should not be subservient to divine truth and authority. But this relationship to faith helps the human mind in two ways. Faith protects philosophy's falling into significant errors, and divine truth guides and helps the philosophical enterprise (no. 9). Toward the end of *Aeterni Patris* Leo insists that domestic and civil society, which were suffering so much, would have a more peaceful and serene existence if the philosophy of Thomas Aquinas were known and taught. Aquinas has much to offer. His teaching on the true understanding of liberty that is not license, the divine origin of all authority and laws, the paternal and just rule of princes, obedience to the higher powers, and mutual charity for all would have a beneficial effect on human society (no. 29). One sees here Leo's strong opposition to political liberalism and using Aquinas to refute it.

The encyclical speaks of Scholasticism but for all practical purposes identifies Scholasticism with the work of Thomas Aquinas. Near the end of the document, Leo XIII exhorts the bishops of the world to restore the golden wisdom of Thomas Aquinas and to spread it far and wide for the defense and beauty of the Catholic faith, the good of society, and the advantage of all the sciences. He writes that carefully schooled teachers should show the solidity and excellence of Aquinas over all others, and that Catholic universities that are already existing and that are coming into existence should use Thomas Aquinas to refute the prevailing errors of our day. But this section also contains a caveat: The Scholastics may at times have proposed some things carelessly or too subtly, or something that disagrees with the discoveries of a later age or seems improbable. Such things should not be taught today (no. 31).

Leo XIII and the Modern World

One of the principal aims of Leo's pontificate was to address the modern social order on the basis of Thomistic principles. In the United States in 1954, the distinguished Thomist philosopher Etienne Gilson brought together nine of Leo's encyclicals, which he published under the title *The Church Speaks to the Modern World: The Social Teachings of Leo XIII.* The first encyclical in the book is *Aeterni Patris,* followed by encyclicals on human liberty, Christian marriage, freemasonry, civil government, the

Christian constitution of states, socialism, the rights and duties of capitalism, and Christian citizenship.[31]

In these encyclicals Leo strongly opposed the fourfold liberalism of the day. First, he firmly attacked religious liberalism. The human being by necessity of nature is totally subject to the most faithful and enduring power of God. To deny the existence or authority of God and refuse to submit to it is the act of a human being who treasonably abuses one's freedom. The chief and deadly vice of liberalism lies in its unwillingness to accept the authority of God. This is the greatest perversion of liberty. Leo characterizes such an understanding not as liberty but as license. One is not free to do whatever one wants. True freedom is to do the will of God and what is good.[32]

Liberalism denies the authority of God and of the Church. The thrust of all these encyclicals is to prove that the Church has the God-given role to propose what is true and good for life in this world and in this way works for the greater good of the state and all humankind. The Church cannot be reduced to operating only in the private sphere, but it must contribute to the good of public society and political life. The Church teaches the natural law, which is based on the very eternal law of God. True freedom recognizes and accepts the law of God.[33]

Leo opposes philosophical liberalism, usually referring to it as rationalism or naturalism. The fundamental doctrine of rationalism is the supremacy of human reason independent of God, which then constitutes itself as the ultimate source and judge of all truth. Every human being becomes a law to oneself. This approach substitutes license for true liberty.[34]

These encyclicals by their very nature discuss at great length the third kind of liberalism—political liberalism. Leo strongly argues against a separation of church and state. The state receives its power and authority from God. Consequently, the state must recognize its indebtedness to God by the public profession of religion. To the obvious question of what is the true religion, Leo responds that it is not difficult to know. Proofs are abundant and striking, such as the fulfillment of prophecies, numerous miracles, the rapid spread of the Catholic Church despite so much opposition and persecution, and the witness of many martyrs.[35]

Leo's view of the state is authoritarian or paternalistic at best. He is willing to accept different forms of government provided they recognize that God is the paramount ruler of this world. The people are not sovereign; God is sovereign.[36] The Leonine encyclicals stress the hierarchical nature of society. Leo's favorite word for rulers is "princes."[37] He refers to the citizens as the untutored or ignorant multitude that need to be led and protected by the rulers.[38] However, the princes should not rule as masters but rather as fathers, for God—the source of the authority of civil rulers—rules in a most just way, always tempered with a father's kindness.[39] With his hierarchical approach, Leo does not promote equality as a value either for the individual or for society. Inequality is a fact of nature and necessary for all human life. Differences exist in human beings with regard to health, beauty, intelligence, thought, and courage. These natural inequalities form the basis for social inequalities, which are necessary for the good of everyone and the good of society.[40] Leo, however, does recognize a basic equality of all human beings with regard to their origin, value, and end.[41]

Leo strongly condemned the modern liberties in all these encyclicals, especially *Libertas praestantissimum*. Liberty of religion or worship goes against the "chiefest and holiest duty," which calls for the worship of the one true God in the one true Church. With regard to freedom of speech and the press, Leo maintains that the excesses of an unbridled intellect result in chaos in society. Law must protect truth in the same way that it protects the weak and the sick from violence and harm. There is no right to teach what is false, either in the natural order or the supernatural order. At best, public authority can tolerate what is opposed to truth and justice for the sake of avoiding greater evils or preserving some good.[42] This toleration of evil served as the basis for accepting religious freedom in some countries such as the United States until Vatican II's "Declaration on Religious Freedom."

Especially in his 1891 encyclical, *Rerum novarum*, the pope condemned economic liberalism with its emphasis on the freedom of owners and capitalists to do whatever they wanted in opposition to any government interference in economic affairs. *Rerum novarum* maintains that when the general interest of any particular class suffers or is threatened with evils that cannot be met in any other way, public authority must step in to deal with these evils. The law, however, must not undertake more than is necessary to remedy these evils or remove the danger.[43]

The primary target of *Rerum novarum*, however, is socialism (no. 4). Thus Leo begins the encyclical with a strong defense of the right to private property. The main tenet of socialism, the community of goods, must be ultimately rejected (no. 4–15). Socialism also gives too great a role to the state. The individual and the family are prior to the state and should not be absorbed by it (no. 35). The encyclical also spells out various rights of workers: the right to just wages, decent working conditions, proper rest, limited hours of work, and above all to form associations to work for their good (no. 37–56).

In disagreeing with the socialists, Leo defends the basic dignity and rights of the individual and of workers—a position that has some similarities with liberalism. In a sense, *Rerum novarum* set the parameters for the future development of Catholic social teaching by opposing the two extremes of liberalism with its deification of the reason, freedom, and conscience of the individual, and socialism, which gives too great a role to the state and fails to recognize the true dignity and rights of the individual, especially with regard to private property.

Other Developments

Neo-Scholasticism presented Leo XIII and the Church (papacy and Church were beginning to be closely identified) with an approach to counter modern liberalism in all its forms. But this Christian philosophy also provided the First Vatican Council a way to deal with the relationship between faith and reason that had surfaced in the nineteenth-century condemnations of the extremes of fideism and rationalism. The fideists were wrong because in positing a primitive divine revelation as the basis for the human knowledge of the first principles of metaphysics and ethics, they denied the proper role and autonomy of reason itself. On the other hand, rationalists gave too much importance to natural reason as providing an intuition of God that can only come from divine grace. Semirationalists such as the German theologians Anton Günther and Georg Hermes claimed that reason could make true judgments about Christian mysteries. Neo-Scholasticism maintained that reason could prove the existence of God, know the natural law, and show the credibility of the Christian faith and the Church, but only faith can provide knowledge of the Christian mysteries.[44]

Subsequent popes continued to legislate and authoritatively call for Catholic theology and philosophy to be based on Thomas Aquinas. In a document of June 1914 (*Doctoris Angelici*), Pope Pius X insisted that "scholasticism" meant the principal teachings of Thomas Aquinas, and that all teachers of philosophy and theology should not deviate so much as an iota from Aquinas. Pius X went on to assert that all universities granting pontifical degrees had to use the *Summa* as the textbook in theology. A month later the Congregation of Studies issued a list of twenty-four fundamental theses in philosophy that had to be taught. The Code of Canon Law (Canon 1366), which went into effect in 1918, required all professors of philosophy and theology to hold and teach the method, doctrine, and principles (*rationem, doctrinam, et principia*) of Thomas Aquinas. Pope Pius XI, in a document issued on the sixth centenary of the canonization of St. Thomas, insisted that Aquinas should be called not only the Angelic Doctor but also the Common or Universal Doctor of the Church because the Church had adopted his philosophy as her own. In 1931, Pius XI proposed that all institutions granting pontifical degrees should teach theology according to the principles and doctrine of Thomas Aquinas. Philosophy faculties should teach Scholastic philosophy according to the method, teaching, and principles of St. Thomas Aquinas. In his 1950 encyclical *Humani generis*, Pope Pius XII condemned what was called the "New Theology" and insisted again in accord with the Code of Canon Law that future priests be instructed in philosophy according to the method, doctrine, and principles of Thomas Aquinas.[45]

There can be no doubt that Leo and the subsequent popes used Thomas Aquinas to prevent any dialogue with contemporary thought in their struggle with modernity. Their instruction to go back to the time-tested, true teaching of the past was intended to refute the errors of the contemporary world. As a result of these directives and legislation, Thomism became identified with Catholic theology and philosophy.

This imposition of Aquinas as *the* Catholic theology and philosophy involves a great irony. Aquinas himself was not content merely to repeat what had been said in the past, but he used the newly translated works of Aristotle to better understand and explain Christian faith. The nineteenth- and twentieth-century popes used Aquinas precisely to prevent dialogue with the modern world. If Church authorities had earlier decreed that theology be taught according to the method, doctrine, and principles of Augustine, there never would have been a Thomas Aquinas! A number of consequences followed from this papal imposition of Aquinas.

EFFECTS OF THE IMPOSITION
OF NEO-SCHOLASTICISM

First, as a part of this opposition to the modern world there developed a Catholic interest in and even nostalgia for the Middle Ages.[46] The Middle

Ages were regarded as a golden period in human history and in the Church. Unfortunately, since that time deterioration had set in beginning with the Protestant Reformation and continuing with the Enlightenment and political liberalism. Protestants and others had often attacked the Church by pointing to the Dark Middle Ages. Catholic apologetes then stressed the positive contributions of the monasteries and universities to the culture and intellectual life of the time.

Especially in light of Leo's encyclicals, an idealistic vision of the Middle Ages became an alternative social model in contrast with the many problems of the modern world. The medieval world of cooperation and working together in an organic unity strongly criticized the individualism and acceptance of industrial capitalism in the nineteenth and even twentieth centuries. The distributist approach of English Catholics such as Gilbert Chesterton and Hilaire Belloc even in the twentieth century argued for a social and artistic approach based on the Middle Ages. In Germany and Austria the economic system of corporatism appealed to the guilds of the Middle Ages as a way to oppose the devastating effects of industrial capitalism and the war between capital and labor. These Catholics looked upon the Middle Ages as the pinnacle of civilization and religious life. In the United States, this spirit was best captured in the widely read book of James J. Walsh, *The Thirteenth, Greatest of Centuries*.[47]

Emphasis on Philosophy, Not Theology

The imposition of Thomism as the approach of the Catholic Church begun by Leo XIII in 1879 had the effect of putting primary emphasis on Thomistic philosophy and not Thomistic theology. As a result, Thomism was seen primarily as a philosophy, and its basic theological orientation and aspects were put into the background. It was precisely this philosophy that Leo and his successors in the papacy used to try to change contemporary life and society. In his famous 1891 encyclical *Rerum novarum*, Leo XIII used the Thomistic philosophy to address the problems that revolutionary change had brought about in the economic order. This encyclical began what has often been called "Catholic social teaching"—the encyclicals and Church documents dealing with the social order that have continued to be written down to the present day. In a sense these documents form a substantial whole, often cite the previous documents in the series, and are frequently collected together in one volume.[48]

The subsequent documents of Catholic social teaching continue to appeal heavily to Thomistic philosophy and not theology as the basis for their teaching right up to and including the 1963 encyclical *Pacem in terris* of Pope John XXIII.[49] This encyclical does not appeal to Jesus or the Holy Spirit or grace as the basis for its teaching on peace but to the fact that the Creator of the world has imprinted in the human heart an order that conscience reveals and enjoins us to obey. The laws governing the relationships of human beings with one another, with states, and the relationship of states to one another are to be found where the Father of all things wrote them, that is, in human nature.[50]

The US Scene

Throughout the Catholic world after Leo, and especially in the United States, much more attention was paid to neo-Thomistic philosophy than theology. The large number of Catholic colleges in the United States was a unique characteristic of US Catholicism. One would immediately think that theology would play a central role in these institutions, but such was not the case. Sandra Yocum Mize, who wrote the history of the College Theology Society (CTS), points out, "Theology had a relatively marginal status as an academic discipline in most undergraduate curricula at Catholic colleges and universities in the mid-twentieth century."[51] The first annual meeting of what was then called the Society of Catholic College Teachers of Sacred Doctrine took place at Trinity College in Washington, DC, in 1955 with 143 attendees. The ponderous name evoked some controversy among the members. "Theology" was identified with the manuals of theology used in Catholic seminaries but many thought a different pedagogy should be used in Catholic colleges. "Religion" was too broad a term and did not recognize the Catholic nature of the discipline. "Sacred doctrine" was the term most often used by Thomas Aquinas himself in the *Summa* and was incorporated into the title of the society despite some opposition. In 1967 the name was changed to the College Theology Society.[52]

The primary reason behind the founding of the society was the woefully weak quality of college theology and religion courses. Accrediting associations and others had begun to point out this problem. The founders of the CTS recognized that this criticism was justified, and the society came into existence to ensure the academic quality of these courses. The courses were inadequate and superficial in content and did not meet the standards proposed for the academic recognition of other courses in these Catholic institutions.[53]

For the most part, these courses were catechetical rather than academic. The teachers were religious or priests, most of whom had no academic degree in their disciplines. Any person with a religious habit or a clerical collar was deemed qualified to teach such courses. In the years before the founding of the CTS there had been some calls for improvement in these courses, but for the most part courses in Catholic religion and theology were not truly academic. As a result of the founding of the CTS, Catholic institutions of higher learning began graduate programs to train professors to teach these courses.[54] But even then the process of becoming more academic was not achieved overnight. Gerard Sloyan, in 1967 the head of the Department of Religious Education at Catholic University of America and president of the CTS, pointed out the slow progress that had been met in making the teachers of colleges of theology equal to professors in other disciplines at Catholic institutions.[55]

What was the most important discipline in the curriculum at Catholic colleges in the developing twentieth century? The answer: neo-Scholastic philosophy. Philip Gleason, in his history of Catholic higher education, claims that it was axiomatic among Catholic intellectuals that neo-Scholasticism provided a rational justification for religious faith, supplied the principles for applying faith to personal and social ethics through the natural law, and thus guided the Catholic effort to reorder society and culture in light of the Catholic understanding. Neo-Scholastic metaphysics is based on a God who was the first cause and creator of all. The human person is the image of God because, like God, she has intellect, free will, and the power of self-determination. Natural theology could prove the existence of God and show the credibility of Catholic faith and the Church, although it could never reach the realm of faith. The natural law as the participation of the eternal law in the rational creature provides the moral direction and compass for individual and social life. Neo-Scholasticism became the integrating element in the undergraduate curriculum and provided the students with a philosophy of life. This neo-Scholastic core and basis gave identity to Catholic colleges and distinguished them from other American institutions of higher learning. There were debates about how the curriculum itself should be developed and in what order the different parts of philosophy should be taught, but all agreed that neo-Thomistic philosophy was the integrating principle of the curriculum. Philosophy courses were required and often involved about twenty-six credit hours of the whole curriculum.[56]

This insistence on a distinctive Catholic identity for Catholic higher education based on neo-Thomistic philosophy created some tensions among Catholic educators themselves. In 1938, George Bull, SJ, the dean of the graduate school of Fordham University, strongly opposed the generally accepted approach of American higher education that the primary role of graduate education was research. Contemplation of the truth and not research constituted the highest intellectual activity for Catholics. Modern American education wanted to discover more and more facts, but such a frantic search only highlighted the disintegration and dehumanization of such an approach. Philosophers learned more facts, but they could not philosophize.[57] This was an extreme position that other Catholics challenged, but it shows how some Catholic higher educators saw their approach as totally opposed to what the rest of American higher education was doing.[58]

The central importance of neo-Scholastic philosophy in Catholic higher education in the first half of the twentieth century occasioned a growing academic interest in this discipline. In January 1925, the first issue of the scholarly journal *The Modern Schoolman* appeared from the Jesuits of Saint Louis University. In 1926, James H. Ryan and Edward Pace of the Catholic University of America founded the American Catholic Philosophical Association, which continues to exist and publishes the proceedings of the annual meetings. Pace and Ryan also began the scholarly journal *New Scholasticism* in 1927, which later changed its name to *American Catholic Philosophical Quarterly*.[59] Catholic intellectuals were greatly heartened by the championing of Aristotle and Aquinas by the non-Catholics Robert Hutchins and Mortimer Adler of the University of Chicago.[60]

The emphasis on neo-Scholasticism in the 1920s and '30s in the United States sparked a Catholic revival spearheaded by an elite group that tried to revitalize American life. This revival by its very nature was countercultural and attempted to put into practice the idea of a Catholic culture over against and in opposition to contemporary culture.[61] Catholic Action, with its strong distinction between the natural and supernatural orders, came to the fore both in the universal Church and in the Church in the United States. The role of the laity was to transform the temporal society especially by living out Catholic social teaching with its bases in Thomistic philosophy. A personal one-on-one approach cannot change a milieu or ethos. The lay apostolate was the way for Catholics to transform the world based on the teaching of the papal encyclicals. Again, only a comparatively few Catholics in the United States heard about and participated in Catholic Action, but those who did were an elite that tried to have a broader influence. The Catholic Church, especially through the role of the apostolate of the laity, could and should bring about change in society.[62]

The Catholic Action movement came out of a very triumphalistic ecclesiology. A good illustration of this triumphalism is the song of Student Catholic Action, often called "An Army of Youth."

> An army of youth flying the standards of Truth
> We're fighting for Christ the Lord
> Heads lifted high, Catholic Action our cry,
> And the Cross our only sword.
> On Earth's battlefield
> Never a vantage will yield
> As dauntlessly on we swing.
> Comrades true, dare and do
> Neath the Queen's white and blue,
> For our flag, for our faith
> For Christ the King.[63]

This Catholic revival tried to bring about in this country a Catholic culture heavily based on neo-Scholastic philosophy. A strong force in trying to bring about this Catholic culture came from Catholic associations and societies to promote these ideas. A plethora of such associations or societies came into existence especially in the late 1920s and early 1930s. One would naturally expect to see the development of some organizations dealing with specific Catholic institutions such as the Catholic Hospital Association or the National Catholic Education Association, or with a particular Catholic field of study such as the American Catholic Historical Association. But there were also Catholic professional societies involving lawyers, doctors, and psychiatrists. Academic societies dealing with the arts, poetry, and literature also stressed the importance of the Catholic perspective in these areas. Two academic associations were founded to show how the Catholic approach should affect secular disciplines. The American Catholic Sociological Society, which published the journal *The American Catholic Sociological Review*, came into existence in 1938 and had a peak membership of five hundred. This society did not want to cut itself off from academic sociology but strove to apply Catholic social principles based on neo-Scholasticism to the social realities in the

United States. A few years later, the Catholic Economic Association was founded with similar aims and with its own journal. Both societies and their journals no longer exist in their original form but have new names and a much broader focus—the Association for the Sociology of Religion and the Association for Social Economics, respectively.[64]

In 1939, Paulist Press published *Five Great Encyclicals: Labor, Education, Marriage, Reconstructing the Social Order, and Atheistic Communism* with discussion club outlines by Gerald C. Tracey.[65] These five encyclicals came from Leo XIII and Pius XI and helped to spur the Catholic attempt to create a Catholic culture in the United States. According to Amazon .com, this book was reprinted forty-four times with the last reprinting occurring in 1962.[66] This call for a Catholic culture based on Thomistic philosophy did not significantly influence the average Catholic in the pew but was an elite movement that stirred the imagination and involvement of many Catholic intellectuals. The Catholic Commission on Intellectual and Cultural Affairs founded in 1946 well illustrates such an approach, but after World War II the Catholic revival with its attempt to bring about Catholic culture in the United States was already on the wane.[67] Neo-Scholasticism was flourishing in Roman Catholicism in the United States in 1950, but then an abrupt and radical change occurred.

Three factors brought about this change. From a sociological perspective, Catholics were becoming middle-class Americans and more and more assimilated into American life and culture.[68] From a Catholic philosophical perspective, some within the Thomist tradition itself began to criticize the neo-Scholasticism associated with Third Thomism and Leo XIII.[69] From a theological perspective in the 1960s, Vatican II introduced a different theological perspective.

The picture painted of the central integrating role of neo-Scholasticism given earlier was somewhat theoretical. The practice did not always live up to the theory. The textbooks often merely repeated what the neo-Thomistic commentators had said without any serious historical and philosophical study of the actual text of Aquinas. The papal legislation did not really stimulate a return to the true spirit and thought of Aquinas. The closed and sterile textbooks of neo-Scholasticism claimed they could quickly and easily dispose of all the arguments proposed by modern philosophical approaches. A living Thomism must be open to the many new and valuable insights that have been proposed by modern thinkers. Thomism by its very nature should be capable of embracing truth wherever and by whomever it was discovered. This includes dialoguing with historicism, existentialism, evolutionism, dialectical materialism, linguistic analysis, and phenomenology. The neo-Scholasticism of the textbooks, for all practical purposes, was a caricature of the best of Thomism. Such is the judgment of neo-Scholasticism in practice as proposed by the highly acclaimed biographer of Aquinas, James A. Weisheipl.[70]

No Change in the Manuals of Moral Theology

What effect did the imposition of Thomism have on the manuals of Catholic moral theology? In light of the more centralized and authoritarian understanding of the Catholic Church in the latter part of the nineteenth and early twentieth century, one would naturally expect a great effect. The reality is entirely different. The manuals of moral theology remained exactly as they were and were not at all changed.

The manuals of moral theology showed no influence whatsoever from the theological aspects of the moral theology found in Aquinas. As Pinckaers points out, the manuals themselves had no treatises on beatitude, grace, the New Law, and the gifts of the Holy Spirit, while the virtues received scant attention. The manuals of moral theology emphasized human action, law as the objective norm of morality, conscience as the subjective norm of morality, and sins. The whole purpose of the role of the manuals was to train future confessors to know what is sinful and what is not sinful.[71]

In addition, the basic ethical methodology and principles of Thomas Aquinas were not the method and approach of the manuals of moral theology. In the United States, Thomas Bouquillon, the first professor of moral theology at the new Catholic University of America in Washington, strongly criticized the manuals of moral theology at the end of the nineteenth century and pointed out how they differed from Aquinas. Bouquillon, a convinced neo-Scholastic, came to Catholic University from his native Belgium. In a rather long historical discussion of theology and moral theology, he divides this history into three periods. The first period from the late twelfth century to the "pseudo-Reformation" (his term) includes the golden period that reached its highest point with Thomas Aquinas. The second period from the pseudo-Reformation to 1830 was an age of decline, perversion, and falling into ruin marked by a tedium and lassitude with regard to Scholastic questions. Practical questions were preferred to more theoretical issues and questions. New philosophical positions from the Cartesian to the Kantian came to the fore, and Aquinas was no longer front and center in Catholic intellectual life. The third stage beginning in 1830 marked a period of renewal with the reclamation of the theology and philosophy of Thomas Aquinas.[72]

Catholic moral theologians at that time would have been startled to find St. Alphonsus Liguori and his work on moral theology placed in the period of perversion and ruin in Catholic moral theology. Bouquillon recognizes that Alphonsus's approach had been strongly supported and endorsed by Church authorities. However, according to Bouquillon, Alphonsus is eminent in the areas of casuistry and the prudential aspects of moral theology but not as a scientific moral theologian.[73]

In 1899, Bouquillon, on the basis of his neo-Scholastic approach, wrote a stinging criticism of the manuals of moral theology that followed the approach of Liguori. The treatise on the ultimate end and the destiny of human beings, the very foundation of the science of moral theology, is seldom found. The treatment of human acts is jejune and deprived of its ontological, psychological, and supernatural aspects. Little or nothing is written on the passions and habits with their twofold aspects of virtues and vices. The theological aspects of the law are often omitted. The manuals propose God's law in a very superficial way while canon law is insisted upon. Much of the problem comes from the fact that moral theology became separated from dogmatic theology and the cognate disciplines of ascetical and liturgical theology. Moral theology also lost contact with its relevant sciences—ethics, sociology, politics, and economics. Moral theology has limited itself only to the laws of private life, and its primary interest here has been with conclusions and applications rather than with the principles of morality.[74]

The manuals of moral theology employ a deontological model, whereas Aquinas used an intrinsic teleological model. For the manuals, law was the objective norm of morality, and obedience to law was what was required of all. Aquinas, on the other hand, is an intrinsic teleologist. Recall that the very first consideration in the moral theological aspect of the *Summa* is the question of happiness. Happiness is the ultimate end of human beings. Aquinas's ethic is not primarily an ethic of obligation but an ethic of human flourishing. For Aquinas, something is commanded because it is good, whereas for the manuals, something is good because it is commanded. There can be no doubt that the manuals are not Thomistic in their approach to moral theology, and this was recognized even in the nineteenth and early twentieth centuries.[75]

Why did the authoritative imposition of Aquinas's theology and philosophy have no effect whatsoever on the manuals of moral theology, which even in those days were recognized by some not to be Thomistic in their approach? A number of factors help to explain what seems to be a radical inconsistency.

First, one can distinguish but not separate the theological and ethical aspects of Thomism. It is somewhat easier to explain why the theological aspects of Thomistic moral theology were not incorporated into the manuals of moral theology. It is true that Church authority called for both theology and philosophy to use the method, doctrine, and principles of Aquinas, but neo-Scholasticism itself stressed the philosophical aspects of Thomism. The fact that the theological aspects of Aquinas's moral theology were not incorporated into the manuals of moral theology shows just how strong was the emphasis on philosophy in neo-Scholasticism. But the ethical and philosophical aspects of Thomism were also not incorporated into the manuals. Further reasons are necessary to explain this reality.

Second, the very nature, purpose, and focus of the manuals would have to change dramatically if they followed a Thomistic approach. The focus of the manuals was to train confessors to know what acts are sinful and the degree of sinfulness. This approach by definition was minimalistic, legalistic, and casuistic. In the *Summa*, Aquinas proposed a systematic and thematic study of the whole Christian moral life seen as the journey of the Christian back to a loving God. In the late nineteenth and early twentieth centuries, the focus and purpose of the manuals was not going to change. The sacrament of penance played a very significant role in the life of Catholics. The ministry of "hearing confessions" remained a very important part of the ministry of the priest. Future priests had to be prepared to carry out this role.

Third, the nineteenth- and twentieth-century papacy not only called for Catholic philosophy and theology to be taught according to the method and approach of Thomas Aquinas but also strongly endorsed the moral theology of Alphonsus Liguori. Alphonsus himself was strongly identified with the ultramontanist approach to papal centrality and power. He had always been a strong supporter of the papacy, an ardent promoter of Marian devotion, and a staunch opponent of the intellectual and political developments associated with the Enlightenment and liberalism. In 1803, the Congregation of Rites, with the approval of the pope, declared that nothing in Liguori's voluminous writings was deserving of censure.

The Sacred Penitentiary in 1831 maintained that confessors in the sacrament of penance could safely follow all the opinions of Liguori. In 1839, he was canonized; in 1871, made a doctor of the Church; and in 1950, Pope Pius XII made Alphonsus Liguori the patron of moral theologians and confessors.[76] As a result, the moral theology of Alphonsus Liguori was in no way going to be criticized by the papacy or the hierarchical Church.

Fourth, Liguori himself testified to the important role of Aquinas in moral theology and maintained that he followed Aquinas. In the preface to his four-volume moral theology, Liguori claims to use the work of Aquinas assiduously, the only theologian he mentions by name in that context.[77] In his discussion of conscience he refers to Aquinas as the most distinguished (*princeps*) of theologians.[78]

Fifth, the manuals based their moral teaching on natural law. Natural law was closely associated with the method of Aquinas. It was very easy at this time for moral theologians to forget that natural law played a lesser role in Thomas Aquinas than it did in the manuals. The emphasis on natural law in the manuals seemed to show that the manuals were truly Thomistic in their method and approach.

In conclusion, the imposition of Thomistic philosophy and theology had a significant influence in the life of the Catholic Church in the nineteenth and twentieth centuries but never changed or even challenged the approach of the manuals of moral theology that by their very nature were not Thomistic.

SIGNIFICANT CHANGES

Two significant changes occurred as the twentieth century developed because of which Catholic philosophy and theology were no longer identified with the method, the teaching, and the principles of Thomas Aquinas. The first significant change concerned the move from opposition to democracy and freedom, which was often associated with political liberalism to an acceptance of democracy and the important role of freedom. This development well illustrates the dramatic change at Vatican II with its insistence on dialogue with the modern world and not opposition to it. The second significant change, building on the first, now recognized a pluralism of theologies and philosophies within the Catholic Church. No longer was Catholic philosophy and theology identified only with Thomism.

Change Concerning Freedom and Democracy

A significant change occurred as the twentieth century progressed with regard to the attitude of the Church to freedom and democracy. In the nineteenth century, the primary problem from the Catholic perspective was liberalism with its emphasis on the separation of church and state and the freedom of the individual. However, already in Leo's time the new development of socialism and communism was on the horizon as a problem for the Catholic approach. Thus, in *Rerum novarum* Leo defended the dignity and rights of workers and the right to private property. In the Catholic understanding, socialism and communism continued to grow as problems. But also more right-wing totalitarian governments came to the fore in Europe in the 1930s with the rise of Nazism and Fascism. In the 1930s, Pope Pius XI wrote encyclical letters condemning Fascism, Nazism, and Communism. Against these totalitarian approaches the Catholic Church began to defend and support democracy and fundamental human rights and liberties.[79]

With regard to democracy, Leo XIII proposed an authoritarian and paternalistic view of government and opposed liberalism and its freedoms. But he did not explicitly condemn democracy in his encyclicals. The generally accepted Catholic approach at the time was the "indifference" of the Church to forms of government. Rulers, whether they were kings, emperors, or elected presidents, had to govern justly. The emphasis was on the function of government and not on the form that it takes. But change occurred here, too. In his Christmas message of 1944, Pope Pius XII cautiously pointed out that a democratic form of government appears to many people as a postulate of human reason today.[80] As time went on, the Catholic Church became a strong supporter of democracy. George Weigel, the self-proclaimed neoconservative Catholic, calls the strong Catholic support for democracy the second twentieth-century revolution; the first was the Russian Bolshevik revolution involving Communism in 1917.[81]

Support for democracy went hand in hand with support for the rights and freedom of the human person, another important development in the Catholic approach. Even in *Rerum novarum*, rights language appeared in relationship to workers. The first full-blown discussion in defense of human rights in Church documents occurred in Pope John XXIII's 1963 encyclical, *Pacem in terris*. Here, human rights based on human nature constitute a most important reality in social ethics. The pope insists on different kinds of rights: the right to life and a decent standard of living, rights regarding moral and cultural values, the right to worship according to one's conscience, the right to freely choose one's state in life, economic rights, political rights, rights of meeting and association, the right to emigrate and immigrate. Yes, in the twentieth century the Catholic Church came to accept human freedom and rights, but this did not involve a total acceptance of individualistic liberalism. Unlike liberalism, *Pacem in terris* insists not only on rights but also on duties. Also, *Pacem in terris* supports not only political rights such as the basic freedoms of speech, assembly, and religion but also social and economic rights such as the rights to food, clothing, shelter, education, and health care.[82] Too often, liberalism accepted only political rights and not social and economic rights. The Catholic tradition cannot accept the philosophical individualism often associated with liberalism.

With regard to freedom, Pope John XXIII's 1963 encyclical, *Pacem in terris*, shows a marked advance over his 1961 encyclical *Mater et magistra*. In a major part of *Mater et magistra*, the pope insists that the ideal social order rests on the three values of truth, justice, and love.[83] *Pacem in terris* adds a fourth element to this triad—truth, justice, love, and freedom. Thus, freedom has an important role to play in human life and society, but it exists alongside other important values.[84]

Later documents of Catholic social teaching continued to emphasize the importance of freedom. The best illustration is the 1974 document, *Octogesima adveniens*, of Pope Paul VI, which maintains that in light of historical developments, the human aspirations to equality and participation—two forms of human dignity and freedom—have come to the fore. Recall that Leo had strongly opposed freedom, equality, and participation in human society, but Paul VI, in the changed contemporary context, strongly defends and supports these realities.[85]

Vatican II marked a most significant change with its acceptance of religious freedom. The very first paragraph of the final document clearly highlights the Church's support for the importance of freedom. A sense of the dignity of the human person has become more present in contemporary consciousness. As a result, people realize they should act on their own judgment and in a responsible use of freedom. Contemporary consciousness also calls for constitutional limits placed on governments to prevent encroachment on the rightful freedom of persons and associations. This demand for freedom chiefly regards the quest for the highest values involving the human spirit, especially the free exercise of religion in society. The Council notes these desires of contemporary persons and declares them to be greatly in accord with justice and truth.[86]

This remarkable paragraph, despite its prosaic language, marks a direct contradiction with the position of Leo and his immediate predecessors. The "Declaration on Religious Freedom" strongly supports democracy and the need for religious freedom. But perhaps even more significantly, the document recognizes that the fathers of Vatican II learned from the experience of the modern world.

The acceptance of religious freedom illustrates the Vatican II emphasis on dialogue with the modern world as contrasted with the older approach of opposition to the modern world. Leo XIII had imposed Thomism because he was so defensive against modern thought and the modern world. The chapter on Vatican II will develop this emphasis on dialogue with the world that also greatly affected the Church's relationship to Thomism.

Changes in Thomism

As the twentieth century progressed, it became clear that a pluralism existed among Thomistic approaches. The neo-Scholasticism associated with Third Thomism and Leo XIII was not the only form of Thomism. One of the unintended consequences of the imposition of Thomism involved a return to the texts of Aquinas and the historical situation in which he wrote. Marie-Dominique Chenu, on the basis of the texts and historical setting of Aquinas, maintained that the neo-Scholasticism of the twentieth-century philosophical manuals basically distorted the true approach of Aquinas. True followers of Aquinas do not dismiss modern thinkers with trite and summary condemnations of positions about which they are quite ignorant. The true followers of Aquinas should honestly discuss the problems legitimately posed by the philosophy of religion, biblical exegesis, and the history of dogma. But Chenu did not simply study the past for the sake of history. He insisted that it is unacceptable to conserve without creating. Chenu played a major role in the pastoral developments that occurred in France after 1940. Among his intellectual achievements was his insistence on the importance of "the signs of the times," which played a central role at Vatican II.[87]

Historical study of the texts of Aquinas in his own historical and cultural circumstances also led James Weisheipl to similar conclusions. For most of the first part of the twentieth century, serious historical and philosophical study of the actual texts of Aquinas had been lacking. The manuals of neo-Scholastic philosophy were often merely a pseudo or half-understood brand of Thomism. A living Thomism must embrace truth wherever and by whomever it is developed. Many important discoveries have occurred since Aquinas wrote. Think of the growth of history and historical method, the insights of psychology and psychoanalysis, the new developments in demography, archeology, philology, modern physics, chemistry, genetics, and anthropology. Contemporary philosophy has also provided important insights for any philosophical approach. The disastrous distinction made by many neo-Scholastics between the perennial philosophy of Aquinas and what is contemporary only led to many false problems. A truly living Thomism must always be open to new knowledge and insight.[88]

Leo XIII and Church authority in the imposition of Thomism wanted a unitary method for Catholic philosophy and theology. But, ironically, Catholic scholars, in going back to the texts and historical circumstances of Aquinas, opened the door to a pluralism even within Thomism. The manuals of neo-Scholasticism were criticized for their failure to give enough importance to historicity and the subject. Precisely in light of the shortcomings of neo-Scholasticism, thinkers such as Joseph Maréchal, Bernard Lonergan, and Karl Rahner developed a transcendental Thomism. Gerald McCool describes four historical stages in the development of Thomistic pluralism as the twentieth century developed. The pluralism within Catholic philosophy and theology then also began to go beyond the Thomistic approach and embrace other philosophical methods.[89]

The chapter on Vatican II shows that the emphasis on dialogue with the modern world opened the Church to dialogue with contemporary philosophies. No longer is Thomism the only approach in Catholic theology and philosophy. However, since the Vatican Council, Thomistic scholars have made significant contributions, and Thomism remains an important approach in contemporary Catholicism even if it exists together with other different approaches.

NOTES

1. Thomas Franklin O'Meara, *Thomas Aquinas, Theologian* (Notre Dame, IN: University of Notre Dame Press, 1997), 51; and Leonard E. Boyle, "The Setting of the *Summa Theologiae* of St. Thomas—Revisited," in *The Ethics of Aquinas*, ed.

Stephen J. Pope, 1–16 (Washington, DC: Georgetown University Press, 2002). For acclaimed biographies of Aquinas, see James A. Weisheipl, *Friar Thomas D'Aquino: His Life, Thought, and Work* (Garden City, NY: Doubleday, 1974); and Jean-Pierre Torrell, *St. Thomas Aquinas*, vol. 1, *The Person and His Work*, trans. Robert Royal (Washington, DC: Catholic University of America Press, 1996).

2. Marie Dominique Chenu, *Aquinas and His Role in Theology*, trans. Paul Philibert (Collegeville, MN: Liturgical Press, 2002); O'Meara, *Thomas Aquinas, Theologian*; Servais Pinckaers, *The Sources of Christian Ethics*, trans. Sr. Mary Thomas Noble (Washington, DC: Catholic University of America Press, 1995); John Berkman and Craig Steven Titus, eds., *The Pinckaers Reader: Renewing Thomistic Moral Theology*, trans. Sr. Mary Thomas Noble (Washington, DC: Catholic University of America Press, 2005); Jean-Pierre Torrell, *St. Thomas Aquinas*, vol. 2, *Spiritual Master*, trans. Robert Royal (Washington, DC: Catholic University of America Press, 2003).

3. For the text of the *Summa*, see Thomas Aquinas, *Summa theologiae*, 4 vols. (Rome: Marietti, 1952); and St. Thomas Aquinas, *Summa theologica: First Complete American Edition*, 3 vols., ed. Fathers of English Dominican Province (New York: Benzinger Brothers, 1947). For a very helpful and complete commentary on the ethics of Aquinas, see Stephen J. Pope, ed., *The Ethics of Aquinas* (Washington, DC: Georgetown University Press, 2002).

4. Louis Vereecke, "Moral Theology, History of (700–Vatican Council II)," *New Catholic Encyclopedia*, 13 vols. (New York: McGraw-Hill, 1967), 9, 1120.

5. O'Meara, *Thomas Aquinas, Theologian*, 57.

6. Berkman and Titus, *Pinckaers Reader*, 78–79. I am heavily dependent on Pinckaers in this section.

7. Ibid., 82–142. The text will refer to the specific places where the material is found—q = question, a = article, c = corpus or body of the article.

8. Ibid., 7, 115ff.

9. O'Meara, *Thomas Aquinas, Theologian*, 113.

10. Paul J. Wadell, *Friendship and the Moral Life* (Notre Dame, IN: University of Notre Dame Press, 1989).

11. For an overview of the ethics of the *Summa*, see Stephen J. Pope, "Overview of the Ethics of Thomas Aquinas," in *Ethics of Aquinas*, ed. Pope, 30–53.

12. I. C. Brady, "Medieval Scholasticism," in *New Catholic Encyclopedia* 12:1156.

13. Torrell, *St. Thomas Aquinas*, 1:296–316.

14. Louis Vereecke, *De Guillaume d'Ockham à Sainte Alphonse de Liguori* (Rome: Collegium S. Alfonsi de Urbe, 1986), 149–214.

15. Berkman and Titus, *Pinckaers Reader*, 211–15, 364–65.

16. Marilyn McCord Adams, *William Ockham*, 2 vols. (Notre Dame, IN: University of Notre Dame Press, 1987).

17. O'Meara, *Thomas Aquinas, Theologian*, 158–59.

18. Ibid., 160–67.

19. Louis Vereecke is recognized as the leading authority on the history of moral theology, but his major work on the general history of moral theology exists in the form of printed notes for his students, which have been made available for public sale; see Louis Vereecke, *Storia della teologia morale*, 4 vols. (Rome: Accademia Alfonsiana, 1980). Vol. 2, *Storia della teologia morale in Spangna nel XVI° secolo e origine delle "Institutiones Morales,"* develops in detail what is very briefly summarized here about the school of Salamanca.

20. James A. Weisheipl, "The Revival of Thomism as a Christian Philosophy," in *New Themes in Christian Philosophy*, ed. Ralph M. McInerny (Notre Dame, IN: University of Notre Dame Press, 1968), 168; see also Weisheipl, *Friar Thomas D'Aquino*; Weisheipl, "Scholasticism: Contemporary Scholasticism," *New Catholic Encyclopedia*, 12:1165–70; and "Thomism," *New Catholic Encyclopedia*, 14:126–35.

21. Pope Pius IX, "Syllabus," in *Enchiridion symbolorum definitionum et declarationum de rebus fidei et morum*, 32nd ed., ed. H. Denzinger et al. (Barcelona: Herder, 1963), no. 2901–80.

22. For the best history of the nineteenth-century relationship of the Catholic Church to liberalism, which is closely followed here, see Roger Aubert, *The Church in the Age of Liberalism*, vol. 8 of *History of the Church*, ed. Herbert Jadin and John Dolan (New York: Crossroad, 1981). For my exposition of the reaction of Catholic approaches to liberalism in the early twentieth century in the United States, see Charles E. Curran, *American Catholic Social Ethics: Twentieth Century Approaches* (Notre Dame, IN: University of Notre Dame Press, 1982), 103–7.

23. Pope Leo XIII, *Rerum novarum*, in *The Papal Encyclicals, 1878–1903*, ed. Claudia Carlen (Wilmington, NC: McGrath, 1981), 17–27.

24. Aubert, *Church in the Age of Liberalism*, 304–30.

25. Gerald A. McCool, *Catholic Theology in the Nineteenth Century: The Quest for a Unitary Method* (New York: Seabury, 1977), 18–19.

26. Bernardino M. Bonansea, "Pioneers of the Nineteenth Century Scholastic Renewal in Italy," *New Scholasticism* 27 (1954): 1–37.

27. McCool, *Catholic Theology in the Nineteenth Century*, 226–27.

28. Pope Leo XIII, *Inscrutabili Dei consilio*, no. 2 and 13, in *The Papal Encyclicals*, ed. Claudia M. Carlen (Wilmington, NC: McGrath, 1981), 5–89. Subsequent references to this and the other encyclicals of Leo XIII will give in the text the paragraph number of the encyclical as found in Carlen.

29. Pope Leo XIII, *Aeterni Patris*, in *Papal Encyclicals*, ed. Carlen, 17.

30. Leonard Boyle, "A Remembrance of Pope Leo XIII: The Encyclical *Aeterni Patris*," in *One Hundred Years of Thomism: Aeterni Patris and Afterward: A Symposium*, ed. Victor B. Brezik (Houston: Center for Thomistic Studies, University of St. Thomas, 1981), 7.

31. Etienne Gilson, ed., *The Church Speaks to the Modern World: The Teachings of Leo XIII* (Garden City, NY: Doubleday Image, 1954).

32. Pope Leo XIII, *Libertas*, no. 36–37, in *Papal Encyclicals*, ed. Carlen, 179.

33. Ibid., no. 8–10, in *Papal Encyclicals*, ed. Carlen, 171–72.

34. Ibid., no. 17, in *Papal Encyclicals*, ed. Carlen, 174.

35. Pope Leo XIII, *Immortale Dei*, no. 6–7, in *Papal Encyclicals*, ed. Carlen, 108–9.

36. Ibid., no. 31, in *Papal Encyclicals*, ed. Carlen, 113–14.

37. John Courtney Murray, *The Problem of Religious Freedom* (Westminster, MD: Newman, 1965), 55–56.

38. Pope Leo XIII, *Libertas*, no. 23, in *Papal Encyclicals*, ed. Carlen, 176.

39. Pope Leo XIII, *Immortale Dei*, no. 5, in *Papal Encyclicals*, ed. Carlen, 108.

40. Pope Leo XIII, *Quod apostolici muneris*, no. 5–6, in *Papal Encyclicals*, ed. Carlen, 13.

41. Pope Leo XIII, *Humanum genus*, no. 26, in *Papal Encyclicals*, ed. Carlen, 917.

42. Pope Leo XIII, *Libertas*, no. 19–37, in *Papal Encyclicals*, ed. Carlen, 175–79.

43. Pope Leo XIII, *Rerum novarum*, in *Papal Encyclicals*, ed. Carlen, 241–61.

44. *Concilium Vaticanum I*, in *Enchiridion*, ed. Denzinger, no. 3015–20. For the influence of Scholasticism on Vatican I, see McCool, *Catholic Theology in the Nineteenth Century*, 216–26.

45. Weisheipl, "Revival of Thomism," 180–83.

46. Philip Gleason, "American Catholics and the Mythic Middle Ages," in *Keeping the Faith: American Catholicism Past and Present* (Notre Dame, IN: University of Notre Dame Press, 1987), 11–34.

47. James J. Walsh, *The Thirteenth, Greatest of Centuries* (New York: Catholic Summer School Press, 1907). The twelfth edition was published in 1952, James J. Walsh, *The Thirteenth, Greatest of Centuries*, 12th ed. (New York: Fordham University Press, 1952).

48. David J. O'Brien and Thomas A. Shannon, eds., *Catholic Social Thought: The Documentary Heritage* (Maryknoll, NY: Orbis, 2010).

49. For my analysis of these documents, see Charles E. Curran, *Catholic Social Teaching 1891–Present: A Historical, Theological, and Ethical Analysis* (Washington, DC: Georgetown University Press, 2002).

50. Pope John XXIII, *Pacem in terris*, no. 1–7, in *Catholic Social Thought*, ed. O'Brien and Shannon, 137–38.

51. Sandra Yocum Mize, *Joining the Revolution in Theology: The College Theology Society: 1954–2004* (Lanham, MD: Rowman & Littlefield, 2007), 31.

52. Ibid., 9–30; and Rosemary Rodgers, *A History of the College Theology Society* (Villanova, PA: College Theology Society, 1983), 5–9.

53. Rodgers, *College Theology Society*, 11.

54. Mize, *Joining the Revolution*, 9–26; and Rodgers, *College Theology Society*, 5–20.

55. Mize, *Joining the Revolution*, 82.

56. Philip Gleason, *Contending with Modernity: Catholic Higher Education in the Twentieth Century* (New York: Oxford University Press, 1995), 104–49.

57. George Bull, "The Function of a Catholic Graduate School," *Thought* 13 (1938): 364–80.

58. Martin R. P. McGuire, "Catholic Education in the Graduate School," in *Vital Problems in Catholic Education in the United States*, ed. Roy J. Deferrari (Washington, DC: Catholic University of America Press, 1939), 114.

59. Gleason, *Contending with Modernity*, 135–36.

60. Ibid., 163–64.

61. Ibid., 146.

62. Ibid., 148–55.

63. Daniel Lord, "For Christ the King," included in the page "Table Talk," by Fred Moleck, www.giamusic.com/sacred_music/tabletalk/63.cfm.

64. Gleason, *Contending with Modernity*, 148–63.

65. Gerald C. Treacy, ed., *Five Great Encyclicals: Labor, Education, Marriage, Reconstructing the Social Order, Atheistic Communism* (New York: Paulist, 1939).

66. *Five Great Encyclicals* (New York, Paulist, 1962).

67. Patrick J. Hayes, *History of the Catholic Commission on Intellectual and Cultural Affairs, 1945–65* (Notre Dame, IN: University of Notre Dame Press, 2011).

68. For changing developments in Catholic education in this period, see Gleason, *Contending with Modernity*, 282–322.

69. For developments in Catholic philosophy at this time, see McCool, *Catholic Theology in the Nineteenth Century*, 241–67.

70. Weisheipl, "The Revival of Thomism," 184.

71. Berkman and Titus, *Pinckaers Reader*, 79–83.

72. Thomas Joseph Bouquillon, *Institutiones theologiae moralis fundamentalis* (Bruges: Beyaert-Defoort, 1873), 92–167.

73. Ibid., 140n7.

74. Thomas Joseph Bouquillon, "Moral Theology at the End of the Nineteenth Century," *Catholic University Bulletin* 5 (1899): 244–68.

75. Th. Deman, "Probabilisme," *Dictionnaire de la théologie catholique* 13, col. 417–619. Deman concludes his article by noting there is an irreconcilable difference between St. Alphonsus and St. Thomas that cannot be overcome.

76. Marciano Vidal, *La Morale di Sant'Alfonso: Dal rigorismo alla benignità* (Rome: Editiones Academiae Alphonsianae, 1992), 201–16.

77. Alphonsus de Ligorio, *Theologia moralis*, vol. 1, ed. Leonardus Gaudé (Vatican City: Typographia Vaticana, 1905), lvi.

78. Alphonsus, *Theologia moralis*, 1:26.

79. For my analysis of this development, see Charles E. Curran, *Tensions in Moral Theology* (Notre Dame, IN: University of Notre Dame Press, 1988), 94–96.

80. Paul E. Sigmund, "Liberalism and Liberal Democracy," in *Catholicism and Liberalism: Contributions to American Public Philosophy*, ed. R. Bruce Douglass and David Hollenbach (Cambridge: Cambridge University Press, 1994), 217–41.

81. George Weigel, "Catholicism and Democracy: The 'Other Twentieth Century Revolution,'" in *Morality and Religion in Liberal Democratic Societies*, ed. Gordon L. Anderson and Morton A. Kaplan (New York: Paragon, 1992), 223–50.

82. Pope John XXIII, *Pacem in terris*, no. 11–38, in *Catholic Social Thought*, ed. O'Brien and Shannon, 139–43.

83. Pope John XXIII, *Mater et magistra*, no. 212–65, in *Catholic Social Thought*, ed. O'Brien and Shannon, 123–32.

84. Pope John XXIII, *Pacem in terris*, no. 35–36, in *Catholic Social Thought*, ed. O'Brien and Shannon, 142–43.

85. Pope Paul VI, *Octogesima adveniens*, no. 22, in *Catholic Social Thought*, ed. O'Brien and Shannon, 289.

86. Declaration on Religious Freedom, no. 1, in *The Documents of Vatican II*, ed. Walter M. Abbott (New York: Guild, 1966), 675–76.

87. Chenu, *Aquinas and His Role in Theology*; see also O'Meara, *Thomas Aquinas, Theologian*, 182–84; and Kristophe Potworowski, *Contemplation and Incarnation: The Theology of Marie-Dominique Chenu* (Montreal: McGill-Queens University Press, 2001).

88. James A. Weisheipl, "Thomism as a Christian Philosophy," 184–85.

89. McCool, *Catholic Theology in the Nineteenth Century*, 241–67; see also Fergus Kerr, *Twentieth Century Catholic Theologians: From Neoscholasticism to Nuptial Mysticism* (Malden, MA: Blackwell, 2007).

CHAPTER 3

STRAND THREE

Natural Law

FROM EARLY IN THE HISTORY of the Western world until the present day, intellectuals and others have referred to the natural law. Greek poets and historians spoke of a natural law that is divine, universal, and known to all. Natural law has been discussed in a number of different contexts. Philosophers have proposed natural law as a law for how human persons should act morally. Theologians have also dealt with natural law in light of Paul's Letter to the Romans 2:14: the Gentiles do by nature what the law requires and are a law unto themselves. Theologians discuss natural law in a twofold context. From a theological perspective, natural law has focused attention on the existence of sources of moral wisdom and knowledge that the Christian shares with all other people. There has been a long discussion in Christian ethics about the existence and extent of such sources of wisdom and knowledge, such as reason, that the Christian shares with all others. In addition, theologians have also shared with philosophers the ethical aspect of natural law as a law for determining how people should live their lives.

Jurists and social theologians and philosophers have also contributed much to the understanding of natural law. Every society must have a civil law in order to exist. But then fundamental questions come to the fore. Are all the laws of a given society just? How do we determine if a law is just or not? What is the criterion? The natural law has been proposed as an answer to these questions. Civil law must be in accord with natural law and cannot be opposed to it.

However, others have denied the existence and reality of natural law. Natural law partisans in the mid-twentieth century pointed out that as often as natural law appears to be dead, it comes back to life again. Writing from a Catholic perspective, A. P. d'Entrèves notes that since the

nineteenth century natural law has been assailed from many sides as criti-
cally unsound and historically pernicious. Although the natural law has
often been declared to be dead and never to rise again from its ashes, it
has survived and still calls for discussion.[1] In 1937, Thomas R. Hanley
translated and made a revised edition of Heinrich A. Rommen's book,
which was titled in English *The Natural Law*. But the original German
title referred to the eternal return of natural law.[2] John Courtney Murray,
an American Jesuit, explicitly referred to Rommen's book when he
devoted the second to last chapter of *We Hold These Truths* (1960) to the
death of natural law and the last chapter to the eternal return of natural
law.[3]

Thus, discussions about the natural law have occurred in the West for
more than two thousand years. The Roman Catholic tradition has given
great importance to the natural law, but the concept has also been discussed at length outside the Catholic tradition. This chapter first discusses
the approach to natural law outside the Catholic tradition and then in the
Catholic tradition itself, with emphasis on the work of Thomas Aquinas.

NATURAL LAW OUTSIDE
THE CATHOLIC TRADITION

This section proves and defends the thesis that outside the Catholic tradition there does not exist the concept of natural law as a monolithic theory
or method with an agreed-upon body of ethical content. Many thinkers
have referred to natural law, but by no means have they always meant the
same thing by it. In addition, they often came to different conclusions
about what the natural law called for in human conduct.

To prove this thesis it is only necessary to point out in different periods
of history that authors have used the term natural law but have understood it in very different ways. Cicero (d. 43 BCE) based his understanding of natural law somewhat on the Greek Stoics. His approach to natural
law greatly influenced subsequent discussions. Cicero described the natural law as the supreme reason implanted in nature, which commands what
ought to be done and forbids the opposite. It is implanted in us by a kind
of innate instinct. This right reason is a true law known to all people that
calls to duty by its precepts and deters from evil by its prohibitions. Neither the Senate nor the people can loosen us from this law. There is not
one law for Rome and another for Athens, but the same law unchanging

and eternal binds all races at all times. There is one common master and ruler—God—the author, promulgator, and mover of this law. Whoever does not obey this law departs from one's true self, condemns the nature of human beings, and inflicts upon oneself the greatest penalties.[4] Note here the identification of natural law with human reason and the attributes of natural law that have often been accepted by subsequent writers.

A different understanding of natural law was proposed by the famous Roman jurist Ulpian (d. 228). In the sixth century, the emperor Justinian compiled the *Digest*, a collection or digest of Roman law. Ulpian appears in the *Digest* more than any other jurist and thereby had a significant future influence. For example, his definition of justice as the constant and perpetual will of giving to everyone what is just or due has been often cited and accepted. His understanding of natural law as found in the *Digest* maintains that natural law is what nature has taught all the animals. This law is not proper to human beings but is common to all animals, whether born on land or in the sea, and also includes birds. From this law comes the conjunction of male and female, which we call marriage, and the procreation and education of children. Other animals, even wild animals, come under this law. The natural law is thus distinguished from the *ius gentium*, which is observed by human beings. Since Ulpian's understanding of natural law was accepted by Justinian, it acquired great authority.[5] Obviously, it stands in opposition to Cicero's definition.

The Catholic approach to natural law is associated with the Scholastic period and subsequent developments after Scholasticism. New approaches to natural law came in with the Protestant Reformation and then the Enlightenment. Hugo Grotius (d. 1650), a Dutch scholar, especially described natural law in relationship to international law. Grotius, in his own way, was heavily influenced by the previous Scholastics. He was a believing Protestant, but he insisted that if, contrary to his own belief, there were no God, there would still be natural laws of right and wrong. This opened the door to later Enlightenment approaches that separated the natural law from God in theory and in practice and served as a justification for the greater autonomy of the state vis-à-vis God and the Church. Grotius also believed that human beings originally lived in a state of nature under a law of nature.[6] Note here a move away from the Scholastic metaphysical view of nature to a more historical view, which again was expanded upon by subsequent philosophers and thinkers.

Samuel von Pufendorf (d. 1694) did not hold for a teleologically inclined metaphysical human nature and the social nature of all human beings as in Scholasticism. Individuals living in the state of nature developed society because it was to the advantage of the individual to do so. Future philosophers and natural law thinkers developed these ideas. Enlightenment thinkers emphasized rationality, the autonomy of the state, the state of original nature, and a more individualistic understanding of the human being. The move to the autonomy of the state did not immediately give rise to democracy. Monarchies remained the primary form of government until the revolutions at the end of the eighteenth century. In this context, natural law became the basis for asserting the rights of the people against the divine right of kings. Thomas Hobbes (d. 1679) and John Locke (d. 1704) both developed their approach based on the individuals existing in a state of nature before they entered into a contractual society in order to protect their individual interest. But their view of the original state of nature was quite different. For Hobbes, the state of nature was nasty, solitary, brutish, and chaotic, but for Locke it was a place of peace and mutual cooperation.[7]

Considerations of natural law arose in different contexts with correspondingly different understandings of what the natural law was. In addition to a long article on the philosophical and theological aspects of natural law including its historical development, the *New Catholic Encyclopedia* has three separate articles on natural law and jurisprudence, natural law in economics, and natural law in political thought.[8] This brief discussion of natural law outside the Catholic tradition is sufficient to prove the thesis that in history there have been many different understandings of the natural and natural law. There has never been a coherent, monolithic theory of natural law with an agreed-upon body of ethical content existing throughout history.

THE SCHOLASTIC PERIOD: THE BEGINNING OF THE CATHOLIC TRADITION

The Catholic theological and scholarly tradition came to the fore in the twelfth century and has continued to the present day. The first stage has been called the Scholastic period, which roughly corresponded with the beginnings of universities in the West. This section proves the same thesis about the Scholastic tradition as the previous section proved about the natural law tradition outside the Catholic tradition. The natural law theory as a monolithic philosophical and theological method with an agreed-upon body of ethical content did not exist in the Scholastic tradition.

The Scholastics from the twelfth century and later basically looked to the past for their understandings of natural law, but they faced different approaches that did not agree among themselves on an appropriate definition or description of natural law.[9] The primary sources for the understanding of natural law were scripture and the patristic authorities of the Church, the older philosophical traditions going back to Greece and Rome, the Roman law jurists, and the canonical understandings beginning with the *Decretum* (*Decree*) of Gratian in the twelfth century.

Very important sources for understanding natural law were scripture and the teachings of the fathers of the Church. Since the natural law is related in some way to eternal and divine law, one would naturally expect theologians to pay attention to scripture. The scriptures themselves did not give any specific definitions or descriptions of natural law. The most explicit scriptural text in terms of dealing with natural law is Romans 2:12–14—the Gentiles do by nature the works of the law. The Scholastics themselves frequently referred to the accounts of creation in Genesis. The relationship of natural law to divine law was discussed by the Scholastics in light of the three types of law found in the Hebrew Bible—the moral, the ceremonial, and the juridical, with special emphasis on the moral law of the Decalogue. Scripture itself provided both negative and positive formulations of the Golden Rule, which was so central in later natural law development. The patristic writings were often mediated through the *Glossa ordinaria*, a collection of patristic sayings on the scriptures.

The Scholastics frequently cited Origen and especially Augustine. Augustine enlarges the term "natural law" and sees it as a temporal expression of the eternal law. He connects the natural law with the unwritten law of the Gentiles (Rom 2:14–15) and to the Golden Rule and Decalogue as found in scripture. The natural law is an expression of the rational soul, which is an image of God.

The Scholastics also knew the work of the Roman jurists who treated natural law at some length, especially in the context of the *ius civile* (civil law) and the *ius gentium* (the law of nations). Gaius, in the second century, as found in the emperor Justinian's sixth-century *Digest*, distinguished these two types of law. The civil law is proper to each people while the law of nations is the common lot of humanity dictated by natural reason. The law of nations is not a positive law made for particular people, and the senate cannot change it. Before any human determination or convention according to the *ius gentium*, things belonging to no one belong to the one who first finds them or occupies the land, prisoners belong to their conquerors, and slavery is recognized by the law of nations.[10]

The most significant jurist in Justinian's *Digest* is Ulpian. Justinian's *Digest* begins with Ulpian's definition of natural law. Instead of the two-fold division of civil law and law of the nations as Gaius and earlier writers had proposed, Ulpian proposes a threefold division—*ius naturale* (natural law), law of the nations, and civil law. According to Ulpian, natural law is what nature has taught all the animals. The law of nations is what is observed by human beings and is proper to humans alone, and it falls short of the natural law, which is common to humans and all animals. This sets the stage for future discussions and disputes about the natural law and its relation to the *ius gentium* both among the Roman jurists themselves and among the later canon lawyers and theologians. By the Middle Ages, Ulpian's definition of natural law was generally called the definition of the jurists. The jurists who studied secular law at this time are often called the civilians to distinguish them from the canon or church lawyers.[11]

A very important figure in discussions among the Scholastics about natural law is Isidore of Seville (d. 636). Isidore was in most respects not an original thinker. The fifth book of his *Etymologies* made available to subsequent generations many of the writings of the earlier Roman lawyers. (The *Digest* of Justinian was not well known or often cited by others until 1070.[12]) However, Isidore did show creativity in his discussion of natural law. He maintained the threefold division of civil law, natural law, and the law of nations, but he totally rejected Ulpian's definition of natural law. Natural law is common to all nations and contains what is known to humans by rational instinct and not by a constitution or human-made law, such as the joining together of man and woman; the procreation and education of children; the common possession of all things; the freedom of all humans; the acquisition of things that may be captured in the air, the water, or the earth; the restitution of what has been loaned; and self-defense by force against violence. Note here the rejection of Ulpian's definition of natural law, although Isidore puts under his understanding of natural law the conjunction of male and female in the procreation and education of offspring, which was the characteristic illustration that Ulpian used for his different definition of natural law.

Isidore's approach also raised further questions for medieval Scholastics because he affirmed the common possession of all things and the freedom of all human beings as belonging to the natural law, whereas the

Scholastics accepted both private property and some slavery. For Isidore, the civil law is proper to particular people, the natural law is common to all nations, and the law of nations is what is in use among almost all people. He extended the law of nations to include treaties and matters of international law. Isidore also proposed another division of laws. All laws are either divine or human, and he identifies the natural law with the divine law. This too became the source for further discussion and disagreement among the Scholastics.[13]

A most significant figure in the natural law discussions among Scholastics was the twelfth-century Bolognese canon lawyer Gratian. His *Decretum* (*Decree*) of about 1140 was a private collection to bring some harmony into the existing conflicting canons. It was later incorporated into the *Corpus Iuris Canonici*, which was the canon law of the Church until 1918, when the Code of Canon Law came into force. Gratian has rightly been called the father of canon law. The *Decretum* actually begins with his discussion of natural law.

> The human race is ruled by a twofold rule, namely, natural law and custom. The natural law is that which is contained in the law and the Gospel by which each person is commanded to do to others what he would wish to be done to himself, and forbidden to render to others that which he would not have done to himself. Hence, Christ [says] in the Gospel, "All things whatever that you would wish other people to do to you, do the same also to them. For this is the law and the prophets."[14]

Gratian refers to Matthew 7:12 in the precept of doing unto others as we would wish others to do to us, and to Tobit 4:15 in the corresponding prohibition of not doing to others what we would not wish to have done to ourselves.[15]

Gratian accepts the threefold division of natural law, the law of nations, and civil law, and in his discussion of natural law in this context, he repeats the definition and understanding of Isidore. Natural law is common to all peoples because it is everywhere present by an instinct of nature and not by decree as exemplified in the union of man and woman, the procreation and education of children, the holding of all things in common and the equal freedom of all persons, and so on. Gratian does not accept Ulpian's definition of natural law, but he does incorporate some of its content into his understanding of natural law.[16]

Gratian's understanding of natural law differs sharply from any understanding previously mentioned. For Gratian, the natural law is found in the Law (Old Testament) and the Gospel (New Testament). The Law and the Gospel tell us about the Golden Rule to do unto others what you would wish other people do to you. Gratian goes on in the *Decretum* to point out that the natural law is contained in the Law and the Gospel, but not everything that is found in the Law and the Gospel belongs to natural law. Here he distinguishes certain moral precepts of the Law, such as do not kill, and mystical or sacrificial precepts, such as that concerning a lamb and other similar precepts. The moral commands belong to the natural law, and therefore they can be shown to be immutable.[17]

Gratian dealt explicitly with the issue of the immutability of natural law when he discussed the possibility of dispensation from the natural law. According to Gratian, no dispensation is allowed against the natural law unless it happens that two evils can be so pressing that it is necessary to choose one or the other. Gratian appeals to the Eighth Council of Toledo that if an unavoidable danger compels one to do one of two evils, do the one that obliges us to acknowledge the lesser debt. He also recalls the words of Gregory the Great, who, in such a situation where no path of escape lies open, maintains that lesser sins are always to be chosen.[18] This question of the immutability of natural law and dispensations would become quite central, especially when theologians had to deal with the fact that God gave commands in the Hebrew Bible that were seemingly against natural law teachings.

The commentators on the *Decretum* are called the decretists. Among many other things, they deal with the definition of natural law and the question of immutability. Rufinus of Assisi (d. circa 1190), perhaps the most influential of the decretists, maintained that Ulpian's definition is not relevant for his purposes. He defines natural law as a certain power of the human creature put in place by nature to do what is good and to avoid what is contrary to the good. This natural law consists of commands, prohibitions, and *demonstrationes*. Rufinus describes the *demonstrationes* as what nature neither commands nor prohibits but shows something as good. With regard to the immutability of natural law, the natural law cannot be modified by subtraction with regard to the commands and prohibitions. However, the counsels (*demonstrationes*)—which are not commands or prohibitions but only point to the good, such as the individual freedom of all human beings and the common possession of property—can be changed by the civil law.[19] Rufinus is dealing with the problem created by Isidore, who maintained that the freedom of all humans and the common possession of property belonged to the natural law. However, in actuality, the Church and the civil law accepted both slavery and private property.

A good number of the decretists simply list various definitions of natural law. Huguccio of Ferrara at the end of the twelfth century recognizes four different understandings of natural law but insists that there are only two proper senses of natural law—reason proper to man and the natural instinct of all living creatures. He identifies Gratian's definition of natural law as what is found in the Law and the Gospel with human reason directing us to the good and avoiding evil. Natural law thus exists subjectively in human reason and objectively in the law as found in scripture.[20]

The Scholastic theologians who emerged in the twelfth and thirteenth centuries inherited a tradition that included several different definitions and understandings of natural law (an innate force, human reason, what is common to humans and all the animals, and what is found in the Law and the Gospel) as well as different understandings of the relationship between natural law and the law of nations. How did they react to these differences? Again, our concern is not to give a full history but simply to illustrate the diversity.

Peter Lombard (d. 1160) wrote the *Four Books of Sentences*, which became the standard textbook of theology until the sixteenth century. Many subsequent theologians including Thomas Aquinas wrote commentaries on the *Sentences*. Peter Lombard has no discussion of natural law as a specific topic and scarcely even mentions it. But he did deal with the problems inherited from the canonists about the actions God commanded in the Hebrew Bible that seemed to be against the teachings of the Decalogue, such as polygamy, lying, and stealing. Apparently the first Scholastic theologian to devote a separate question to natural law was William of Auxerre, writing around 1220. William recognizes three different ways of understanding the natural law. The wide sense is Ulpian's definition—that which is common to humans and all the animals. The strict sense sees natural law connected with reason, which is somewhat intuitive. He also added a third, even wider sense—natural law is synonymous with the harmony of creation.[21]

Bonaventure (1221–75) has no specific treatment of natural law as a subject in itself, but he recognizes three different definitions of natural law—Gratian's, which is the common acceptance; Isidore's—what is common to all nations—which is the more precise definition; and Ulpian's, which is the most exact. On the other hand, Albert the Great

(1206–80) strongly insisted there can be no natural law common to humans and all animals.[22]

THOMAS AQUINAS

Thomas Aquinas himself testifies to the diverse definitions of natural law even as he finally developed his own approach to natural law. To understand Aquinas's reaction to the diverse definitions found in the tradition, one has to appreciate the approach of Scholastic theologians to "the authorities." The Scholastic method employed a systematic exposition of authoritative teachings. They paid great respect to the existing authorities and were often reluctant to disagree with them.[23] This characteristic is very evident in Aquinas himself. He seldom directly disagrees with an authority, but as a result of accepting what diverse authorities said, he sometimes tends to create confusion even about his own position. This approach is clearly present in his discussion of natural law.

Aquinas's understanding of natural law developed and matured over the years. In his *Commentary on the Sentences* dealing with the question of polygamy in the Hebrew Bible, Aquinas acknowledges three different understandings of the natural law—Cicero's, "the innate force"; Gratian's; and Ulpian's. He claims that in the most strict sense, natural law is what is common to humans and the animals.[24] In the *Summa*, Aquinas develops his own approach to natural law. Natural law is situated in the context of his discussion of law in general as an ordering of reason for the common good made and promulgated by one who has charge of the community. In this context the natural law is the participation of the eternal law in the rational creature. However, in the process of his discussion, Aquinas refers to the definitions of many of the authorities already mentioned, and he never directly refutes these views. Indeed, he tries to fit them into his own understanding. As a result, at times his acceptance of such approaches from earlier authorities creates some confusion and tension even with regard to his own approach. The example of his acceptance of the definitions of Isidore of Seville and of Ulpian will suffice to illustrate this problem.[25]

It seems that in the *Summa*, Aquinas definitively rejects Ulpian's approach by insisting on the rational aspect of natural law. Irrational creatures share in the eternal law in their own way. But the rational creature shares in it intellectually and rationally, and therefore the participation in the eternal law by the rational creature is properly called a law since law is a function of reason. In the irrational creature, it is not shared rationally and consequently cannot be called a law except by a similitude (*Ia IIae*, q.91, a.3; Aquinas makes a similar point in *Ia IIae*, q.92, a.5).

In *Ia IIae*, q.94, which deals explicitly with natural law, the position of Ulpian appears in a very significant way. The natural law follows the order of the inclinations of the human being. There are three such levels of inclination. The first is what humans share with all substances: the inclination to conserve oneself in being, and thus to conserve one's life, belongs to the natural law. Second is the inclination that humans share with all animals, and thus what nature teaches all the animals: the coming together of male and female and the education of children belong to natural law. The third inclination of human nature is the rational inclination proper to human beings: to know the truth about God and to live in human society, and hence that human beings should avoid ignorance, not offend others in society, and similar things belong to the natural law (*Ia IIae*, q.94, a.2). This explanation refers to the ontological basis of the natural law in terms of human nature that has these three inclinations. Here Aquinas seems to give some acceptance to Ulpian's definition of natural law.

Ulpian's definition of natural law appears again in the next question, *Ia IIae*, q.95, a.4, which deals with Isidore of Seville's understanding of the relationship between natural law and the law of nations. Aquinas had addressed this issue in his earlier commentary on the *Nichomachean Ethics* and concluded that the law of nations belongs to the natural law and not to the category of civil or human law. But he comes to a different conclusion in the *Summa*, especially because he does not want to contradict what he believes to be the position of Isidore of Seville. In this article he responds to the objection that the law of nations should belong to natural law and not to civil law. He believes that Isidore of Seville held that the law of nations belongs to the civil law, and he responds sharply and simply—the authority of Isidore suffices. But now he has to defend the position (which earlier he had opposed). Here he invokes the approach of Ulpian as one way to defend the position he attributes to Isidore. In one sense it can be said that the law of nations belongs to the natural law since it is based on reason and is derived from natural law by a conclusion not far removed from the first principles of natural law. However, it is distinguished from the natural law especially because the natural law is common to all animals. Michael Bertram Crowe discusses at some length

Aquinas's puzzling use of Ulpian in light of the Angelic Doctor's insistence that the natural law is rational. Crowe concludes that Ulpian was a strong authority that Aquinas was unwilling to accept yet loathed to cast aside.[26] For our purposes, Aquinas cannot bring himself to clearly oppose the definitions of authorities such as Ulpian and Isidore, even if it results in some confusion and apparent tensions in his own positions. Thus, Aquinas himself recognizes and uses diverse and pluralistic definitions and understandings of natural law.

To understand the theory of natural law in Aquinas, one needs to see it in the broader context of his ethics or moral theology as such. In my judgment, three characteristics of Aquinas's moral theology (Aquinas himself did not use this term; it first appeared in Alan of Lille [d. 1203][27]) stand out—the role of mediation, a teleological approach, and an intrinsic morality. First, mediation. The primary definition of natural law is the participation of the eternal law in the rational creature (*Ia IIae*, q.91, a.2). The eternal law is the reason of divine wisdom directing all actions and movements (*Ia IIae*, q.93, a.1). The natural law mediates the eternal law to the rational creature. Human reason reflecting on what God has made can determine what God is calling human beings to do. Human beings do not go immediately to God to ask what should be done. Rather, by using God-given reason and reflecting on what God has made, the rational creature can determine what is the plan of God.

Second, Aquinas's moral theology is teleological in its methodology. The first question for Aquinas is what is the ultimate end for human beings. The answer is happiness (*Ia IIae*, q.1). I call the Thomistic approach an intrinsic teleology, as distinguished from the extrinsic teleology of utilitarianism. For utilitarianism, something is good if it contributes to the greatest good of the greatest number. But for Aquinas, something is good because it contributes to the good of the person, whose ultimate good or end is happiness or fulfillment. Third, Thomistic morality is intrinsic. Something is commanded because it is good and not the other way around.

Most beginning scholars are very surprised by the comparatively minor role that natural law has in Aquinas. The *Summa* devotes only one question (*Ia IIae*, q.94) to natural law as such, but of course it is mentioned in many other places. For Aquinas, virtue is much more important than law in his ethics. He develops a special moral theology considering all specific human actions in this world not on the basis of laws such as the Ten Commandments but on the basis of the theological and cardinal virtues.

The virtues are perfective of the human person and again show that morality for Aquinas is based on what is good or perfective of the person.[28]

In the *Ia IIae*, Aquinas treats law after his discussion of virtue. Law in general for Aquinas is the ordering of reason for the common good made by one who has charge of the community and promulgated (*Ia IIae*, q.90, a.4). Note that all law for Aquinas is an ordering of reason and not primarily an act of the will. Such an emphasis coheres with his insistence on an intrinsic morality. Something is commanded because it is good. The will of the legislator does not make something right or wrong.

In discussing the precepts of the natural law, Aquinas compares the precepts of practical reason with the principles of speculative reason. The first principle of practical reason, like the first principle of speculative reason, is self-evident. The first self-evident principle of speculative reason is founded on being and recognizes that the same thing cannot be affirmed and denied at the same time. This is called the principle of non-contradiction—contradictory principles cannot at the same time both be true. Practical reason does not deal with being but with the good, and good has the nature of an end. Note again the teleological character of this ethics. The good is sought as perfective of the person. The first principle of practical reason is founded on the reason of the good. Hence, the first precept of the natural law is that good is to be done and pursued and evil is to be avoided. All other precepts of the natural law are particularizations of this first precept.

How are the other precepts developed? All those things to which human beings have a natural inclination are apprehended by reason as being good and consequently as objects of pursuit. The order of the precepts of natural law is based on the order of the three natural inclinations of the human being, which were developed in the earlier discussion of Ulpian's definition of natural law.

In his discussion of natural law in *Ia IIae*, q.94, a.4 and 5, Aquinas deals with the universality and immutability of natural law. He develops his thought by once again distinguishing between speculative reason and practical reason. Speculative reason deals with necessary things that cannot be other than what they are. Hence, its conclusions, like its first principles, are always true in reality. Practical reason deals with contingent matters. The general principles (e.g., good is to be done) are always true in reality, but the more one descends into specifics, the more defects can occur. In other words, as one descends to particulars, one cannot claim the same degree of certitude as in the general principles. Aquinas concludes from this that the natural law with regard to first principles is always and every way true. But in more specific or concrete matters that are conclusions, as it were, of the first principles, they are generally true but may not be true in a few cases because of what we today call extenuating circumstances. Aquinas gives one example. Borrowed goods should be returned to the owner when the owner asks for them. This is true most of the time, but not if the owner wants the goods back in order to fight against one's country. In treating the moral precepts of the Old Law (*Ia IIae*, q.100, a.1 and 3), Aquinas proposes a threefold distinction: the naturally known first principle, the precepts that can be known almost immediately and with very little consideration in light of the first principles, and other precepts that involve more complex reasoning and require the work of experts.

In addressing the question of the unchangeableness of natural law precepts (often referred to today as the absolute character of natural law norms), Aquinas, like all the medieval Scholastics, had to deal with the seeming exceptions to natural law precepts found especially in the Hebrew Bible. In discussing this question, Aquinas responds to the problems created by scripture. The slaying of the innocent, adultery, and theft are negative precepts of the natural law. But God commanded Abraham to kill his innocent son, and the Jews to take the vessels of the Egyptians, and Hosea to marry a harlot. There are also other examples, such as Abraham lying about the fact that Sarah was his wife and the widespread practice of polygamy. Also, Aquinas himself brings up the objection that, according to Isidore, the possession of all things in common and the freedom of all are matters of natural law, but in Aquinas's day private property and slavery were accepted.

Aquinas responds by saying that, with regard to subtraction (what was previously against natural law is now acceptable), the natural law is altogether unchangeable in its first principles. With regard to the secondary principles, the natural law can be changed in a very few cases because of some causes impeding the observance of the precept, as discussed earlier.

With regard to the scriptural problems, there is no injustice in these cases. By the command of God, death can be inflicted on anyone, guilty or innocent. Intercourse with any woman by the command of God is neither adultery nor fornication. With regard to theft, whatever is taken by the command of God to whom all things belong is not taken against the will of the owner, which is the malice of theft.

With regard to the objection from Isidore, something can belong to the natural law in two ways. In the first way, natural law inclines to this particular thing as, for example, injury should not be done to another. In the second way, nature does not call for the contrary. In this sense, for a human being to be naked is of the natural law. Nature does not give human beings clothes but art has supplied them. In this sense, the common possession of all things and universal freedom are of the natural law, but reason called for private property and slavery in order to benefit human life. The law of nature has been changed by addition, which is acceptable, but not by subtraction, which is always wrong.

Aquinas considered the possibility of dispensation from the precepts of the Decalogue in *Ia IIae*, q.100, a.8. Precepts that involve the preservation and protection of the common good or the very ordering of justice and virtue contain the intention of the legislator and thus cannot be dispensed from. The precepts of the Decalogue contain the intention of the legislator who is God, and therefore they cannot be dispensed from. Aquinas then uses this understanding to show that the examples in the Hebrew Bible did not involve dispensations given by God. For example, Abraham, in intending to kill his son, did not commit murder. To kill at the command of God is not against the natural law because God is lord of life and death.[29]

This is not the place to discuss in any detail the merits of Aquinas's approach to the universality and immutability of natural law in the Decalogue. But it should be pointed out that the unwillingness to accept dispensations given by God and the call for a rational explanation in these cases coheres with the Thomistic insistence on law as an ordering of reason, not as an act of the will, and that morality is intrinsic and not extrinsic. Likewise, according to Porter, it indicates some flexibility in applying natural law to particular cases.[30]

AFTER AQUINAS

Even the Scholastics after Aquinas often proposed quite different understandings of natural law. Scholars coming out of the neo-Scholasticism of the nineteenth and early twentieth century are quick to point out that Voluntarism and Nominalism in the centuries following Aquinas are radically different from and opposed to his natural law approach.[31] Voluntarism gave primacy to the will, whereas Aquinas stressed the intellect in his approach to natural law. Nominalism denied the existence of universals such as human nature, whereas Aquinas built his theory on human nature. For these neo-Scholastics, the problem began with John Duns Scotus (d. 1308), a Scottish Franciscan friar, and reached its zenith in the work of William of Ockham (d. 1348), an English Franciscan friar. According to Yves Simon, Ockham held that nothing is right or wrong by nature, but the morality of our actions is determined by arbitrary decrees of the divine will. For Aquinas, such words are sheer blasphemy.[32] A. d'Entrèves maintains that the vindication of the primacy of the will in Voluntarism made God's will the foundation of ethics. All moral laws are then reduced to the inscrutable manifestation of divine omnipotence. Natural law is no longer a standard of good and evil based on an eternal and immutable order that can be known by all human beings.[33] According to Heinrich Rommen, for Ockham an act is not good because of its suitableness to essential human nature but because God so wills. However, God could have willed the precise opposite. The natural law in this case is pure will without any foundation in reality based on the essential nature of things.[34]

Some scholars maintain that the neo-Scholastics were too one-sided in their interpretation of Scotus and Ockham. For example, with regard to Scotus, Hannes Möhle points out that one can find three different interpretations in the secondary literature about Scotus's understanding of ethics and natural law: (1) the rational accessibility of ethics is substantially reduced; (2) an extreme version claims that moral knowledge can be obtained only through revelation; and (3) an attempt to hold fast to some residual rationalism in Scotus's thought is contrasted with a radical Voluntarism. Möhle himself opts for the third approach, which leads neither to the abandonment of rational ethics nor to the destruction of its philosophical character.[35]

The Scholastics in the sixteenth century, especially in Spain and at Salamanca in what has been called the Silver Age of Scholasticism, went back to the writings of Thomas Aquinas.[36] According to the neo-Scholastic Heinrich Rommen, they successfully rehabilitated natural law on its true ontological foundation in the eternal law of God and human nature. The natural law is not related in a simplistic manner to the will of God. The natural law is related to God's essence and reason from which comes the eternal law itself. The natural law is the participation of the eternal law in the rational creature. The proximate principle of natural law is the essential nature of human beings.[37] The acknowledged leading figure at Salamanca was Francisco de Vitoria (d. 1546), who first introduced the *Summa* of Aquinas as the textbook in ethics and wrote extensively on questions of international law with special emphasis on the rights of natives in the Americas. Vitoria helped settle the long-standing debate that existed from the time of the Roman lawyers about the exact relationship between natural law and the *ius gentium*. The *ius gentium* is not the natural law but the quasi-positive law of the international community founded on custom and treaties.[38] However, even in what has been called the Silver Age of Scholasticism, which went back to the approach of Aquinas, some neo-Scholastics still saw unfortunate influences coming from Ockham and Voluntarism. The Jesuit Francisco Suárez (d. 1617) accepted Ockham's understanding of freedom as absolute indifference. With regard to the natural law, Suárez still gave too much importance to the will and not enough to reason and the intellect.[39] William E. May, a contemporary defender of the method and content of papal teaching, recognizes that Suárez's understanding of natural law is quite different from that of St. Thomas.[40]

In conclusion, this comparatively short overview convincingly shows that Scholasticism from its origins in the twelfth century to its end in the late sixteenth century contained a number of very different theoretical understandings of the natural law. There was no agreement on a coherent method and theory accepted by everyone. The secondary literature bears out this conclusion. Yves Simon claims that to speak of a Scholastic doctrine of natural law is nonsensical and misleading.[41] Jean Porter, in her study of the Scholastic theologians and canonists up to and including the thirteenth century, insists there is no one developed theory of natural law, but these texts propose a distinctive concept of natural law, less comprehensive than a systematic theory but more than simply ad hoc and fragmentary comments.[42] D. J. O'Connor likewise maintains there is no single theory of natural law, but he describes the common core as maintaining in some sense or other that the basic principles of morals are objective, accessible to reason, and based on human nature.[43]

NEO-SCHOLASTICISM AND ITS AFTERMATH

As mentioned in chapter 2, Thomism had very little influence in Catholic scholarship in the seventeenth, eighteenth, and nineteenth centuries until the neo-Scholastic movement, strongly supported by Leo XIII in the nineteenth century. With his 1879 encyclical *Aeterni Patris*, Leo XIII urged Catholic scholars and universities to employ the approach of Thomas Aquinas, which obviously included also the natural law approach.

The Manuals and other Philosophical Writings on Natural Law before Vatican II

As pointed out earlier, however, the manuals of moral theology did not really change their basic methodological approach despite Leo's insistence on the need for Thomism. Even before neo-Scholasticism, the manuals appealed to natural law, but they paid very little attention to the theory of natural law. As the twentieth century began and developed, the approach of the manuals of moral theologians was fearful of any innovative and creative aspects and continued merely to repeat what had been said in the past.

The manual of Aloysius Sabetti, written in Latin for Jesuits and other seminarians in the United States at the end of the nineteenth century, discusses different species of law—natural law, divine positive law, ecclesiastical law, irritating laws, custom, and privileges. However, the discussion of natural law takes up only one page.[44] Not only do the manuals of moral theology not develop in depth and breadth the more theoretical aspects of moral theology, but they also distort the basic Thomistic understanding of natural law. As pointed out earlier, natural law for Aquinas is a teleological approach to ethics based on the internal drive of the human person to happiness as the ultimate end. This approach proposes an intrinsic morality according to which something is commanded because it is good. The manuals, however, employ a deontological approach to moral theology based on a legal model in order to determine what is sinful and the degree of sinfulness. Alphonsus Liguori (d. 1787), the officially declared patron of moral theologians, accepted the deontological approach of the earlier manuals with their very practical focus. According to Alphonsus, there is a twofold rule of human actions—the remote or material rule is divine law, and the proximate and formal rule is conscience.[45] This basic understanding determines the structure of the fundamental moral theology of the manuals with two very large treatises on conscience and law. This basic structure of the manuals continued until Vatican II. For example, the Noldin manual frequently used in the United States follows the same approach.[46] The understanding and role of natural law in the manuals of moral theology thus differs considerably from the method and approach of Aquinas. Neo-Scholastics have recognized that the moral theory of natural law of the manuals of moral theology is not the theory and natural law of Aquinas. At the end of the nineteenth century, Thomas Bouquillon excoriated the manualists for not truly following Aquinas.[47] Thomas E. Davitt, writing in 1951, pointed out that most manuals of moral theology and canon law do not follow the Thomistic understanding of natural law.[48]

Germain Grisez, a staunch defender of the moral teachings of the papal magisterium, called the approach of the manuals primarily Suárezian, and not Thomistic. Grisez points out that the approach of the manuals is inevitably static. There is no basis here for creativity and innovation. The intrinsic linkage between human moral life and the supernatural life is slighted. As a result of these defects, this theory fails to offer convincing arguments concerning current moral issues.[49] The assertion made by Grisez can be amply supported. For example, Peter Scavini, in his manual written in 1851, specifically adopts the position of Suárez that the obligation in the natural law does not arise from the nature of things but from the divine will.[50] The 1952 manual of Marcellinus Zalba frequently cites Suárez in the footnotes dealing with natural law.[51]

Before Vatican II some Catholic scholars criticized aspects of the neo-Scholastic revival, especially its failure to go back to the very writings of Aquinas.[52] On the question of natural law, Jacques Maritain, the renowned French Thomist who exercised a considerable influence in the United States and Latin America, made a significant contribution to the Thomistic understanding of natural law by disagreeing with its deductive character. The manuals of theology as exemplified in the work of Zalba refer to the primary conclusions of the natural law with a clear and evident connection to the first principle of natural law as being deduced by an immediate application of the first principle to the concrete realities, such as parents are to be honored. The secondary principles are deduced by a more difficult reasoning process and hence need a special expertise.[53] Michael Crowe also refers to the primary common principles as deduced by an immediate consideration from the first principle, whereas the other deductions require a more involved reasoning process that calls for the expertise of a specialist.[54] Aquinas's own treatment could serve as a basis for the emphasis on a deductive approach. Aquinas speaks of the conclusions of the first principle and compares the modes of practical reason

with speculative reason, which moves from the first principle to the conclusions derived from that principle.[55]

However, Maritain maintains that for Aquinas the conclusions from
the first principle of natural law were not derived through a rational reasoning process with concepts and conceptual judgments but involved
knowledge through inclination. Such knowledge is not clear knowledge
through concepts and conceptual judgments but is obscure, unsystematic,
vital knowledge by connaturality or congeniality in which the intellect
consults and listens to the inner melody that the vibrating strings of abid-
ing tendencies make present in the subject. As a result, Maritain claims
that Aquinas's views call for a more historical approach and a philosophical acceptance of the idea of development that the Middle Ages were not
equipped to carry into effect. In fact, Maritain uses this approach to justify
democracy and human rights in his discussion of social ethics.[56]

Papal Social Teaching and Catholic Philosophical Social Ethics

Although Leo's insistence on using Thomism had little or no effect on
the manuals of moral theology, it had a very enduring and significant
effect on papal social teaching and the social ethics proposed by Catholic
philosophers. *Aeterni Patris* itself set the direction for this significant
future development. Thomistic philosophy is the best approach to restore
a sound and just social order.[57] Leo himself used this Scholastic approach
in his many encyclicals speaking to the modern world.[58] Leo XIII's 1891
encyclical *Rerum novarum* (often called in English "On the Rights and
Duties of Capital and Labor") began a long line of subsequent papal
encyclicals using Thomistic philosophy in general and the natural law in
particular to point out what is a just social order.[59] Since these papal
documents were primarily teaching documents for the whole Church,
they do not develop the theoretical understanding of natural law but
apply natural law to show what the just society should be and to point out
deficiencies in other approaches. For example, Leo XIII begins *Rerum
novarum* by insisting that private property is based on "human nature"
and "natural law" (no. 6–7, O-S, 16–17). The "most sacred law of
nature" demands that a father provide food and necessities for his children (no. 9, O-S, 18). Socialism is "against natural justice" and "contrary
to the natural rights of workers" (no. 11 and 12, O-S, 19). Thus, natural
law grounds the basic teachings of *Rerum novarum*. Subsequent papal documents in what became known as the tradition of Catholic social teaching

continued to use the natural law approach. Pius XI's *Quadragesimo anno* (1931) and John XXIII's *Mater et magistra* (1961) commemorated anniversaries of *Rerum novarum* and applied its principles to new circumstances and conditions with the emphasis on the approach of human reason, human nature, and natural law. John XXIII, in *Mater et magistra*, for example, continued the same methodology by proposing a "social message based on the requirements of human nature itself and conforming to the precepts of the Gospel and reason" (no. 15, O-S, 86).

Papal social teaching used such a natural law approach exclusively until Vatican II. *Pacem in terris*, the 1963 encyclical of John XXIII, well illustrates this approach, which does not appeal to any uniquely Christian warrants. The very first paragraphs of *Pacem in terris* spell out the methodology to be followed in the whole encyclical.

> Peace on earth, which all people of every era have most eagerly yearned for, can be firmly established only if the order laid down by God be dutifully observed. . . . The Creator of the world has imprinted in the human heart an order which conscience reveals to us and enjoins us to obey. . . . [Many] think that the relationships between people and States can be governed by the same laws as the forces and irrational elements of the universe, whereas the laws governing them are of quite a different kind and are to be sought elsewhere, namely where the father of all things wrote them, that is, in the nature of human beings. (no. 1–6, O-S, 137–38)

Gaudium et spes, the Pastoral Constitution on the Church in the Modern World, insisted on overcoming the split between faith and daily life. Faith, grace, scripture, and Jesus Christ should have some effect on all aspects of social, political, and economic life (no. 43, O-S, 201–3). Subsequent papal documents gave more emphasis to the specifically Christian approach, but they still recognized the need for these documents to appeal to all people of goodwill on the premises that could be accepted by all.

In his 1986 encyclical *Sollicitudo rei socialis*, John Paul II found a creative way to recognize the role for a specifically Christian approach and at the same time to address all people of goodwill. He dedicated section five of the encyclical to "a theological reading of modern problems." Here he dealt with the specifically Christian aspects of the structures of sin, the need for conversion, and the virtue of Christian solidarity. But even in this specifically Christian theological analysis in this one section, he hopes

that women and men of goodwill without an explicit faith would be convinced of the need to recognize and overcome the obstacles to integral
human development (no. 35–40, O-S, 449–557).

Since *Aeterni Patris* dealt with the restoration of Christian philosophy,
it had a strong influence on Catholic philosophers who used Thomistic
philosophy and natural law to address the social issues of the modern
world. A group of German scholars associated with the Königswinter
Circle included such figures as Oswald von Nell-Breuning (the primary
drafter of Pius XI's encyclical *Quadragesimo anno*), Gustav Gundlach SJ,
Goetz Briefs, and Theodore Brauer. Heinrich Rommen, whose book was
mentioned earlier, was also a member of this group.[60] The French philosopher Jacques Maritain had a worldwide influence in his attempt to use
Thomism and natural law to deal with human rights and democracy. John
Courtney Murray, an American Jesuit, used natural law to provide the
structural foundations of the political, social, and economic orders as they
should exist in the United States. In fact, Murray lamented the fact that
in America the natural law ethic, which launched Western constitutional-
ism and gave essential form to the American system of government,
has now ceased to sustain the structure and direct the action of this
commonwealth.[61]

These Catholic philosophers did not speak with and write only for
Catholics. In the middle part of the twentieth century and in light of the
world wars and the atrocities connected with them, others outside the
Catholic Church took an interest in natural law. Natural law provided a
way for judging the unjust regimes and laws of particular countries and
also for preserving and promoting the human rights of all. Jacques Maritain, for example, stayed in the United States during World War II and
taught at both Princeton and Columbia Universities.[62] John Courtney
Murray was frequently involved in dialogue with many leading American
thinkers through the think tank Center for the Study of Democratic Institutions and other groups.[63]

Murray was not a philosopher but a theologian. However, he accepted
and based many aspects of his approach on the neo-Scholastic distinction
between the natural order and the supernatural order. The natural order
refers to the temporal aspect of existence as distinct from the spiritual,
that is, to life in the world. This life is governed by the natural law.
Catholic theologians influenced by this neo-Scholastic approach saw the
natural law as governing all social ethics in this world. However, even
before Vatican II some Catholic theologians and Thomistic scholars

objected to this approach and argued that this distinction or even separation was not a correct interpretation of Aquinas's own approach.[64] After Vatican II, as pointed out with regard to papal social teaching, the strong distinction between the natural order and the supernatural order was no longer accepted. Grace, faith, and Jesus Christ had to affect everything in our world. However, grace is mediated in and through the human.

Personal Ethics

Today Catholic moral theologians are hesitant to see a great division between personal and social ethics, but in a pre–Vatican II era this distinction was frequently made and observed. Although the teaching of the manuals of moral theology did not adopt the basic Thomistic approach to the moral life, Catholic moral theologians regularly used natural law to explain and defend their teaching on sexual ethics.[65] Joseph Fuchs gave significant attention to the theory of natural law.[66] He developed a sexual ethic on the basis of human nature—the essence of the human sexual faculty and its act. In his 1963 book, Fuchs strongly defended the existing Catholic teaching but later changed his mind with regard to both the understanding of natural law and the teaching on such sexual issues as contraception.[67]

Medical ethics became a special area in Catholic moral theology in the middle of the twentieth century. Catholic medical ethicists used the natural law as the basis for their teaching, but their discussion of the theory of natural law was brief and cursory. For example, in his 1956 book, *Medical Ethics*, Edwin F. Healy, an American Jesuit teaching at the Gregorian University in Rome, began by discussing natural law. Human beings freely choose to act. God imposes on them the obligation to act in accord with their rational human nature. God has given us certain commandments and prohibitions, the observance of which enables us to accomplish the purpose for which God made us. These fundamental commands and prohibitions form what is commonly referred to as the natural law. Healy devoted fewer than five pages to the development of natural law.[68]

Authoritative papal moral teaching on personal ethics in the twentieth century before Vatican II insisted on its natural law basis. One of the most authoritative of such teachings was Pope Pius XI's 1930 encyclical, *Casti connubii*, with its strong condemnation of artificial contraception for spouses. "Any use whatsoever of matrimony exercised in such a way that the act is deliberately frustrated in its natural power to generate life is an offense against the law of God and of nature."[69]

Pope Pius XII (1939–58), who succeeded Pius XI, authoritatively taught much more than any previous pope on issues in moral theology. John Kenny, in his book *Principles of Medical Ethics*, reports that Pius XII gave seventy-five allocutions in the area of medical ethics alone. The pope used these many allocutions and addresses to various groups to express his teaching. However, these addresses were not only to Catholic groups but also to many secular groups. Within a three-year span the pope spoke to the following groups: The First International Conference on Histopathology of the Nervous System (1952), The Fifth International Congress of Psychotherapy and Clinical Psychology (1953), The Twenty-Sixth Congress of the Italian Society of Urology (1953), and the Eighth Assembly of the World Medical Association (1954).[70] The natural law served as the basis for Pius XIII's moral teachings. For example, "artificial fecundation violates the natural law and is contrary to justice and morality."[71] "Direct sterilization, either permanent or temporary, of man or of woman, is illegal by virtue of the natural law from which, as you are aware, the Church has no power to dispense."[72]

VATICAN II AND *HUMANAE VITAE*

The two most significant ecclesial realities affecting the Catholic Church in general and moral theology in particular in the latter part of the twentieth century were the Second Vatican Council (1962–65) and Pope Paul VI's 1968 encyclical *Humanae vitae*. Vatican II's effect on the discussion of natural law was both direct and indirect. Chapter 5 develops this effect in greater detail. For our purposes, it is sufficient to point out that the Pastoral Constitution on the Church in the Modern World lamented the split between faith and daily life. This split deserved to be counted among the more serious errors of our age (no. 43, O-S, 202). In its own methodology dealing with the understanding of the human person, human community, and human activity, the Pastoral Constitution appealed not only to creation but also to the roles of sin, redemption, and in the discussion of human activity, to eschatology (no. 12–39, O-S, 181–98). Such an approach replaced the older distinction and even practical separation between the supernatural and the natural orders, which had characterized both papal teaching and much of Catholic social ethics in the period from neo-Scholasticism to Vatican II. This aspect of natural law has been called the theological aspect of natural law. This aspect maintains that the Church and Christians accept human sources of moral wisdom and knowledge and use the sources almost exclusively in addressing the world and its issues. The philosophical aspect of the natural law discussion concerns what is meant by human nature and human reason. The Council did not directly deal with the philosophical concept of natural law, but chapter 5 shows in detail that the Council indirectly opened the door to the possibility of rethinking natural law with its emphasis on *ressourcement*, *aggiornamento*, and dialogue.

The issue of artificial contraception became the lens for discussing the philosophical aspect of natural law in the Catholic Church in the 1960s and subsequently.[73] Papal teaching continued to repeat the natural law–based condemnation of artificial contraception. The discovery and marketing of the birth control pill in the 1950s created a widespread conversation about the pill and contraception. On September 12, 1958, in an address to the Seventh International Conference of Hematology, Pius XII used the natural law approach to condemn the use of the pill as a means of preventing birth. Immediately after the address the moral theologians who wrote on the subject unanimously agreed with and explained the papal teaching. However, change and discussion were in the air.

In the United States in 1963, John Rock, a Catholic doctor who played a major role in the development of the birth control pill, published his book advocating that the Catholic Church accept the pill for contraceptive purposes. It was only in late 1963 that three articles appeared in respected Catholic theological journals in Europe arguing for using the pill for contraceptive purposes. The authors were Fr. Louis Janssens, the well-respected professor of moral theology at the University of Louvain in Belgium; William van der Marck, a young Dutch Dominican; and Joseph M. Reuss, the auxiliary bishop of Mainz, Germany. On June 23, 1964, Pope Paul VI announced the existence of the commission that was studying the birth control issue, but the existing norms were still in effect. The pope also took the issue of contraception out of the agenda of the ongoing Second Vatican Council. Discussions pro and con occurred throughout the Catholic world while awaiting the work of the commission and the final decision by the pope.

Finally, on July 29, 1968, the Vatican released the encyclical *Humanae vitae* of Paul VI. The pope repeated the condemnation of artificial contraception based on the natural law. Spouses must conform their activities to the very nature of marriage and its acts. By its intimate structure, the conjugal act capacitates spouses for the generation of new lives according to laws inscribed in their very being. Consequently, the Church, calling people back to the observance of the norms of natural law as interpreted by constant doctrine, teaches that each and every marriage act must be open to the transmission of life. Human beings do not have dominion over their generative faculties as such because of their intrinsic orientation toward raising up life.[74] The magisterium has been entrusted by God as the guardian and authentic interpreter of all the moral law, not only the law of the Gospel but also the natural law, which is an expression of the will of God, the fulfillment of which is necessary for salvation.[75]

The contraception issue was the occasion for the broader discussion of natural law in the Catholic Church. But discussion of some other issues, especially in the area of sexuality, also influenced the debate about natural law. Three basic positions emerged among Catholic theologians—the revisionist approach, the new natural law approach of Germain Grisez, and a defense of the papal approach and its teachings.

The Revisionist Approach

The revisionist approach challenged the papal and manualistic understanding of natural law on three counts—the problem of physicalism, the lack of historical consciousness, and the emphasis on the teleology of the faculty with the failure to give primary importance to the person and the person's relationships.[76] First, the charge of physicalism or biologism criticizes the hierarchical approach for identifying the moral and human act with the physical or biological aspect of the act. For example, in the case of artificial contraception for spouses, the physical aspect of the conjugal act becomes normative. One cannot interfere with the physical process for any reason. This is the basis for the papal condemnation of both artificial contraception and artificial insemination even with the husband's seed.[77] In both cases one interferes with the physical structure of the sexual act itself, even though the purpose and intention of such artificial insemination is to have a child. The insistence that every act of sexual intercourse must be open to procreation also serves to condemn masturbation and homosexual acts. In many and almost all other circumstances, the Catholic teaching accepts the need to interfere in the physical and biological for an acceptable reason such as medicine's need to amputate or remove part of the body to save the whole. The human or moral aspect is more than just the physical or biological aspect of the human. The human or moral aspect brings together every single particular aspect of the human such as the physiological, the sociological, the psychological, the eugenic, the hygienic, and so on. You cannot absolutize any one of these partial perspectives of the human. The Catholic tradition has always distinguished between the physical act of killing and the moral act of murder.

Some have seen here the influence of Aquinas's threefold inclinations, especially the second inclination based on Ulpian's definition of natural law as what humans share with all animals, such as sexual intercourse and the education of offspring. Thus, Aquinas's anthropology involves a three-layer approach—what humans share with all substances, what we share with all animals, and what is proper to humans in keeping with their rational nature. Such an approach seems to canonize what nature teaches human beings and all the animals and does not allow human reason to interfere in these biological and animal structures.[78]

Second, revisionists agree that a historically conscious approach should replace the classicism of the accepted natural law theory. Bernard Lonergan pointed out that the primary shift that occurred at Vatican II involved a methodological shift from a classicist approach to a more historically conscious approach.[79] Classicism begins with an unchanging element named human nature. Then one works methodically from the abstract and universal toward the more concrete and particular. In so doing, one is involved in the casuistry of applying universals to concrete reality. One begins with the definition of a human being that applies to every human being with properties verified in every person. One thus knows the human being as such, which is unchangeable. On the other hand, the historically conscious approach begins from people where they are performing intentional acts that give meaning and significance to human living. Just as meaningful, performance is constitutive of human living, so common meaning is constitutive of community. This understanding sees humankind as a concrete aggregate developing over time and not something totally fixed and immutable. Human nature itself is historically developing and changing.[80]

In light of Lonergan's approach, one can develop an understanding of these two different methodologies. The classicist methodology tends to be abstract, a priori, and deductive. It begins with the abstract essence that is universal and immutable. Thus, in natural law theory the first principle of morality is established and then other universal norms of conduct are deduced from it. There is no doubt that the manuals of moral theology generally employed such a deductive methodology. The first and most universal principle of natural law according to Aquinas is that good is to be done and evil is to be avoided. This principle is self-evident and implicitly contains the whole natural law. The primary and secondary conclusions of the natural law are deduced from the first principle.[81] The historically conscious methodology tends to be concrete, a posteriori, and inductive.

Proponents of revisionism point out that a historically conscious methodology can account for the changes that have occurred in Catholic moral teaching over the years—religious freedom, democracy, human rights, capital punishment, slavery, the role of women, the ends of marriage, and the role of pleasure in the marital act.[82]

A more historically conscious methodology cannot claim the same certitude for its proposals that a classicist approach does. By its very nature, historical consciousness recognizes that practical reason deals with contingent realities and circumstances and in very specific issues one cannot claim moral certitude. To its credit, the Thomistic approach recognized that the secondary principles of the natural law oblige in general and can admit of exceptions. But papal teaching has on occasion claimed great certitude for its teaching on very controversial issues. Pope John Paul II in *Evangelium vitae* strongly condemned direct abortion and the direct taking of human life.[83] This condemnation is based on the nineteenth- and twentieth-century understanding of the difference between direct and indirect. This distinction is based on a very complex philosophical understanding. As a result, one really cannot claim for this position a certitude that excludes the possibility of error. The very fact that the contemporary Catholic understanding of direct and indirect abortion only evolved in the late nineteenth and early twentieth century in the midst of much theological discussion and controversy well indicates that one cannot claim certitude for such a position.[84]

Third, revisionists maintain that an emphasis on the person and the person's relationships should replace the emphasis on the faculty or power. The sexual teaching of the manuals and of the hierarchical teaching office is based on a teleology of the faculty. Thus, Joseph Fuchs, in the 1963 edition of his book on sexuality, gives as the first reason for the condemnation of artificial contraception for spouses that it goes against the finality of the sexual faculty as taught by *Casti connubii*. Fuchs makes an analogy with the condemnation of lying. Lying is a perversion of the

natural ordering because it involves an abuse of the faculty of speech that
exists for the purpose of communicating to others what is in one's mind.[85]
A few years later, Fuchs changed his position on these questions of sexuality and became one of the leading revisionist moral theologians.[86] A personalist and more relational understanding of the person would come to
a different judgment on the morality of artificial contraception. For the
good of the person or of the relationship, one could interfere with the
teleological ordering of the faculty. This same approach could be applied
to other sexual issues, such as homosexual acts.

In the twentieth century, some Catholic theologians recognized a
problem with the malice of lying based on the teleology of the faculty of
speech with its definition of a lie as speech that goes against what is in
one's mind. The ultimate malice of lying rests on the relational criterion
of the violation of my neighbor's right to truth. Sometimes (e.g., when
the Gestapo inquires if a person is hiding Jews in her house) the neighbor
does not have the right to truth. In that case, when the person denies
hiding Jews to the Gestapo, what is involved is false speech but not the
moral reality of lying.[87] A fascinating development concerning the morality of lying occurred in the *Catechism of the Catholic Church*. The 1994
edition understands a lie as "to speak or act against the truth in order to
lead into error someone who has the right to know the truth."[88] Thus,
the *Catechism* accepted the newer approach to lying. When the definitive
Latin edition of the *Catechism* appeared in 1997, Cardinal Ratzinger, the
prefect of the Congregation for the Doctrine of the Faith, issued a short
list of changes or corrections to what was found in the 1994 edition but
did not give the reason for these corrections. Among these corrections is
that the description of lying should now read: "To lie is to speak or act
against the truth in order to lead someone into error."[89] The malice of
lying here does not consist in the violation of the neighbor's right to
truth. Ratzinger well knew that many Catholic theologians today use the
analogy of lying to argue against the faculty analysis with regard to human
sexuality.

This section does not attempt to present an exhaustive development of
a revisionist approach to moral theology. It has merely pointed out its
more pertinent criticisms of the natural law theory employed by the papal
magisterium and some other Catholics. There is no doubt that a very
large number of Catholic moral theologians, including myself, fit under
this umbrella of revisionism.

The New Natural Law Theory

In the context of the discussion about contraception and other moral issues in relationship to natural law, Germain Grisez and, later, John Finnis developed what has been called the "new natural law theory." Grisez is a US-trained philosopher and prolific author on ethical issues who, after the 1960s, concentrated on Catholic moral theology, first enunciated his natural law theory in the context of contraception, and eventually wrote a three-volume text in moral theology.[90] Finnis, an Australian, studied and taught jurisprudence and philosophy at Oxford and more recently also teaches at the University of Notre Dame Law School.[91] Grisez and Finnis have staunchly defended the teaching of the papal and hierarchical magisterium on particular contentious moral issues.

According to Grisez, Aquinas's first principle of practical reason—good is to be done and pursued and evil is to be avoided—is not a moral precept as such. For Grisez, the first principle of morality is this: "In voluntarily acting for human goods and avoiding what is opposed to them, one ought to choose and otherwise will those and only those possibilities whose willing is compatible with a will toward integral human fulfillment."[92] Grisez then develops modes of responsibility as intermediate principles that are somewhat formal in nature and involve not moral actions but ways of choosing and acting that spell out this first general moral principle. The first mode of responsibility, for example, holds that one should not be deterred by inertia from acting for intelligible goods. The most significant of the modes of responsibility for the defense of the absolute moral norms taught by the hierarchical magisterium is the eighth and final mode: one should not be so moved by desire for one instance of an intelligible good that one chooses to destroy, damage, or impede some other instance of an intelligible good to obtain it. In other words, one cannot go against a basic human good in trying to achieve some other basic human good. For Grisez, basic human goods are incommensurate; there is no common denominator for judging what the greater good is.[93]

What are these basic human goods? Grisez maintains there are eight self-evident basic human goods that are not deduced from any first principle or derived from our understanding of human nature. Grisez does not want to accept an ethic that is based on human nature. We know these goods just by knowing the meaning of their terms. Four are existential goods—integration, practical reasonableness or authenticity, friendship and justice, and religion or holiness. Three are substantive goods—life and bodily well-being, knowledge of truth and appreciation of beauty, and skill for performance and play. The eighth good is the complex good of marriage and family. The permanent good of man and woman that normally unfolds in parenthood and family life is both substantive and reflexive. This is a substantive good insofar as it fulfills the capacity of men and women to complement one another, have children, and bring them up; but it is also a reflexive good insofar as it includes the free choices of a couple marrying and committing themselves to fulfill all the responsibilities of marriage.[94]

Grisez explicitly recognizes that his theory differs from what he calls the "Scholastic natural law theory," which is based on human nature.[95] According to the Scholastic natural law theory, actions that conform to human nature are good; those that do not conform are evil. God has commanded us to do what is in harmony with our created nature and to refrain from doing what is not. Grisez points out several positive aspects about this Scholastic natural law perspective, especially in the light of other theories that deny that moral norms are truths, or others such as intuitionism and cultural relativism, which recognize moral norms as truths but are seriously defective in other ways. In the Scholastic natural law theory, morality is not arbitrary since creation has meaning and value placed there by God. To do what is morally right is to act in accord with the truth about ourselves. This theory does not reduce morality to a mere adjunct to society and its requirements for survival and good functioning since human nature is more basic than human society. Scripture itself speaks of a natural law written in the heart.

However, this Scholastic natural law theory is inadequate. Central to the theory is a logically impermissible leap from human nature as given to the way human beings are morally obliged to choose and act. Logically, one cannot derive an "ought" from an "is." The fact of how reality is does not by itself tell us how to respond to reality, which is a moral norm. The theory furthermore misunderstands the normative character of nature, which is not the same as the normative character of morality. Morality is conferred with free choices. Nature might call for monkeys to eat bananas rather than hamburgers, but that has nothing to do with choice. A fundamental confusion underlies a moral theory that confuses the normativity of nature with the normativity of human practical reason. Scholastic natural law theory does not adequately grasp the role of free choice and self-determination. In this perspective, choice merely triggers behavior that is or is not in conformity with nature. The creativity of moral reflection with respect to possibilities and the self-determining role of freedom is overlooked.

In light of this, Grisez finds inadequate arguments on behalf of certain moral norms. Why is contraception wrong? The Scholastic natural law theory maintains it is wrong because it perverts the faculty that is naturally oriented toward procreation. It goes against the God-given nature of the faculty toward procreation. If that is a good argument, then it is also a good argument to say that chewing gum after the sugar is gone is wrong because it perverts the faculty that is naturally oriented toward nutrition. In Grisez's theory, contraception is a choice to prevent the passing on of human life, but this is a choice to impede the basic human good of life in a particular instance.

Grisez also sees Scholastic natural law theory as contributing to other defects in classical moral theology. Those who equate moral goodness with conformity to nature, and moral evil with failure to conform, place emphasis on what does not fit the pattern. But this leads to the negativism and minimalism of classic moral theology. This approach is inevitably static. Thus, there is no basis for creativity and innovation. The role of human beings as cocreators, coredeemers, and cooperators with God in bringing about the fullness of the kingdom gets short shrift. In addition, the intrinsic linkage between human moral life and supernatural life is slighted. Grisez proposes his theory of natural law as a better way to defend and support the traditional teachings proposed by the hierarchical magisterium.

A Defense of the Papal Approach to Natural Law

A third group of Catholic scholars opposes both the revisionist position and the new natural law theory while strongly supporting the natural law theory that serves as a basis for the current papal and hierarchical teaching on issues disputed by others in the Catholic Church in the last fifty years. Basically, they are working in the mainline realism of Thomistic natural law theory as it existed in the pre–Vatican II period. A good example of this third approach is the work of the late Notre Dame philosopher Ralph McInerny. McInerny was a well-known and published neo-Scholastic who dealt with many different areas of Thomism but also wrote on Thomistic ethics. In developing his approach to natural law he sharply differed with the new natural law theory and with the revisionist approach and its dissent from papal teachings.[96]

Romanus Cessario, a much-published Dominican priest now teaching on the faculty at St. John's Seminary in Boston, has written extensively on Thomas Aquinas with a special emphasis on the virtues.[97] He develops his Thomistic understanding of the natural law in his 2001 *Introduction to Moral Theology*.[98]

Martin Rhonheimer is a Swiss-born priest teaching at the Opus Dei University in Rome whose many writings on Thomas and natural law have recently been translated into English. He understands natural law as a cognitive reality that formally belongs to human reason embedded in the strivings of the natural inclinations and their ends. The precepts of the natural law are the first principles of practical reason and moral reasoning, but they are dependent on the natural inclinations understood as goods of reason. He avoids reducing the natural law either to human reason alone or to nature but claims that he has been wrongly accused of both of these extreme positions. Rhonheimer vigorously defends the positions and norms proposed by the papal magisterium. He spends the most time refuting the revisionist approach and gives special attention to Joseph Fuchs, Franz Böckle, and Richard McCormick, but he also has differences with Grisez and Finnis and with Servais Pinckaers.[99]

Pope John Paul II defended the papal theory of natural law in his 1993 encyclical *Veritatis splendor*. This encyclical differs from all his other encyclicals because it is addressed only to his brother bishops and not to all the faithful and all people of goodwill. The reason for this restricted audience comes from the fact that in this encyclical, the pope addresses the more theoretical question of the very foundations of moral theology. The occasion for *Veritatis splendor* was the existence in the Church of a genuine crisis involving a widespread dissent among theologians calling into question both the theoretical aspects of natural law teaching and many practical conclusions taught by the papal magisterium. The theoretical errors come from detaching human freedom from its constitutive relationship to truth and denying the universality and immutability of the precepts of natural law.[100]

In response to these two major theoretical problems, *Veritatis splendor* insists that natural law properly understood recognizes there is no conflict between freedom and law precisely because freedom depends on truth. God, not human beings, determines what is right or wrong. The eternal law is the divine wisdom itself, and the natural law is the participation of the eternal law in the rational creature. The natural law thus grounds a participative theonomy, which avoids the two extremes of autonomy (human beings determine their own law) and heteronomy (human beings are governed by an outside force). The natural law proposes both what is the law of God and what is the law of human nature, which entails what is good for human beings and contributes to their happiness and well-being. Human freedom depends upon the truth of who we are as human beings (no. 37–44).

Veritatis splendor insists on the two characteristics of natural law—its universality and immutability. In defending these characteristics, the pope responds to the criticisms of physicalism and the lack of historical consciousness made by revisionist theologians but never mentions any of these theologians by name. In response to the charge of physicalism or biologism, *Veritatis splendor* insists on the unity of the human person whose rational soul is per se and *essentialiter* the form of the body. The body is not just a raw datum devoid of meaning and value that can be shaped by human freedom for whatever purposes it wants. Any teaching that disassociates the moral act from the bodily dimensions of its exercise is contrary to the teaching of scripture and tradition (no. 48–50).

The pope also rejects the appeal to historical consciousness that emphasizes cultural changes and calls into question the universality of the natural law and the existence of absolute objective moral norms. Yes, human beings exist in different cultures, but there is something in human beings—human nature—that transcends culture and is the measure of culture. For the pope, unchanging human nature is the basis for both the universality and immutability of natural law. The encyclical does not deny a proper individuality for the person and a proper recognition of some historical development, but there are negative precepts of the natural law that are universally valid for all human beings in all circumstances (no. 51–53).

One cannot expect even an encyclical of this type to develop in depth its natural law theory, but there are two aspects of the Thomistic theory of natural law that are not developed here. First, there is no mention of how the universal and immutable precepts of natural law are arrived at by the method of natural law. Natural law refers primarily to the precepts of natural law and not to the natural law as a method. The encyclical also occasionally mentions inclinations in human nature, but it never develops the threefold inclinations found in the Thomistic anthropology. However, unlike the general approach of neo-Scholasticism and its philosophy, the pope insists that given the present state of fallen nature, divine revelation is needed for knowing moral truths even of the natural order (no. 36).

Thus, in the period after Vatican II and *Humanae vitae* there has been a lively debate within Catholicism about the theory and practical conclusions of natural law. This recent history also proves again the basic thesis of this chapter, that there has been no such reality of the natural law understood as a monolithic philosophical system with an agreed-upon body of ethical content that has existed throughout the Catholic tradition.

Other Approaches to Natural Law

Near the end of the twentieth century two Catholic scholars, Russell Hittinger and Jean Porter, maintained that natural law is a theological and not just a philosophical concept for the Scholastics and Aquinas. Porter has developed the argument in more historical detail and will be followed here. She is strongly committed to defending the definition of Gratian and its theological implications. Porter first points out that Gratian's definition did not come out of the blue but has a solid basis in earlier Christian teachings. The Scholastics after Gratian locate the natural law within scripture. Scripture provides the definitive formulation of the natural law through the negative and positive formulations of the Golden Rule found in Tobit 4:15 and the Gospels (Mt 22:39–40 and parallels). The more specific content of the natural law is found in the Decalogue. The Scholastic reliance on scripture as a source of moral reflection leads them to consider some human inclinations as centrally more important than others—nonmaleficence, love of neighbor as oneself, and equality.[101]

Porter thus rejects understanding natural law as based on the order of nature as in the generally accepted neo-Scholastic and manualistic approach or as based on the human mind in the Grisez approach. In developing her approach, she appeals to Alasdair MacIntyre's notion of rationality as "tradition guided inquiry." Situating natural law within a tradition calls for recognizing the theological and metaphysical component of that tradition. There can be more than one authentic natural morality. However, Porter insists that her understanding of natural law recognizes some universality and is open to criticism from other rational and theological perspectives.[102]

Other considerations appear to give some support to Porter's thesis. As already pointed out, the neo-Scholastic approach emphasized that natural law was based solely on human reason and human nature, but the reason for this is the very strong distinction they made between the natural order and the supernatural order. However, other Thomists pointed out that such a clear distinction is not found in Aquinas himself. Likewise, in the later twentieth century, some Thomists have insisted that Aquinas is primarily a theologian and not a philosopher.[103]

Although Porter and Hittinger agree that natural law is not based on human reason and human nature totally separate from any theological influences, they strongly disagree on the basic understanding of natural law and what it calls for in specific cases. Porter understands natural law as a fundamental capacity for moral judgment, not primarily as a set of specific precepts derived from first principles. Natural law more broadly conceived includes specific moral norms, but there is considerable room for both legitimate variation and sinful distortion at the level of particular norms. On specific questions Porter disagrees with hierarchical teaching condemning suicide and physician-assisted suicide for individuals near death. She also maintains that the early-stage fetus is not a person.[104] On the other hand, Hittinger staunchly supports the existing hierarchical Church teaching on all moral issues.[105] Whereas Hittinger strongly supported John Paul II's 1993 encyclical *Veritatis splendor* in its theory and its defense of the traditionally accepted intrinsically evil moral actions, Porter strongly disagreed with both the theory and the defense of some intrinsically evil moral actions as set forth in the encyclical.[106]

The discussion in this section focuses on the approach to natural law within the Roman Catholic tradition by Catholic authors addressing that tradition. However, discussion has also occurred about natural law in the broader human and secular worlds in terms of the understanding of the moral good today. Today, many in the broader philosophical community dispute the possibility of moral agreement in our diverse world and profess the impossibility of coming to agreement on a common morality. Different theories of the moral good have been proposed, but strong disagreement continues and no one position has been able to convince others to accept its understanding of the moral good.

Philosopher Alasdair MacIntyre has been a very significant voice in the contemporary discussion in the United States about the role of reason in determining the good. In his later books—*After Virtue* (1981), *Whose Justice: Which Rationality?* (1988), *Three Rival Versions of Moral Inquiry* (1990), and *Dependent Rational Animals* (1999)—he has developed his approach.[107] He has consistently been critical of modernity and its proposals for the human good from the time of his early support of Marxism. MacIntyre opposes what he calls the Enlightenment Project of providing a defense of morality that all rational people can accept. On the contrary, MacIntyre accepts that diversity and disagreement characterize our political and moral discourse and will continue to do so. The Enlightenment Project has failed to overcome this radical diversity. As a result, is relativism the only acceptable answer? MacIntyre strongly claims to reject relativism.

Yes, there exist different traditions of moral reason and incompatible theories of the rational determination of the good. However, in his complex theory, MacIntyre maintains that one can adhere to a theory as true without basing the claim on a reputed universal rational standpoint that MacIntyre maintains does not exist. MacIntyre also insists that one can concede that the adherents of other traditions can be rational without becoming a relativist. At the same time, he argues that one tradition can be shown to be superior to all other traditions by explaining how the tradition succeeds better than all others in explaining the deficiencies of other traditions. MacIntyre himself argues for a revised Aristotelian-Thomistic tradition. As one might suspect, there have been many discussions and criticisms of MacIntyre's theory, but such a discussion lies beyond the scope of this chapter.[108]

For our purposes, the significant reality is that MacIntyre became a Roman Catholic in the 1980s and has strongly supported hierarchical Catholic teachings in moral issues. In this context, a significant book, *Intractable Disputes about the Natural Law: Alasdair MacIntyre and Critics*, was published by the University of Notre Dame Press in 2009. The preface explains the book's rather unique genesis. In October 2004, Cardinal Joseph Ratzinger, the then prefect of the Congregation for the Doctrine of the Faith, wrote a letter to the president of the University of Notre Dame about the problem of finding a common denominator for the moral principles held by all people. Ratzinger asked that Notre Dame (as well as the Catholic University of America and the Ave Maria Law School) undertake symposia to address aspects of this issue. Notre Dame decided to publish a volume focusing on the discussion of a long essay by MacIntyre, a faculty member at Notre Dame, on the fundamental problem of moral disagreements about natural law. Eight other scholars, many from Notre Dame, wrote reactions to MacIntyre's essay dealing with intractable moral disagreements.[109]

In his long introductory essay and conclusion, MacIntyre develops his position on these disagreements and the understanding of natural law. In keeping with his earlier approaches, he rejects the understanding of natural law as a law established by reason that is universal in its principles and convincing to all humankind. The evidence of the great diversity existing today argues against such an understanding. He goes on to claim that radical moral disagreements themselves can be accommodated within the Thomistic approach. The article discusses in depth the differing approaches of utilitarianism and Thomism. He maintains that Thomism is superior to utilitarianism, but Thomism remains unacceptable and unconvincing to anyone committed to utilitarianism.[110] Thus, it is very clear that MacIntyre's interpretation of Aquinas and natural law differs considerably from the approach of the hierarchical magisterium. MacIntyre's position is added proof that there has never been a monolithic theory of natural law with a coherent method and an agreed-upon body of ethical content existing even within the Catholic tradition.

CARDINAL JOSEPH RATZINGER, POPE BENEDICT XVI

As expected, Pope Benedict XVI continued to appeal to natural law. His 2009 encyclical *Caritas in veritate* extends the development of papal social teaching. Like its predecessors, this encyclical is concerned with the problems and issues that arise, and is not primarily concerned with the development or analysis of the theory of natural law. The primary emphasis of the encyclical, as is evident from its title, is love and truth, but this takes particular form in the criteria that govern moral action, especially justice and the common good.[111] These criteria obviously come from the natural law.

The encyclical explicitly refers to natural law on a number of occasions. Despite cultural differences in our world, cooperation is possible because of the natural law. This universal moral law etched on human hearts provides a sound basis for all cultural and political dialogue and cooperation (no. 59, O-S, 567). Against materialistic and mechanistic understandings of the human being, the natural law provides and protects the true greatness and dignity of the human person but also reveals our wretchedness insofar as we fail to recognize the call to moral truth (no. 75, O-S, 577). But the role of natural law in the encyclical is much more prominent than just the explicit references to it. The pope insists that Catholic social teaching can make a specific contribution to integral human development in the present context of globalization because the teaching is based on the understanding of human beings created in the image of God. This reality serves as the basis for the inviolable dignity of the human person and the transcendent value of natural moral norms (no. 45, O-S, 557). The encyclical continues the natural law tradition of Catholic social teaching with its emphasis on concepts such as the common good, distributive and social justice, the rights of workers, the solidarity of all, and above all the importance of truth and metaphysics. A new aspect of the encyclical is the emphasis on the logic of gift. To be authentically human, economic, social, and political development need to make room for the principle of gratuitousness as an expression of solidarity (no. 34, O-S, 548).[112]

Benedict XVI explicitly addressed natural law in his address in 2007 to an international congress on natural moral law. In the midst of so much disorientation in society today, we need a metaphysical concept of nature, not an empirical one, that serves as the basis for natural law. This is the law that, according to St. Paul, is written on the hearts of human beings and hence accessible to all. The first principle of the natural law, "to do good and to avoid evil," serves as the basis for more particular principles such as respect for human life, the duty to seek the truth, and the demands of justice and solidarity. The natural law precedes all human law, judges such laws, and cannot be overridden by any other law. Natural law is the only valid bulwark against any ideological manipulation today.[113] The address is quite short and obviously unable to develop his understanding of natural law in any depth.

Document of the International Theological Commission

During Benedict XVI's papacy, a fascinating document on natural law came from the International Theological Commission. The commission consists of thirty members appointed by the pope under the presidency of the prefect of the Congregation for the Doctrine of the Faith. Although this commission has no authoritative role as such, it occasionally publishes long statements on particular issues. By reason of the way in which the members are appointed, one can assume that the paper reflects the vision of the congregation and of the papal magisterium itself.[114]

With the exception already noted of *Veritatis splendor*, papal teaching documents do not deal in depth with the theory of natural law. However, this document, of forty-eight pages in the English translation, provides a comparatively in-depth understanding of natural law. As the title indicates, "The Search for a Universal Ethic: A New Look at Natural Law" focuses on the need for a universal ethic in the social and political order in today's global society.[115] This is a complex document, but I will concentrate on those aspects of natural law that have already been discussed in this strand.

In an attempt to show the need for natural law as a basis for political life in our time, the document mentions that the great philosophical and religious traditions of the past have produced a largely common moral patrimony that makes explicit a universal ethical message embedded in the nature of things that everyone is able to decipher (no. 11). At first sight this seems to indicate the existence of natural law as a coherent monolithic theory with an agreed-upon body of ethical content existing throughout history. But a closer reading of the document reveals this is not the case. The International Theological Commission's first chapter refers to convergence in the wisdom traditions and the religions of the world. The paper insists on a metaphysical basis for natural law and laments the lack of a metaphysical understanding today. Some today insist that only relativism can safeguard democracy and pluralism. The document laments the secularization of natural law and the modern rationalist model of natural law. In addition, the Scholastic tradition itself, with the nominalism of Ockham, refused to accept the metaphysical foundations of natural law (no. 28–33 and 70–75). This paper never explicitly enunciates the thesis of this chapter, that the natural law as a coherent, monolithic ethical theory with an agreed-upon body of ethical content has never existed throughout history, but its reasoning supports such a thesis.

In a related issue, the International Theological Commission makes the somewhat unexpected assertion that in the course of history, theology has used natural law to justify positions that consequently have been recognized as conditioned by their historical and cultural context. A more profound understanding of the person as moral subject and a better consideration of historicity with regard to the concrete application of the natural law can avoid such problems. Today, it is important to propose the traditional doctrine of the natural law in terms that better manifest the personal, existential, and historical dimensions of the moral life (no. 10). The document incorporates the greater emphasis on the subjectivity of the person and historical consciousness (although it does not use this word) into its own approach. A legitimate development of the medieval Scholastic tradition today in our more complex cultural context calls for a more vivid sense of moral subjectivity (no. 28).

One later section of the document refers to the historicity of natural law. Morality deals with contingent reality that evolves through time. Moral reflection cannot remain at the general level of the first principles of natural law but must apply these to contingent and concrete circumstances in different cultures. Sometimes the evolving circumstances lead to a better understanding of the existing norms, but sometimes the norms change, as has occurred in questions such as slavery, interest taking, or the death penalty. Since concrete applications can vary throughout time, pure deduction by syllogistic reasoning is not adequate today. The more the moralist deals with concrete situations, the more one must have recourse to the wisdom of experience that integrates the contributions of other sciences and is nourished by contact with women and men engaged in action. The moralist today needs the virtues, especially prudence, that enable one to make a good ethical judgment and discernment in the application of natural law to circumstances. In fact, every human person needs this prudence in order to live out a truly moral life (no. 53–56).

As mentioned previously, other commentators have pointed out this twofold development of greater emphasis on subjectivity and historicity, but papal documents have never explicitly recognized such a development. On the one hand, these papal documents have not concentrated on the theory or method of natural law but with moral teaching on particular issues, and in that light would not be expected to discuss such a change. On the other hand, the papal documents never explicitly disagree with their "predecessors of happy memory," to use the term they frequently employ. Also there is no doubt the popes have insisted on the continuity in Catholic social teaching and hence would not be prone to explicitly recognize discontinuity in the theory behind their approach.

Revisionist Catholic moral theologians have claimed that a greater emphasis on the person as subject and historical consciousness would call for a change in the attitude toward contraception and other sexual issues. Obviously, this document does not accept such an approach. The International Theological Commission's paper supports the teaching condemning artificial contraception by citing both the 1930 encyclical *Casti connubii* of Pius XI and the 1968 encyclical *Humanae vitae* of Paul VI, but there is no extended discussion of contraception and other sexual issues (no. 34).

Papal teaching has emphasized the God-given role of the hierarchical magisterium in authoritatively teaching the natural law. This document recognizes this role of the papal teaching office (no. 34 and 35), but there is very little stress on this role throughout the document.

Papal teaching generally uses natural law to refer to the natural law conclusions and not to the method as such. Again, this is somewhat understandable in light of the teaching role of pope and bishops with regard to the Church. But the International Theological Commission puts much less emphasis on the conclusions and stresses above all the method. In four different places the document sees the natural law primarily as an inspiration and not as a set of norms or inviolable principles. Both the introduction and the conclusion of the document emphasize the nature of the natural law as inspiration. "It is a source of inspiration that always springs up in the search for an objective foundation for a universal ethics" (no. 113, and also 11). "It is not a closed and complete set of moral norms, but a source of constant inspiration . . ." (no. 27). The natural law cannot be presented as a set of rules imposed on the moral subject but is a source of "objective inspiration" for the process of making a decision (no. 59).

In keeping with the emphasis on inspiration, the document stresses that natural law "grounds the possibility of a dialogue with persons belonging to different cultural or religious horizons" (no. 42). "The doctrine of natural law can make its contribution to that dialogue" with a view to a universal ethics (no. 52). There are frequent repetitions of the role of natural law as contributing to the dialogue seeking a universal ethics among people with religious and cultural differences (see no. 35, 38, 50, 54, 112, 114). This emphasis on the natural law as inspiration is something new in the Catholic tradition.

The document also explicitly discusses the conclusions and precepts of natural law. After all, the International Theological Commission insists that they are following the approach of Thomas Aquinas (no. 37) and recognizes the need for a metaphysical understanding of the natural law (no. 62, 72, 73, 78), so the document considers the threefold inclinations in the human being and the primary and secondary precepts of natural law. Even here, however, there are some surprising aspects. The first paragraph dealing with these aspects maintains that on the basis of the maxim "one must do good and avoid evil," the subject recognizes the fundamental laws regulating human actions. Such a recognition does not consist in an abstract consideration of human nature that is proper to theoretical theology and philosophy but rather from the perception of fundamental moral goods, which is immediate, vital, based on the connaturality of the spirit with values, and engaging both the heart and the spirit. This grasp is often imperfect, still obscure and dim, but it has the profundity of immediacy (no. 44).

The document then refers to the basic inclinations or set of natural dynamisms of the human being as found in Aquinas. With these inclinations, one can formulate the first precepts of natural law, but they are very general. On the basis of this generality, discursive reason—also referred to as practical reason as distinguished from the theoretical reason of philosophy and theology mentioned earlier—discovers the secondary precepts of the natural law. The primary precepts are picked up spontaneously by reason, but the secondary precepts require a longer or shorter consideration of practical reason (no. 46–47). For example, the second inclination (that which is common to humans and all animals) regards the survival of the species that is realized by procreation. The dynamism toward procreation is intrinsically tied to the natural inclination that brings husband and wife together, but nothing is explicitly said that every single marital act must be open to procreation. From the third inclination comes the recognition of the equal dignity of every individual regardless of creed or culture and respect for all humanity, especially the smallest and the least appreciated of its members (no. 49–51).

Then, on the basis of these fundamental inclinations, we arrive at "a set of precepts and values that, at least in their general formulation, can be considered as universal . . . [and having] the character of immutability" (no. 52). There follows a section on the application of the common precepts: historicity of the natural law. It is impossible to remain at the general level of the first principles of the natural law. But to the degree that moral reflection confronts more concrete and contingent situations, to that degree its decisions are more characterized by variability and uncertainty. The document explicitly quotes Aquinas that the general principles of morality have a certain necessity, but the more particular the matters that are examined, the more uncertain the conclusions become. Here the document also refers to the changes that have occurred in the teachings on slavery, interest taking, and the death penalty (no. 53).

The tone and even the substance of the International Theological Commission document on natural law differs somewhat remarkably from the approach in *Veritatis splendor*. Some of the difference can be accounted for by the fact that this document deals primarily with a universal ethic in a pluralistic contemporary society, whereas *Veritatis splendor* had the focus of defending the existence of intrinsically evil acts and norms that are always and everywhere true. Still, many revisionists like myself can find much to agree with in this understanding of natural law.

The final chapter, "Jesus Christ, Fulfillment of the Natural Law," explicitly mentions the role of sin with regard to the natural law. Sin has gravely obscured the image of God in human beings. Human beings are so harmed by sin that they do not recognize the profound meaning of the world and interpret it in terms of pleasures, money, or power (no. 104). Catholic social teaching has seldom if ever pointed this out, but it has always been a part even of pre–Vatican II Catholic theology. Catholic systematic theology traditionally has taught that fallen human beings without grace are not able for a long time to observe the whole natural law with regard to its substance. This thesis finds support in the teaching of the Council of Trent that even the justified person needs the special help of God to overcome the temptations of the world, the flesh, and the devil, and to persevere in grace. There is a dispute about the opinion of some of the older Scholastics in this matter. Suárez taught that older Scholastics such as Scotus, Durandus, and Biel held that a human being without grace could avoid all sins against the natural law. Other theologians interpreted these older Scholastics to only deny the need for habitual grace and not the need for actual grace in order to observe the natural law or that they were conceding only the physical possibility and not the moral possibility of observing the natural law.[116]

Catholic social teaching, however, does not mention this important reality in talking about natural law as a basis for all people working together for the good of society. The logical question is why did Catholic social teaching as a whole not mention this important aspect of the Catholic teaching on grace? Recall that Pope Leo XIII saw Catholic philosophy and not theology as the way for Catholics to address the modern world. Philosophy as such deals only with human reason and does not directly consider the reality of human sinfulness. The fact remains, however, that the papal documents of social teaching involving natural law fail to propose the full Catholic teaching that without grace human beings cannot for a long time observe the substance of natural law. In this area and many others, this remarkable document on natural law from the International Theological Commission proposes aspects and nuances about natural law that are not found in official papal teachings.

Cardinal Ratzinger's Own Approach to Natural Law

In his writings before becoming pope, Cardinal Ratzinger frequently lamented the crisis of contemporary culture and its opposition to the Catholic understanding. The book that became known as the *Ratzinger Report*, which involved a long interview of Cardinal Ratzinger with Vittorio Messori, originally appeared in a shorter version in the Italian journal *Jesus*. The title given to the article was "Behold Why the Faith Is in Crisis."[117] In this article, Ratzinger talked about the crises of faith that come from contemporary culture. The crises take a different form depending on the particular culture involved. In Europe, the mood is one of disinterestedness and disenchantment. In Africa and Asia, the crisis comes from a problematic appeal to inculturation. The crisis in South America comes from a too-ready acceptance of Marxism, which presents a false human messianism. In North America, we see a world where riches are the measure and where the values and style of life proposed by Catholicism appear more than ever as a scandal. The moral teaching of the Church is seen as extraneous and opposed to the American culture.

The Cardinal Prefect of the Congregation of the Doctrine of the Faith in his discussion of Europe at the end of the twentieth and beginning of the twenty-first century again saw a true crisis with regard to his contemporary European culture. The problem is a rationalistic positivistic philosophy that dominates this culture.[118] In reality, this is a mutilation of reason and cannot be considered rational at all. Such an approach is totally relativistic. For many today, relativism is the only solid basis for law and public policy that involves the consensus held by the majority of citizens. Any other approach is a dogmatism that undermines self-determination, deprives citizens of their rights to make decisions, and obliterates their freedom. This is an empty concept of freedom. It is pure subjectivism. The state itself is not the source of truth and morality. The state cannot accomplish its own purposes without a freedom that has some content. A meaningful and viable ordering of civic life requires a minimum of truth and a knowledge of the good. A state can only receive this truth from outside itself.[119]

The positivistic reason predominant today is a-metaphysical and post-metaphysical. A radical evolutionism has replaced the Christian concept of creation and the order put into the world by the Creator God. Today's culture can no longer recognize moral principles inscribed in being because nothing is inscribed if being is only the product of chance and evolution. Freedom needs the guidance and direction of truth.[120] This positivistic reason makes freedom the absolute and supreme value. Human beings have increasingly gained the possibility of doing many things through science and technology. But if this knowledge does not find its operating criteria in a true moral norm, it becomes a power for destruction as is evidenced in our world. We know how to clone human beings and how to build nuclear weapons and even threaten to use them. Even terrorism finds its roots in the primacy of human self-authorization.[121]

Ratzinger recognizes that in the culture of Europe humanity has made some significant gains. These include not only the tremendous techno-logical advances but also some valuable moral claims—religions must be accepted in freedom and cannot be imposed by the state; fundamental human rights must be respected; powers in democracy must be separated. But even these positive aspects of positivistic philosophy are grounded in a self-imitation of reason that recognizes neither God nor metaphysics. In reality, this is not the voice of reason. The cardinal refers to this approach as being not only incomplete but radically incomplete. The emancipation of human beings from God and metaphysics stands in opposition to the true understanding of human dignity based on the rec-ognition of God and the order that the creator has inscribed in the world.[122]

Much of Ratzinger's considerations about the crisis of culture were occasioned by the debate in Europe about mentioning Europe's Christian origins in the Constitution of the European Community. But even before that time, he had addressed the problem in his 1991 book, *Turning Point for Europe?* Ratzinger had a more negative view of what was occurring in Europe than most other observers. Unlike many academics, the head of the Congregation for the Doctrine of the Faith living in Rome feared that what was happening in Europe would be paradigmatic for what was to happen in the rest of the world. He was fearful that European civiliza-tion was denying its Christian origins and pursuing modernity's logic with an understanding of the world that totally denies the transcendent, building its foundations only on a technological rationale that has no other foundation than itself.[123]

Ratzinger's negative reading of the signs of the times and his approach to contemporary culture derive in great measure from his Augustinian theological perspective. In the last pages of *A Turning Point for Europe?* he cites Augustine's understanding of world history as the struggle between two kinds of love—love for self, which goes so far as despising God, and love for God, which goes so far as despising oneself. He formulates his approach for today in terms of history as marked by the confrontation between love and the inability to love, which is a devastation of the soul that comes when the only values that count are quantifiable ones. The capacity to love, which involves the capacity to wait in patience for what is not under our control and to let oneself receive this as a gift, is suffocated by the need for quick fulfillment. This destruction of the capacity to love is the poisoning of the human person and gives rise to lethal boredom. Today we are called to choose love.[124]

On the basis of Ratzinger's quite negative view of human reason's work today, one might not expect him to appeal to natural law as the way to overcome the present impasse. But in reality, he insists on the important role of natural law. Here he raises a perspective that is quite new to the Catholic discussion of natural law—the evidential character of natural law morality. One might hope that the pure insight of reason could recognize the full breadth and depth of the human person as being more than the quantifiable, the empirical, and the materialistic. Unfortunately, such is not the case. A pure evidential quality of morality independent of history does not exist. Metaphysical and moral reason become effective and persuasive only in a historical context.[125]

The Catholic and Christian traditions give great importance to the Logos, the creative reason, the power of the divine knowledge that grounds a truly rational understanding of the world. John's Gospel begins with the assertion that in the beginning was the Logos (the Word); the Creator Spirit provides the rational basis for determining what is human. A truly rational approach has to be grounded in the rationality given by the Creator Spirit. The historical tradition of Christianity and Catholicism can supply the historical tradition that provides the evidential and persuasive character of human morality. Reason has come to maturity in this historical tradition.[126] The true source for politics and life in the world is not Christianity as revealed religion but Christianity as a leaven and a form of life that has testified to the good in the course of history.

Only God can provide the true basis for the rationality that grounds the meaning of human beings and human existence. Since this is a truth of reason, it does not try to convince others by force or violence but rather by the power of reason itself. The Christian tradition provides the context in which reason can know true rationality as the basis for governing life in this world.[127]

In the light of this understanding, what is the role of the Church today? According to Ratzinger, the Church is a creative minority working for what is the truly human good in our world.[128] The Church today has a tremendous responsibility for humanity.[129] How should the Church carry out this function? The Church's role is to be true to herself. She is not first and foremost a means for social progress; nor should the Church try to justify itself by her deeds of working for social reform. The Church must bear evidence to her basic reality—seek first the kingdom of God and God's righteousness, and the rest will be given to her. She cannot hide her basic doctrines and symbols. Her task is to make God known and to proclaim the kingdom. Only on this foundation can she make known to the world the moral dimension of true humanity. She makes this accessible to nonbelievers only through the means of freedom with the use of reason, will, and emotion. The Church must prepare space for the divine not through power and institutional strength, but through the witness of her life, love, and suffering. She helps society to find its true moral identity. She bears witness to the ability to love in our world.[130] We need Christian people today who by their lives show to others what true humanity means. We need people like St. Benedict, who made his foundation at Monte Cassino the "city on the hill" where in the midst of so many ruins a new world was formed, and Benedict, like Abraham, became the father of many peoples.[131]

Donal Dorr maintains that the role of the Church and its social mission in Pope Benedict's social encyclicals is in keeping with this understanding and differs from some previous approaches. Pope Benedict is clearly committed to having the Church work for justice in the world, but he has a somewhat controversial view about the way in which this should be done. He apparently feels that the balance has swung too much in the direction of having Church leaders and Church agencies directly involved in the struggle for justice. He maintains that the official Church and Church leaders should not be *directly* involved in promoting justice. Their role, rather, is that of educating the consciences of Christian people and evoking the spiritual energy of laypeople to engage in a *personal* capacity in the work of justice. Such an approach obviously differs from what has been proposed by many others with regard to the role of Church leaders in working for justice, especially in unjust situations.[132]

There are also indications in *Caritas in veritate* about the role of the Church as a creative minority. The encyclical calls for the creation of a new type of business between the traditional two models of profit-based companies and nonprofit organizations. Based "on an economy of communion," these businesses would not exclude profit but would consider it as a means to achieve truly human and social ends. Benedict does not expect this type of business to replace all existing for-profit businesses, but they can influence the for-profit businesses to appreciate aspects other than profit (no. 46, O-S, 558).[133]

On a practical level, Ratzinger addresses the Church's teaching on abortion in light of its role as a creative minority. Ratzinger recognizes that widespread public opinion feels that it is exaggerated, inopportune, and downright distasteful for the Church to remind contemporary society about the issue of conceived and unborn human life as a decisive question. Why not recognize in the light of what has occurred in almost all Western cultures that we have lost this battle and that it would be better to dedicate our energies to issues that can find support in a broader social consensus? After all, no one is forced to have an abortion; all remain free to act according to their own conscience on this very disputed issue. However, on the basis of Genesis 9:5–6, God claims the life of human beings as God's own possession, under God's direct and immediate protection. As a result, the respect of every human life is an essential condition for every truly human society. When humanity loses respect for life as sacred, humanity itself loses its own identity. We must not give up the fight![134]

In the light of his understanding of the problem today and its solution, Ratzinger makes an invitation and proposal for what people outside the Church should do. The problem is that contemporary reason is blind to the nonmaterialistic dimensions of reality. The reason for this is the contemporary inability to recognize the rationality in the world put there by the Creator. The Catholic historical tradition possesses an evidential quality that is rational and can convince others of its rationality. His proposal for those outside the Church is to try to live and direct their lives as if God did indeed exist. In developing his proposal, Ratzinger appeals to history. In the early age of the Enlightenment the attempt was made to understand the essential norms of morality and the human by saying these would be valid even if God did not exist (*etsi Deus non daretur*). Such an approach made great sense at that time. In the midst of the Protestant and Catholic antagonisms, it was better to keep the essential moral values outside the controversy and to recognize an evidential quality in those values independent of the strong religious divisions. At the time, understandings created by Christianity were still in place and deemed accessible to reason. But such is not the situation today. The crisis in contemporary culture comes from a failure to recognize true human values and their grounding. Today we should reverse the axiom of the early Enlightenment and propose a new one—even those who do not believe in God ought to try to live and direct their lives *veluti si Deus dareteur*—as if God did indeed exist.[135]

Readers should be careful not to misunderstand what Ratzinger is saying here. He is not asking nonbelievers to become Christians. He carefully distinguishes between the recognition of moral truth in the historical tradition, which is a work of reason, from belief in the truth of the Christian revelation, which is a work of faith. His proposal is based on two presuppositions—that Christianity as a historical tradition has embodied moral truth about humanity, and that its evidential character remains even when the foundational theological claims of the Christian tradition are rejected.[136]

Ratzinger's basic theory helps us to understand better his strong and frequent disagreement with the European Constitution's failure to refer to God and to mention the Christian roots of Europe. He denies that the mention of the Christian roots of Europe would offend the feelings of all other religious persons living in Europe. That Europe has Christian roots is simply a historical fact that cannot be denied. Muslims are not threatened by the Christian roots of Europe but by the cynicism of a secularized culture that denies its own foundations. Jewish citizens would not be offended because the Christian roots of Europe go back to Mt. Sinai. Other believers in Europe are opposed to the attempts to construct the human community in a manner that excludes God and to exclude the mention of God in the constitution. The refusal to refer to God is not an expression of tolerance to protect the dignity of nonbelievers but an attempt to see God eradicated once and for all from public life and shut up in the subjective spheres of cultural residues from the past.[137] If Europe does not recognize God and its Christian roots, it will never be able to see in the Christian historical tradition the true understanding of humanity and morality.

I have five comments with regard to Ratzinger's approach to natural law. First, Ratzinger does not base his approach on the work of Thomas Aquinas. Popes and other Catholic moral theologians dealing with natural law have invariably insisted on the Thomistic understanding of natural law. But Ratzinger does not ground his theory on the work of Thomas Aquinas. In fact, there is no substantial mention of Thomas Aquinas in the four books in which Ratzinger develops his approach. In the light of the Catholic tradition on natural law, this passing over the role of Aquinas is somewhat surprising.

Second, his lack of reference to Aquinas in a consideration of natural law might partially be explained by the fact that Ratzinger in these books pays no attention to the philosophical understanding of natural law although he strongly opposes the false philosophies of relativism and secularism. By philosophical understanding of natural law I mean how one understands the meaning of human nature and of human reason and how moral precepts and norms are derived from these understandings. There is no doubt even in these books that Ratzinger strongly supports the moral teachings proposed in the Catholic Church today that have been consistently grounded in natural law theory. But in this discussion Ratzinger never develops his philosophical understanding of natural law and how moral precepts and norms are derived from it. He jumps from the contention that the Catholic moral tradition proposes with an evidential quality the true rationality of the human and of human morality to the conclusions that he accepts on specific moral issues. One might excuse this jump on the basis that most of the material in these books dealing with the topic of natural law comes primarily from previously given lectures and essays; consequently, he is not really attempting here to give an in-depth scholarly presentation of natural law. Still, the huge jump from the true rationality of the human and morality in the Catholic tradition to its very particular moral precepts and norms cannot be taken for granted.

Third, Ratzinger has proposed here an approach to natural law that is quite different from what has been a part of the Catholic tradition in general and the papal magisterium in particular. In the mainstream Catholic approach there has been no reference to the fact that the evidential quality of natural law can be found only in the context of the Catholic and Christian moral tradition. The very fact that Pope Leo XIII drew on Thomistic philosophy to address the modern world shows his recognition of the evidential quality of the natural law itself. Denying the evidential character of reason itself and natural law and calling for the Catholic and

Christian tradition to supply this evidential characteristic is quite different from what the Catholic tradition has proposed, especially in its modern development of papal teaching since Leo XIII. The traditional
Catholic understanding of natural law, as well illustrated in the document
of the International Theological Commission, saw natural law as the basis
for dialogue with contemporary culture in light of the need for a global
ethic. But Ratzinger, with his emphasis on the crisis of contemporary
culture, emphasizes the opposition between contemporary culture and
the natural law's understanding of morality.

Fourth, Ratzinger proposes Christian civil religion and not natural law
as the primary solution to the crisis of European culture. The cardinal
has often pointed out that the primary problem for the Church today is
secularism. This emphasis moves him to see a basic agreement among all
the different religions that are opposed to secularism. All these religions
argue that God has a role to play in society.[138] In two different places
Ratzinger contrasts the situation in Europe with the situation in the
United States. Europe has denied its Christian roots, embraced a secular-
istic approach to public life, and reduced God and religion to the private
sphere. But such is not the case in the United States. Alexis de Tocque-
ville, in *Democracy in America*, points out that democracy in the United
States functions well because of the thriving Christian-inspired contributions of religious and moral convictions in American society. This moral
and religious foundation is greater than that of any single denomination.
Even today in the United States, the sphere involving religion, cultural,
and social aspects also has a public character. The United States has separation of church and state, but religion still has a public role. Catholics
have made a significant contribution to maintaining a Christian consciousness in the United States. This contribution is more important than
ever now because traditional Protestant communities are becoming more
secularized; on the other hand, Catholics are discovering their surprising
commonality with evangelicals. The United States, unlike Europe, still
acknowledges a public role for religion.[139]

These convictions about the public role of religion in the United States
do not stem from any one particular Christian church. One hopes the
same situation could occur in Europe, but unfortunately secularism has
become ever more entrenched in Europe since the 1960s.[140] What can be
done in Europe today to overcome this secularism? Ratzinger's answer is
a "Christian civil religion" that would actualize and revitalize the values
that are necessary for truly human life in this world. But how can Europe

attain a Christian civil religion that sustains society? This is the role of creative minorities who have discovered the pearl of great price (Mt 13:45ff) and live in a manner that is convincing to others. These minorities can become the yeast that can affect the whole.[141]

Note in this perspective that the contribution of the understanding of what it means to be truly human based on reason and natural law does not play a primary role. The Christian values of the different Christian churches do not come from a natural law grounded understanding of humanity and morality. The working together of various Christian churches and other religions in the struggle against secularism does not in itself support the role of rationality and natural law as the basis for this upholding of such values in society.

Fifth, what about Ratzinger's invitation to secularists and nonbelievers today to direct their lives as if God indeed does exist so that they might find in the Catholic tradition the persuasive and evidential aspect of natural law? What Ratzinger proposes might be an interesting thought experiment for intellectuals, but it has no chance of becoming effective in practice. A realistic perspective recognizes that such an invitation or proposal will never be accepted and become a reality in our world.

In conclusion, the official documents of Benedict XVI's papacy have continued the general approach to natural law found in the tradition of Catholic social teaching. However, the document of the International Theological Commission and Ratzinger's own writings before becoming pope have proposed surprisingly different understandings of natural law.

FURTHER AMBIGUITIES

The historical section has shown that there is no such thing as the natural law understood as a monolithic theoretical system with an agreed-upon body of ethical content existing from the medieval Scholasticism to the present day. This section points out four further ambiguities in the Catholic natural law tradition—the relationship between theory and practice; natural law as method, as conclusions, or as both; the relationship between natural law and authority; and the different approaches to natural law in papal social and sexual teaching.

Relationship between Theory and Practice

The ultimate question here is, what came first—theory or practice? Many of the moral teachings of the Church were accepted and worked out long before the development of Scholastic natural law theories. In fact, the method came along later to explain systematically and thematically why particular positions were accepted or condemned. As time went on, the natural law theory was used to discuss new issues, but in the overall picture it is a mistake to see that the morality of the action was always determined by the application of the method to the particular issue.

History shows that the Church in the first thousand years had dealt with many different moral issues and had come to conclusions about whether they were good or bad. Think, for example, of the teachings on murder, theft, lying, breaking promises, blasphemy, obedience to parents and authorities, service in the military, adultery, fornication, and many other issues. How did the Church at this time come to a moral judgment about these and other actions when there was no well-developed theory that everyone agreed upon as the method to apply to particular issues as they came along?

In all these areas the Christian community went through a discernment process that involved many different aspects—the teaching of Scripture, the tradition of the Church, and the role of the Holy Spirit in the individual Christian and in the life of the community. Discursive reason was also involved in this process, but reason involved not only a discursive analysis but also a connatural and prudential approach. This discernment process involves not only the intellectual and the rational but also the affective and intuitive aspects of the human and the Christian. There was considerable writing in the early Church about the discernment of spirits in determining whether something was prompted by a good spirit or a bad spirit, and the discernment of the Spirit in terms of determining what should be done about a particular issue.[142]

Even today it is erroneous to see the discernment process as only going from the theory of natural law to the solution of particular issues. The discernment process briefly described earlier is much more inclusive than any of the different theories of natural law. Discernment cannot be reduced simply to the application of natural law theory to particular issues. Natural law theories deal with the objective aspect of the act. Discernment brings together the subjective and the objective. The individual person or subject discerns what is to be done. In this process the Holy Spirit, the emotions, the virtues, the background, and the past experiences all come together. More subjective criteria, such as the peace and joy of the decision made, are proposed as the signs of having made a good decision. However, the discernment process, which itself can result in wrong choices, must always give due importance to the objective aspect of the act.[143] The Church as the community of the disciples of Jesus goes through an analogous discerning process regarding the morality of actions.

A reciprocal relationship exists between the theory or method and the discernment of particular issues. A theory of natural law can help to discover whether an action is morally good or evil, but history again reminds us of examples of how discernment of a particular act modified the existing theory. The early Church condemned marital relations done for the sake of pleasure, but in the light of experience this was changed. The early Church also accepted the practice of slavery, but later on (unfortunately too much later on) this was changed. Reference has already been made to the changed understanding of the malice of lying in light of the experience of the Christian community. Lying is not wrong because it involves the perversion of the faculty of speech whose purpose is to put on my lips what is in my mind; it is wrong because it violates the relational criterion of my neighbor's right to truth. The recognition of religious freedom changed the theoretical understanding of church–state relationships. The fact that the existential discernment process about the morality of a particular act is broader than the application of an existing theory or method of natural law to particular issues also helps to explain how change has occurred on these issues within the Church.[144] Thus, there exists a reciprocal relationship between the theory or method of natural law and the discernment of a particular action.

A more historically conscious and personalist approach to natural law would be more open to seeing a reciprocal relationship between general theory and particular issues, but even a more classicist understanding cannot deny this reality in light of what has historically occurred. The reason for this reciprocal relationship between theory and practice of natural law or between method and conclusions comes from the fact that the discernment process both for the individual and for the community of the Church is wider and broader than the rational approach of applying a method to a particular issue. It is interesting that Pope John Paul II in *Veritatis splendor* recognized this broader reality of conscience formation. To prove what is the will of God and what is good and acceptable, according to the pope, the knowledge of God's law in general is certainly necessary but not sufficient. What is essential is a sort of "connaturality between man and the true good." Such a connaturality is rooted in and developed through the virtuous attitudes of the individual herself—

prudence and the other cardinal virtues, and even before these, the theo-logical virtues of faith, hope, and charity.[145]

In my judgment, the rational method of a natural law theory is helpful in assisting individuals and the community in their attempts to arrive at moral truth about a particular issue, but the broader discernment process involves more than the rational application of a method. Also, one has to recognize that it is impossible to claim absolute certitude for a particular method of natural law. The historical fact that there has never been a monolithic moral system called natural law with an agreed-upon body of ethical content also indicates the possible imperfections of any method and its openness to the need for modification and correction.

Natural Law: Method or Conclusions?

Another ambiguity concerns the relationship between the method of nat-ural law and its conclusions. What does natural law primarily refer to—the method or the conclusions? Historically, it has been used to refer to both. However, from a more theoretical perspective, the method is the controlling reality. It is by using the method that one comes to the conclusions.

However, in papal teaching the emphasis is on the conclusions as con-stituting natural law and not the method. The papal office has a teaching role in the Church. As a teacher, the Bishop of Rome is not, however, primarily interested in theories but in giving directions and guidance to members of the Church. Even in the encyclical *Veritatis splendor*, which deals with more theoretical issues, the understanding of natural law as a method is never fully developed. As pointed out, the encyclical never explicitly shows how the conclusions are derived from the theory of natu-ral law. But it is the conclusions that the papal magisterium emphasizes and equates with natural law.

Papal teaching as illustrated in *Veritatis splendor* insists on the charac-teristics of natural law as universal and immutable precisely because it is inscribed in the rational nature of the human person. These characteris-tics refer to the conclusions of the natural law. The negative precepts of the natural law are universally valid. They oblige each and every individ-ual always and in every circumstance. They forbid an action *semper et pro semper* (always and forever). They oblige everyone regardless of the cost.[146] So papal teaching sees the natural law primarily in terms of con-clusions that are universally applicable and unchanging.

Relationship between Natural Law and Authority

The role of the papal magisterium in teaching the conclusions of the natural law logically raises the question of the relationship between natural law and authority in determining what is right or wrong. The best of the Catholic tradition has insisted, in accord with Thomas Aquinas, on an intrinsic morality. Recall that, for Aquinas, law is an ordering of reason and not primarily an act of the will. Something is commanded because it is good and never the other way around. An intrinsic morality insists that morality is perfective of the person and what is for the good of the person. Something is commanded because it is good. In this case, the legislator or authority must conform to what is the good; authority itself does not make something good.

Veritatis splendor in theory agrees with such an approach. The first two sections of the second part of the encyclical deal with the understanding of freedom and law and conscience and truth.[147] There can be no conflict between freedom and divine or natural law. God's law and the natural law prescribe what is good for the human person. Freedom is not license. By submitting to divine and natural law, freedom consents to the good of creation. Patterned on God's freedom, human freedom is not negated by obedience to the divine law; in fact, only through this obedience does human freedom cohere to the truth and conform to human dignity. In other words, divine and natural law propose what is good for human beings in accord with their God-given dignity and nature. Likewise, conscience itself seeks the truth. There is no conflict between conscience and truth, just as there is no conflict between true freedom and law. Conscience discerns the truth about what it means to be and act as a creature of God.

However, the practice is much different from the theory. When the rubber meets the road, the authoritative teaching trumps reason. Unfortunately, the best illustration of this primacy of authority comes in the 1968 encyclical *Humanae vitae*. In this document, Pope Paul VI restated the condemnation of artificial contraception for spouses. The outline of the document itself clearly shows the primacy of authority. The very first section is titled "New Aspects of the Problem and Competency of the Magisterium."[148] Here the pope refers to recent developments related to the use of contraception and some of the reasons proposed against the existing teaching of the Church. In the first place, among the noteworthy changes that have occurred is the demographic problem. Fears exist that the world population is growing more rapidly than the available resources. In addition, the modern economic situation makes providing the proper education for a large number of children today very difficult. The role of women in society and the value of conjugal love with regard to the marriage relationship itself have changed. The stupendous contemporary progress in the control of natural forces calls for the extension of this domination and control to the human body, to psychic life, to social life, and even to the laws that regulate the transmission of life.

These new developments, according to the pope, raise new questions. In light of the changed social, economic, and cultural conditions and the newer approaches to the conjugal relationship, is it not advisable to change the existing ethical norms, especially when they cannot be observed without sacrifices, sometimes even heroic sacrifices? Could it not be admitted that the principle of totality (a part can be sacrificed for the good of the whole) could justify a less abundant but more rationally justified fecundity? Could it not be admitted that the finality of procreation pertains to all of the conjugal life and not just to the single individual acts? In view of the increased responsibility of human beings today, is it not time for reason and will rather than biological rhythms to direct the task of regulating births?

The pope recognizes that questions have required the teaching authority of the Church to instigate a new and deeper reflection on the moral teaching on marriage, a teaching that has been based on natural law illumined and enriched by divine revelation. All Catholics recognize that the teaching authority of the Church is competent to interpret even the natural law. It is indisputable that Jesus Christ, in communicating to Peter and the Apostles his divine authority to teach all nations his commandments, constituted them as guardians and authentic interpreters of all the moral law, not only of the law of the Gospel but also of the natural law, which is also an expression of the will of God. The faithful fulfillment of the natural law is equally necessary for salvation. In conformity with this mission, the Church has produced a coherent teaching about marriage. Conscious of this mission, the pope himself confirmed and enlarged the study commission instituted by Pope John XXIII in 1963 concerning marriage and the regulation of birth. This commission included experts in the pertinent sciences and married couples themselves with the purpose to gather the opinions on the new questions of conjugal life and in particular the regulation of birth so that the magisterium could give an adequate reply to the faithful and the world on this issue. The pope expressed his gratitude to all those participating in this study, including his brother bishops.

The next paragraph of the encyclical deserves to be cited in its entirety:

> The conclusions at which the commission arrived could not, nevertheless, be considered by us as definitive, nor dispense us from a personal examination of this serious question; and this also because, within the commission itself, no full concordance of judgments concerning the moral norms to be proposed had been reached, and above all because certain criteria of solutions had emerged which departed from the moral teaching on marriage proposed with constant firmness by the teaching authority of the Church. Therefore, having attentively sifted the documentation laid before us, after mature reflection and assiduous prayers, we now intend, by virtue of the mandate entrusted to us by Christ, to give our reply to these grave questions.[149]

It was well known that the commission was divided but with the majority of the commission favoring changing the existing teaching.[150] The pope explicitly recognized this fact. However, he maintained that the conclusion favoring change could not be accepted as definitive because of the primary reason of the emergence of solutions that departed from the existing moral teachings, which had been proposed with constant firmness by the teaching authority of the Church. He goes on in the second section of *Humanae vitae* to develop the doctrinal principles and natural law arguments supporting the condemnation of artificial contraception for spouses.[151] Thus, the encyclical itself manifestly makes clear that it is primarily the teaching authority of the Church that makes artificial contraception morally wrong. Various interpretations of natural law, human reason, or the experience of Christian people (the *sensus fidelium*) could not go against what the papal magisterium had taught. *Humanae vitae* set the parameters for any further discussion about morality in the Catholic Church. The authoritative teaching of the pope cannot be changed. Sexuality has been the primary area in which most challenges have been raised against official Catholic teaching. Calls for change have arisen on such issues as masturbation, sterilization, artificial insemination, in vitro fertilization, homosexuality, divorce, premarital sexuality, and aspects of the abortion issue. But in all cases, the answer has been the same—the authoritative teaching of the Church cannot be changed and trumps whatever reasons are proposed against it.[152]

The papacy has been unwilling to change its teaching on any of these issues. It has often been pointed out that Catholic spouses practice contraception in the same basic number as other Americans, but the pope and bishops continue to maintain that contraception is a grave moral evil.[153] The discrepancy between hierarchical teaching and the practice of married Catholics raises serious questions about the credibility of the hierarchical teaching office. Many wonder why the pope and bishops have not changed the teaching. In my judgment, a major reason for not changing the teaching now is that such a change logically would open the door to the call for change in other areas as well. There is no possibility for change in any other area of negative moral absolutes if the hierarchical magisterium does not change on the issue of artificial contraception for spouses.

Two Different Contemporary Papal Approaches to Natural Law

Papal and hierarchical teaching have employed natural law in dealing with personal ethics, especially sexual and medical ethics, and on issues of social ethics. However, there are some fascinating differences between the two approaches. As previously pointed out, within the Church the teachings, especially on sexual ethics, have met with dissent from a good number of Catholic theologians while, for all practical purposes, there has been no dissent from the hierarchical teachings on political, economic, and social issues. What explains this dramatic difference?

The lack of dissent in social teachings cannot be accounted for by the fact that there are no disagreements between and among Catholic social ethicists. In general, there are three different approaches found among Catholic scholars—neoconservative, progressive or liberal, and radical approaches. Sometimes proponents of one of these approaches are charged with dissenting from Church teaching, but none of the proponents themselves claim to be dissenting from papal teaching.[154]

A partial explanation comes from the fact that the teaching on social issues tends to be more general and less specific than on sexual issues. Consider, for example, the issues of peace and war. The hierarchical teaching propounds a just war doctrine but recognizes that pacifism is a legitimate option for individuals within the Church. The just war theory proposes the conditions necessary for going to war (*jus ad bellum*) and the conditions necessary in carrying out a just war (*jus in bello*). The conditions required for having a just cause and going to war in the first place are by definition somewhat general, that is, just cause, hope for success, the good to be accomplished must outweigh the evil.[155] These conditions by definition are quite general and can be interpreted differently by different people. In the United States, many Catholic social ethicists have condemned the US wars in Iraq and Afghanistan, but others have supported these wars on the basis of just war criteria. The one quite specific teaching on peace and war is the *jus in bello* criterion of noncombatant immunity. One cannot directly kill innocent civilians. However, no group of Catholic ethicists has publicly disagreed with or dissented from this teaching, which was a traditional part of just war theory over time.[156]

There is no doubt that hierarchical teaching on sexual issues is much more specific than it is on social issues. Concrete actions such as contraception, direct sterilization, artificial insemination, homosexual acts, direct abortion, and divorce and remarriage are always wrong, but papal social teaching seldom speaks out on specific concrete actions, although the teaching on no direct killing of innocent civilians is somewhat of an exception to the general rule. The more general teachings by their very nature allow for a variety of interpretations and different specific applications.

Another factor also partially explains the lack of dissent among Catholics in the area of hierarchical social teaching. Those who dissent from some of the sexual teachings point to the problems created by physicalism and by the moral criterion based on the nature and purpose of the faculty. Such criticisms apply to many of the negative moral norms proposed in sexual issues, but these problems do not exist in social ethics. The human or the moral is not identified with the physical structure of the act in papal social teaching. Social teaching does not rely on the nature and purpose of a faculty but on the good of the human person. Thus, two of the methodological problems pointed out by dissenters in the area of sexual issues do not exist in the area of social teachings.

But another reason has had the greatest influence on the lack of dissent within the Catholic Church concerning papal social teaching. The methodology supporting papal social teaching itself over the years has developed and changed, whereas such a change has not occurred in the methodology involved in sexual teachings. A primary change here has been the acceptance of historical consciousness in the methodology behind papal social teaching as time elapsed. There is no doubt that the pre–Vatican II documents employed both a classicist approach with an emphasis on the immutable and unchanging, and a deductive methodological approach. As is to be expected, Pope Leo XIII used the neo-Scholastic approach to natural law when addressing social issues. The emphasis is on the givenness of "human nature" and "natural law" to determine what is right, although he does not develop the theory of natural law in his 1891 encyclical *Rerum novarum*. Private property is based on "human nature" and "natural law."[157] The "most sacred law of nature" demands that a father provide for his children. Socialism is "against natural justice."[158]

Quadragesimo anno, the 1931 encyclical of Pope Pius XI, recognizes that natural law manifests God's will (no. 53, O-S, 56). The pope insists on the existence of "unchanging principles" and later refers to principles that are "fixed and unchangeable" (no. 11 and 79, O-S, 45 and 62). These laws and principles (e.g., subsidiarity) are universal and unchanging, but they are somewhat general and leave room for public authority and individuals to specify them. In addition, the approach in the encyclical is basically deductive. "But reason itself clearly deduces from the nature of things and from the individual and social character of human beings what is the end and object of the whole economic order assigned by God the Creator" (no. 42, O-S, 52). The most innovative part of the encyclical based on a deductive approach calls for a moderate corporatism or solidarism in which all the groups (capital, labor, and consumers) work together for the common good rather than the existing struggle between capital and labor (no. 81–87, O-S, 62–64).

Pope John XXIII's 1963 encyclical *Pacem in terris* explicitly calls attention to its natural law and deductive methodology in its opening paragraphs. The laws governing the relationships between and among human beings are to be sought where the Father of all things wrote them, that is, in human nature. These laws teach us how we should conduct our mutual dealings among ourselves, how citizens should relate to states, how states should relate to one another, and how the community of all people should act toward each other (no. 6–7, O-S, 138). The pre–Vatican II documents thus employ a deductive approach, but within this framework they recognize room for some historical developments.

Vatican II's Pastoral Constitution on the Church in the Modern World (*Gaudium et spes*) definitely employs a more inductive methodology connected with historical consciousness. This document in part 2 considers five particular areas of social issues—marriage and the family, culture, socioeconomic life, political life, and peace. Each of these considerations begins not with natural law but with a section on the signs of the times.[159] Contrast this with *Pacem in terris*, which has a section on the signs of the times only at the end of its discussion of each part.[160]

There is no doubt that *Octogesima adveniens*, the 1971 letter of Pope Paul VI to Cardinal Maurice Roy, the president of the Council of the Laity and of the Justice and Peace Commission, incorporates a historically conscious methodology more than any other papal document. The document recognizes the great diversity of situations in which Christians find themselves today—diversity of regions, sociopolitical systems, and cultures—and then goes on to say:

> In the face of such widely varying situations, it is difficult for us to have a unified message and to put forward a solution which has universal validity. Such is not our ambition, nor is it our mission. It is up to the Christian communities to analyze with objectivity the situation which is proper to their own country, to shed on it the light of the Gospel's unalterable words, and to draw principles of reflection, norms of judgment, and directives for action from the social teaching of the Church. . . . It is up to these Christian communities, with the help of the Holy Spirit in communion with the bishops who hold responsibility and in dialogue with other Christian brethren and all men of good will, to discern the options and commitments which are called for in order to bring about the social, political, and economic changes seen in many cases to be urgently needed. (no. 4, O-S, 281)

John Paul II retreated from Paul VI's emphasis on historical consciousness. He never explicitly said so (popes never explicitly disagree with their predecessors!), but he reverted to a more classicist approach. His first social encyclical, *Laborem exercens* (1981), comes from a more universal perspective, trying to explain the meaning of work for all people and deducing conclusions from his anthropology. He did not begin with the signs of the times, but also he did not turn his back on particular developments with regard to issues. For example, based on his personalism, he strongly supported human rights. Two reasons—one internal and one external—help to explain his differences with Paul VI. First, John Paul II was trained in neo-Scholastic philosophy under his doctoral dissertation director, Réginald Garrigou-Lagrange. To his credit, John Paul II also incorporated into his approach more mystical and spiritual elements, phenomenology, and personalism, but the more classicist method was still there.[161]

The external influence came from the stimulus of Marie-Dominique Chenu's book, published in the late 1970s in Italian and French with the provocative French title *The "Social Doctrine" of the Church as Ideology*.[162] Chenu criticizes the "social doctrine of the church" as an ideology based on abstract and prefabricated understandings that claim to be the eternal and unchanging demands of natural law. This was an authoritative, deductive, top-down approach coming from the hierarchical Church to the faithful. Chenu sees John XXIII but especially Vatican II and Paul VI's *Octogesima adveniens* as using a very different, more inductive approach arising from the bottom up. Social change comes from the active involvement of the people themselves and the oppressed. Chenu emphasizes the discontinuity between Paul VI and earlier papal teaching, pointing out that Vatican II and Paul VI no longer referred to the concept of the social teaching or doctrine of the Church.

Without mentioning Chenu by name, John Paul II responded to the book by claiming a great continuity within the documents themselves, and even by reviving the term "the social doctrine of the Church." In this context the opening of his encyclical *Sollicitudo rei socialis*, written on the twentieth anniversary of Pope Paul VI's *Populorum progressio* (1967), is most instructive. In writing this document the pope had two objectives—to pay homage to the esteemed document of Paul VI and "to reaffirm the *continuity* of the social doctrine as well as its constant *renewal*." This continuity and renewal are a proof of the perennial value of the teaching of the Church. This teaching is constant, for it remains identical in its fundamental inspiration, in its "principles of reflection," in its "criteria of judgment," in its basic "directives for action," and above all as a vital link to the Gospel. The three characteristics in quotation marks in the previous sentence are found with these quotation marks in the encyclical itself and they refer to paragraph four of *Octogesima adveniens*. Thus, this document uses the very encyclical on which Chenu based his theory of discontinuity to prove the continuity in the social doctrine of the Church.[163]

In addition to the shift from a classicist approach to a greater appreciation of history and historical consciousness, the documents of papal social teaching also shifted from an emphasis on human nature to a greater appreciation of the human person as subject with the new and different characteristics of the personal subject today. Once again, *Octogesima adveniens* stands as the beacon of this change and sees it in conjunction

with the move to historical consciousness. "While scientific and techno-
logical progress continues to overturn man's surroundings, his patterns
of knowledge, work, consumption, and relationships, two aspirations consistently make themselves felt in these new contexts, and they grow
stronger to the extent that he becomes better informed and better educated: the aspiration to equality and the aspiration to participation, two
forms of man's dignity and freedom" (no. 22, O-S, 289).

At the end of the nineteenth century, Leo XIII had a very different
understanding of the person. He did not advocate freedom, equality, and
participation; in fact, he denied all three. As pointed out in chapter 2, Leo
strongly condemned modern liberalism in his encyclicals as well illustrated in his 1888 *Libertas praestantissimum*. Freedom of worship goes
against the chief and holiest duty that calls for worship of the one true
God in the one true Church. Freedom of speech and the press mean that
nothing will remain sacred. Nature is not indifferent to truth and falsehood. There is no right to teach or speak what is false. The authority of
law must prohibit such freedoms to spread error.[164]

Leo recognized the basic equality of human beings with regard to origin, value, and end.[165] But there are differences in abilities and powers of
mind and body that call for inequalities in the institutions of civil life. The
natural inequalities of family, beauty, intelligence, thought, and courage
involve social inequalities that are essential for the good functioning of
society.[166]

In keeping with his views on freedom and inequality, Leo proposes a
very hierarchical and authoritarian view of society with no participation
of the ordinary people in running government. His favorite word for rulers is "*principes*." Leo even quotes the maxim *Qualis rex talis grex* ("as the
king, so the flock").[167] The people are the untutored or ignorant multitude that must be led and protected by the rulers.[168] At its best, Leo's
approach can be described as paternalistic, as when he compares the rulers' subjects to children who need the guidance and direction of their
father.[169]

The opposition to freedom, equality, and participation came from
Leo's strong opposition to liberalism and the Enlightenment. The fatal
flaw of the Enlightenment and liberalism was the exaltation of the freedom of individual human reason with no recognition of God and God's
law represented and mediated by the Church in the spiritual sphere and
by the rulers in the temporal realm.[170]

Chapter 2 has already explained how the shift occurred in papal social teaching from opposition to acceptance of freedom, equality, and participation. Leo opposed these because of his opposition to liberalism. But as the twentieth century developed, the primary problem for the Church came not from liberalism but from totalitarianism and communism. In opposition to these approaches, the popes emphasized the importance of freedom, equality, and participation.

Although John Paul II retreated from Pope Paul VI's emphasis on historical consciousness, he steadfastly embraced the emphasis on the person as subject. This methodology shows itself in two very important developments in his first encyclical, *Laborem exercens*. First, he emphasizes the priority of the subjective aspect of work over the objective aspect. The subject who does the work has primacy over the object or thing that is done. The pope goes on to point out that such an understanding practically does away with the basis for the older differentiation of people into classes based on the type of work they do (no. 5–6, O-S, 357–60). Second, *Laborem exercens* goes on to extol the priority of labor over capital. Capital is only a means or an instrument that is always subordinated to the person (no. 12, O-S, 367–68). In his papacy John Paul II strongly condemned authoritarian governments throughout the world and supported human rights and democracies. He played a most significant role in the ultimate collapse of communism in Poland. Samuel P. Huntington, a Harvard political scientist, pointed out that very few of his generation would have expected the Catholic Church to be one of the strongest supporters of democracy in the latter part of the twentieth century.[171]

Papal sexual teaching has not accepted historical consciousness and a more inductive methodology. In addition, papal sexual teaching is based on the finality of the sexual faculty and does not recognize the primacy of the person. The natural law method employed in papal social teaching thus differs considerably from the natural law method used in papal sexual teaching.

Natural law is the third strand in the development of moral theology in this volume. This chapter, focusing on the historical development of natural law in the Catholic tradition and recognizing ambiguities within the tradition, has demonstrated that there is no such theory as the natural law understood as a coherent ethical theory with an agreed-upon body of ethical content existing both now and in the past in the Catholic tradition.

NOTES

1. A. P. d'Entrèves, *Natural Law: An Introduction to Legal Philosophy* (London: Hutchinson, 1951), 7.

2. Heinrich A. Rommen, *The Natural Law: A Study in Legal and Social Philosophy*, trans. Thomas R. Hanley (St. Louis: B. Herder, 1947), iii.

3. John Courtney Murray, *We Hold These Truths: Catholic Reflections on the American Proposition* (New York: Sheed and Ward, 1960), 275–336.

4. Michael Bertram Crowe, *The Changing Profile of Natural Law* (The Hague: Martinus Nijhoff, 1977), 36–40.

5. Ibid., 43–51.

6. Yves R. Simon, *The Tradition of Natural Law: A Philosopher's Reflection*, ed. Vukan Kuic (New York: Fordham University Press, 1965), 35–36.

7. Rommen, *Natural* Law, 76–109.

8. *New Catholic Encyclopedia*, 13 vols. (New York: McGraw-Hill, 1967), 10:251–71.

9. Jean Porter, *Natural and Divine Law: Reclaiming the Tradition for Christian Ethics* (Grand Rapids, MI: Eerdmans, 1999), 124–27; and Odon Lottin, *Le Droit Naturel chez Saint Thomas d'Aquin et ses prédécessurs* (Bruges: Beyaert, 1931), 7.

10. In this section I am heavily dependent on Crowe, d'Entrèves, Rommen, Simon, and Lottin, *Le Droit Naturel*, 7.

11. Crowe, *Changing Profile of Natural Law*, 43–51.

12. Porter, *Natural and Divine Law*, 45.

13. Lottin, *Le Droit Naturel*, 9–11; and Crowe, *Changing Profile of Natural Law*, 68–71.

14. This translation comes from Porter, *Natural and Divine Law*, 129–30.

15. Crowe, *Changing Profile of Natural Law*, 77.

16. Lottin, *Le Droit Naturel*, 11–12.

17. Porter, *Natural and Divine Law*, 131–37.

18. Ibid., 148.

19. Lottin, *Le Droit Naturel*, 13–15.

20. Crowe, *Changing Profile of Natural Law*, 104–5.

21. For a detailed discussion of the theologians before Aquinas, see Lottin, *Le Droit Naturel*, 23–57.

22. Crowe, *Changing Profile of Natural Law*, 118–22.

23. Porter, *Natural and Divine Law*, 42–44.

24. Lottin, *Le Droit Naturel*, 61–62.

25. In the following paragraphs I am heavily dependent on Crowe, *Changing Profile of the Natural Law*, 136–91. Part of this section depends on his earlier essay, "St. Thomas and Ulpian's Natural Law," in *St. Thomas Aquinas, 1274–1974*, ed. Armand A. Maurer, Etienne Gilson, Joseph Owens, Anton C. Pegis, John F. Quinn, Edward Synan, and James A. Weisheipl (Toronto: Pontifical Institute of Medieval Studies, 1974), 261–82. For Aquinas, see Thomas Aquinas, *Summa theologiae*, 4 vols. (Rome: Marietti, 1953).

26. Crowe, *Changing Profile of Natural Law*, 142–55.

27. Giuseppe Angelini and Ambrogio Valsecchi, *Disegno storico della teologia morale* (Bologna: Dehoniane, 1972), 88.

28. For the best one-volume discussion of Thomistic ethics, see Stephen J. Pope, ed., *The Ethics of Aquinas* (Washington, DC: Georgetown University Press, 2002).

29. For a more in-depth discussion of Aquinas on the universality and immutability of the natural law, see Lottin, *Le Droit Naturel*, 74–96.

30. Porter, *Natural and Divine Law*, 146–56.

31. Crowe, *Changing Profile of Natural Law*, 186.

32. Simon, *Tradition of Natural Law*, 34.

33. d'Entrèves, *Natural Law*, 68–69.

34. Rommen, *Natural Law*, 59.

35. Hannes Möhle, "Scotus's Theory of Natural Law," in *The Cambridge Companion to Duns Scotus*, ed. Thomas Williams (Cambridge: Cambridge University Press, 2003), 312–31.

36. Crowe, *Changing Profile of Natural Law*, 212–22.

37. Rommen, *Natural Law*, 64–65.

38. Louis Vereecke, *Storia della teologia morale in Spagna nel XVIo secolo e origine delle 'Institutiones Morales'*, *1520–1600* (Rome: Accademia Alphonsiana, 1980), 52–53. Four volumes of Vereecke's *Storia della teologia morale* were published in mimeograph form at the Accademia Alphonsiana but have been available for public sale.

39. Thomas E. Davitt, *The Natural Law* (St. Louis: B. Herder, 1951), 88–108.

40. William E. May, "On the Existence of Moral Absolutes: The Teaching of Theologians from St. Thomas Aquinas until Vatican Council II," *Eternal World Television Network*, www.ewtn.com/library/theology/FR92202.htm#3. (From the Summer 1992 issue of *Faith & Reason*.)

41. Simon, *Tradition of Natural Law*, 34.

42. Porter, *Natural and Divine Law*, 50.

43. D. J. O'Connor, *Aquinas and Natural Law* (London: Macmillan, 1967), quoted in Fergus Kerr, *After Aquinas: Versions of Thomism* (Oxford: Blackwell, 2002), 98.

44. Aloysius Sabetti, *Compendium theologiae moralis*, 7th ed. (New York: Pustet, 1892), 74–84.

45. Alphonsus de Ligorio, *Theologia moralis*, vol. 1, ed. Leonardus Gaudé (Rome: Typographia Vaticana, 1905), 3.

46. Hieronymous Noldin, *Summa theologiae moralis*, vol. 1, *De principiis*, 33rd ed. (Innsbruck: Rauch, 1960), 106–240.

47. Thomas Bouquillon, "Moral Theology at the End of the Nineteenth Century," *Catholic University Bulletin* 5 (1899): 244–68.

48. Davitt, *Nature of Law*, 226.

49. Germain Grisez and Russell Shaw, *Fulfillment in Christ: A Summary of Christian Moral Principles* (Notre Dame, IN: University of Notre Dame Press, 1991), 44–48.

50. Petrus Scavini, *Theologia moralis universa*, 4th ed. (Innsbruck: Veladini, 1851), 128.

51. Marcellinus Zalba, *Theologiae moralis summa*, vol. 1, *Theologia moralis fundamentalis* (Madrid: Biblioteca de autores Cristianos, 1952), 345–69.

52. For a good discussion of many of these Catholic scholars, see Fergus Kerr, *Twentieth Century Catholic Theologians: From Neoscholasticism to Nuptial Mysticism* (Oxford: Blackwell, 2007).

53. Zalba, *Theologiae moralis summa*, 1:357.

54. Crowe, *Changing Profile of Natural Law*, 183.

55. Aquinas, *Summa theologiae*, Ia IIae, q.94, a.4, 6.

56. Jacques Maritain, *Man and the State* (Chicago: Phoenix Books, University of Chicago Press, 1956), 89–93.

57. Pope Leo XIII, *Aeterni Patris*, no. 28–29, in *The Papal Encyclicals 1878–1903*, ed. Claudia Carlen (Wilmington, DE: McGrath, 1981), 25.

58. Etienne Gilson, ed., *The Church Speaks to the Modern World: The Social Teachings of Leo XIII* (Garden City, NY: Doubleday Image, 1954).

59. For the text of the documents that compose Catholic social teaching, see David J. O'Brien and Thomas A. Shannon, eds., *Catholic Social Thought: The Documentary Heritage*, exp. ed. (Maryknoll, NY: Orbis, 2010). Subsequent references to the documents of Catholic social teaching will appear in the text giving the paragraph number (no.) of the document and the page number from O'Brien-Shannon (O-S). I have used inclusive language whereas the language of the documents is exclusive. For the best available commentary on all these documents, see Kenneth R. Himes, ed., *Catholic Social Teaching: Commentaries and Interpretations* (Washington, DC: Georgetown University Press, 2005).

60. Rommen, *Natural Law*, 3.

61. Murray, *We Hold These Truths*, 293–94.

62. Joseph W. Evans, ed., *Jacques Maritain: The Man and His Achievement* (New York: Sheed and Ward, 1963).

63. Robert W. McElroy, *The Search for an American Public Theology: The Contribution of John Courtney Murray* (New York: Paulist, 1989).

64. Francis Schüssler Fiorenza, "The New Theology and Transcendental Thomism," in *Modern Christian Thought*, vol. 2, *The Twentieth Century*, 2nd ed., ed. James C. Livingston and Francis Schüssler Fiorenza (Minneapolis: Fortress Press, 2006), 197–208.

65. John C. Ford and Gerald Kelly, *Contemporary Moral Theology*, vol. 2, *Marriage Questions* (Westminster, MD: Newman, 1963).

66. Joseph Fuchs, *Natural Law: A Theological Investigation* (New York: Sheed and Ward, 1965).

67. Josephus Fuchs, *De castitate et ordine sexuali*, 3rd ed. (Rome: Gregorian University Press, 1963), 39; and Mark Graham, *Josef Fuchs on Natural Law* (Washington DC, Georgetown University Press, 2002), 116–202.

68. Edwin F. Healy, *Medical Ethics* (Chicago: Loyola University Press, 1956), 4–9.

69. Pope Pius XI, *Casti connubii*, no. 56, in *The Papal Encyclicals 1903–1939*, ed. Claudia Carlen (Wilmington, DE: McGrath, 1981), 400.

70. John P. Kenny, *Principles of Medical Ethics*, 2nd ed. (Westminster, MD: Newman, 1962), vii; see also Charles E. Curran, *The Catholic Moral Tradition Today: A Synthesis* (Washington, DC: Georgetown University Press, 1999), 203.

71. Kenny, *Principles of Medical Ethics*, 96.

72. Ibid., 174.

73. For the theological history of the period that I am following here, see Ambrogio Valsecchi, *Controversy: The Birth Control Debate 1958–1968* (Washington, DC: Corpus 1968), 1–36; and Robert Blair Kaiser, *The Politics of Sex and Religion: A Case History in the Development of Doctrine, 1962–1984* (Kansas City, MO: Leaven, 1985).

74. Pope Paul VI, *Humanae vitae*, no. 10–12, in *The Papal Encyclicals 1958–1981*, ed. Claudia Carlen (Wilmington, DE: McGrath, 1981), 225–26.

75. Ibid., no. 4, p. 224.

76. For an earlier development of this revisionist position, see my *Contemporary Problems in Moral Theology* (Notre Dame, IN: Fides, 1970), 97–158.

77. Pope Pius XII, "Christian Norms of Morality (Sept. 29, 1949)" and "Fundamental Laws Governing Conjugal Relations (Sept. 29, 1951)," in *Medical Ethics: Sources of Catholic Teachings*, ed. Kevin D. O'Rourke and Philip Boyle (St. Louis: Catholic Health Association, 1989), 60–62.

78. Michael Crowe maintains that Thomas does not accept Ulpian's definition of natural law despite some inconsistencies in his approach; see Crowe, *Changing Profile of Natural Law*, 141–54.

79. Bernard Lonergan, "The Transition from a Classicist World-View to Historical-Mindedness," in *Law for Liberty: The Role of Law in the Church Today*, ed. James E. Biechler (Baltimore: Helicon, 1967), 126–33.

80. See also Thomas J. McPartland, *Lonergan and Historiography* (Columbia, MO: University of Missouri Press, 2010).

81. Zalba, *Theologiae moralis summa*, 1:356–57.

82. John T. Noonan Jr., *A Church That Can and Cannot Change: The Development of Catholic Moral Teaching* (Notre Dame, IN: University of Notre Dame Press, 2005); and Charles E. Curran, ed., *Change in Official Catholic Moral Teachings: Readings in Moral Theology No. 13* (New York: Paulist, 2003).

83. Pope John Paul II, *Evangelium vitae*, no. 57, 62, in *The Encyclicals of John Paul II*, ed. J. Michael Miller (Huntington, IN: Our Sunday Visitor, 2001), 724–29.

84. For the history of the debate about direct and indirect abortion at this time, see T. Lincoln Bouscaren, *Ethics of Ectopic Operations*, 2nd ed. (Milwaukee: Bruce, 1944), 3–24; and John R. Connery, *Abortion: The Development of the Roman Catholic Perspective* (Chicago: Loyola University Press, 1977), 225–303.

85. Fuchs, *De castitate*, 52–54.

86. Graham, *Josef Fuchs*, 83–241.

87. Julius A. Dorszynski, *Catholic Teaching about the Morality of Falsehood* (Washington, DC: Catholic University of America Press, 1949).

88. *Catechism of the Catholic Church* (Liguori, MO: Liguori, 1994), no. 2483, p. 595.

89. Joseph Ratzinger, "Vatican List of Catechism Changes," *Origins* 27 (1997): 262.

90. Germain G. Grisez, *Contraception and the Natural Law* (Milwaukee, WI: Bruce, 1964); Grisez, *The Way of the Lord Jesus*, vol. 1, *Christian Moral Principles* (Chicago: Franciscan Herald, 1983); Grisez, *The Way of the Lord Jesus*, vol. 2, *Living a Christian Life* (Quincy, IL: Franciscan, 1993); and Grisez, *The Way of the Lord Jesus*, vol. 3, *Difficult Moral Questions* (Quincy, IL: Franciscan, 1997). For a very readable,

succinct, and accurate summary of the basic theory, see Grisez and Shaw, *Fulfillment in Christ*. For a personal and intellectual overview of Grisez's life and work, see Russell Shaw, "The Making of a Moral Theologian," *Church World Report* (March 1996), available at www.ewtn.com/library/homelibr/grisez.txt. For discussion and evaluation of Grisez's theory, see Robert P. George, ed., *Natural Law and Moral Inquiry: Ethics, Metaphysics, and Politics in the Work of Germain Grisez* (Washington, DC: Georgetown University Press, 1998); and Nigel Biggar and Rufus Black, *The Revival of Natural Law: Philosophical, Theological, and Ethical Responses to the Finnis-Grisez School* (Burlington, VT: Aldershot, 2000).

91. Finnis's most significant works include: John Finnis, *Fundamentals of Ethics* (Washington, DC: Georgetown University Press, 1983); Finnis, *Moral Absolutes: Tradition, Revision, and Truth* (Washington DC: Catholic University of America Press, 1991); and Finnis, *Natural Law and Natural Rights* (Oxford: Clarendon, 1980).

92. Grisez and Shaw, *Fulfillment in Christ*, 80.

93. Ibid., 305–14.

94. Ibid., 54–56.

95. This and the following paragraph summarize Grisez and Shaw, *Fulfillment in Christ*, 44–48.

96. Ralph McInerny, *Ethica Thomistica*, rev. ed. (Washington, DC: Catholic University of America Press, 1997); and McInerny, *What Went Wrong with Vatican II? The Catholic Crisis Explained* (Manchester, NH: Sophia Institute, 1998).

97. Romanus Cessario, *The Virtues, or The Examined Life* (New York: Continuum, 2002); and Cessario, *The Moral Virtues and Theological Ethics* (Notre Dame, IN: University of Notre Dame Press, 2009).

98. Romanus Cessario, *Introduction to Moral Theology* (Washington, DC: Catholic University of America Press, 2001), 52–99.

99. Martin Rhonheimer, "Natural Law and Moral Reasoning: At the Roots of Aquinas's Moral Epistemology," *Josephinium Journal of Theology* 17 no. 2 (2010): 341–81; see also Rhonheimer, *Natural Law and Practical Reason: A Thomistic View of Moral Autonomy* (New York: Fordham University Press, 2000).

100. Pope John Paul II, *Veritatis splendor*, no. 1–5, in *Encyclicals of Pope John Paul II*, ed. Miller, 584–87. Subsequent references in the text will give the paragraph number of the encyclical.

101. Porter, *Natural and Divine Law*, 121–86.

102. For a summary of her position, see Porter, *Natural and Divine Law*, 203–17; see also Jean Porter, *Nature as Reason: A Thomistic Theory of the Natural Law* (Grand Rapids, MI: Eerdmans, 2005), 378–400.

103. Kerr, *Twentieth Century Catholic Theologians*.

104. Jean Porter, *Moral Action and Christian Ethics* (Cambridge: Cambridge University Press, 1995), 110–24; and Porter, *Natural and Divine Law*, 187–302.

105. Russell Hittinger, "Natural Law and Catholic Moral Theology," in *A Preserving Grace: Protestants, Catholics, and Natural Law*, ed. Michael Cromartie (Washington, DC: Ethics and Public Policy Center, 1997), 1–3; and Hittinger, *First Grace: Rediscovering Natural Law in a Post-Christian World* (Wilmington, DE: ISI Books, 2003).

106. Russell Hittinger, "Natural Law a Single 'Law': Reflections on the Occasion of *Veritatis Splendor*," *American Journal of Jurisprudence* 39 (1994): 1–32; and Jean Porter, "The Moral Act in *Veritatis Splendor* and Aquinas's *Summa Theologiae*," in *Veritatis Splendor: American Responses*, ed. Michal E. Allsopp and John J. O'Keefe (Kansas City, MO: Sheed & Ward, 1995), 278–95.

107. Alasdair MacIntyre, *After Virtue: A Study in Moral Theory* (Notre Dame, IN: University of Notre Dame Press, 1981); MacIntyre, *Whose Justice: Which Rationality?* (Notre Dame, IN: University of Notre Dame Press, 1988); MacIntyre, *Three Rival Versions of Moral Inquiry: Encyclopedia, Genealogy, and Tradition: Being Gifford Lectures Delivered in the University of Edinburgh in 1988* (Notre Dame, IN: University of Notre Dame Press, 1990); and MacIntyre, *Dependent Rational Animals: Why Human Beings Need the Virtues* (Chicago: Open Court, 1999).

108. See, for example, Mark C. Murphy, ed., *Alasdair MacIntyre* (Cambridge University Press, 2003); and Lawrence S. Cunningham, ed., *Intractable Disputes about the Natural Law: Alasdair MacIntyre and Critics* (Notre Dame, IN: University of Notre Dame Press, 2009). In Cunningham's book I found especially helpful the essay of Gerald McKenny, "Moral Disagreement and the Limits of Reason: Reflections on MacIntyre and Ratzinger," 195–226.

109. Lawrence S. Cunningham, "Preface," in *Intractable Disputes about the Natural Law*, vii–xi.

110. Alasdair MacIntyre, "Intractable Moral Disagreements," and "From Answers to Questions: A Response to the Responses," in *Intractable Disputes about the Natural Law*, ed. Cunningham, 1–52 and 313–51.

111. Pope Benedict XVI, *Caritas in veritate*, no. 6, in *Catholic Social Thought: The Documentary Heritaage*, exp. ed., ed. David J. O'Brien and Thomas A. Shannon, 528–29 (Maryknoll, NY: Orbis, 2010). Subsequent references in the text will give the paragraph number from the encyclical and the page number from the book: O-S.

112. For a perceptive commentary on *Caritas in veritate*, see Drew Christiansen, "Metaphysics and Society: A Commentary on *Caritas in veritate*," *Theological Studies* 71 (2010): 3–28.

113. Benedict XVI, "Address of His Holiness Benedict XVI to the Participants in the International Congress on Natural Moral Law (2007)," *Vatican* website, www.vatican.va/holy_father/benedict_xvi/speeches/2007/february/documents/hf_ben-xvi_spe_20070212_pul_en.html.

114. For the statutes and membership of the International Theological Commission, see the Vatican website at www.vatican.va/roman_curia/congregations/cfaith/cti_index.htm.

115. The website of the Holy See has French, German, Italian, and Spanish versions of this document; for the Italian, see www.vatican.va/roman_curia/congregations/cfaith/cti_documents/rc_con_cfaith_doc_20090520_legge-naturale_it.html. For an unofficial English translation by Joseph Bolin, which will be followed here with checks from the Italian, see International Theological Commission, "The Search for Universal Ethics: A New Look at Natural Law," at www.pathsoflove.com/universal-ethics-natural-law.html. Subsequent references in the text will give the paragraph number.

116. Severinus González Rivas, *Tractatus De Gratia*, in *Sacrae Theologiae Summa*, vol. 3, 3rd ed. (Madrid: Biblioteca de autores Cristianos, 1956), no. 49–59, pp. 521–29.

117. Vittorio Missori, a colloquio con il Cardinale Josef Raztinger, "Ecco Perché La Fede È in Crisi," *Jesus* (November 1984): 67–81. For the expanded English translation of the book developed from the original interview, see Joseph Ratzinger with Vittorio Missori, *The Ratzinger Report: An Exclusive Interview* (San Francisco: Ignatius, 1985).

118. Joseph Ratzinger, *Christianity and the Crisis of Cultures* (San Francisco: Ignatius, 2005), 39–45.

119. Joseph Ratzinger, *Values in a Time of Upheaval* (New York: Crossroad, 2005), 61–68.

120. Joseph Ratzinger, "The Renewal of Moral Theology: Perspectives of Vatican II and *Veritatis Splendor*," *Communio* 32 (2005): 363–65.

121. Ratzinger, *Christianity and Crisis*, 41–42.

122. Ibid., 39, 43–45.

123. James V. Schall, "Foreword to the Second Edition," in Joseph Ratzinger, *A Turning Point for Europe? The Church in the Modern World: Assessment and Forecast*, 2nd ed. (San Francisco: Ignatius, 2010), 11–16.

124. Ratzinger, *A Turning Point for Europe?*, 179–80.

125. Ratzinger, *Values in Time of Upheaval*, 64–69.

126. Ratzinger, *Christianity and Crisis*, 47–49.

127. Ratzinger, *Values in Time of Upheaval*, 64.

128. Joseph Ratzinger and Marcello Pera, *Without Roots: The West, Relativism, Christianity, Islam* (New York: Basic, 2006), 80 and 120–27.

129. Ratzinger, *Christianity and Crisis*, 31–32.

130. Ratzinger, *Turning Point*, 177–79.

131. Ratzinger, *Christianity and Crisis*, 52–53.

132. Donal Dorr, *Option for the Poor and for the Earth: Catholic Social Teaching* (Maryknoll, NY: Orbis, 2012), 390.

133. For a further development of this "economy of communion," see ibid., 368–93.

134. Ratzinger, *Christianity and Crisis*, 57–60.

135. Ibid., 50–51.

136. McKenney, "Moral Disagreement." I have found this article very helpful and used it in developing this section.

137. Ratzinger, *Christianity and Crisis*, 32–33, 44–45. Note also the title of the book coauthored by Ratzinger and Marcello Pera, *Without Roots*.

138. Ratzinger, *Christianity and Crisis*, 32–34, 44–45.

139. Ratzinger and Pera, *Without Roots*, 109–13; and Ratzinger, *Values in Time of Upheaval*, 51.

140. Ratzinger, *Turning Point*, 157–64.

141. Ratzinger and Pera, *Without Roots*, 120–24.

142. Joseph T. Lienhard, "On 'Discernment of Spirits' in the Early Church," *Theological Studies* 41 (1980): 505–29; and Jacques Guillet et al., *Discernment of Spirits*

(Collegeville, MN: Liturgical, 1970). This book is the authorized English translation of the article that originally appeared in the *Dictionnaire de spiritualité*.

143. See, for example, Richard M. Gula, *Moral Discernment* (New York: Paulist, 1999); and Jules Toner, *Discerning God's Will: Ignatius of Loyola's Teaching on Christian Decision Making* (St. Louis: Institute of Jesuit Sources, 1991).

144. See Noonan, *A Church That Can and Cannot Change*; and Curran, *Change in Official Catholic Moral Teachings*.

145. John Paul II, *Veritatis splendor*, no. 64, in *Encyclicals of John Paul II*, ed. Miller, 625.

146. Ibid., no. 51–52, pp. 617–19.

147. Ibid., no. 35–54, pp. 607–26.

148. Pope Paul VI, *On the Regulation of Birth: Humanae Vitae* (Washington, DC: United States Catholic Conference, 1968), no. 2–6, pp. 2–4.

149. Ibid., no. 6, p. 4.

150. Kaiser, *Politics of Sex and Religion*, 129–215; and Robert McClory, *Turning Point* (New York: Crossroad, 1995), 38–146.

151. Paul VI, *On the Regulation of Birth*, no. 7–19, pp. 4–12.

152. Charles E. Curran and Richard A. McCormick, eds., *Readings in Moral Theology No. 8: Dialogue about Catholic Sexual Teaching* (New York: Paulist, 1993).

153. Reuters, "98 Percent of Catholic Women Use Birth Control Banned by the Church," *Huffington Post: Religion*, April 14, 2011, www.huffingtonpost.com/2011/04/14/98-percent-catholic-women-birth-control_n...849060.html.

154. For my overview of contemporary Catholic social ethics, see Charles E. Curran, *Catholic Moral Theology in the United States: A History* (Washington, DC: Georgetown University Press, 2008), 252–62.

155. For the best presentation of hierarchical teaching on peace and war, see US Catholic Bishops, "The Challenge of Peace: God's Promise and Our Response (1983)," in *Catholic Social Thought*, ed. O'Brien and Shannon, 604–88.

156. For my summary discussion of these issues, see Curran, *Catholic Moral Theology*, 262–66.

157. Pope Leo XIII, *Rerum novarum*, no. 6–7, in *Catholic Social Thought*, ed. O'Brien and Shannon, 16–17.

158. Ibid., no. 9–13, 18–19. Subsequent references will be given in the text to the paragraph number (no.) of the papal documents and the pages from *Catholic Social Thought*, ed. O'Brien and Shannon (O-S).

159. *Pastoral Constitution on the Church and the Modern World*, no. 47, 54, 63, 73, 77, in *Catholic Social Thought*, ed. O'Brien and Shannon, 205–6, 212, 219–20, 226–27, 230–31.

160. Pope John XXIII, *Pacem in terris*, no. 39–45, 75–79, 126–29, in *Catholic Social Thought*, ed. O'Brien and Shannon, 143–44, 150–51, 158–59.

161. See, for example, Kerr, *Twentieth Century Catholic Theologians*, 163–82. For a generally sympathetic biography of Garrigou-Legrange, see Richard Peddicord, *The Sacred Monster of Thomism: An Introduction to the Life and Legacy of Réginald Garrigou-Legrange* (South Bend, IN: St. Augustine's, 2005).

162. Marie-Dominique Chenu, *La dottrina sociale della chiesa: origine e sviluppo 1891–1971* (Brescia Queriniana, 1977); and Chenu, *La doctrine sociale de l'église comme idéologie* (Paris: Cerf, 1979).

163. Pope John Paul II, *Sollicitudo rei socialis* no. 3, in *Catholic Social Thought*, ed. O'Brien and Shannon, 425.

164. Pope Leo XIII, *Libertas praestantissimum*, no. 19–29, in *The Papal Encyclicals 1878–1903*, ed. Claudia Carlen (Wilmington, NC: McGrath, 1986), 175–78.

165. Pope Leo XIII, *Humanum genus*, no. 26, in *The Papal Encyclicals 1878–1903*, ed. Carlen, p. 97.

166. Pope Leo XIII, *Quod apostolici muneris*, no. 5–6, in *Papal Social Encyclicals 1878–1903*, ed. Carlen, 19.

167. John Courtney Murray, *The Problem of Religious Liberty* (Westminster, MD: Newman, 1965), 55–56.

168. Pope Leo XIII, *Libertas*, no. 3, in *Papal Social Encyclicals 1878–1903*, ed. Carlen, 176.

169. Pope Leo XIII, *Immortale Dei*, no. 5, in *Papal Encyclicals 1878–1903*, ed. Carlen, 108.

170. Ibid., no. 23–24, p. 112.

171. Samuel P. Huntington, "Religion and the Third Wave," *National Interest* 24 (Summer 1991): 30.

CHAPTER 4

STRAND FOUR

Papal Teaching Office

CATHOLIC MORAL THEOLOGY differs from its Protestant sibling by its recognition of the role of what is called the hierarchical magisterium or the teaching office of popes and bishops in the area of morality. This unique characteristic of moral theology is explored and developed in this chapter.

Catholic faith recognizes the unique role of the pope in the Church. According to the Constitution on the Church of the Second Vatican Council, Jesus placed Peter over the other apostles and instituted in him a permanent and visible source and foundation of unity and fellowship. The pope is called the successor of Peter, the Vicar of Christ, and the visible head of the whole Church. This papal role in a general way is called the papal primacy.[1] The First Vatican Council (1870) addressed only the papal role in the Church. Vatican II emphasized the role of the bishops as successors of the apostles who, together with the pope as visible head of the Church, govern the house of the living God. The pope and bishops constitute the hierarchical office and role in the Catholic Church (no. 18–29).

According to Catholic faith, the papacy grew out of the role and mission of Peter (the Petrine office), who according to reliable but not irrefutable evidence lived and died as a martyr in Rome. In the New Testament, Peter appears as the first of the apostles in the various lists. 1 Corinthians 15:5 refers to Jesus after the resurrection appearing first to Peter, then to the others. In Matthew 16:13–19 Jesus gave Simon a new name—Peter, the rock upon which he would build the Church. Jesus gave to Peter the power of the keys to bind and loose. Similar powers are also given to the other apostles (Mt 18:18), but Peter has these powers in a special way. Jesus prayed for Peter and his faith so that he might be a support for his brothers (Lk 22:27–32). Despite Peter's threefold denial of Jesus (Jn 18:15–27), after the resurrection following a threefold questioning about Peter's love for him, Jesus gave Peter the call and responsibility to feed his sheep (Jn 21:15–19). In the Acts of the Apostles, Peter appears as a recognized leader of the apostles and disciples of Jesus. The Catholic Church believes that the bishop of Rome, known as the pope since the sixth century, continues the Petrine office of leadership in the Church.[2]

In the beginning of the Christian community in Rome, the role of the papacy was very rudimentary indeed and developed greatly over time. It is a fatal mistake to take the exercise of primacy by the papal office today and see it as the model for what has always occurred throughout history. This chapter shows that the primacy has been exercised in many different ways throughout its historical development.

A number of significant relationships within the Church have profoundly influenced and, to a certain degree, limited papal primacy and the way in which this primacy has been exercised in governing and in teaching. As mentioned, Catholic faith believes in a hierarchical Church with the offices of pope and bishops. Bishops either singly or as members of what is called the college of bishops have a very significant role to play in the life of the Church. Vatican II emphasized the role of bishops in the Church precisely because Vatican I had time to consider only the papal office, thus leaving the impression that the Church is truly a monarchy. Throughout history, the role of bishops in the Church has influenced the way in which the papal primacy has been exercised. The Church also has consistently recognized the presence of the Holy Spirit in all the baptized faithful. Contemporary theology insists on the fact that all the baptized share in the threefold offices of Jesus as priest, teacher, and ruler. As a result, then, all the faithful also have a role to play in the teaching function in the Church. From earliest times, theologians have exercised a teaching role in the Church. But over time, all these different roles have been understood in different ways and the relationship among them has not always been exactly the same.

In the ancient Church until the eighth century there were five patriarchates in the Church—Rome, Constantinople, Alexandria, Antioch, and Jerusalem. Even today, the pope bears the title of "Patriarch of the West." But little or nothing is said about his role as Patriarch of the West because the role of the five traditional patriarchates has only a small and vestigial role in the Church. After the rise of Islam in the seventh and eighth centuries, three of the original patriarchates—Alexandria, Antioch, and Jerusalem—ceased to have much influence in the life of the Church. With the final division of the Church between the East (Constantinople) and the West (Rome) in 1054, the older patriarchal structure for all practical purposes ceased to exist.[3]

The roles of popes and bishops have also been greatly affected by their relationships with secular rulers, whether emperors, kings, or local dukes. To this day the title Defender of the Faith given by the pope to King Henry VIII continues to be used by the English monarch. Perhaps no one has had a greater influence on the development of the Church than the Emperor Constantine in the early fourth century.[4] For well over a thousand years the popes themselves were also civil rulers. Bishops likewise often played a similar role in some countries. For example, only in the nineteenth century did the pope nominate most of the bishops in the world. Before that time kings, civil rulers, and local clergy and people had nominated bishops.[5]

Factors outside the Church also had a leading role in the development of papal primacy. Think, for example, of the modern developments of transportation, communication, and the social media. All of these realities have contributed immensely to the present understanding of the role of papal primacy in the Catholic Church. Renowned historian of the papacy and the early modern Church John W. O'Malley pointed out the huge change that occurred in the Catholic Church with regard to the papacy in the second millennium. Today the primary understanding of what it means to be a Catholic is to obey the pope. Not only Catholics but all others are familiar with the role of the pope in the Catholic Church; and in the United States, for example, practically everyone can identify the present pope. But all this is a phenomenon that developed in the second millennium and has gradually become ever more important and focused. From the earliest years the bishop of Rome claimed a special role in the Church. But in the first millennium the pope did not "rule" the Church. Popes did not define doctrines, did not write encyclicals, did not choose the vast majority of bishops in the world, and did not require bishops to come to Rome to report directly to the pope. The popes in the first millennium were primarily local church leaders dealing with local problems and were not primarily world-renowned leaders.[6]

The three developments in this secular world mentioned earlier greatly influenced this change. Many Catholics in the United States are quite surprised when they learn that the first Catholics in Maryland wanted the liturgy celebrated in the vernacular.[7] After all, this was the New World and called for a new approach. Rome (Vatican City did not exist at this time) was far away and not readily accessible. Transportation to Rome was long and difficult. There were no steam engines, to say nothing of airplanes. There were no telegraphs or phones. In the light of these circumstances one can well understand why and how local churches throughout the world made many of their decisions on their own. It would be impossible for the bishop of Rome to be involved in the daily life of the local churches throughout the world since the contact with them was so difficult and minimal even as late as the eighteenth century.

What a difference the modern means of communication have accomplished. Only in the fifteenth century did Johannes Gutenberg start the printing revolution with his invention of mechanical movable type printing. The development of the modern media has made contact between Rome and the universal Church possible, feasible, and very easy. Now with telephones, cell phones, and the internet, Rome is in instantaneous communication with the whole Church throughout the world. Newspapers, radio, television, and the internet have focused on the pope as the head of the Catholic Church. Every major and even minor papal pronouncement is immediately made available throughout the world. No pope before Paul VI (1963) traveled overseas. Pope John Paul II made 104 overseas trips and visited 129 countries in addition to 146 trips within Italy.[8] The press and media coverage of these visits in the individual countries and even throughout the world was enormous. As a result, John Paul II has been accepted by many as one of the most influential leaders of the twentieth century. But before the second millennium, very few people in the world even knew who was the bishop of Rome.

This section focuses on the role of the pope as an authoritative teacher of morality in the Catholic Church. To adequately understand this role, it is necessary to consider the broader framework of the papal primacy in general and the papal teaching office in matters of faith as well as morals. The focus is on the authoritative teaching role of the pope but not on the persons of the popes as such. Popes are human beings like everyone else and are subject to the same limitations and temptations. The history of the papacy does not always make for edifying reading. Not without reason did the English historian Eamon Duffy title his history of the papacy *Saints and Sinners: A History of the Popes.*[9]

This section attempts to cover a huge amount of historical material. Much work has already been done on the issues of papal primacy and the papal teaching office in general. I summarize much of this work that has been done by others, try to organize it in a coherent manner, and develop the papal teaching role in morals in the context of the broader developments. In light of some of the more general approaches to the papal primacy and teaching role, the material here is divided into historical periods—the first millennium, from Pope Gregory VII to the Council of Trent, from Trent to the nineteenth century, the nineteenth century and subsequent developments, and Vatican II and afterward.[10]

THE FIRST MILLENNIUM

The early Church in Rome followed the same general trajectory of development as other early churches in the infant Church. At first the local church in a city or area consisted of household churches or neighborhood meeting assemblies and did not have a single leader. This process also took place in Rome, and there probably was not a single leader or monarchical bishop until well into the second century. The origins of the monarchical episcopate in Rome (and elsewhere) came about because of a need for greater organization, for example, in taking care of the needs of widows and the poor and in response to the existing differences with regard to both belief and practice. However, even earlier there was a feeling that Rome constituted one community that, because of the generally accepted understanding of its relationship to Peter and Paul, had preeminence among the other local communities. A number of testimonies from this time bear witness to such a preeminence of the Church at Rome. But there is no real historical evidence to support the existence and role of those who are listed as the first bishops of Rome and popes, that is, Linus, Anacletus, Clement, and others. Only in the middle of the second century did a monarchical episcopacy come to the fore in Rome—that is, one bishop as the leader of the local Christian community.[11]

Development of the Papal Primacy

Similarly, it took time for recognition of some primacy of the Church of Rome, and especially the bishop of Rome, to come to the fore. The greatest influence on the history of the Church and even the bishop of Rome came from Constantine, who was the Roman emperor from 312 to 337. In his decisive battle at the Milvian Bridge in 312, Constantine attributed his victory to his vision of the Cross, with the words "In this sign, you will conquer." A year later he issued the Edict of Milan, giving toleration to Christians and, in fact, favoring and endowing the Christian Church throughout the empire, but especially in Rome and later Constantinople. In Rome he built a number of famous churches, such as St. Paul's Outside the Wall, Holy Cross in Jerusalem, St. Peter's, and St. John Lateran, which he designated as the cathedral of the bishop of Rome. In 321, he declared Sunday, the Christian feast day and celebration of the resurrection, to be a public holiday. He saw himself as a super bishop to ensure orthodoxy in the Church. All bishops including the bishop of Rome paid him deference, but Constantine also respected their authority as bishops. He later moved the empire to the city of Constantinople, named after him. Many, especially in the East, have called him the Thirteenth Apostle. John O'Malley maintains that, with the exception of Peter, Constantine was more important for the papacy and for Christianity than any other pope. From Constantine on emerged the close union of church and state, which ceased to exist in theory only at the Second Vatican Council. The close relationship of the spiritual with the temporal undoubtedly had deleterious effects on the Church in general and the papacy in particular.[12]

The primary way of exercising authority in the early Church and of settling doctrinal and pastoral disputes was through local synods and councils. Many problems came to the fore, ranging from discussions about how Jesus was both divine and human to the way of reconciling those Christians who had lapsed during the time of persecution. These local synods were held in all parts of the Christian world and dealt with the problems and questions that arose there. The conversion of the empire brought with it increased communication possibilities and paved the way for the movement from local synods and councils to what have been called general or universal councils to secure communion among all the ecclesiastical provinces throughout the Christian world. These councils dealt with heresies and often matters of faith including such significant issues as the divinity and humanity of Jesus (two natures, divine and human, in one person) and the Trinity (three persons in one God). It should be noted that these councils dealt primarily with what was taught by various bishops and, with a few exceptions, not with what an individual theologian taught. There were eight ecumenical councils recognized by the Roman Catholic Church in the first millennium—First Nicea (325), First Constantinople (381), Ephesus (431), Chalcedon (451), Second Constantinople (553), Third Constantinople (680–81), Second Nicea (787), and Fourth Constantinople (869–70). Note that all these councils took place in the East and not in the West. The first seven councils are also recognized as such by the Eastern Orthodox Churches.[13]

Emperors played the primary role in the early councils, but the bishops of Rome were not totally uninvolved, especially in the acceptance of the early councils. Augustine in the fifth century maintained that confession by the whole Church constitutes the ultimate guarantee of truth. Integral to that acceptance is the concurrence of Rome. All seven councils were finally accepted only after a considerable period of time. Nicea did not prevail for a comparatively long time. Other councils, for example, Sardica (343), Rimini (359), Ephesus (449), and Constantinople (454), were convened as ecumenical councils but never recognized as such. There was no a priori means of distinguishing an ecumenical council from others. Also at this time there was never an appeal to the authority of a general council as such, which occurred in the later period of conciliarism in the Church. The appeal at this time was always to a particular council. As time went on, the bishop of Rome played a greater role, and it was recognized that the council had to be accepted by the bishop of Rome.[14]

Likewise, as time went on, the bishop of Rome himself claimed a greater role in the life of the Church. Leo the Great, pope from 440–61 and one of two popes called "the Great," was a strong advocate in theory and in practice for the authoritative role of the bishop of Rome's leadership in the Church. He was the first bishop of Rome to claim to be the heir of Peter, with all the rights and duties of Peter. Standing in the place of Peter, he exercised authority over all the faithful and the bishops. He exercised his authoritative role not only in Italy but also to some extent in Spain, Gaul, and Africa. The East, however, was not willing to accept his strong papal claims. Yet the universal papal role was by no means a day-to-day function of the life of the bishop of Rome. The emperor, for example, convened the Council of Chalcedon in 451, which ultimately ratified the Christological teaching of Leo himself. Leo had wanted the council to take place in Italy but was unable to bring that about. In addition, he strongly objected to the never approved Canon 28 at the Council of Chalcedon, granting Constantinople the same prerogatives and dignity in the East that Rome enjoyed in the West.[15]

With no emperor in Rome, the bishops in Rome became more than just ecclesiastical leaders, taking on many secular duties. History especially remembers Leo for saving Rome from invasion by Attila the Hun and Geiseric the King of the Vandals. His role in taking responsibility for the city of Rome served as the basis for the fact that for 1,500 years his successors saw the protection and defense of Rome as part of their sacred duty.[16]

Gregory I, bishop of Rome from 540 to 640, was the second and last pope to be called "the Great." He was a monk, a person of virtue, a reformer, a good administrator, and an author who saw his role even in Rome as primarily one of service. Even in his time, the authority of the pope was fragile. He had difficulties in the East with the emperor and with many of the bishops. In the West, he could not assume he would be obeyed in his efforts at reform. His success there was based on his persuasion, coaxing, and scolding. He also refused to be addressed as "universal pope." History above all remembers Gregory for sending Augustine of Canterbury to evangelize England. But in Rome the local clergy did not strongly support him because he had given power to monks rather than to the clergy.[17]

Gregory wrote much, but his writings were not official papal documents such as we have today. They were the work of a bishop, a scholar, a monk, and a spiritual leader. His *Pastoral Care* was a handbook for properly carrying out the roles of pastor and bishop. His *Moralia* was a mystical and spiritual reflection on Job that served for many centuries as spiritual guidance for Christians. Thomas Aquinas in the second part of the *Summa theologiae* cites Gregory 374 times. Gregory's writings were on the practical side and often derived from others, but he was recognized as one of the four original "Doctors of the Western Church," together with Ambrose, Augustine, and Jerome.[18]

After Gregory the Great, problems continued for the bishop of Rome. On the theological front, the heresy of monothelitism (Jesus had only one divine will and not a human will as well) came to the fore and exacerbated the relationships with the bishops of the East. Growing tensions also were felt between the bishop of Rome and the emperor in the East. The barbarians had taken over the West since the fifth century. The Lombards had become converted to Christianity, and even they threatened to invade the city of Rome. In the latter part of the eighth century the bishop of Rome tilted to the empire of the Franks. Pepin, the leader of the Franks, in what later became known as the "Donation of Pepin," gave extensive

lands in Italy to the pope, thus solidifying the role of the pope as a temporal ruler over a rather expansive territory in what is known today as Italy.
In 800 in St. Peter's Basilica, Pope Leo III crowned Charlemagne as
emperor. Charlemagne definitely wanted to reform the Frankish Church,
but there were growing tensions with the bishop of Rome. John O'Malley
questions whether Charlemagne was a savior or a master.[19]

The papacy had its ups and downs in the course of history, but there
is general agreement that in the tenth century and first part of the eleventh century the papacy was at its lowest. The popes were almost totally
subordinated to the ruling German emperor and to the local Roman aristocracy. Twelve of the twenty-five popes elected between 955 and 1057
were appointed by the German emperors and no fewer than five of these
were also dismissed by the emperors. The papacy was also deeply
involved in the internecine warfare of the Roman nobility with the papacy
itself frequently becoming a commodity for sale or barter. Thirteen popes
in this period were appointed by the local Roman aristocracy. The
eleventh-century papacy in many respects had become a local institution
as well as a prisoner of the geography and politics of Rome.[20]

The holders of the papacy at this time involved many more sinners
than saints. At least five popes in this time frame were assassinated. Ser-
gius III (904–11) ordered the murders of his predecessor, Leo V, and the
antipope, Christopher. Stephen VIII (939–42) and John XIV (983–84)
were imprisoned and mutilated or starved to death. Stephen VI in 896
ordered Pope Formosus's body (891–96) to be exhumed nine months
after his death and put on trial in what was called "The Cadaver Synod,"
presided over by Stephen himself. The deceased pope was found guilty
and his body was mutilated before being thrown into the Tiber. "The
Cadaver Synod" divided the Roman Church and was a major factor in
the election of subsequent popes.[21]

Popes in the first millennium claimed a special primacy in the Church,
but the historical reality was often a far cry from these theoretical claims.
Brian Tierney, a distinguished medieval historian, points out that after
Gregory the Great, chaos became worse in Western Europe after a brief
revival under Charlemagne. From the eighth century, the pope became a
temporal ruler of central Italy, a petty Italian duke, as well as head of the
Church. As a result, the local Roman nobility sought out and struggled
for the papacy as they did for secular leadership. The behavior of some of
these popes was truly scandalous. Popes like this exercised no significant
control over other bishops in the West. These other bishops for the most

part were controlled by local kings and dukes. Ironically, as the Church seemed to be dead in its center, there was quite a bit of vitality at the periphery with increased missionary activities in different areas such as Scandinavia and among the Slavs and the Poles.[22]

Popes as Teachers

There is no doubt that the popes in the first millennium did not play a primary teaching role in the Church with regard to what was later called "faith and morals." Avery Dulles maintains that in this time frame, the primary hierarchical teaching role in the Church came in the form of local, regional, and more general synods and councils. Even here there is no doubt that the earlier general councils saw the primary role coming from the emperor. But the conviction gradually grew that the Holy Spirit is present where the bishops of the Church are gathered together in councils. As noted, there were eight recognized general councils together with many other local and regional synods and councils in the early church. Dulles sees these councils as an attempt to obtain unity "from below" through the consensus coming from the local and regional churches. The flow was not from the top down but from the bottom up. In the last centuries of the millennium, there was lesser synodal and conciliar activity as a result of the tensions and struggles that were briefly mentioned earlier.[23]

The general or ecumenical councils primarily dealt with issues of faith centering on the fundamental doctrines of the Trinity and the person of Jesus. These were not only central matters of faith but also contentious issues in local churches and in the broader general Church. But these councils did not deal in any depth with issues of morality, even though there was no shortage of moral issues that arose for life in the Church. Since the papacy did not play a major initiating or prescribing role in teaching in general, even in the faith controversies, it logically follows that the papacy played no major role in proposing moral teachings for the universal Church. How then was this teaching role in morality carried out?

Any knowledge of the early Church shows there was no shortage of moral issues that came to the fore. These issues included attitudes to the world, to wealth and poverty, to sexuality, and to violence in the political order with emphasis on the legitimacy of Christians serving in the military.[24] Who were the teachers with regard to these moral issues? In keeping with the New Testament recognition of a separate function of teachers, the first few centuries recognized teachers who were not clergy. In the church of Alexandria, Clement and Origen stand out as playing a teaching role even though they were not part of the priestly ministry of the Church. But Origen himself later had to accept being ordained to what we call today priestly ministry. But after that time, catechists and what we call theologians were generally identified with the role of priests and bishops. The West remembers especially Ambrose, Augustine, Gregory the Great, and Jerome. The East recalls the fourth-century Cappadocians, Basil of Caesarea, Gregory of Nazianzus, and Gregory of Nyssa as well as John Chrysostom and John Damascene.[25]

It is neither necessary nor possible here to go into detail about the moral teaching of these "Fathers of the Church."[26] Volumes have been written on the moral teaching of Augustine alone. The teaching on usury or the condemnation of taking interest on a loan will suffice as an example. Robert P. Maloney has studied the teaching of the patristic authorities on usury.[27] The writings of Clement of Alexandria (c. 150–215) are among the earliest extant writings condemning usury. Maloney then develops and explains the approach taken by a large number of subsequent Fathers of the Church, both Eastern and Western—Apollonius, Cyprian of Carthage, Lactantius, Hilary of Poitiers, and especially Basil the Great, Gregory of Nyssa, Ambrose, Chrysostom, Jerome, Augustine, and Gregory the Great. Usury is a grave sin for all Christians and not just for clerics. These fathers appealed especially to the Old Testament texts and to the general Christian teaching of love for the poor and those in need. The Lucan text (6:34–35), maintaining that one should lend expecting nothing in return, played only a minor role in their approaches, even though Pope Urban III in the twelfth century made it a primary argument against usury. The argument based on the nature of money as fungible or perishable also received some attention. One has to return only what has been used or perished, as true of all other fungible goods such as food. Aristotle had used this argument, and at a later date medieval Christian authorities gave great importance to it.

Early local and regional synods or councils forbade usury. Usury or the taking of interest was forbidden to clerics by the 44th of the Apostolic Canons, by the First Council of Arles (314), and by the First General Council of Nicea (325). The First Council of Carthage (345) forbade laity to engage in usury.[28] In a letter to three Italian bishops, Pope Leo the Great also condemned usury.[29]

In conclusion, in the first millennium, popes claimed to have a universal primacy in the whole Church, but in reality that was not found in any substantial way. The relationship and even dependency of the papacy on secular rulers and even Roman aristocracy limited its spiritual role. The role of the bishops of Rome as temporal rulers also took away from their claim to primacy in spiritual matters. As a matter of fact, the primary way of teaching or settling disputes of faith and practice was through local, regional, and general councils, with recognition of some role for the pope in these general councils. The papacy did not play a significant role with regard to teaching morality to the universal Church.

FROM THE GREGORIAN REFORM (ELEVENTH CENTURY) TO MARTIN LUTHER

The eleventh century witnessed a reform movement to restore the papacy and the life of the Church. Even in the tenth century, a movement to renew Christian life in general and monastic life in particular began in France and Germany. The monastery of Cluny was the most famous of these reforming communities. Some individual bishops also worked for reform in the spiritual life of the Church. But in the eleventh century the papacy itself became the leading force in the reform of the whole Church and of the papacy. Leo IX (1049–54) and Nicholas II (1058–61) began the work of reform. To institutionalize reform Nicholas II's Lateran Synod in 1059 promulgated a new procedure for papal elections to prevent papal appointments coming from emperors or the Roman aristocracy. The choice was to be made by the cardinal bishops with the subsequent approval of the cardinal priests and deacons. The cardinals were the senior clergy of Rome. There was also need for subsequent assent by the people and a grudging recognition for some imperial approval.[30]

The Gregorian Reform

It was Gregory VII (1073–85), the former monk Hildebrand, who spearheaded this reform that is generally referred to as the "Gregorian Reform." This reform movement strongly influenced the next few centuries in the life of the Church. The problems facing Gregory VII were immense—the fact that bishops were often appointed and chosen by emperors, dukes, and other civil rulers, which was called the "lay investiture" problem. In addition, simony, the buying and selling of Church offices and spiritual goods, was rampant; nepotism was present in the papacy and in many other areas of the Church; and clerical concubinage was accepted in various parts of the Christian world. Especially since the vast majority of bishops saw themselves primarily as fulfilling secular duties, carrying out their spiritual role and functions was not a priority.[31]

To bring about the reform, Gregory emphasized the prerogatives and powers of the papacy. He first asked Peter Damian to put together from the decrees and acts of popes all the material that favored the authority of the popes.[32] Gregory himself set out his understanding of the papacy in twenty-seven short affirmations, the *Dictatus Papae* (The Memorandum of the Pope). Gregory made claims for the papacy that went far beyond previous understandings. The pope alone can depose and reinstate bishops. He can depose emperors and also relieve subjects of their oath of fealty to unjust rulers. The pope is judged by no one. The Roman Church has never erred, nor shall it err for all eternity.[33]

By making law the primary instrument of reform, Gregory VII was influential in the growth and importance of canon law. The eleventh century showed a tremendous development in this area. The Bolognese monk Gratian in 1140 put together what was called *Concordia discordantium canonum* (Harmony of the Discordant Canons) that became popularly known as the *Decretum* (Decree). Gratian made the significant contribution of bringing some systematization and order to a situation that had been not only disorderly but chaotic. His work included not only previous papal documents but also forgeries such as "The Donation of Constantine," which tended to exalt papal primacy and powers. Gratian's own work associated with the University of Bologna gave a great impetus to the study of canon law as a most important discipline in the next centuries. The study of canon law spread rapidly to all parts of Europe. Gratian's work was that of a private scholar, but soon other official papal decrees and decretals were added to what later became known as the compendium of all canon law—*Corpus Iuris Canonici*, which served as the law of the church from 1500 until the new Code of Canon Law in 1918.[34]

In reality, Gregory VII's strong vision of reform was bound to create conflicts. The most famous of these conflicts involved the pope and Henry IV, the emperor of the Holy Roman Empire. The emperor challenged the pope by deposing both claimants to the prestigious archbishopric of Milan and installing his own candidate. Gregory rebuked him

and orally threatened excommunication. The emperor responded by calling a synod of his bishops at Worms and called the pope a "false monk"
and deposed him—a sentence later accepted by the bishops of Lombardy.
But many princes became disaffected with Henry and demanded that he
revoke his deposition of the pope and swear religious obedience to him.
History has recorded the famous scene at Canossa of the emperor, bare-
foot in the snow, begging for absolution, which Gregory ultimately gave.
Gregory had won an astounding victory, but it did not last. A short time
later, Henry appointed as antipope Clement III and in the process cut off
much of Gregory's income. In 1084, Henry entered Rome, took over St.
Peter's, and had the antipope Clement crown him as emperor. Gregory,
abandoned by most of his cardinals, was holed up in the fortress of Castel
Sant'Angelo. Gregory was rescued by Robert Guiscard, the leader of the
Normans in Sicily and southern Italy, who then sacked Rome. Gregory
was forced by the disenchanted Romans to flee and died shortly thereafter
in bitter exile in Salerno.[35]

In concrete and immediate terms, Gregory accomplished very little.
His efforts to excommunicate many bishops were not successful; Henry
the emperor outlived him and saw Gregory die in exile. But Gregory's
vision and actions on behalf of the freedom of the Church from political
and secular control in spiritual matters ultimately won out. The subsequent papacy would enjoy this freedom thanks to Gregory. Eamon Duffy
concludes his analysis of Gregory VII by saying, "No pope for a hundred
years, perhaps no pope ever, would loom so large on the European scene
as he had done."[36]

Richard McBrien points out that two very different evaluations of
Gregory VII and his successors have emerged in the Church. For some,
Gregory and his successors represent the apex of the glory, grandeur, and
power of the papacy. Others view the developments associated with the
Gregorian Reform as an aberration that has to some degree distorted the
basic idea of the Church and the papacy. One significant representative of
such an approach is Yves Congar, one of the most distinguished Catholic
theologians of the twentieth century and a significant contributor to Vatican II who was made a cardinal by Pope John Paul II in 1994, the year
before he died.[37]

For Congar, the turning point in ecclesiology is the eleventh century,
embedded especially in the person and work of Gregory VII. Congar
recognizes the huge problems that Gregory faced, both in relation to the

emperor and civil rulers and with regard to reforming the role and function of bishops in the Church. The Church above all should be understood as a spiritual communion based on the word of God received in faith and grace with a strong emphasis on the role of the sacraments. The communion of grace as the free loving action of God in Christ through the power of the Spirit gathers together a people in sacrament and prayer to continue in time and space the work of the risen Lord. But Gregory's approach to reform put primary emphasis on the legal aspect of the Church and not the sacramental.[38]

The Church had to oppose the intrusion of the temporal powers into its spiritual affairs, but in the process it adopted the same understanding and approach as the temporal power itself. The Church began to see itself as a society with power to exercise over others in the same way that temporal rulers exercised their power. The Church became a society like temporal and political society and failed to stress that it was a sacramental communion with ministers and servants as its leaders. The Church became primarily a legal institution. The legal thus took priority over the sacramental. This change in approach can be seen in the ways in which the term *corpus Christi* (body of Christ) and *corpus mysticum* changed in the middle of the twelfth century. These two concepts originally referred to the Eucharist, the sacramental body of Christ. But the mystical body now began to refer to the Church as a society with its hierarchical functions similar to temporal societies.

The shift from the sacramental to the legal understanding of the Church also brought about a new chapter in the history of the notion and concept of authority in the Church. This development was not based entirely on the new juridical and legal understanding of the Church. The growth and attraction of this understanding of authority also owed much to the mystique surrounding it and the powerful personalities involved in it beginning with Gregory VII. Gregory did not claim these powers and rights for his own personal aggrandizement; he did not seek power for himself. What was involved here was truly a theocracy, a justice coming from God expressed in the law of the Church and the power and the rights of the papacy. This was the will of God.[39]

Such an approach gave a legalistic interpretation to certain themes and texts that were previously understood in light of a spiritual anthropology and not a legalistic application to the popes. Jeremiah 1:10—I have set you over the nations and kingdoms to root up and pull down—became an assertion of the authority of the pope to depose kings. 1 Corinthians

2:15—the spiritual person judges all things and himself is judged by no one—proved the canonical assertion that the First See (Rome) is judged by no one. 1 Corinthians 6:3—we will judge angels and even more so secular realities—justified the right of popes to judge secular rulers. What originally referred to spiritual anthropology in general now was understood as supporting the power and rights of the papacy.

This development brought about a new understanding of the bishop of Rome. In a true sense, it is at best an anachronism to refer to the bishop of Rome as pope before Gregory VII. Gregory himself decreed in 1073 that the title "pope" should be restricted to the bishop of Rome. Before that time the title "pope" applied to every bishop in the West.[40] The most traditional title given to the bishop of Rome after the fourth century was the Vicar of Peter. Not until the pontificate of Eugenius III (1145–53) did the title "Vicar of Christ" refer explicitly and exclusively to the pope. "Vicar of Christ" is today probably the most used title for the pope.[41]

At its best, according to Congar, the title "Vicar of Christ" has a sacramental and iconological understanding—the transcendent and heavenly power is actually active in the earthly representative, the pope. There is a continuing vertical descent from above, which is then present in and through the pope. But with the Gregorian Reform comes a more legalistic understanding that from then on predominates. This power is given by Christ to his vicar, who takes his place. The power is attached to the papal office. The predominant feature is not a continued vertical gift and actual presence, nor an iconological representation. The power now becomes the possession of the person who becomes pope, who uses it in the same way that temporal authority is used by secular powers. The pope now has a title to this power. The authoritative role of the pope has shifted from a sacramental, representational, and iconological understanding of God present and acting through his representative to a power that now belongs by legal right to the pope.[42]

The legalistic approach to papal authority began with Gregory VII and has continued through the vicissitudes of history to the present day. Canon 331 of the new Code of Canon Law is the first canon dealing with the Roman pontiff: "The bishop of the Roman church, in whom continues the office given by the Lord uniquely to Peter, the first of the Apostles, and to be transmitted to his successors, is the head of the college of bishops, the Vicar of Christ, and pastor of the universal Church on earth.

By virtue of his office, he possesses supreme, full, immediate, and universal ordinary power in the Church, which he is always able to exercise
freely."[43]

The popes carried out their responsibility with the help of others. Synods and councils were often held. From 1123 to 1275, six general or ecumenical councils were held to carry out the work of reform—the councils
of Lateran I, II, III, and IV, and Lyons I and II. Unlike the eight ecumenical councils of the first millennium, these were clearly under control of
the pope, but there was often free and unfettered discussion. The pope
now also relied more on the cardinals who assumed a greater responsibility in the life of the Church. The curia (the term was introduced by Urban
II, 1088–92), including to some extent the role of the cardinals, was the
administrative bureaucracy of the papacy; it expanded greatly, taking on
a more significant role in light of Rome's status as the executive center of
the Church. Many of the popes were themselves canon lawyers, who used
papal decrees or formal letters to carry out the work of reform. About
one thousand of these papal documents from the twelfth century have
survived. The curia and all this administrative bureaucracy was financed
primarily by fees for services. Papal finances even at this time were not
secure, and the possibility of abuse and corruption became ever present.
The ongoing financial needs paved the way for the later granting of indulgences in exchange for financial contributions.[44]

Popes and Problems after Gregory

A number of significant figures served as popes after Gregory. Urban II's
call at Claremont in 1095 for a crusade or holy war to free Jerusalem from
Muslim control well illustrated the greater role and primacy of the papacy
as many responded to this call. The granting of an indulgence—
technically the remission of temporal punishment due to sin but often
commonly understood to mean the forgiveness of all sin—was a powerful
motive for people to join this crusade. According to Eamon Duffy, the
papacy of Innocent III (1198–1216) may represent the pinnacle of papal
power and influence. Innocent intervened in the life of political rulers to
defend Christian morality and the role of the papacy. He summoned and
led the ecumenical council, Lateran IV, an important reform council.
Innocent approved and supported the new religious approaches of the
Dominicans and the Franciscans in their renewal efforts. He used papal
legates to increase the power of the papacy at the expense of local bishops.

Innocent strongly opposed heretics and used the Dominicans to put down the Albigensian heresy, which tended to identify the material world with evil, in Southern France. But he later used the sword in a crusade against the Albigensians.[45]

Boniface VIII, whose papacy extended from the end of the thirteenth to the beginning of the fourteenth century, illustrated both the good and the bad aspects of the medieval concept of papal supremacy. He supported papal reform by inaugurating the first Holy Year in 1300, insisting on an education for the clergy, codifying canon law, and founding a university in Rome. But he also used his office to enrich his own family and put down their traditional rivals. Boniface was involved with political rulers, most disastrously in a conflict with the king of France. In this context he issued the Bull *Unam Sanctam*, which claimed that it is altogether necessary for salvation that every human creature be subject to the Roman pontiff. French forces ultimately humiliated the pope in his palace at Anagni, and he died soon afterward. His claims to ultimate temporal power were overcome by the reality of his humiliation and defeat by the king.[46]

As time progressed, the problems of seeking protection from secular rulers—usually against other rulers, especially in this case the king of France—continuing struggles with the aristocrats in the city of Rome, and divisions among the cardinals themselves continued. Two somewhat related events—the Babylonian Captivity of the Papacy in Avignon (1309–77) and the Great Western Schism (1378–1470)—greatly weakened the papacy. The seventy-year exile of the popes in Avignon was a disaster for the Church, but it came about almost by accident. The papal conclave in 1304–5 was split between those seeking revenge against what the king of France had done to Boniface and those seeking reconciliation with the French king. After eleven months of wrangling, the latter group won out with the election of Clement V (1305–14). To please the French king, Clement V had himself crowned in Lyons. His intent was to stay only a short time, but in Avignon he and his six successors came very much under the influence of the French king, and the papacy itself became French. Despite the protestations of the Avignon popes, their presence in Avignon affected perceptions of what the papacy was and contributed to growing questions about its claim to supremacy in the Church. The exile in Avignon came to an end when Gregory X (1370–78) returned to Rome at the instigation of Catherine of Siena and many others. But an even greater problem was imminent—the Great Western Schism with three different contenders for the papal crown.[47]

Just after the papal return to Rome in 1378, a papal conclave divided between the French and Italian factions finally elected an Italian as pope, Urban VI. But a short time later, the same cardinals deposed Urban and elected a Frenchman, Clement VII, who went back to Avignon. Thus began the Great Western Schism with two different popes and their successors. There had been many antipopes previously, but the problem here was that the same cardinals elected both popes! No compromise or dual resignation was possible. Many came to the conclusion that a council was needed to solve the problem. A council was held at Pisa in 1409, but this only succeeded in adding a third pope—Alexander V. Finally the Council of Constance in 1417, after deposition and resignation of the three claimants, elected Martin V. The role of the council in this case raised issues about conciliarism in the Church and the relationship of the papacy to a general council. The majority opinion, which was apparently accepted at Constance, held that in certain circumstances an ecumenical council might act against a pope, but a more radical approach made the council supreme over the pope on a general basis. Obviously, this schism further affected the influence and role of the papacy. Constance itself ordered that councils should be held regularly, but in the midst of the tensions later popes did not go along with this. In the fifteenth century the Council of Basle-Ferrara-Florence made a futile attempt to unite the Western and Eastern churches.[48]

Nicholas V (1447–56) was the first of the Renaissance popes who did much to promote the art and architecture of Rome. The Renaissance papacy, however, despite all its accomplishments with regard to buildings and art, was chronically resistant to reform. Throughout the Christian world came cries for reform—for example, from Savonarola in Florence and Erasmus in Rotterdam. Many felt the need for a reform council. Julius II convened a fifth Lateran Council, but this did not deal with the real problem of reform.[49] According to Richard McBrien, the self-interest of those most involved—the popes, the bishops, and the secular rulers—militated against any real reform.[50] The growing disenchantment created the powder keg ignited by Martin Luther and other reformers.

Luther's first objection was against the giving of indulgences by Julius II and, later, Leo X to fund the rebuilding of St. Peter's in Rome. Raising donations by giving spiritual blessings was by no means new in the Church, but the preaching of this indulgence in Germany was riddled with corruption. In the ensuing controversy, the role of the papacy together with the importance of the scripture and the doctrine of justification became primary issues. The complex details of all that occurred between Luther and the pope, together with the role of secular rulers, are too complex to go into here. However, the result is familiar: the Lutheran reform resulted in the division in Western Christianity between the Catholic and Protestant churches.[51] Church reform had been a primary issue beginning with Gregory VII in the eleventh century, but Gregory certainly never imagined that his call for reform would end with the Protestant Reformation and a further diminishment of the influence and power of the papacy.

Teaching Role of the Popes

As one would expect, the popes and bishops carried on a teaching role in this period, but it was quite different from the teaching role in the first millennium and was very closely connected with governing power in the Church. In the earlier period, the content of the teaching was primarily doctrinal matters referring to basic Christian beliefs such as the Trinity and the divinity and humanity of Jesus. Most of the bishops, including the bishop of Rome, were looked upon as theologians. There were no autonomous individual theologians or groups of theologians after the third and fourth centuries. The milieu of the period of the Gregorian Reform was quite different. The primary problems involved the independence and freedom of the papacy and the Church from secular powers, and the reform of the Church. Canon law had now taken over the central importance that theology had in the first millennium. Most of the popes themselves were canon lawyers, and law was the primary means they used to bring about reform in the Church.

The popes in the earlier period of the Gregorian Reform used what we call today ecumenical councils as a primary way of carrying on their work of legislating and teaching. In the course of two centuries there were seven of what today are recognized as ecumenical councils—Lateran I (1123), II (1139), III (1179), and IV (1215); Lyons I (1245) and II (1274); and Vienne (1311). These councils differed from the recognized eight ecumenical councils in the first millennium by the fact that they were all called and presided over by the pope himself.[52] This is obvious proof of the recognition of the primacy of the pope that had developed since the first millennium.

Pope Callistus II invoked and presided over Lateran I. No records of the deliberations have survived, but the council promulgated twenty-two (or, according to some, twenty-five) canons. The canons often restated earlier legislation and dealt primarily with ordinations, offices, and spiritual administrations; with clerics; and with the protection of churches, property, places, and persons. The Fourth Lateran Council marks the high point of medieval papal legislation and is sometimes called the Great Council. The council and its profession of faith condemned the heresies of the Albigensians and the Waldensians without explicitly mentioning them, and proposed transubstantiation for understanding the change in the Eucharistic species. Seventy canons dealt with the general state of the Church as well as a good number of political issues. Unfortunately, the last section of canons imposed restrictive legislation against Jews, such as the need to wear distinctive dress. These canons were promulgated in the name of the pope and included in the official collection of canon law. The Fourth Lateran Council marks the culminating point in medieval papal legislation and leadership. Subsequent councils dealt with similar issues.[53] The Second Council of Lyons tried but failed to bring about union with the Eastern Church. The Council of Constance (1414–18) brought a solution to the Great Western Schism.[54] During this time the struggles with secular rulers continued, but the zeal for reform within the Church dwindled.

These councils were the primary and most authoritative way in which the popes at this time carried on their ministry of governing and teaching. But the popes also used letters, especially to bishops. Thus, for example, Denzinger lists three letters of Pope Alexander III that deal with the incorrupt body of Mary after her death, the errors of Peter Lombard about the humanity of Christ, and other errors dealing with the humanity of Christ.[55]

What about papal teaching on moral issues during the time of the Gregorian Reform to the Reformation? The example of the teaching on usury, the condemnation of taking interest on a loan, again serves as a good example of teaching on a moral issue.

The Decree of Gratian, trying to find some harmony among the discordant canons (circa 1140), discussed usury in two different places. In a section dealing with clerics and impediments to ordination, eight canons forbade clerics from demanding usury and declared that those guilty of usury cannot be ordained. If one is already in orders, he is to be deposed. In the second part of his work, Gratian raises questions concerning the practice of usury by everyone—cleric or lay. Specifically, Gratian raises three questions: can clergy and laity engage in usury? May alms be given by what is acquired by usury? Is restitution required before penance can be done for taking usury? The canons cited all come from the fourth, fifth, and sixth centuries, and in this case of usury there is little novelty and no contradictions about the prohibition. To demand, receive, or lend expecting to receive something above the capital is to be guilty of usury. The prohibition against usury holds for laity as well as for clerics, but the latter will be more severely punished.[56]

The issue of usury rose again in the time frame from the Gregorian Reform to the Reformation, in light of increasing mercantile and economic activities. As noted, the emphasis of Church governing and teaching at this time was to achieve moral reform within the Church and do away with existing evils. Canon 13 of the Second Lateran Council (1139) condemned the greed of usurers, a practice condemned as despicable and blameworthy by divine and human law and denounced in both testaments of scripture. Those who do not repent will be deprived of Christian burial. The twenty-fifth canon of the Third Lateran Council (1179) recognized that the crime of usury had become firmly rooted nearly everywhere, and lamented that many practice usury and in no way notice that it is forbidden in both the Old and the New Testaments. Notorious usurers should not be admitted to communion or receive Christian burial if they die in their sin. The twenty-ninth canon of the Ecumenical Council of Vienne (1311) declared that those involved in taking usury incur the sentence of excommunication. If one affirms pertinaciously (this adverb implies that the condemnation here does not apply to all usurers) that the practice of usury is not sinful, such a one is to be punished as a heretic. These conciliar considerations are in keeping with the framework of using legislation and punishment to achieve moral reform. However, these punishments are based on the fact that usury is a serious moral evil.[57]

As noted in general, in addition to the popes using councils, they also governed and taught by their letters and responses to bishops and others. The Archbishop of Palermo wrote to Pope Alexander III (1159–81) asking if he could dispense from the prohibition of usury to raise funds to ransom captives from the Saracens. The pope even in this case stood by the principle that usury is always wrong. The Archbishop of Canterbury asked about the obligation of debtors to pay usury they had sworn to pay. The papal answer was that the debtors are not bound because usury is a detestable crime. Urban III in 1196 issued the first official statement that Luke 6:34 proved that usury is always wrong. The popes also condemned practical attempts to evade the condemnation of usury.[58] Thus, in this time frame of the Gregorian Reform and afterward, the papal teaching either in conjunction with an ecumenical council or on its own condemned usury. The example stands for many of the cases in which morally wrong acts were condemned, often in the context of legislation or punishment aimed at reform in the Church.

Theological Faculties and Universities

A new teaching reality appeared in this period—theologians and universities. In the first few centuries, there were independent theologians who were not bishops, but after that time the categories of theologian and bishop tended to merge somewhat. Monastic schools with theology had emerged before the end of the first millennium, but something new and different came in the twelfth century. At that time, the West experienced an outpouring of creativity—population exploded, cities became more important, the Crusades sparked imagination, and cathedrals began to be built. In this context, schools were established with a new mode of doing theology. Unlike the monastic theology, this new theology emphasized a rational method with stress on analysis and systematization. By the end of the twelfth century, universities began to flourish with theology as the queen of the sciences.[59]

In this context there emerged three governing groups in society—*sacerdotium*, *imperium*, and *studium*—the Church, the empire, and the university. These were three powers analogous to three persons in the Trinity; according to some authors these were symbolized by the three points of the stylized fleur-de-lis on the arms of the king of France. The thirteenth century is recognized as the golden age of Scholastic theology. The rise of the universities, together with the newly founded medieval orders (the Dominicans and the Franciscans with their *studia generalia*), provided a locus for the rational systematization of Catholic theology, with Thomas Aquinas eventually recognized as the most significant figure. Note that the theologians were not just treated as individuals, but they were members of a guild or a particular university faculty with the obligations, duties, and privileges attached to such relationships. At this time, society was not egalitarian. These three leading groups had obligations, leadership roles, and privileges in keeping with their function.[60]

This developing role of theologians, *studia*, and universities recognized a significant distinction between power and knowledge. The role of the theologians and universities constituted one of the three ruling aspects in the world. As a result, there arose a somewhat autonomous and independent role for theology. From the time of St. Bede there existed a distinction between two types of keys (*claves*)—the key of power (*potestas*) and the key of knowledge (*scientia*). Thus, theology emerged as a separate and somewhat autonomous reality within society at large and within the Church. The most prominent university at the time was the University of Paris. Francisco de Vitoria (d. 1546) affirmed that one would sin mortally if, after Paris had determined that a particular contract was usurious, one held the contrary position.[61]

From the middle of the thirteenth century the university faculties of theology censured errors in theology on their own initiative independently of pope and bishops. In 1241, for example, the theological faculty of Paris condemned ten propositions of Etienne de Venisy; in 1254, it reproved thirty-one propositions of Gerard de Borgo San Donnino. At the time of the Great Schism, theology had a stronger role in the light of the weakening of the papacy. At the end of the period we are considering, Melchior Cano, in his famous *De locis theologicis*, gives extraordinary authority to the work of the school theologians. It is theologically reckless to ignore the common opinion of Scholastics because in any discipline one must trust the experts. The unanimity of these theologians can only come from the Holy Spirit. An opinion contrary to the common teaching of the Scholastics in a matter of faith or morals is at least "close to heresy." Cano applied to theologians the New Testament text—the one who hears you, hears me; and the one who rejects you, rejects me.[62] In the twentieth century the ordinary papal magisterium applied these words to the pope.[63]

What was the precise relationship, then, between the role of theologians and the role of the papacy, which had been given great prominence in the Gregorian Reform? The canonists recognized the papal role in solving disputes and correcting errors. Perhaps the best understanding of the two different roles is found in the distinction between inquiry and authority, two different but complementary charisms in the Church. The pope possessed the authority to clarify doubtful issues, but by authority and not by inquiring as the theologians did. Despite some absolute-sounding statements about the role of theologians, the final decisions belonged to the pope.[64]

However, popes recognized the need to learn from theologians and to employ these theologians in developing their own positions. Yes, popes saw their role as censuring erroneous positions, but they relied heavily on committees of theologians. Congar mentions this heavy reliance on commissions of theologians in the papal condemnations of *L'Evangile éternal* (1255), William of Holy Love (1256), John Peter Olivi (1324–26), and the Fraticelli (1318, 1322) in addition to the well-known condemnations of Wyclif and Luther, which involved a significant role for theologians.[65]

Avery Dulles has succinctly summarized the role of universities and theological faculties in determining the teaching of the Church during this period. The doctrinal decrees of several general councils (Lyons I, 1245; Lyons II, 1274; and Vienne, 1312) were officially submitted to universities for approval before being officially published. The theological faculties received corporate invitations to attend the fifteenth-century reform councils. At the Council of Constance (1415), Pierre d'Ailly successfully contended that the doctors of sacred theology should have a deliberative vote, since they have received the authority to preach and teach everywhere—an authority that exceeds that of an individual bishop or of an ignorant abbot. The universities during this period were accustomed to pass on the orthodoxy of new opinions and to prepare theological censures.[66]

In this period, theologians were involved in the work of what were called the general councils of the West, some of which were recognized as ecumenical councils by the Roman Church. According to Nelson Minnich, in nine of these councils held from 1409 to 1563, theologians had deliberative voting rights equal to bishops in the first six general councils held before 1450 but did not have such voting rights in the later three councils studied—Pisa-Milan-Asti-Lyons (1511–12), Lateran V (1512), and Trent (1545).[67]

What explains the change? A number of factors have been proposed but two stand out. The first is a change in ecclesiology from the *congregatio fidelium* (congregation of the faithful), with its ascending power, to the *corpus mysticum* (mystical body), with power descending from the pope. The earlier councils mentioned gave greater credence to the conciliarist claim that a council should represent all the constituencies in the Church with the doctors of theology present and voting. The corporatist model, which was in ascendancy in the early sixteenth century, restricted voting in council only to those who had jurisdiction from the pope. Second, in the shift from late medieval to Renaissance times, emphasis was placed on the ancient Church as the model in general and the model in councils, where only bishops had a vote. To give such a vote to theologians was an anomaly and corruption of the ancient practice. However, even in the later councils such as Trent, the theologians played a significant role even if they did not have a deliberative vote. They drew up the articles for debate, clarified the issues, helped to draft the decrees, and even prevented decrees with which they disagreed from being accepted and consented to those that were passed.[68]

The reasons given for the role of theologians in the work of the councils even to the point of having a deliberate vote in the earlier councils studied have some lasting validity for today. The roles of bishops and theologians are not the same. In complex issues regarding theology, the bishops need the expertise of theologians. By definition, bishops do not necessarily have theological skills. In the present day with the phenomenal growth of specialization, it is impossible for most bishops with their already overburdened role of exercising oversight over all aspects of Church life, including running a large corporation, to have the skills of a theologian. During the period we are studying, the bishops explicitly recognized that they needed the help of theologians, even if in the later years the theologians did not have a deliberative vote in the councils. The Council of Trent decreed that bishops should have some competency in theology. Studies have shown that in the mid-sixteenth century in France, only 4 percent of bishops had degrees in theology and by the third quarter of that century only 12 percent had theological degrees. At the same time, a much greater percentage of bishops in France had degrees in canon law. This emphasis on canon law obviously comes with the importance that the Gregorian Reform gave to canon law in its role in governing and reforming the Church. Yes, it belongs to bishops to determine questions of faith and doctrine in the governance of the Church, but they need the help of theologians to carry out this function.[69]

The shift from bishop-theologians in the first millennium to a more independent role of a rational and Scholastic theology after Gregory VII resulted in a new context for the papal, conciliar, and episcopal roles. There were still problems of heresy and schism to contend with. The Inquisition came into existence during this time. But now more than ever before, the positions of theologians entered into the picture. Thus, the theses of Berengarius of Tours on the Eucharist were examined by six councils directly under the pope and by eight provincial councils. Some positions of Abelard, seen especially through the perhaps discolored lens of Bernard of Clairvaux, were censured by the Councils of Soissons (1121) and Sans (1140). Other censures and condemnations included Peter Lombard's Christology at the Council of Tours (1163) and by Pope Alexander III, and Joachim de Flora's Trinitarian ideas at Lateran V (1215).[70]

As Avery Dulles points out, there was a downside to this new emphasis on the teaching role of theologians. In the latter part of this period especially, popes and councils were drawn into disputes of a Scholastic character and were often distracted from the primary role of passing on the apostolic faith. Too often the popes and the councils of the later Middle Ages dealt with threats to papal power and with abstruse theological issues, such as the body–soul relationship, the mysteries of the afterlife (e.g., purgatory), and the intricacies of the Trinitarian processions. The papal and episcopal commissions tended to be caught up in the disputes between rival theological schools. The most notorious example involves the condemnation by the bishops of Paris and Canterbury of certain unexceptionable theses attributed to Thomas Aquinas.[71] However, this interest by popes, councils, and bishops in more abstract theological questions did not involve extensive consideration of areas of what today we know as moral theology.

Excursus on the Word "Magisterium"

This context of the development of a more rational and systematic approach to theology associated with the universities and the *studia* of religious orders in the Middle Ages furnishes a proper place to discuss the changing understanding of the word "magisterium" in Catholic theology. Only since the nineteenth century has the term "magisterium" been understood as the office of popes and bishops as authentic (meaning authoritative[72]) teachers in the Church. The Latin term *magisterium* originally referred to a master or leader in any type of activity, such as a master of horsemen or a commander of troops. The activity involved could also be that of teaching. With the rise of Scholastic theology in the Middle Ages, the distinction between doctrinal scholarly teaching and pastoral teaching came more to the fore. Two teaching roles or magisteria were recognized in the medieval Church. The pastoral teaching role is linked to the public teaching office or jurisdiction that belongs to the popes and bishops. The magisterium of the theologians or doctors in the

Church had some authority to make decisions and call for submission. Thomas Aquinas clearly recognizes these two different teaching roles in the Church. Sometimes he refers to the two functions as that of *praelitio*, attributed to bishops, and that of *magisterium*, attributed to theologians. He also speaks of two kinds of teaching—*doctrina praedicationis* (preaching), which is the task of bishops, and *doctrina scholastica* (Scholastic teaching), which is the task of theologians. On one occasion he refers to the bishops as having *magisterium cathedrae pastoralis* (a pastoral magisterium) and the theologians as exercising a *magisterium cathedrae magistralis* (a magisterial magisterium).[73]

There is no doubt that after Gregory VII the emphasis on papal authority in the Catholic Church grew, as illustrated by a number of attributes given to papal authority in the Roman Church—the Roman Church has never erred in faith; heresy is an approach that does not agree with the faith of the Roman Church; the papal function of judgment as putting an end to debate takes primacy over the papal function of witness and preaching; and the pope authorizes, invokes, and presides over councils. However, the magisterium of theologians, even with some authority in the Church, was also recognized.[74] In the nineteenth century the term "magisterium" became limited only to the hierarchical teaching office, and no authoritative role was given to the teaching of theologians. A subsequent section discusses this period in much greater detail.

FROM THE COUNCIL OF TRENT TO THE NINETEENTH CENTURY

The Catholic Church and the papacy had been weakened by the Avignon papacy and the Great Western Schism. The reform movement started by Gregory VII had also lost much of its strength. In the fifteenth century, calls for reform began to surface. But, in the sixteenth century, Martin Luther's call for reform resulted in the birth of Protestantism. The Catholic response to these circumstances came especially from the Council of Trent (1545–63).

The Council of Trent and Its Aftermath

The Council of Trent gave the impetus to a much more centralized and defensive church and papacy. In the context of Vatican II deliberations,

Trent became synonymous with the fact that the pre–Vatican II Church had become more centralized, more defensive, and more authoritarian than it had ever been in its history. At the first session of Vatican II, Bishop Émile-Joseph de Smedt of Bruges, Belgium, criticized the first draft of the proposed text on the Church as unacceptable because of three characteristics—triumphalism, clericalism, and juridicism.[75] For many supporters of Vatican II, de Smedt's comments reflected what they thought was the Tridentine spirit and approach that had to change. John W. O'Malley, however, has pointed out the important distinction between the Council of Trent and "Trent." "Trent" refers to the general approach and understanding of the Church and papacy that arose after the council in light of many circumstances, including a strong papal role in interpreting, carrying out, and specifying the reforms of the Council of Trent.[76]

The Council of Trent itself did not emphasize or for that matter even deal with the papal primacy; rather, it gave important roles to theologians. Avery Dulles points out, somewhat ironically, that the Council of Trent "represents a high point of successful collaboration between bishops and theologians." The pope invoked the council, presided over it through his delegates, and generally maintained control of it, but theologians still played a significant role.[77] Nelson Minnich disagrees somewhat with Dulles because some of the earlier councils before Trent had given a deliberative vote to theologians, but Trent did not. Minnich, however, recognizes that the theologians at Trent enjoyed more than just a consultative vote. Congregations of minor theologians (as distinguished from major theologians who were prelates with theological expertise) debated theological issues among themselves while the bishops listened. Minor theologians also drafted some statements for debate by the bishops. They could also criticize in private and raise questions about what the bishops had done.[78]

Pope Leo X excommunicated Luther in 1521. But the Council of Trent did not begin until many years later, in 1545. The delay came from two sources. Pope Clement VII (1523–34) feared that the council might invoke conciliaristic positions to depose him, whereas King Francis I of France (1515–47) feared that a council would strengthen the political hand of his great rival, Charles V. The most surprising and astonishing aspect of the Council of Trent when it finally did meet, especially in light of Luther's attitude on the papacy, was that the council said nothing about the papacy. The council fathers could not agree on what to say about the papacy, so they eventually said nothing.[79]

What did the Council of Trent do? It met in three sessions over an eighteen-year period and enacted a number of decrees and documents on scripture and Tradition, original sin, justification, and reform of the offices of bishop and pastor in the Church, and it spent a great deal of time on the sacraments. The issue of justification was at the center of the differences with Luther. Despite the polemics of the time, the decree on justification was quite well done.[80] In contemporary times, and in light of a more ecumenical spirit, Catholic theologians have pointed out that the teaching of Trent is compatible with the position of many orthodox Protestants with regard to justification.[81] A few years ago, Lutherans and Catholics officially agreed on a mutual understanding of justification.[82]

How did the Council of Trent lead to "Trent" with its heavy emphasis on papal prerogatives? The papacy gradually took charge of the reform programs in the Catholic Church. The council gave over to the pope several issues it had not been able to deal with—the index of forbidden books, the Roman Catechism which had a great influence on Catholic reform, and the reform of the Roman breviary and missal.[83] Charles Borromeo (1538–84), the archbishop of Milan and the great implementer of Trent, for all practical purposes rewrote the decrees of the council, giving them a specificity and rigor they lacked and even supplying what he thought the council failed to do. The papal curia moved along similar lines in interpreting and implementing the council. A good illustration of a greater specificity and rigor coming from the council comes from one of the "ten rules" that the council passed on to the pope for his consideration. The fourth rule put severe restrictions on the practice of reading the Bible and allowed it only with permission of the bishop or the local inquisitor. These rules were not an official decree of the council, but this one in particular eventually encouraged a virtual crusade against the reading of the Bible in Catholic cultures. By the seventeenth century, Rome had for the most part made itself the effective interpreter of the council and presented the council as a systematic, complete, and exhaustive response to every problem. Under the umbrella of the council, the papacy and Catholic theology closed a great number of questions that at Trent were recognized to be open. As a result, there was a false identification of the certainties of faith with theological intransigence. Thus the Council of Trent became "Trent."[84]

Other factors also played into this development. The polemical relationship between Catholics and Protestants that extended for a number
of centuries obviously caused both sides to be very defensive, with the
Catholic side extolling the rights and primacy of the papacy. The papacy
was also strengthened by the need to resist the variety of nationalistic
movements within the Church. The decline of the great medieval universities also took away the corporate role of theologians in the Church.[85] In
addition, there never was another ecumenical council after Trent until
Vatican I in 1870. The papacy thus became ever more central in the life
of the church based on a model analogous to monarchy.

Institutional and structural change also gave greater prominence to
the authoritative teaching role of the pope. There had been a policy of
condemning books throughout Church history, but this was intensified
and institutionalized in the papacy as a result of the Council of Trent,
which appointed a commission to revive the index of forbidden books
published in 1559 by Pope Paul IV. The commission came up with a list
of forbidden books and ten general norms proposing regulation concerning the condemnation of books in the future. In 1571, the pope established the Congregation of the Index as a part of the Roman Curia to
handle all matters pertaining to the condemnation of books. As time went
on, many types of books were put on the index, including novels, belles
lettres, and books of biography, history, economic and political science,
education, philosophy, and religion. The Congregation for the Index thus
institutionalized a very important teaching role for the papacy. The index
was later abolished by Pope Paul VI after Vatican II.[86]

A more important structural development definitely contributed to the
growing papal role as an authoritative teacher of morality and a judge of
erroneous theological opinions on morality. In 1542, in the bull *Licet*,
Paul III established a new Roman commission staffed with cardinals and
other functionaries and given the highest powers to defend the integrity
of faith and to prosecute errors and false teachings. The commission was
to investigate, judge, condemn, and punish those who were guilty. Pope
Sixtus V gave it the name of the Congregation for the Holy Inquisition
and ranked it first among all the parts of the Roman Curia. The name
was changed to the Holy Office in 1904 and the Congregation of the
Doctrine of the Faith in 1965. Pope Sixtus V also built the palace now
called the Palace of the Holy Office next to St. Peter's Basilica, which
remains today the office of the Congregation for the Doctrine of the
Faith.[87]

One of the functions given originally to the Roman Inquisition was to investigate and punish those who were guilty of heresy and denying matters of faith. However, the Roman Inquisition (sometimes called the Roman Universal Inquisition) should not be confused with the Spanish Inquisition. John Tedeschi concludes his study of the Roman Inquisition by noting that it is impossible to condone the coercion, torture, and other horrors perpetrated in the name of religion in the Reformation era. Such approaches were common to all legal proceedings in the sixteenth century. But these coercive means were used less frequently, with greater moderation, and with a higher regard for human rights in the tribunals of the Roman Inquisition.[88] For our purposes, the Roman Inquisition became an important vehicle used by the papacy to defend Catholic teaching and condemn deviations also in the area of moral theology.

Papal Teaching on Moral Issues

As a result of the aftermath of the Council of Trent, the papacy exerted an ever more central role in the life of the Church in general and in particular with regard to the area of what today we call moral theology. The council tried to bring about a reform in the Church and root out existing abuses. In the moral realm one of those abuses was the growing practice of usury understood as the taking of interest on a loan. A developing mercantile and banking environment was behind the growing practice of usury. The nascent Protestant movement reacted with significant differences to this issue of usury. Martin Luther was generally opposed to usury but allowed for its practice. John Calvin staunchly defended the right to lend money at interest. The Anabaptist movements strenuously opposed such practice.[89]

The Roman Catechism, also called the Catechism of the Council of Trent, condemned as usury whatever was received beyond the principal and based the condemnation on quotations from Ezekiel and the famous passage from Luke, "Lend, hoping for nothing in return." But in practice, many Catholics were involved in usury, and some theologians tried to justify such a practice. Here the theologians applied a casuistic method to argue from accepted business contracts to justify usury in many areas. Theologians proposed three different ways to justify usury based on other types of contracts recognized as acceptable within the Church. First, profit could be made by investment in partnerships, and one could also

charge for insurance. Putting these two together, some theologians justified the so-called triple contract, which allowed for interest. A second
approach was based on annuities—one could buy the right to some annual
return from some fruitful property such as a farm. A third approach to
profit on a credit transaction involved the purchase of foreign currency.
There is no need here to go into the intricate complexities of these issues,
but it is sufficient to note that these approaches presented ways to circum-
vent and ultimately undermine the existing moral teaching on usury.
Within a period of seventeen years, 1569–86, three different popes issued
papal bulls (Pius V, *Cum onus*; Pius V, *In eam*; Sixtus V, *Detestabilis avari-
tia*) that condemned these attempts to overturn the prohibition of usury.[90]

John T. Noonan Jr., whose work I depend on throughout this section,
demonstrates that the practice of the faithful and the reasoning of the
theologians by the end of the sixteenth century had changed and even
overturned the papal teaching in the documents mentioned earlier. My
purpose here is simply to illustrate how after Trent the papal teaching
office was the primary vehicle for defending the condemnation of usury.
In the period before Trent, the councils had played the primary moral
teaching role with regard to condemning usury.[91] But this history also
shows the role of reception by the whole Church of papal teaching even
after Trent.

The seventeenth century saw a violent controversy in the area of moral
theology. The *Institutiones morales* were the textbooks that had the limited
purpose of training future priests for their role, especially as judges, in
the sacrament of penance. The extreme positions were described as laxist,
with some Jesuits and others accused of such a position, and rigorist, often
associated with Jansenism. The specific issue at stake in moral theology
concerned how to move from practical doubt about the existence of a
law or obligation to the moral certitude necessary to act. The textbooks
basically employed a legal model of seeing law as the objective norm of
morality and conscience as the subjective norm of morality. So the question was, what happens if there is doubt about the law? The safest position
(tutiorism) said one always had to follow the position in favor of the law
even if it were weaker than the position against the law. The laxist position was not spelled out in exact terms but basically held that one could
follow even a very weak position claiming there is no law. Eventually the
controversy played out between these two extremes and involved what
is called probabilism, or a probable position. Note that the Latin word
"*probabilis*" means provable and is really not the same as the English word

"probable." Probabiliorists required that the argument for freedom from the law or obligation had to be more probable than the law's existence in order to free one from the obligation. Probabilists held that the reason for freedom from the obligation had to be truly probable even if less probable than the position favoring the law. They justified such a position using the reflex principle that a doubtful law does not oblige. However, they rejected the use of a tenuously probable argument, which was the equivalent of laxism.[92]

This intellectual controversy became even more contentious in light of other factors involved. The controversy was a significant part in the bitter dispute over Jansenism, especially in France and Belgium. The controversy also exacerbated the tensions between secular and religious clerics and especially between Dominicans and Jesuits. Some Jesuits were accused of laxism; the majority were probabilists; a very few were probabiliorists. The Dominicans before 1665 embraced probabilism as illustrated in the work of Bartolomé de Medina. With some urging from Pope Alexander VII and the Dominican General, subsequent Dominicans became strong supporters of probabiliorism. Earlier in the seventeenth century, the Dominicans and Jesuits were involved in a very acrimonious debate, "de auxiliis," which concerned the relationship between grace and human freedom. Different popes intervened at different times. In the end, the popes did not try to decide this contentious debate but told both sides to avoid acerbic words and to not accuse the other of heresy. The discussions over probabilism were equally contentious, with authors sometimes writing under pseudonyms in order to attack their adversaries.

The papal intervention in this controversy marked the first detailed involvement of the papacy in specific issues of moral theology as such with condemnations of various positions. In general, the papacy condemned the two extreme positions of laxism and tutiorism (rigorism). In 1665, Pope Alexander VII intervened through the Holy Office to condemn forty-five propositions that were prepared for condemnation from sources in France and especially from the University of Louvain, where there had been strong opposition to laxism and even to probabilism itself. These propositions were condemned "*prout sonant*" (as they stand) as scandalous, and it was forbidden under pain of excommunication to put them into practice. Denzinger, a collection of papal and hierarchical teaching, gives specific names of authors who held these propositions. However, since the propositions were taken out of context, one has to be very careful here.[93] Alexander VII himself was known as not favoring probabilism, but only two propositions deal with probabilism (D 2046–47). They do not condemn probabilism in any way but simply illustrate the laxism involved. The two condemned propositions are (1) when a judge is faced with equally probable opinions, he can take a bribe to decide in favor of one rather than the other, and (2) the opinion in a book written by a recent contemporary author (the Jansenists insisted on the importance of scripture and the fathers rather than contemporary authors) can be considered probable provided that it has not been explicitly rejected by the Apostolic See. The laxist character of the other propositions is quite evident: a husband does not sin if he kills his wife found in the act of adultery (D 2039); a person who very often eats a little on a fast day does not break the fast even if the small amounts eaten result in a very notable intake of food (D 2049).

In 1679, Pope Innocent XI condemned 65 propositions emanating from the list of 115 dogmatic and moral propositions sent by the University of Louvain for papal condemnation. For some reason the pope did not condemn the dogmatic propositions but chose 65 dealing mostly with morality. In regard to probabilism, the Holy Office condemned the use of the less probable or tenuously probable opinions (D 2102, 2103). Likewise, in conferring the sacraments, it was forbidden to follow a probable opinion leaving behind a more safe opinion (D 2101). A good illustration of the laxist position comes from the condemned proposition that stated, "it is sufficient to make an act of faith only once in a lifetime" (D 2178).

The intrigue and intensity in the entire debate is well illustrated in the case of Thyrsus Gonzalez de Santalla, a Jesuit professor of moral theology at Salamanca who wrote a book dedicated to the General of the Jesuits, Father Giovanni Paolo Oliva, in which he advocated probabiliorism. The fact that Father Oliva refused permission to publish the book came to the attention of Pope Innocent XI, who then issued a decree through the Holy Office in 1680. The Holy See told Gonzalez to intrepidly preach, teach, and defend the teaching about the more probable opinion. In the second part, the decree ordered the General of the Society of Jesus not only to permit Jesuits to write in favor of the more probable opinion but also to inform all Jesuit universities that scholars are free to write in favor of the more probable opinion. It seems the decree was never communicated as such to the members of the Society of Jesus. But the plot thickens. Gonzalez, with some help from the pope, was elected General of the Jesuits in 1687, but his assistants blocked publication of his book. Only in

1694 did Gonzalez succeed in publishing a version of the book he had originally written in 1671.[94]

In a short papacy (1688–91), Alexander VIII issued two decrees concerning morality. He first condemned two laxist propositions dealing with the objective goodness of the moral act and philosophical sin (D 2290–91); but, in 1690, he condemned thirty-one errors of the Jansenists. After the early condemnations of laxist propositions, Jansenism and rigorism continued to be associated with the University of Louvain, but the bishops of Belgium wanted the pope to condemn some of these Jansenist positions. The condemned propositions went to the heart of the Jansenistic position with regard to morality: Ignorance of the natural law does not excuse from sin (D 2302). Christ died only for the faithful (D 2303). Every deliberate act comes from either the love of God or the love of the world, and thus infidels necessarily sin in every act (D 2307–8). The intention of doing good and avoiding evil based on the motive of gaining heaven is neither correct nor pleasing to God (D 2310). Those who do not have the most pure love of God should be excluded from Holy Communion (D 2323). Despite the condemnation, rigorism remained strong in practice in France and Belgium as illustrated in the Assembly of the French Clergy of 1700, which strongly attacked probablism.[95]

The papal condemnations gave impetus to a new genre of moral theology—commentaries on the papal decrees. These started in the seventeenth century and continued well into the eighteenth century. These commentaries came from both the probablist and probabiliorist camps. Some of these books were placed on the index of forbidden books. In the judgment of Th. Deman, these commentators did not really contribute much to the development of moral theology.[96]

On the whole, there was much less authoritative papal involvement in the eighteenth century in moral theology. But the seventeenth-century condemnations continued to play an important role in the discipline. In 1713, Pope Clement condemned 101 Jansenistic propositions found in the work of Pasquier Quesnel, who had become the leader of the Jansenist faction. A few of these dealt with moral theology but added nothing important to what had already been condemned (D 2400–2502). Something should be said here about the response expected of papal condemnations as illustrated in the case of Cornelius Jansen. In 1653, Pope Innocent X condemned five errors of Jansen as heretical (D 2001–7). In 1705, Clement XI said that everyone had to give not just external submission or *silentium obsequiosum* but true internal assent and acceptance. Such is the obedience required of apostolic constitutions (D 2390).

In 1745, Pope Benedict XIV issued an encyclical to the bishops of
Italy, *Vix pervenit*, dealing with usury—the last mention by a pope of
usury (D 2546–51). In the centuries before the encyclical, theologians
had been finding ways to justify taking interest on most loans. Benedict
repeated the condemnation of usury as taking interest on a loan, but he
admitted that extrinsic titles (e.g., theologians had pointed out that one
could financially be rewarded for the loss that would come from not
investing the money in a profitable business enterprise) or licit contracts
distinct from a loan (e.g., the annuities mentioned before) could justify a
profitable return. The pope explicitly said he was pronouncing no judgment on titles or contracts discussed by theologians. Thus the door was
open to justify taking profit from many such transactions, as significant
theologians such as the Jesuits Leonardo Lessius and Juan de Lugo had
argued.[97]

The period after Trent saw the first sustained involvement of the papal
teaching office in authoritatively teaching on disputed issues in moral
theology. But note that the teaching only went so far as to condemn
the extremes. Finding solutions within these parameters was left to the
theologians. In actuality, in the eighteenth century the moderate probabilism proposed by St. Alphonsus Liguori significantly helped to overcome
the crisis in moral theology. The nineteenth-century papacy declared
there was nothing in Alphonsus's writings deserving of censure and made
him a saint and a doctor of the church. He became identified with ultramontanism, and his own approach to moral theology became somewhat
distorted by those who claimed to be his followers. Ironically, Alphonsus,
the one who recognized his own doubts and hesitations, was later used by
the Church authority as a guarantee of doctrinal certitude.[98]

However, the eighteenth century saw a weakening of the role of the
Church and the papacy because of intra-Church tensions and circumstances brought about by developments in the secular world. There arose
a disparity between the world that was fast developing in the economic,
social, political, and cultural spheres and the clerical hierarchy, which
could not differentiate between the essentials of faith and the nonessential
accoutrements that the Church had embraced and accepted. The Church
was holding on to obsolete positions. Two factors in particular contributed to the diminishment of the papacy. The first was the growth of a
national spirit and an anti-Roman animus in the Church, especially in
France but also later in Germany and Austria. These countries resented
the greater centralization in Rome and stressed the national character of

the Church. This movement first began with Gallicanism in France but then spread through Germany with Febronianism and to Austria with Josephinism. Some of these approaches appealed to the earlier conciliarism. Recall how the French Church had a history of promoting and defending its national roots. These movements thus tried to diminish the spiritual supremacy of the pope.[99]

The second intra-Church factor contributing to a lessening of papal prestige and authority came from the Papal States, which was handicapped by a very traditional and even oppressive institutional structure. As a result, the Papal States and the papal temporal rule became the objects of widespread criticism. In addition, in order to protect and defend the Papal States, the pope found himself in a rivalry among the monarchs in Vienna, Paris, and Madrid, forcing him to make allegiances with different rulers at different times in order to defend the territory of the Papal States. Therefore, the pope was seen primarily as an intriguing temporal ruler and not as the spiritual leader of the Church.

In the broader secular society, the Enlightenment was the most significant development affecting all aspects of life. The Enlightenment began with the thinkers of the seventeenth century but played a major role in the thinking and life of the eighteenth century. Despite differences among the philosophers and thinkers about particular aspects, the general approach of the Enlightenment was clear. The Enlightenment put heavy emphasis on human reason rather than tradition and authority. Many thinkers so exalted human reason that they became atheists. Morality was not based on the law of God but on human reason. In the political sphere, reason and freedom of the individual person became primary. The Enlightenment was closely associated with liberalism, which is discussed in chapter 2. Again, there are many different aspects to liberalism. The *New Catholic Encyclopedia*, for example, speaks of personal liberalism, political liberalism, and economic liberalism. However, what is common to all aspects of liberalism is the emphasis on the reason and freedom of the individual.[100]

The Enlightenment and liberalism were behind the political movements in the late eighteenth and nineteenth centuries in favor of revolution against existing monarchies and implementing democracy. At first, some Catholics were sympathetic to the French Revolution, but the Revolution ultimately turned anti-Church and anticlerical. As a result, the Catholic Church identified itself with the *ancien régime*, not only in France but in all parts of Europe, and opposed the new revolutionary and democratic movements. Thus the stage was set for the nineteenth century.

FROM THE NINETEENTH CENTURY TO THE EVE OF VATICAN II

Two factors strongly influenced the Church and the papacy in the nineteenth century—the opposition to liberalism and the positive impact of ultramontanism, which championed the spiritual supremacy of the papacy. In general during the nineteenth century, the Catholic Church strongly opposed liberalism, although there were some attempts to bridge the gap between the Church and aspects of liberalism. As mentioned in chapter 2, under the leadership of Felicité de Lamennais, some Catholics in France and Belgium argued against the union of altar and throne. Catholic liberalism, however, was a very distinctive approach. Lamennais staunchly rejected the Enlightenment's insistence on individual reason. In addition, he was a strong ultramontanist—the term originally referred to those north of the Alps looking south toward Rome as the supreme spiritual center of the Catholic Church. Lamennais argued that the Church would be much better off by abandoning its dependence on kings and monarchs and supporting the people with the political freedoms of conscience, press, and education. His Catholic liberalism advocated the acceptance of political liberalism as the best way to support and protect the spiritual supremacy of the pope in the Church. He went to Rome and sought the support and approval of Pope Gregory XVI.[101]

Pope Gregory XVI ended up strongly condemning both liberalism and Lamennais's approach in the encyclical *Mirari vos* (1832).[102] The encyclical denounced the separation of church and state. Gregory called freedom of conscience not only erroneous but a *"deliramentum"* (madness).[103] The pope condemned the freedom of the press as harmful and never sufficiently denounced. All authority comes from God and princes must be obeyed. Both divine and human law cry out against those who advocate treason and sedition by inciting people to lose confidence in their rulers and princes.

There were indications that the next pope, Pius IX (1846–78), harbored some liberal sympathies, but in the light of developing circumstances, especially the attempt to unite Italy at the expense of the Papal States, Pius IX became an intractable foe of liberalism. In 1864, Pius IX issued the encyclical *Quanta cura* and "The Syllabus of Errors," which was primarily a summary or collection of previous statements and denunciations. The strongest statements came at the end of the syllabus with the condemnations of religious freedom and freedom of the press. The last proposition that was condemned stated that the pope should reconcile himself with progress, liberalism, and recent civilization. Some attempts were made, especially by Bishop Felix Dupanloup in France, to mitigate the absoluteness of the syllabus, but the basic opposition of Pius XI to liberalism in all its forms, including the quite mitigated Catholic liberalism, was very clear.[104]

The Rise of Ultramontanism

The nineteenth-century Church and papacy especially opposed liberalism, but the constructive thrust in the nineteenth century was ultramontanism, with its support for the spiritual primacy of the pope and centralization of the Church in Rome. Ultramontanism did not begin in Rome but, as the name suggests, began in northern Europe looking south over the Alps to Rome. Ultramontanism had to overcome the emphases on national Churches that had been associated with Gallicanism, Febronianism, and Josephinism. Gallicanism in France had been the oldest and strongest of these national movements, but Gallicanism was on the wane as the nineteenth century moved forward. Loyalty to the monarchy had been the foundation of Gallicanism, but now the old monarchy was no longer in power. The anticlericalism of much of the French political elite also pushed Catholic people toward Rome. Seminaries began to embrace a more ultramontane approach. Dom Prosper Guéranger led the campaign for a Roman liturgy to replace the particularistic local French liturgies that had been associated with Gallicanism. In Germany and Austria, a similar development occurred, but more slowly. The growth of religious orders with their headquarters in Rome, especially the Jesuits, also contributed to the ultramontanist cause.[105]

Ultramontanism, like many of the movements discussed, was not a unified whole, but the basic commitment to the spiritual primacy of Rome and centralization was always at its core. Ultramontanism insisted on the freedom of the Church and especially the pope to act for the good of the Church, but it generally opposed diversity in the intellectual and pastoral life of the Church itself. Jeffrey von Arx has gathered together the ultramontanist approach of six different non-Italian bishops including the leading episcopal figures in Germany, England, Ireland, and the United States and a significant bishop in France. They each supported the basic principles of ultramontanism, but each in light of his own needs and context.[106]

Although ultramontanism did not begin in Rome, Gregory XVI in his later years and especially Pius IX strongly supported it. Mauro Cappellari in 1799, long before he became Pope Gregory XVI in 1831, published *Il Triumfo della Sancta Sede* (*The Triumph of the Holy See*), which maintained that the Church is a monarchy, the papacy is totally independent of any civil authority, and the pope is infallible as its chief pastor. Only after he had become pope did this book receive much attention and translations into other languages. Obviously, Gregory was very open to ultramontanism. Pius IX came to symbolize the triumph of ultramontanism. The ultimate triumph came with the First Vatican Council's solemn declaration of the infallibility of some papal teaching. At the time there was opposition on the part of some bishops, with a small minority opposing infallibility itself and a larger group opposed to the feasibility of defining it at this time. But the infalliblists, with the help of the pope, won out. Vatican I never completed discussing such aspects of the Church as the role of bishops and the people of God because it could not continue after the outbreak of the Franco-Prussian war.[107]

The concept of the infallibility of the papal teaching office as it was finally defined at Vatican I was in reality quite limited. The vast majority of papal teaching was noninfallible. However, the definition of infallibility created an aura about the pope that permeated all he said and did. The circumstances that prevented Vatican I from discussing other aspects of the Church also accentuated the supreme role of the pope in the Church. As a result, most Catholics after Pius IX understood that the pope ruled the Church.[108]

The uniformity of discipline coming from Rome also secured the triumph of ultramontanism. Apostolic nuncios, whose original role was to represent the Church in foreign countries, now involved themselves much more deeply in supervising the internal life of the local Church. At the beginning of the nineteenth century, practically all episcopal nominations outside the Papal States were made under local patronage. But gradually the pope reserved to himself all the nominations and appointments of bishops throughout the world. Pius IX also revived the practice of bishops making an *ad limina* visit to report to the pope in Rome. He supported the older national colleges of seminarians in Rome and encouraged the establishing of new ones such as the Polish, French, Spanish, and North American colleges. The adoption of Roman policies was reinforced by the conferring of Roman titles such as "monsignor" on priests. Pius IX created more monsignors in thirty years than his predecessors had done in two centuries. Anyone familiar with the Church in the United States knows how common it became to name priests monsignors, especially in the later years of the pre–Vatican II period. The role of the College of Cardinals decreased, except for the role of the election of the pope, but even in the nineteenth century more non-Italians were made cardinals. This growth in the number and diversity of cardinals spread rapidly in the twentieth century until the present day. Since cardinals are appointed by the pope, they assume leadership over other bishops in the area and have a significant role in determining the direction of local churches in accord with the papal approach. The Roman Curia developed and deepened to a great extent its role in governing the whole Church, especially through the papal encouraging of local bishops to submit disputed issues of worship, discipline, and even of theology to the curia.[109]

The promulgation of the New Code of Canon Law in 1917, which became effective on Pentecost 1918, incorporated many of the aspects supporting the centralization of the Church in Rome. In 1904, Pope Pius X announced his intention to have a complete and orderly compilation of the laws of the Church. Such a compilation had not been done since Gratian in the twelfth century, and Gratian's was not an official code as such. The new Code of Canon Law also intensified the importance of canon law in the Church with its centralizing features.[110]

Ultramontanism did more than just emphasize the papal structure in the Church. It involved a total transformation of Catholicism within a generation. For all practical purposes, ultramontanism became the face and reality of the Catholic Church throughout the world. Ultramontanism established a Roman approach to devotion, discipline, and theology throughout the Catholic world. There emerged a devotional piety that was both spiritually powerful and in service of the new ecclesiology with its emphasis on papal privileges. Marian devotion flourished with the papal pronouncement of the dogma of the Immaculate Conception in 1854. A number of apparitions by the Blessed Mother in France—Besançon (1803), Paris (1830–40), Blangy (1840 and 1846), and La Salette (1846)—gave support to the ultramontanist cause, which became identified strongly with the promotion of Marian devotion. The most

famous of all these appearances, in 1858 at Lourdes, strongly reinforced
the papal declaration of the dogma of the Immaculate Conception a few
years earlier. Marian devotion under the patronage of Rome spread
throughout the Catholic world. Other Roman and Italian devotions such
as perpetual adoration of the blessed sacrament and "Forty Hours"
quickly spread throughout the Church.[111]

Whatever his shortcomings might have been, Pius IX was a very like-
able person with an outgoing personality. After King Vittorio Emmanuele
invaded the Papal States and conquered Rome, the pope locked himself
in the Vatican as a prisoner. The Catholic people as a whole then developed a great respect and sympathy for the pope in his plight. For the first
time in history, many Catholics felt a personal relationship with the pope.
Modern means of communication greatly assisted this new devotion to
the pope. This only increased as the nineteenth and twentieth century
evolved, with many Catholics understanding their religion primarily in
terms of the papal role and often having a picture of the pope in their
homes.[112]

The second chapter discussed at length the philosophical and theological aspects of the more general ultramontanist movement. The papal
insistence on Thomistic philosophy and theology as *the* Catholic approach prevented any dialogue with contemporary thought, most of
which was strongly influenced by the Enlightenment. At the same time,
it opposed any real pluralism in Catholic philosophy and theology. The
pope and the Roman Curia continued to condemn opposing positions
throughout the nineteenth and twentieth centuries before Vatican II.

In 1899, Leo XIII issued his apostolic letter *Testem benevolentiae*, which
condemned Americanism. His condemnation obviously referred only to
the United States, but this was another strong indication of the Vatican
insistence on centralization and the dangers of any particularistic
approaches within the Catholic communion. The liberal wing of the
American hierarchy (Archbishop John Ireland, bishops Denis O'Connell
and John Keane, and James Cardinal Gibbons of Baltimore, to a great
extent) urged the Americanization of immigrants and a greater accommo-
dation of the Church to American culture, with its strong support for the
separation of church and state as it existed in the United States. The more
theological controversy on Americanism primarily took place in Europe
as a result of the French translation and introduction by Felix Klein of
the biography of Isaac Hecker, the founder of the Paulist Fathers. Hecker
was convinced that many Americans would convert to Catholicism if the

Church accommodated itself more to American culture. Leo XIII condemned Americanism for accommodating the Catholic faith to American culture in order to gain converts and for its emphasis on the active virtues over the passive virtues and the natural virtues over the supernatural. The more liberal bishops such as those mentioned earlier maintained that they agreed totally with everything in the encyclical, but the encyclical did not portray what actually was occurring in the United States.[113]

In September 1907, Pope Pius X issued the encyclical *Pascendi dominici gregis*, which condemned modernism. As had been the case with liberalism in the previous century and with Americanism, modernism was described and defined by the pope. The general thrust of the modernist approach was to call for an evolution in development and faith that would recognize the historical aspect of all human knowledge. The danger, of course, was an uncritical acceptance of contemporary thought. The pope specifically condemned Alfred Loisy for maintaining that Christianity went through historical developments and evolutions in the very beginning that were not envisioned by Jesus. The pope also condemned the writings of Irish Jesuit George Tyrrell for emphasizing the experiential basis of revelation and the metaphorical character of religious language. There never was a single well-defined movement called "modernism." Modernism, however, was coined as a pejorative term around 1905 by neo-Scholastic theologians. The modernist crisis played out primarily in Europe, but there were some ramifications of it even in the United States.[114]

The condemnation of modernism created an intellectual climate in the Church that was fearful of theological creativity and innovation and insisted on neo-Scholasticism as the Catholic philosophy and theology. There was to be absolutely no dialogue with modern thought. To ensure that the condemnation of modernism would have practical implications, all Catholic priests and professors had to take the oath against modernism. Vigilance committees were set up in every diocese to make sure that modernism never again surfaced. Historical consciousness and critical thinking were allowed no room in the Church. This condemnation had a very negative effect on Catholic intellectual life throughout the world and on the development of theology and philosophy. In this atmosphere of suspicion and caution, the manuals of theology and philosophy, which were discussed in previous chapters, flourished.[115]

This emphasis on papal primacy and a juridical understanding of the Church was incorporated in the ecclesiology found in the theological manuals that served as the textbooks for future priests. At this time the only place theology was taught was in the seminaries, which came under the governing authority of the pope and curia. Before Vatican II, there were some calls for a renewed ecclesiology, but the manuals reigned supreme. Richard McBrien agrees with Avery Dulles that these manuals employed a juridical approach to the Church as a perfect society founded by Christ with the pope depicted as ruler of the whole Church.[116]

This section has developed the historical basis of the judgment of John W. O'Malley, that without doubt the most significant discontinuity in the second millennium of the Catholic Church was the papalization of the Church. O'Malley goes on to say that not only does the role of the papacy dramatically change in the second millennium, but this change in the papacy has also changed all of us who are the Church.[117]

The Papal Teaching Role in General

When the role of the papacy as the supreme authority in the Church developed in the nineteenth and twentieth centuries, the teaching role of the papacy also greatly increased. Starting with Gregory XVI in the nineteenth century, a series of popes condemned modern thinking, especially about the state and the relationship between faith and reason, in a frequent and energetic manner. The increase in papal teaching continued in the long pontificate of Pius IX, who was the first pope to define a dogma (the Immaculate Conception) on his own authority. His Syllabus of Errors received much attention, both pro and con. The First Vatican Council defined the primacy of the pope and the infallibility of papal teaching under certain limited circumstances. Leo XIII authoritatively made the approach of Aquinas the Catholic approach to philosophy and theology, and his 1891 encyclical *Rerum novarum* began the long series of papal teachings on social issues. The condemnation of modernism highlighted the extensive teaching role of Pius X. This vigorous papal teaching role grew even more in the work of Pius XI and Pius XII. Pius XI is best known for his encyclicals on social issues, Christian education, marriage, and artificial contraception. Pius XII was the first pope after Vatican I to infallibly define a dogma—the Assumption of Mary into heaven. No pope in history exercised his teaching office more than Pius XII.[118] The Vatican published twenty volumes containing the discourses and radio messages of Pius XII.[119]

In the nineteenth and especially in the twentieth century, the most important noninfallible papal teachings were often found in encyclical letters. An encyclical is a formal pastoral letter written to all the bishops in the entire Church. The first modern use of the encyclical came from Benedict XIV in 1740, but only since Gregory XVI and Pius IX have encyclicals become a frequently used genre by the authoritative papal teaching office. Thus, the ever expanding papal teaching office basically developed this new genre to carry out its function.[120]

With the intensification of the teaching role of the pope comes a new name for this teaching office—the magisterium. This chapter has been emphasizing the papal teaching office, which has been the most used exercise of the hierarchical magisterium. However, the hierarchical teaching office or magisterium includes the pope, ecumenical councils, and bishops either as a college or as individuals. The current use of magisterium as the authoritative teaching office in the Church was introduced in eighteenth-century theology but especially by German canonists in the nineteenth century. Gregory XVI as early as 1835 used the term in this sense. Pius IX also used the term magisterium to refer to the teaching office.[121] The term "ordinary magisterium" first appeared in an official Church document in Pius IX's 1863 papal brief *Tuas libenter*, where it refers to the infallible exercise of the college of bishops distributed throughout the world when they teach something to be held definitively by the faithful.[122] *Humani generis*, Pius XII's 1950 encyclical, used the term "ordinary magisterium" to refer to noninfallible papal teaching.[123] The magisterium therefore can teach infallibly (e.g., *ex cathedra* papal statements, definitions by a general council or a teaching to be held as definitive as taught by all the bishops) or noninfallibly, which obviously involves most of the teaching.[124] As Yves Congar has pointed out, the ordinary magisterium of popes has assumed predominant importance in light of the incredible flow of encyclicals, speeches, and various interventions of popes in the years before Vatican II.[125]

This development is not just terminological because a new understanding of the teaching role of the Church came into being as a result. Recall that in the Middle Ages everyone recognized that theologians had a magisterial role, but now that role is not authoritative. As a result of the new approach, a significant distinction was made between the *ecclesia docens* (the teaching church, with the hierarchical teaching office) and the *ecclesia discens* (the believing or learning church, which involves all other people in the Church).[126]

Yves Congar points out the significance of the development. In an earlier period, the basic norm of faith had been the apostolic tradition that had been handed down. The teaching office was to preserve and defend the faith of the Church. What happened in the nineteenth and twentieth centuries was that the *quo* replaced the *quod*. The *quod* was that which was handed down. The *quo* was the instrument by which the faith was handed down. But now the instrument became more important than the substance it originally defended and explained. The teaching role primarily had the twofold role of preserving and explaining the faith of the Church. But now the role of explaining or defending had become primary. The magisterium had become, as *Humani generis* in 1950 said, the proximate norm of truth.[127]

Michael Place describes the theological change in the understanding of the teaching role of the pope and bishops as the move from solicitude to magisterium. In this period the general understanding of the Church became more juridical. In the earlier period, the solicitude of the hierarchical teaching role saw itself as being in the service of the mysteries of the faith, which were more basic and important than the teaching office. But now, rather than serving, the teaching office itself becomes the organ of the truth.[128]

This new understanding of the teaching office of the magisterium had a strong juridical flavor to it. In Catholic ecclesiology, the powers of the papacy (and the hierarchy in general) are the powers of order and jurisdiction. The power of orders deals with sanctification, whereas the power of jurisdiction deals with the governing of the Church. The teaching role is seen as part of the governing or jurisdictional power. The teaching role of preserving and defending the unity of the Church is a function of the power of governing. In the nineteenth century, some theologians insisted on teaching as a power in its own right in addition to the power of jurisdiction. Even in such an understanding, teaching was still seen as a power. Thus the teaching role of the magisterium tended to be overlaid with very juridical and governing overtones.[129]

What effect did this new understanding of the magisterium as the authoritative papal and episcopal teaching office in the Church have on Catholic theology? Pius XII's 1950 encyclical *Humani generis* clearly explains what had been developing since the new understanding of magisterium came into existence in the nineteenth century. In *Humani generis*, Pius XII addressed the papal teaching authority found in encyclicals. This involves the ordinary papal magisterium (the English translation of "magisterium" here is "teaching authority") where the popes are not exercising the supreme power of their magisterium. Encyclicals involve the ordinary papal magisterium (that which deals with noninfallible teaching) as distinguished from the extraordinary magisterium, which involves infallible teaching. But it is true to say of the ordinary papal magisterium the scriptural words, "He who hears you, hears me" (Lk 10:16). Our divine redeemer has given only to the magisterium the role of authoritatively interpreting the deposit of faith. The task of theology is to point out how the authoritative teaching of the living magisterium is to be found either explicitly or implicitly in scripture and Tradition. It is unacceptable to try to clarify the teaching of the magisterium from what is obscurely found in scripture and Tradition. Pius XII cites his predecessor, Pius IX, as giving a similar description of the noble office of theology.[130]

This approach to theology—especially to what was called dogmatic theology, which deals with matters of faith and belief—has been called "Denzinger theology." Henry Denzinger was a German priest theologian who in 1854 published his *Enchiridion symbolorum et definitionum*. This was a collection of the early creeds, particular and ecumenical councils, and papal teaching that brought together in one volume what the Church authoritatively teaches. The *Enchiridion* needed to be frequently updated as new documents became available.[131] The Denzinger theology begins with the teaching of the magisterium as found in the *Enchiridion* and then shows how this teaching is found in scripture, in tradition, and supported to some extent by reason. One further comment about Denzinger: Denzinger was not the first book (in theological parlance Denzinger became the name of the book and not just the name of the original editor) to bring together the documents containing the official teaching of the Church. One of the best-known predecessors was the three-volume work *Collectio iudiciorum de novis erroribus* by Charles du Plessis D'Argentré, a professor at the University of Paris who died as Bishop of Toul in 1740. D'Argentré also included in his three volumes decisions by medieval and counterreformation university faculties of theology.[132] For Denzinger and the subsequent Catholic understanding, theologians no longer had such an authoritative teaching role in the Church. Part of the reason was that such university theological faculties ceased to exist after the French Revolution.

Papal Teaching on Moral Issues

What effect did this new role and function of the papal magisterium beginning in the nineteenth century have on moral theology? As developed in a previous chapter, the manuals or textbooks of moral theology mostly used the Ten Commandments as their outline but now added any appropriate intervention by the ordinary papal magisterium.

In the nineteenth century, a very frequent approach involved the responses of the Roman Curia to particular questions sent to them, especially those sent by local bishops. The requests for specific guidance from Rome grew considerably in the ethos of emphasizing papal supremacy. The primary instrumentalities in these responses were the Sacred Penitentiary, which responded to questions of what should be done in the sacrament of penance, and the Holy Office, which responded to questions of what should be the moral teaching on a particular issue. This mode of proceeding marked a very significant development. In the 1600s, the Holy Office intervened to condemn the extreme positions and left to theologians the discussion of what should be done within these limits. But now the Holy Office gave very specific conclusions and condemnations.

With regard to the penitentiary, for example, John T. Noonan Jr. reports on nineteenth-century responses with regard to artificial contraception. In 1842, questions were raised to the Sacred Penitentiary: Can spouses confessing artificial contraception be in good faith about this and thus be excused from grave sin? Can the practice of some confessors of not inquiring if spouses practice artificial contraception be accepted? The response of the penitentiary was quite lenient. It accepted the position that contraception could be practiced with innocence of its sinful nature, and it gave at least tacit approval to confessors not questioning penitents about the use of contraception.[133] As the nineteenth century progressed, contraception was becoming more prevalent in France. To an 1886 inquiry by an anonymous French bishop, the Sacred Penitentiary responded that "regularly" the good faith of the penitent would not be a defense against grave guilt in the practice of contraception, and "regularly" the confessor should not abstain from questioning the penitent about the use of artificial contraception.[134]

Most instructive for our purposes is the intervention of the Holy Office in specific questions dealing with abortion at the end of the nineteenth and beginning of the twentieth centuries. The issue here was not abortion in general but the very complex issues of conflict situations involving the lives of the mother and the fetus and of the meaning of direct abortion. These issues had been hotly debated by respected moral theologians, but the Holy Office intervened to settle the disputed questions that had arisen.[135] Craniotomy of the fetus was being employed with some frequency in cases to save the life of the mother. The Holy Office responded in 1884 to a question from the archbishop of Lyons that it cannot safely be taught that craniotomy is permissible if necessary to save the mother's life and thereby avoid the death of both mother and fetus (D 3258).

Soon afterward, questions arose about other surgical procedures. In 1886, the bishop of Cambrai sent six sets of cases to the Holy Office. The response to these cases in 1889 did not deal with the individual cases but set down the general principle that direct killing of the mother or the fetus by a surgical procedure cannot be safely taught. This response, however, did not settle all the questions. The archbishop of Cambrai then submitted a specific question to the Holy Office. To save the life of the mother, can the physician remove the fetus from the womb? To kill the fetus in the womb would be a direct killing and wrong, but in this case the fetus is not killed but only removed from the womb even though it is not viable and cannot live outside the womb. In 1895, the Holy Office replied that this procedure could not be safely used in accord with the earlier 1884 and 1889 decrees (D 3298).

In 1898, the Holy Office responded to three questions proposed by another bishop. To the questions involving acceleration of birth and the use of caesarian section in difficult situations, the response was basically positive, with the stipulation that the lives of both mother and fetus must be supported. The Holy Office also responded positively to the use of a laparotomy in extreme cases for the removal of ectopic conceptions, provided that serious and opportune provision was made as far as possible for the life of both the fetus and the mother (D 3336–38). This reply left some doubt about its exact meaning. Another response was made by the Holy Office in 1902 to the question of the removal of an ectopic pregnancy before viability. The answer was negative (D 3358). The conclusion from all these interventions was clear—the direct removal of a nonviable fetus, both in the uterus and outside the uterus (ectopic), to save the life of the mother is not morally acceptable.

This last intervention went against the position proposed by the American Jesuit moral theologian at Woodstock College, Aloysius Sabetti. Sabetti had previously maintained that the ectopic fetus was not where it should be; hence it was a materially unjust aggressor. Outside the womb one may directly kill a materially unjust aggressor if this is necessary to save one's own life. Logically, the same principle is true in the womb.[136] As a result of the Holy Office interventions, there was more protection for the fetus in the womb than for the person outside the womb because such a person could be killed as a materially unjust aggressor if it were necessary to save the life of the person being attacked.

As time went on, T. Lincoln Bouscaren and others came up with a morally acceptable way to deal with the ectopic pregnancy. The fetus in the fallopian tube by its very nature begins to burrow into the tube, and the tube becomes infected and diseased. The physician then can remove the infected and diseased fallopian tube, which unfortunately contains a fetus. But one can never directly target or attack or remove the fetus itself.[137] This whole controversy for the first time involved the intervention of the papacy in a very specific moral issue, which included the implicit condemnation of the positions of many well-respected Catholic moral theologians, such as Pietro Avanzini, Giuseppe Pennacchi, Antonio Ballerini, Giuseppe Cardinal D'Annibale, August Lehmkuhl, and many others.[138]

Papal interventions in moral issues grew in the twentieth century. Frequent decrees came from the Holy Office. Pius XI in 1930 issued the encyclical *Casti connubii*, which strongly condemned artificial contraception for spouses (D 3700–3724). Papal teaching on specific moral issues in the twentieth century reached its zenith with the many pronouncements and interventions of Pius XII (1939–58). Recall that there are twenty volumes of the discourses and radio messages of Pius XII. Pius XII also used a new genre of intervention in terms of the addresses he gave to both Catholic and secular groups. This pope spoke on many disputed issues in moral theology, but he especially addressed issues of medical ethics. He was frequently asked by secular medical associations, usually meeting in Rome, to address them on moral issues. Within a three-year span the pope spoke to the following groups: the First International Conference on the Histopathology of the Nervous System (1952), the Fifth International Congress of Psychotherapy and Clinical Psychology (1953), the Twenty-Sixth Congress of the Italian Society of Urology (1953), and the Eighth Assembly of the World Medical Association (1954).[139] In the process of talking to these groups and in other addresses Pius XII gave authoritative teaching about dilemmas in a variety of areas—abortion, anesthesia for the dying, artificial insemination, blood transfusions, care for the dying, cosmetic surgery, experimentation, and extraordinary and nonnecessary means to preserve life. There were comparatively few medical issues of the time that were not directly addressed by the pope. A 1962 American manual of Catholic medical ethics lists in its index forty different issues that the pope addressed.[140] In this ethos Catholics in general and moral theologians in general expected the pope to authoritatively solve specific issues facing human beings and society at large.

The Authority of the Ordinary Papal Magisterium

What is the authority of such papal teaching, and how should Catholics in general and Catholic theologians in particular respond to such papal teachings? Pius X, for example, in 1907 maintained that all are bound by the duty of conscience to submit to the decrees of the Pontifical Biblical Commission just as to the decrees of sacred congregations that pertain to doctrine and are approved by the pope. To impugn such decisions involves disobedience and great sin.[141] In his 1912 encyclical *Singulari quadam*, Pius X maintained that all human actions insofar as they are morally good or bad—that is, whether they agree or disagree with natural and divine law—are subject to the judgment and jurisdiction of the Church. The social question and its associated controversies such as labor unions, strikes, and so on, are not merely economic issues that can be settled apart from ecclesiastical authority.[142]

Pius XII's most significant discussion of the ordinary papal magisterium came in the 1950 encyclical *Humani generis*. One cannot conclude that what the pope teaches in an encyclical does not call for assent on the part of Catholics because the pope is not exercising the supreme power of his magisterium—that is, infallible teaching. In encyclicals, the pope is using his ordinary magisterium (this is the first time the term "ordinary papal magisterium" was used in a document). The words of Luke 10:6, "He who hears you, hears me," apply to this ordinary papal magisterium. If the pope purposely passes judgment on a matter that up to this time has been freely disputed among theologians, then the matter is no longer open to such discussion among theologians. God has given to the Church the living magisterium to explain and make clear what is contained in the deposit of faith only obscurely and implicitly.[143]

Pius XII explicitly saw the papal teaching as involving the natural law and issues pertaining to it. The content, the institution, the interpretation, and the application of natural law belong to the teaching authority of the Church. When the legitimate pastors of the Church—the pope for the universal church and bishops for those committed to their care—teach on issues of natural law, one cannot claim that these judgments have only the authority that comes from the reasons proposed for the teaching. Hence, even if a particular teaching does not seem persuasive on the basis of the reasons given, the obligation of obedience remains (note here how the governing power affects the teaching role).[144]

What did Catholic theologians say about what *Humani generis* called the ordinary papal magisterium—that is, the teaching that does not involve the supreme power of the infallible teaching office? The dogmatic theologians writing after Vatican I recognized the differences between infallible and noninfallible teaching. One aspect of these differences is that noninfallible teaching might be wrong. This difference was recognized at Vatican I. Opponents of defining the infallibility of the teaching office of the Church brought forth the errors found in the teachings of Pope Liberius (352–66), Pope Vigilius (540–55), and Pope Honorius (625–38). Yes, their teachings did contain errors, but they were not teachings of an infallible nature. Nevertheless, these teachings point to the fact that papal teaching in the past has involved some error.[145]

Joseph A. Komonchak, in a very significant essay, studied how the authors of the manuals of dogmatic theology after Vatican I dealt with the assent due to noninfallible teaching. To infallible teaching, one owes the assent of faith, which is absolutely certain and most firm. To noninfallible teaching, a Catholic owes internal religious assent, which is not absolutely or metaphysically certain but is morally certain. This assent, therefore, is to some extent conditional. J. Salaverri expresses the condition as "unless by an equal or superior authority the Church should decree otherwise." For F. Sullivan, the condition is "unless the Church should at some time decide otherwise, or unless the contrary should become evident." For L. Lercher, the condition is "unless a grave suspicion should arise that the presumption is not verified." C. Pesche speaks of the binding force, "so long as it does not become positively clear that they are wrong," and adds that "assent is prudently suspended when there first appears sufficient motives for doubting." D. Palmieri maintains that "religious assent is owed when there is nothing which could prudently persuade one to suspend his assent."[146]

Lercher stands out among these manualists as the only one who explicitly recognizes that others in the Church might correct an error taught by the ordinary magisterium. "The way in which error would be excluded would more probably consist in the assistance of the Holy Spirit given to the head of the Church, by which such an erroneous decree would be prevented. But it is not entirely out of the question that the error might be excluded by the Holy Spirit in this way, namely, by the subjects of the decree detecting its error and ceasing to give it their internal assent."[147]

In practice, however, Catholic moral theologians in the twentieth century recognized even before *Humani generis* that the teaching of the ordinary papal magisterium in its response to disputed moral issues provides the answer for all Catholics and stops all further discussion. A faint criticism of having recourse to Roman congregations to solve all controversial issues came at the end of the nineteenth century from the Belgian Thomas Bouquillon, who was then professor of moral theology at the Catholic University of America. Although Bouquillon was often associated with the American Catholic liberals, he was a convinced neo-Scholastic who strongly supported the program of Leo XIII. As a Thomist, he severely criticized the manuals of moral theology. The manualists are often content merely to list the number of authors who hold a position in order to show that it is probable rather than to delve into the reasoning required to provide an appropriate answer on their own. In this context he criticized the abuse of having recourse to the Roman congregations for decisions when there was no reason to do so. However, the criticism was not directed at the congregations as such. In fact, the congregations even recognized the problem by often responding that the approved authors should be consulted and by not giving a specific answer. When the congregation did reply that the people should not be disturbed in the approach they are now taking, too often the petitioners in particular and moral theologians in general were satisfied and did no more work or research to arrive at the truth.[148]

Despite Bouquillon's criticism of too quick a request from Roman congregations, Catholic moral theologians in the late nineteenth and the twentieth centuries before Vatican II acknowledged that the exercise of the ordinary papal magisterium, including the responses of the Roman congregations, solved the issue under discussion and that the decision of the magisterium had to be held and accepted by Catholics. An earlier section discussed the interventions, especially of the Holy Office at the end of the nineteenth century and the beginning of the twentieth with regard to the meaning of "direct" and "indirect" in relation to abortion. The German moral theologian August Lehmkuhl was an important voice in these discussions and debates. He had originally proposed that craniotomy on the fetus to save the life of the mother is not certainly wrong and can be accepted. However, after the 1884 condemnation of craniotomy by the Holy Office, Lehmkuhl changed his position. He declared that, after the Roman response, his original reasons were spurious and not convincing.[149] Lehmkuhl later held that the removal of a nonviable fetus from the womb in order to save the life of the mother is acceptable and not a direct abortion because the fetus was not killed but only removed from the womb. After the 1895 response of the Holy Office condemning such a procedure, Lehmkuhl changed his position in subsequent editions of his manual.[150]

Lehmkuhl had expressed this opinion in a series published in the *American Ecclesiastical Review* together with contributions by Joseph Aertnys and Aloysius Sabetti. Sabetti disagreed with Lehmkuhl but proposed, as mentioned earlier, that an ectopic pregnancy, precisely because it was where it should not be, constituted a materially unjust aggressor and therefore could be directly removed or killed to save the life of the mother. But, in 1902, the Holy Office declared that it is not licit to remove a nonviable ectopic fetus to save the mother's life (D 3358). Sabetti was dead by the time of this decree, but there is no doubt what his response would have been. Sabetti, as a Neopolitan Jesuit, was a staunch supporter of papal primacy and neo-Scholasticism, and firmly maintained that responses from the Roman congregations settled controversial issues once and for all. The Holy Father makes use of the congregation "in the exercise of his supreme power." "The binding force of this decree is thus the greatest; to disobey it would be a sin."[151] Notice the use of the superlatives "supreme" and "greatest," and the consequent erroneous understanding of papal teaching authority. Sabetti would obviously have recognized that infallible papal teaching involves the supreme power and has the greatest binding force. Sabetti's own exaggerations show how much authority he gave to these decrees of Roman congregations.

T. Lincoln Bouscaren, in his book based on his 1928 doctoral dissertation at the Gregorian University on the subject of direct abortion and ectopic pregnancy, concludes that as a result of the interventions of the Holy Office, the possible acceptance of direct abortion in any form to save the life of the mother is forever closed for Catholic moralists and physicians.[152]

In 1939, US Jesuit Gerald Kelly did an extensive study of the teaching of Catholic moral theologians on the artificial insemination of the wife with the husband's semen, provided that the semen was not obtained by masturbation, which is intrinsically wrong, but by extracting semen directly from the epididymis or by massaging the seminal vesicles. Kelly consulted thirty Catholic moral theologians of whom only thirteen discussed this particular case, and about half of them argued that one could permit such artificial insemination in practice. Kelly himself agreed with this position.[153] But after papal allocutions in September 1949 and October 1951, Kelly said the position was no longer acceptable.[154] The very influential German Jesuit Franz Hürth, who taught at the Gregorian University, maintained in 1946 that such a procedure was morally wrong.[155]

Hürth in 1952 wrote an influential article discussing the proper response of Catholics to what the pope teaches in an address or allocution, which is a lesser type document than an encyclical. As noted, most of Pope Pius XII's teachings on moral matters were found in such allocutions, which were usually addressed to a particular group and not to all the bishops of the world as in the case with encyclicals. In such allocutions the pope speaks in an official capacity and not merely as a private teacher, but he does not act in the full and highest decree of his teaching office. The faithful must give internal and external assent to such teaching. These teachings must be admitted and held as true, but not with an absolute and irreformable assent.[156]

One of the primary reasons why Hürth was so influential came from the well-known fact that he had drafted most of Pius XII's teachings on moral issues and had played a prominent role in Pius XI's encyclical *Casti connubii*.[157] One illustration of this role of Hürth is his commentary on the September 29, 1949, allocution of Pius XII condemning artificial contraception. His commentary appeared in the issue of *Periodica* dated September 15, 1949![158]

A personal reflection makes the same point. I was a student at the Gregorian University in Rome from 1955 to 1961. Even as seminarians we were aware that Hürth was the primary author of Pius XII's pronouncements on moral theology and was heavily involved in the responses of the Holy Office. Edwin Healy, an American moral theologian who taught at the Gregorian, once said in class with a twinkle in his eye, "I hold this opinion even though Father Hürth holds the opposite— even though he writes occasionally under the name of Pius XII." As a seminarian in the large lecture classes, I occasionally talked outside class in Latin with Hürth about moral issues. I did not want to bother him, but he seemed very pleased to have me come to talk with him on occasion. Later, when I had him for a doctoral seminar, we talked more often. Father Francis Furlong, the American who succeeded Healy after his death and was my dissertation director, approached me one day to ask a favor. Dr. Joseph Doyle, a Boston gynecologist, had designed and was promoting what he called the Doyle cervical spoon, which attempted to remedy some infertility problems. The spoon was inserted into the woman's cervix to prevent harmful acids in the vagina from affecting the sperm and thus diminishing the possibilities of conception. Furlong had heard a rumor that the Holy Office or even the pope might condemn the Doyle cervical spoon. He knew that I talked occasionally with Hürth, and asked me to sound Hürth out about the cervical spoon.

My conversation with Hürth was fascinating. He was definitely opposed to the device in accord with his understanding that the proper act of marital intercourse required the depositing of male semen in the vagina of the female. But with the Doyle cervical spoon, the semen was not deposited in the vagina but in what he called a *machina americana*. I tried to make the case for the cervical spoon but obviously failed to convince him. At the end of our discussion, Hürth smiled and said in Latin, "However, this is an American issue and I am not going to get involved in it." He had probably figured out the nature of my mission. I went back to Furlong with the good news that neither Hürth nor the Holy Office nor Pius XII was going to condemn the cervical spoon.

Hürth's role in drafting documents for Pius XII raises a very important issue of papal dependence on theologians for their knowledge and expertise. A pope can and should depend on theologians in making such pronouncements. But the real issue involves what theologian or school of theologians should be chosen. As noted, some prominent Catholic moral theologians before 1949 accepted the practice of artificial insemination, but not Hürth. The pope, with a heavy dependence on Hürth, then condemned artificial insemination with the husband's seed. Today there exists a much greater diversity and pluralism among Catholic theologians, but papal documents are often based on only one school of contemporary theologians. However, in the late nineteenth and early twentieth centuries, there was no doubt that the intervention of the ordinary papal magisterium, even in an allocution or a response of the Holy Office, settled controversial moral issues for everyone in the Catholic Church.

VATICAN II AND AFTERWARD

Vatican II continued to affirm papal primacy in the Church and the infallible teaching office of the pope and all the bishops together with the pope. However, the Constitution on the Church of Vatican II (*Lumen gentium*) definitely changed the primacy of the institutional model in the Church and the monarchical understanding of papacy that had been so strong in the earlier part of the twentieth century. Although the Church is an institution, the institutional aspect is not the only or even the most important aspect of the Church. *Lumen gentium* in its very first chapter describes the Church primarily as a mystery and not as an institution. The Church is a sacrament or sign of intimate union with God and of the unity of all humankind.[159] The second chapter understands the Church as the community or the people of God (no. 9–17). In the original drafts proposed for the Council, the hierarchy was to be considered in the second chapter, but then the fathers of the Council agreed that the hierarchy exists to serve the people of God who are the Church. It is only in the third chapter that the hierarchical office is discussed.[160] The council also emphasizes the role of the local bishop and the local church. The local bishops are not simply appointees of the pope but have the God-given role of presiding over the local Church. In addition, the council stresses the collegiality of all the bishops together with the bishop of Rome in their common solicitude for the Church universal (no. 18–29). Such an approach superseded the concept of a monarchical papacy, which had flourished in theory and even more so in the practice of Catholics before Vatican II.

The council also recognized that the Holy Spirit fulfills its teaching role not only in the hierarchical teaching office, but also in other ways. Through baptism all Christians share in the threefold functions of Jesus as priest, teacher, and ruler. The Holy Spirit distributes special graces and gifts among the faithful of every rank. These charismatic gifts are to be used for the good of the whole Christian community. The body of the faithful, anointed as they are by the Holy One, cannot err in matters of belief (no. 12).

A good illustration of the teaching that the Holy Spirit works not only through the hierarchical teaching office but also through others in the Church and even outside the Church is found in the Declaration on Religious Freedom. In the very beginning this document recognizes the contemporary consciousness and demand for responsible use of freedom, including religious freedom. The Council declares these desires to be greatly in accord with truth and justice.[161] In other words, the fathers of the Council also learned their new teaching on religious liberty from the experience of people.

Vatican II also made Catholics more conscious of the possibility and even a need for change in the Church. Not only did great changes occur in liturgy and pastoral practice, they also occurred with regard to significant teachings such as religious liberty, the relationship between the Catholic Church and other churches, and the understanding of scripture and Tradition and their role in the life of the Church. Vatican II represents both continuity and discontinuity with the past.[162] Such change, especially in many practical cases, made people more conscious of the changes that had already occurred in authoritative teachings in the past on moral issues such as torture, usury, slavery, and the Catholic understanding of sexuality.[163] Thus, Vatican II also contributed to a more nuanced understanding of the role of the ordinary papal magisterium and how it functions.

What specifically did Vatican II say about the magisterium? Five aspects of this teaching are significant for our purposes. First, the Council repeated the generally accepted understanding of the two types of teaching. To infallible teaching one owes the assent of faith. To noninfallible teaching one owes religious *obsequium* of intellect and will. (Since that time much has been written about the exact meaning of religious *obsequium*.[164]) The pope teaches infallibly when he solemnly proclaims in a definitive act a doctrine belonging to faith and morals. Bishops teach infallibly when, dispersed throughout the world in communion among themselves and with the pope, they authoritatively teach a matter of faith and morals that is to be held definitively by the faithful. All the more, the college of bishops in union with the pope in an ecumenical council likewise teaches infallibly when it defines a particular doctrine. Religious *obsequium* of intellect and will is due to the authoritative teaching of the pope even when he is not speaking *ex cathedra*. The teaching of individual bishops in communion with the pope in matters of faith and morals likewise calls for a religious *obsequium* on the part of the faithful (no. 25).

Second, the Constitution on Divine Revelation recognized that the task of authoritatively interpreting scripture has been entrusted exclusively to the living teaching office of the Church—the magisterium. This magisterium is not above the word of God (scripture and Tradition) but serves it, teaching only what has been handed down.[165] Therefore, the magisterium is not above the deposit of faith found in scripture and Tradition but is to serve it and be guided by it.

Third, an important question was raised to the doctrinal commission at the council about paragraph 25 of the Constitution on the Church. What about the case of an educated person confronted with a noninfallible teaching who for solid reasons cannot give internal assent? The response of the commission was that approved theological explanations should be consulted to answer this question. These approved theological authors are the ones mentioned earlier who recognized that the assent to such teaching is conditional and the teaching itself might be erroneous.[166]

Fourth, the Constitution on the Church recognized that the primary teacher in the Church is the Holy Spirit and that all Christians by reason of their baptism share in the teaching of the prophetic office of Jesus. In addition, the Holy Spirit distributes charismatic gifts to many different people in the Church (no. 12). As a result, the older distinction between the teaching Church (*ecclesia docens*) as pope and bishops and the learning Church (*ecclesia discens*) no longer holds. Since that time much has been written about the role of the *sensus fidelium* in the Church.[167] The teaching or magisterial role in the Church involves more than just the hierarchical teaching office. The hierarchical teaching office has an authoritative role, but it does not exhaust the total magisterial function in the Church. Consequently, the teaching office of pope and bishops should more properly be called not the magisterium but the hierarchical magisterium.

Fifth, the original schema or proposed document on the Church presented to the Council fathers included the citation from *Humani generis* that when the pope goes out of his way to pronounce on a controversial issue that has been debated among theologians, the subject can no longer be a matter for free debate by theologians. This schema as a whole was rejected by the Council fathers and the final document does not include the teaching of *Humani generis*.[168] Thus, what the document says about the response to noninfallible teaching is quite significant and somewhat different from earlier understandings.

Dissent from and Disagreement with the Ordinary Papal Magisterium

The role of the ordinary papal magisterium in moral matters came to the fore in the discussion over Pope Paul VI's 1968 encyclical *Humanae vitae*, which condemned artificial contraception for spouses. Probably no document in Church history was as eagerly anticipated by as many people as

this encyclical. Before 1963, no Catholic theologian had publicly disagreed with the teaching against contraception, but in light of the changes
associated with Vatican II, critical discussion about this issue grew. Pope
Paul VI publicly announced in 1964 the existence of a commission originally established by his predecessor to study the issue, but he maintained
the present teaching of the Church was binding. The pope expanded the
commission and removed the issue of contraception from discussion at
Vatican II. The commission met on five occasions. In April 1967, documents were leaked to the press showing that the majority of the commission favored a change in the teaching. But the encyclical released on July
29, 1968, reiterated the existing teaching. The response was headline
news throughout the world. The next day, after having read the document, I acted as a spokesperson for eighty-six Catholic scholars in the
sacred sciences (in the end there were more than six hundred signatures
to the statement) saying that one could be a good Catholic and dissent in
theory and in practice from the specific teaching that artificial contraception for spouses is always wrong.[169]

Contraception at that time was a burning practical issue for Catholic
spouses. Andrew M. Greeley maintained that the encyclical influenced a
large number of US Catholics who left the Church in the decade of 1963–
73.[170] Since that time, the issue of dissent in the Church from noninfallible teaching has loomed ever larger, and volumes have been written on
this issue.[171] The following paragraphs will summarize much of what has
been said in favor of such dissent and disagreement.

Arguments in favor of dissent from the ordinary papal magisterium
come from ecclesiology, moral theology, and history. From an ecclesiological perspective, we are dealing with the category of noninfallible
teaching. By definition, it is plain that such a teaching could be erroneous.
The very word "noninfallible" basically means "fallible." Recall the
aspects mentioned earlier. The positions of the "approved authors" of
the textbooks on ecclesiology have already been discussed in this regard.
The Holy Spirit is the primary teacher in the Church, and the Holy Spirit
assists the hierarchical magisterium but also teaches through others in
the Church. The magisterial function in the Church is broader than the
hierarchical magisterial role. Moral theology deals with issues affecting
human and Christian life. The teaching on artificial contraception is
based not on scripture but on natural law and is therefore quite removed
from the core of faith. One does not deny a core aspect of faith when
dissenting from the teaching on artificial contraception.

Thomas Aquinas and the best of the Catholic tradition, also relying on Aristotle, recognize the difference between speculative and moral truth. A principle of speculative truth is always true. Thus, every triangle has 180 degrees. The first principles of the natural law oblige always and everywhere while the secondary principles generally oblige but can allow exceptions. One should return to the owner a deposit that has been given under the condition that the person must return it when the owner asks for it. But if the owner left you her sword and now comes back raving drunk and threatening to kill people, you should not return the sword.[172] Moral principles and truth do not have the same certitude as speculative principles and truth. The reason for the difference is that morality by its nature involves many contingent aspects or circumstances that in complex matters preclude the type of certitude that can be had in speculative realities. Moral certitude by definition is a special type of certitude that does not claim to be absolutely certain.

History also shows the possibility of dissent from noninfallible hierarchical teaching. The earlier summary of Vatican II clearly opens the door to recognizing the possibility of dissent. Nineteenth- and twentieth-century-approved Catholic theologians recognized that noninfallible teaching could be erroneous. Above all, history shows that the Catholic Church has changed its teaching on a significant number of specific moral teachings—slavery, torture, the right to silence, usury, interest on loans, religious freedom, and the meaning of human sexuality.[173] It is also true that the hierarchical magisterium has learned from others in our world with regard to some of the issues mentioned earlier as well as the importance of human freedom, human rights, and the equal dignity of women.

Confirmation of the legitimacy of such dissent has come from the hierarchical magisterium itself. In a 1967 pastoral letter the West German bishops addressed the issue of the response to noninfallible Church teaching. Such teaching has occasionally been erroneous. In applying the gospel to daily life, even at the risk of error, the hierarchical magisterium gives directives that have a certain degree of binding force, but since they are not *de fide* definitions, they involve an element of the provisional even to the possibility of including error.[174] In 1968, after the issuance of *Humanae vitae* and the reaction to it, the US bishops addressed this issue in their pastoral letter "Human Life in Our Day": "The expression of theological dissent from the magisterium is in order only if the reasons are serious and well-founded, if the manner of the dissent does not question or impugn the teaching authority of the Church, and is such as not to give scandal."[175]

A unique aspect of theological dissent from *Humanae vitae* that has also been frequently used since that time was the public statement issued and signed by a group of theologians. Such public dissent is justified by the public role of theologians within the Church, the need for dialogue within the Church, and the very public nature of the issue under discussion.[176]

The basic problem in the area of noninfallible teaching is that the hierarchical magisterium has claimed too great a certitude for these teachings. Some of this probably could have been alleviated if the hierarchical teaching office simply labeled this teaching as noninfallible. The tendency to claim too great a certitude also comes from the more juridical understanding of the role of teaching. Recall that until the late nineteenth century and to some extent even today, hierarchical teaching was seen as part of the jurisdictional or governing power of the hierarchy. But even today official Catholic teaching refers to the teaching authority of the hierarchical magisterium. Here the noun is "authority," which definitely colors the understanding of teaching.[177]

Some Catholic moral theologians who agree with the basic reality of dissent object to the use of the word "dissent" as too pejorative.[178] But the term helps to ensure that one recognizes there is a presumption in favor of the hierarchical teaching. In the Catholic understanding, the pope is not just another theological voice. Through the assistance of the Holy Spirit, the pope has a special office in the Church, even in noninfallible teachings. However, the pope must use all the human sources of arriving at truth and be in dialogue with others. The pope has always depended on theologians for help in formulating teachings, but the danger is that only theologians of a certain school will be consulted. Nonetheless, the assistance of the Holy Spirit gives a special character to the hierarchical teaching office, which Catholics must always recognize.

Sometimes the issue of dissent is seen in terms of the tension or even opposition between theologians and the hierarchical magisterium or between the conscience of the individual Catholic and the hierarchical magisterium. But there are actually three realities involved and not just two. The primary reality is the truth, which the hierarchical magisterium with the assistance of the Holy Spirit as well as theologians and individual Catholics are trying to discern. The truth remains the ultimate and most important reality, which all in the Church are trying to discover and serve.[179]

Not all Catholic moral theologians support the legitimacy of dissent from noninfallible magisterial teachings, but there is no doubt that the majority of moral theologians publishing scholarly books and articles have accepted the legitimacy of such dissent in some circumstances. Such dissent from hierarchical Church teaching has continued to deepen on many issues and to encompass other issues as time goes on. In practice, many Roman Catholics seem to be acting in disagreement with Church teachings, especially in the area of sexuality. A respected 2005 sociological study found that less than 25 percent of US Catholics looked to Church teachers as the only teaching source on such moral issues as contraception, divorce and remarriage, homosexual behavior, and nonmarital sexuality.[180]

Response of the Papal Magisterium to Such Dissent

John Paul II's 1993 papal encyclical *Veritatis splendor* clearly gives the authoritative papal response to this growing dissent. The pope maintains that there is a genuine crisis in the Church of unprecedented proportion, which needs to be corrected.[181] Official hierarchical and papal documents have been issued that repeat and reinforce the moral teaching in the areas where some dissent exists. In addition, other Vatican documents and actions have insisted that the hierarchical magisterium should have greater control over theologians. John Paul II's 1979 apostolic constitution *Sapientia christiana* and the 1990 apostolic constitution *Ex corde ecclesiae* called for greater control by the hierarchy over teachers of theology in all Catholic colleges and universities.[182] The 1989 Profession of Faith and Oath of Fidelity promulgated by the Congregation for the Doctrine of the Faith emphasized the decisive role of the hierarchical magisterium and the submission required by theologians.[183]

The 1990 "Instruction on the Ecclesial Vocation of the Theologian (*Donum veritatis*)" from the Congregation for the Doctrine of the Faith insists that the theologian is officially charged with the task of presenting and illustrating the doctrine of the faith in its integrity and with full accuracy. This demands that the willingness to submit loyally to the teaching of the magisterium on matters per se not irreformable must be the rule. If, after serious study and true openness, the theologian cannot give internal intellectual assent, the theologian has the obligation to remain open to a deeper examination of the question. In the meantime, the instruction proposes three ways of acting. First, the theologian has the duty to make known to the magisterial authorities with no recourse to the mass media the problems involved in the teaching. Second, the theologian can suffer in silence and prayer with the certainty that truth will ultimately prevail. Third, dissent, which is described as public opposition to the magisterium of the Church and involves serious harm to the community of the Church, cannot be justified. Note the very pejorative description of public dissent. But one could maintain that not all public dissent is forbidden. For example, the instruction comments that the theologian will refrain from giving *untimely* public expression to his or her divergent hypothesis. The document goes on to refute some of the arguments for this unacceptable type of dissent. However, the vast majority of dissenting theologians have not been convinced by the teaching of this instruction.[184]

Up to this point our discussion has concerned noninfallible teaching. But it is necessary to consider the possibility of infallible teaching on moral issues. In June 1998, Pope John Paul II inserted into the Code of Canon Law some changes that first appeared in the Profession of Faith issued by the Congregation for the Doctrine of the Faith in 1989. The 1983 Code of Canon Law referred to two categories of magisterial teaching: the infallible teaching of a divinely revealed truth that must be believed by divine and Catholic faith, and noninfallible teaching to which the faithful owe the religious obsequium of intellect and will. The new category inserted between these two is the definitive (i.e., infallible) teaching by the magisterium of a doctrine concerned with faith and morals that is not directly revealed but is necessarily connected with revelation.[185] In a commentary on the papal document, Cardinal Ratzinger and Archbishop Tarcisio Bertone, the two top officials at that time in the Congregation for the Doctrine of the Faith, mentioned the following teachings as belonging to the second category: the ordination of women, the invalidity of Anglican orders, and the moral teaching on euthanasia, prostitution, and fornication.[186] Although this commentary is not an official Church teaching, it clearly indicates that important Church leaders want to extend infallibility to include some moral issues. In my judgment this is a fallible assertion by significant individuals that certain moral teachings are infallible by reason of being taught by the ordinary and universal magisterium of all bishops together with the pope. This second category inserted by the pope corresponds to what the earlier Catholic theological tradition called the secondary object of infallibility, which was often understood as limited to what is strictly required in order that the magisterium might be able to defend and explain the Gospel.[187]

On the theological front, Germain Grisez maintained that, although the norm against contraception is not contained in revelation, it is at least connected with it as a truth required to guard and faithfully expound the deposit of faith and thereby belongs to what has traditionally been called the secondary object of infallibility.[188] The vast majority of Catholic moral theologians and ecclesiologists maintain that teachings based on the natural law do not and cannot belong to the category of infallible teaching. The determinations of the natural law with regard to specific and complex moral issues are neither formally nor virtually revealed, nor are they so necessarily connected with revealed truth that the magisterium could not defend revelation if it could not teach infallibly in these areas.[189] Of interest here is the 1970 doctoral dissertation of William Levada, the former Prefect of the Congregation for the Doctrine of the Faith, which maintains that matters of the natural law cannot be infallibly taught.[190]

Another important question concerns what is required to verify that the ordinary universal magisterium has infallibly taught a particular point. Vatican II's Constitution on the Church addressed the conditions required in order that something can infallibly be taught by the ordinary universal magisterium. The conditions are that the bishops, dispersed throughout the world but maintaining among themselves and with Peter's successor the bond of communion, authoritatively teach matters to do with faith and morals as something to be held conclusively or definitively by the faithful (no. 25, p. 48). The most significant criterion here concerns the condition that all the bishops must have taught that this matter is to be held definitively by all the faithful. Francis Sullivan, who taught for many years at the Gregorian University in Rome, and others insist that to be held definitively does not mean just to teach something as a serious moral obligation but to maintain that this position is to be held with an irrevocable assent by the faithful.[191] This obviously is not easily proved.

The 1917 Code of Canon Law maintains that nothing is understood to be infallibly defined or declared unless this is clearly established. However, the 1983 Code omits the words "or declared." On this basis Germain Grisez concluded that the fact of infallibility has to be clearly established only when it is a question of judging when a doctrine has been infallibly defined and not in the case of the infallible ordinary universal magisterium. Yet it seems the intent of the statement from the theological perspective applies to any type of infallibility. Thus, if the infallibility is not clearly established, the particular teaching is not infallible.[192]

This chapter has shown how papal teaching on moral matters has become ever more prominent in the last two centuries. Since Vatican II, disputes have arisen in the Church about the response due to such hierarchical moral teachings. There exists significant theological dissent on some noninfallible moral teachings. The hierarchical magisterium has strongly opposed public theological dissent, but there is some slight and rather implicit recognition that such teachings might be erroneous. Some in the Church, including then-cardinal Ratzinger and Archbishop Bertone, maintain that a teaching on a specific moral issue can be infallibly taught by the ordinary universal magisterium—that is, all the bishops in the world together with the pope teaching something to be held infallibly by the Church. However, the conditions required for such infallible teaching are very difficult to fulfill. In addition, the majority of Catholic theologians maintain that a teaching based on natural law is removed from revelation and therefore cannot be taught infallibly.

NOTES

1. "Dogmatic Constitution on the Church," no. 18, in *The Documents of Vatican II*, ed. Walter M. Abbott (New York: Guild, 1966), 37–38. Subsequent references will give the paragraph numbers to the document and the page number to Abbott.

2. Richard P. McBrien, *The Church: The Evolution of Catholicism* (New York: HarperOne, 2008), 93–98.

3. John E. Lynch, "The Magistery and Theologians from the Apostolic Fathers to the Gregorian Reform," *Chicago Studies* 17 (1978): 205.

4. Noel Alinsky, ed., *The Cambridge Companion to the Age of Constantine* (New York: Cambridge, 2008).

5. Ladislas Örsy, "The Papacy for an Ecumenical Age: A Response to Avery Dulles," *America* 183, no. 12 (October 21, 2000): 9–15.

6. John W. O'Malley, "The Millennium and the Papalization of Catholicism," *America* 182, no. 12 (April 8, 2000): 8–16.

7. Jay P. Dolan, *The American Catholic Experience: A History from Colonial Times to the Present* (Notre Dame, IN: University of Notre Dame Press, 1992), 109–10.

8. P. G. Maxwell-Stuart, *Chronicle of the Popes: The Reign by Reign Record of the Papacy from St. Peter to the Present*, rev. ed. (New York: Thames and Hudson, 2006), 234.

9. Eamon Duffy, *Saints and Sinners: A History of the Popes*, 2nd ed. (New Haven, CT: Yale University Press, 2002).

10. See, for example, Avery Dulles, "The Magisterium in History: A Theological Perspective," *Theological Education* 19 (Spring 1983): 7–26. A version of this essay appears in Avery Dulles, *A Church to Believe In: Discipleship and the Dynamics of Freedom* (New York: Crossroad, 1982). The entire issue of *Chicago Studies* 17, no. 2 (1978) deals with the historical development of the magisterium and follows a similar historical division.

11. Duffy, *Saints and Sinners*, 1–5; and John W. O'Malley, *A History of the Popes: From Peter to the Present* (Lanham, MD: Rowman and Littlefield, 2010), 13–16.

12. O'Malley, *History of the Popes*, 23–33.

13. Lynch, "Magistery and Theologians," 194–98.

14. Ibid., 202–4.

15. Richard P. McBrien, *Lives of the Popes: The Pontiffs from St. Peter to John Paul II* (San Francisco: HarperSanFrancisco, 1997), 75–77.

16. O'Malley, *History of the Popes*, 40–42.

17. Duffy, *Saints and Sinners*, 67–72.

18. McBrien, *Lives of the Popes*, 98.

19. O'Malley, *History of the Popes*, 53–74.

20. Duffy, *Saints and Sinners*, 110–14.

21. McBrien, *Lives of the Popes*, 127 and 145–46.

22. Brian Tierney, "Popes and Bishops before Trent: An Historical Survey," in *The Papacy and the Church in the United States*, ed. Bernard Cooke (New York: Paulist, 1989), 14–15.

23. Dulles, "Magisterium in History," 10–15.

24. J. Philip Wogaman, *Christian Ethics: A Historical Introduction* (Louisville, KY: Westminster/John Knox, 1993), 25–62.

25. Lynch, "Magistery and Theologians," 188–209.

26. See, for example, Francis X. Murphy, *The Christian Way of Life*, Message of the Fathers of the Church, vol. 18 (Wilmington, DE: Michael Glazier, 1986).

27. Robert P. Maloney, "The Teaching of the Fathers on Usury: A Study of the Development of Christian Teaching," *Vigiliae Christianae* 27 (1973): 241–65.

28. T. F. Divine, "Usury," *New Catholic Encyclopedia* 14:499.

29. Henricus Denzinger et al., eds., *Enchiridion Symbolorum definitionum et declarationum de rebus fidei et morum*, 32nd ed. (Barcelona: Herder, 1963), no. 280–81.

30. Duffy, *Saints and Sinners*, 112–19.

31. Ibid., 110–21.

32. Yves Congar, "Theologians and the Magisterium in the West: From the Gregorian Reform to the Council of Trent," *Chicago Studies* 17 (1978): 212.

33. O'Malley, *History of the Popes*, 99–100.

34. Anders Wenroth, *The Making of Gratian's Decretum* (New York: Cambridge University Press, 2000).

35. Duffy, *Saints and Sinners*, 123–26.

36. Ibid., 127–28.

37. McBrien, *Lives of the Popes*, 181–82.

38. The following paragraphs come from Bernard Lauret, ed., *Fifty Years of Catholic Theology: Conversations with Yves Congar* (Philadelphia: Fortress, 1988), 40–43.

39. This and the following paragraph come from Yves Congar, "The Historical Development of Authority in the Church: Points for Reflection," in *Problems of Authority: The Papers Read at an Anglo-French Symposium Held at the Abbey of Notre Dame du Bec, April 1961*, ed. John M. Todd, 136–44 (Baltimore: Helicon, 1962).

40. McBrien, *Lives of the Popes*, 181–82.

41. Ibid., 33. O'Malley (*A History of the Popes*, 125–26) claims that Innocent III was the first pope to divest himself of the title Vicar of Peter and appropriate the title Vicar of Christ.

42. Congar, "Historical Development of Authority," 138–39.

43. Canon 331, in *New Commentary on the Code of Canon Law*, ed. John P. Beal, James A. Coriden, and Thomas J. Green, 431–36 (New York: Paulist, 2000).

44. Duffy, *Saints and Sinners*, 128–36.

45. Ibid., 136–51.

46. O'Malley, *History of the Popes*, 129–38.

47. Duffy, *Saints and Sinners*, 163–68.

48. O'Malley, *History of the Popes*, 149–69. For the definitive study on conciliarism, see Brian Tierney, *Foundations of Conciliar Theory: The Contribution of the Medieval Canonists from Gratian to the Great Schism*, enl. ed. (Leiden: Brill, 1998).

49. Duffy, *Saints and Sinners*, 177–200.

50. McBrien, *Lives of the Popes*, 275–76.

51. Duffy, *Saints and Sinners*, 200–208.

52. "Ecumenical Councils," in the *HarperCollins Encyclopedia of Catholicism*, ed. Richard P. McBrien (San Francisco: HarperSanFrancisco, 1995), 453–54.

53. A. Duggan, "Lateran Councils," *New Catholic Encyclopedia* 8:406–10.

54. McBrien, *Encyclopedia of Catholicism*, 453–54.

55. Denzinger, *Enchiridion*, no. 748–50.

56. T. P. McLaughlin, "The Teaching of the Canonists on Usury: XII, XIII, and XIV Centuries," *Medieval Studies* 2 (1940): 82.

57. John T. Noonan Jr., "Authority, Usury, and Contraception," *Cross Currents* 16 (Winter 1966): 60–62; see also John T. Noonan Jr., *The Scholastic Analysis of Usury* (Cambridge, MA: Harvard University Press, 1957).

58. Noonan, "Authority, Usury, and Contraception," 62–63.

59. Congar, "Theologians and Magisterium in the West," 214.

60. Roger Gryson, " The Authority of the Teacher in the Ancient and Medieval Church," in *Authority in the Church and the Schillebeeckx Case*, ed. Leonard Swidler and Piet Fransen (New York: Crossroad, 1982), 182–84.

61. Congar, "Theologians and Magisterium in the West," 220.

62. Gryson, "Authority of Theologians," 185–86.

63. "Pope Pius XII, *Humani generis*," Denzinger, no. 3885.

64. Congar, "Theologians and Magisterium in the West," 223.

65. Ibid., 216–17.

66. Dulles, "Magisterium in History," 16. For more detailed studies, see Guy Fitch Lytle, "Universities as Religious Authorities in the Late Middle Ages and Reformation," in *Reform and Authority in the Medieval and Reformation Church*, ed. G. F. Lytle (Washington, DC: Catholic University of America Press, 1981), 69–97; and

Jacques M. Gres-Gayer, "The Magisterium of the Faculty of Theology of Paris in the Seventeenth Century," *Theological Studies* 53 (1992): 424–50.

67. Nelson H. Minnich, "The Voice of Theologians in General Councils from Pisa to Trent," *Theological Studies* 59 (1998): 420–34.

68. Ibid., 434–40.

69. Ibid., 439–41.

70. Congar, "Theologians and the Magisterium in the West," 215–16.

71. Dulles, "Magisterium in History," 16.

72. The Latin *authenticum* is best translated as "authoritative." See Francis A. Sullivan, *Magisterium: Teaching Authority in the Catholic Church* (New York: Paulist, 1983), 26–28.

73. The original research on this development comes from two articles by Yves Congar: "A Semantic History of the Term 'Magisterium,'" and "A Brief History of the Forms of the Magisterium and Its Relationship with Scholars," in *Readings in Moral Theology* No. 3, *The Magisterium and Morality*, ed. Charles E. Curran and Richard A. McCormick (New York: Paulist, 1982), 297–331. For a summary of Congar's thought, see Avery Dulles, "Magisterium in History," 15. For development in Dulles's understanding of the relationship between theologians and the hierarchical magisterium, see Mark S. Massa, "Avery Dulles, Teaching Authority in the Church, and the Single 'Dialectically Tense' Middle: An American Strategic Theology," *Heythrop Journal* 48 (2007): 932–51.

74. Congar, "Theologians in the West," 318–21.

75. Gerard Philips, "History of the Constitution," in *Commentary on the Documents of Vatican II*, vol. 1, ed. Herbert Vorgrimler (New York: Herder and Herder, 1967), 109.

76. John W. O'Malley, "The Council of Trent: Myths, Misunderstandings, and Misinformation," in *Spirit, Style, Story: Essays Honoring John W. Padberg, SJ*, ed. Thomas M. Lucas (Chicago: Loyola University Press, 2002), 205–23.

77. Dulles, "Magisterium in History," 18–19.

78. Minnich, "Voice of Theologians," 432–33.

79. O'Malley, "Council of Trent," 207 and 214.

80. Ibid., 210–14.

81. E.g., Hans Küng, *Justification: The Doctrine of Karl Barth and a Catholic Reflection* (New York: Nelson, 1964).

82. Lutheran World Federation and the Roman Catholic Church, *Joint Declaration on the Doctrine of Justification* (Grand Rapids, MI: Eerdmans, 2000).

83. Herbert Jedin, "Trent, Council of," *New Catholic Encyclopedia* 14:277.

84. O'Malley, "Council of Trent," 220–23.

85. Dulles, "Magisterium in History," 18.

86. Redmond A. Burke, *What Is the Index?* (Milwaukee: Bruce, 1952), 5–9; and D. Dee, "Index of Forbidden Books," *New Catholic Encyclopedia* 7:434–35.

87. J. T. Catoir, "Doctrine of the Faith, Congregation for," in *New Catholic Encyclopedia* 4:944–46.

88. John Tedeschi, "The Organization and Procedures of the Roman Inquisition: A Sketch," in *The Spanish Inquisition and the Inquisitorial Mind*, ed. Angel Alcelá (New York: Columbia University Press, 1987), 198; see also John A. Tedeschi, *Prosecution*

of Heresy: Collected Studies on the Inquisition in Early Modern Italy (Binghamton, NY: Medieval & Renaissance Texts & Studies, 1991).

89. David W. Jones, *Reforming the Morality of Usury: A Study of the Differences That Separated the Protestant Reformers* (Lanham, MD: University Press of America, 2004).

90. John T. Noonan Jr., "The Amendment of Papal Teaching by Theologians," in *Contraception: Authority and Dissent*, ed. Charles E. Curran, 41–57 (New York: Herder and Herder, 1969); see also Noonan, *Scholastic Analysis of Usury*.

91. Noonan, "Amendment of Papal Teaching," 58–75.

92. For the history of the controversy, I am following the work of Louis Vereecke, who is the recognized authority in the history of moral theology. He has published four volumes of printed notes for his students at the Accademia Alfonsiana in Rome, but they are also available for public sale. For this controversy, see Louis Vereecke, *Storia della telolgia morale nel XVII secolo: la crisi della teologica morale*; see also Th. Deman, "Probabilisme," in *Dictionnaire de théologie catholique* 13, cols. 418–619.

93. Denzinger, *Enchiridion*, no. 1021–65. Subsequent references to Denzinger will be in the text, e.g., D 2046.

94. Vereecke, *Storia III*, 157–61; and Deman, "Probabilisme," 539–47.

95. Vereecke, *Storia III*, 161–68.

96. Deman, "Probabilisme," 566–71.

97. Noonan, *Scholastic Concept of Usury*, 357.

98. Marciano Vidal, *La morale di Sant'Alfonsio: Dal rigorismo alla benignità* (Rome: Editiones Academiae Alphonsianae, 1992), esp. 207–16.

99. Here and in the subsequent paragraph I am following Roger Aubert, "Introduction," in *History of the Church*, vol. 7, *The Church between Revolution and Restoration*, ed., Herbert Jedin and John Dolan (New York: Crossroad, 1981), 3–11.

100. J. H. Hallowell, "Liberalism," *New Catholic Encyclopedia* 8:701–6.

101. Peter Steinfels, "The Failed Encounter: The Catholic Church and Liberalism in the Nineteenth Century," in *Catholicism and Liberalism: Contributions to American Public Philosophy*, ed. R. Bruce Douglass and David Hollenbach, 19–44 (Cambridge: Cambridge University Press, 1994); see also Duffy, *Saints and Sinners*, 281–84.

102. Pope Gregory XVI, *Mirari vos*, in *The Papal Encyclicals 1740–1878*, ed. Claudia Carlan (Wilmington, NC: McGrath, 1981), 235–41.

103. Pope Gregory XVI, *Mirari vos*, in Denzinger, *Enchiridion*, no. 2730.

104. Roger Aubert, "The Syllabus and Its Consequences," in *History of the Church*, vol. 8, *The Church in the Age of Liberalism*, ed. Herbert Jedin and John Dolan, 293–99 (New York: Crossroad, 1981).

105. Roger Aubert, "Progress of Ultramontanism," in *History of the Church*, vol. 8, 3–13.

106. Jeffery von Arx, *Varieties of Ultramontanism* (Washington, DC: Catholic University of America Press, 1998).

107. Duffy, *Saints and Sinners*, 279–301.

108. O'Malley, "Millennium and the Papalization of Catholicism."

109. J. Derek Holmes, *The Triumph of the Holy See: A Short History of the Papacy in the Nineteenth Century* (London: Burnes & Oates, 1978), 135–37.

110. T. Lincoln Bouscaren and Adam C. Ellis, *Canon Law: A Text and Commentary*, 2nd ed. (Milwaukee: Bruce, 1951), 4–6.

111. Holmes, *Triumph of the Holy See*, 135–42. For the effect of ultramontanism on the Church in the United States, see Patricia Byrne, "American Ultramontanism," *Theological Studies* 56, no. 2 (June 1995): 301–25.

112. Holmes, *Triumph of the Holy See*, 135.

113. For the classical study of Americanism, see Thomas E. McAvoy, *Americanist Heresy in Roman Catholicism* (Notre Dame, IN: University of Notre Dame Press, 1963); see also Margaret Mary Reher, "Pope Leo XIII and Americanism," *Theological Studies* 34 (1973): 679–89; and the entire issue of *US Catholic Historian* 11 (Summer 1993).

114. Darrell Jadock, ed., *Catholics Contending with Modernity: Roman Catholic Modernism and Anti-Modernism in Historical Context* (New York: Cambridge University Press, 2000).

115. J. J. Heaney, "Modernism," in *New Catholic Encyclopedia* 9:991–95; see also Gabriel Daly, *Transcendence and Immanence: A Study in Catholic Modernism and Integralism* (Oxford: Clarendon, 1980).

116. McBrien, *Church*, 147.

117. O'Malley, "Millennium and Papalization," 16.

118. John P. Boyle, *Church Teaching Authority: Historical and Theological Studies* (Notre Dame, IN: University of Notre Dame Press, 1995), 5–7.

119. *Discorsi e radiomessagi di Sua Santità Pio XII*, 20 vols. (Città del Vaticano: Typographia Polygatta Vaticana, 1955–59).

120. G. Malone, "Encyclical," *New Catholic Encyclopedia* 5:332–33.

121. Congar, "Semantic History of the Term 'Magisterium,'" 306–7.

122. Boyle, *Church Teaching Authority*, 10–42; see also Richard R. Gaillardetz, *Witnesses to the Faith: Community, Infallibility, and the Ordinary Magisterium of Bishops* (New York: Paulist, 1992), 18–35.

123. Pope Pius XII, *Humani generis*, in Denzinger, *Enchiridion*, no. 3885.

124. For systematic studies of the magisterium, see Richard R. Gaillardetz, *Teaching with Authority: A Theology of the Magisterium in the Church* (Collegeville, MN: Liturgical, 1997); Ladislas Örsy, *The Church: Learning and Teaching: Magisterium, Assent, Dissent, Academic Freedom* (Wilmington, DE: Glazier, 1987); and Sullivan, *Magisterium*.

125. Congar, "A Brief History of the Forms of Magisterium," 325.

126. Ibid., 323.

127. Ibid., 323–26.

128. Michael Place, "From Solicitude to Magisterium: Theologians and the Magisterium in the West: From the Gregorian Reform to the Council of Trent," *Chicago Studies* 17 (1978): 226.

129. Ibid., 232–35.

130. Pius XII, *Humani generis*, in Denzinger, *Enchiridion*, no. 3384–86.

131. Joseph Clifford Fenton, "Father Denzinger's *Enchiridion* and Its First Hundred Years," *American Ecclesiastical Review* 131 (December 1954): 387–95.

132. Ibid., 387–88.

133. John T. Noonan Jr., *Contraception: A History of Its Treatment by the Catholic Theologians and Canonists* (Cambridge, MA: Belknap Press of Harvard University Press, 1965), 401–2.

134. Ibid., 416–17.

135. In the following paragraphs I am following very closely John Connery, *Abortion: The Development of the Roman Catholic Perspective* (Chicago: Loyola University Press, 1977), 283–303; T. Lincoln Bouscaren, *Ethics of Ectopic Operations*, 2nd ed. (Milwaukee: Bruce, 1944), 11–13 and 21–22; and Charles E. Curran, *The Origins of Catholic Moral Theology in the United States* (Washington, DC: Georgetown University Press, 1997), 113–16 and 146–50.

136. Connery, *Abortion*, 301–2; Curran, *Origins of Catholic Moral Theology*, 146–50.

137. Bouscaren, *Ethics of Ectopic Operations*, 147–71.

138. For the position of these and other authors discussing these questions, see Connery, *Abortion*, 225–83.

139. The official versions of these allocutions and addresses can be found in *Acta Apostolicae Sedis*. English translations of the later documents can be found in *The Pope Speaks*, which began publishing in the United States in 1954. This journal itself testifies to the increasing role played by the papacy in the life of the Church at this time.

140. John P. Kenny, *Principles of Medical Ethics*, 2nd ed. (Westminster, MD: Newman, 1962).

141. Pope Pius X, *Praestantia Scripturae*, in Denzinger, *Enchiridion*, no. 3503.

142. Pope Pius X, *Singulari quadam*, in *The Papal Encyclicals 1903–1939*, ed. Claudia Carlan (Wilmington, NC: McGrath, 1981), 136.

143. Pope Pius XII, *Humani generis*, in *Papal Encyclicals 1939–1958*, 178.

144. Pope Piux XII, *Magnificate dominum*, in *American Ecclesiastical Review* 132 (January 1955): 52–63.

145. Charles E. Curran and Robert E. Hunt, with John F. Hunt and Terrence R. Connelly, *Dissent In and For the Church: Theologians and Humanae Vitae* (New York: Sheed & Ward, 1970), 66–69.

146. Joseph A. Komanchak, "Ordinary Papal Magisterium and Religious Assent," in Charles E. Curran, *Contraception: Authority and Dissent* (New York: Herder and Herder, 1969), 108–9.

147. Ibid., 112.

148. Curran, *Origins of Catholic Moral Theology*, 233.

149. Bouscaren, *Ethics of Ectopic Operations*, 14–16.

150. Connery, *Abortion*, 292.

151. Aloysius Sabetti, "Commentary on the Decree *Quemadmodum*," *American Ecclesiastical Review* 6 (1892): 166.

152. Bouscaren, *Ethics of Ectopic Operations*, 13.

153. Gerald Kelly, "The Morality of Artificial Fecundation," *American Ecclesiastical Review* 101 (1939): 109–18; and Kelly, "Current Theology: Notes on Moral Theology," *Theological Studies* 8 (1947): 106–10.

154. Gerald Kelly, *Medico-Moral Problems* (St. Louis: Catholic Hospital Association, 1958), 243.

155. Franciscus Hürth, "La fecondition artificelle: Sa valeur morale et juridique," *Nouvelle revue théologique* 68 (1946): 402–26.

156. Franciscus Hürth, "Annotationes," *Periodica de re morali, canonica, liturgica* 41 (1952): 245–49.

157. Marcelino Zalba, "In Memoriam P. Francisci Hürth," *Periodica de re morali, canonica, liturgica* 52 (1963): 411–16.

158. Gerald Kelly, "Current Theology: Notes on Moral Theology, 1949," *Theological Studies* 11 (1950): 67n101.

159. Dogmatic Constitution on the Church, no. 1–8, in *Documents of Vatican II*, ed. Walter M. Abbott (New York: Guild, 1966), 14–24. Subsequent references will be given in the text to the paragraph number of the Constitution and the page from Abbott. For an in-depth treatment of the Constitution on the Church, see McBrien, *Church*, 151–214.

160. McBrien, *Church*, 167.

161. Declaration on Religious Freedom, no. 1, in *Documents of Vatican II*, ed. Abbott, 675.

162. McBrien, *Church*, 198–204.

163. John T. Noonan Jr., *A Church That Can and Cannot Change: The Development of Moral Theology* (Notre Dame, IN: University of Notre Dame Press, 2005); and Charles E. Curran, ed., *Change in Official Catholic Moral Teachings* (New York: Paulist, 2003).

164. Lucy Blyskal, "*Obsequium*: A Case Study," *Jurist* 48 (1988): 559–89.

165. Dogmatic Constitution on Divine Revelation, no. 10, in *Documents of Vatican II*, ed. Abbott, 117–18.

166. Komonchak, "Ordinary Papal Magisterium and Religious Assent," 104–18.

167. For three essays with different views of the *sensus fidelium* in moral theology, see Paul Valadier, "Has the Concept of *Sensus Fidelium* Fallen into Desuetude?" (187–92); Nathanäel Yaovi Soédé, "*Sensus Fidelium* and Moral Discernment: The Principle of Inculturation and of Love" (193–201); and Giuseppe Angelini, "The *Sensus Fidelium* and Moral Discernment," (202–9), all in *Catholic Theological Ethics in the World Church*, ed. James F. Keenan (New York: Continuum, 2007).

168. Komonchak, "Ordinary Papal Magisterium and Religious Assent," 102–3.

169. For the historical development of this issue, see Robert Blair Kaiser, *The Politics of Sex and Religion: A Case Study in the Development of Doctrine, 1962–1984* (Kansas City, MO: Leaven, 1985).

170. Andrew M. Greeley, William C. McCready, and Kathleen McCourt, *Catholic Schools in a Declining Church* (Kansas City, MO: Sheed & Ward, 1976), 103–54.

171. For an in-depth and broad discussion of the different positions on the legitimacy of such dissent, see Charles E. Curran and Richard A. McCormick, eds., *Readings in Moral Theology No. 3: The Magisterium and Morality* (New York: Paulist, 1982); and Curran and McCormick, eds., *Readings in Moral Theology No. 6: Dissent in the Church* (New York: Paulist, 1988).

172. Thomas Aquinas, *Summa theologiae* (Turin: Marietti, 1952), *Ia IIae*, q.94, a.4.

173. Noonan, *Church That Can and Cannot Change*; and Curran, *Change in Official Catholic Moral Teachings*.

174. Karl Rahner, "The Dispute concerning the Teaching Office of the Church," in Curran and McCormick, *Readings in Moral Theology No. 3*, 112–16.

175. Curran and Hunt, *Dissent In and For the Church*, 133–53; and United States Catholic Bishops, *Human Life in Our Day* (Washington DC: United States Catholic Conference, 1968), 18.

176. Curran and Hunt, *Dissent In and For the Church*, 133–53.

177. For a similar criticism of the excessively judicial understanding of teaching authority, see Boyle, *Church Teaching Authority*, 161–78.

178. Kevin Kelly, "Serving the Truth," in Curran and McCormick, *Readings in Moral Theology No. 6*, 479–80; Linda Hogan, *Confronting the Truth: Conscience in the Catholic Tradition* (New York: Paulist, 2000), 176–79; and Lisa Sowle Cahill, "Sexual Ethics," in *A Call to Fidelity: On the Moral Theology of Charles E. Curran*, ed. James A. Walter, Timothy E. O'Connell, and Thomas A. Shannon (Washington, DC: Georgetown University Press, 2002), 113–14.

179. Yves Congar, "Brief History of the Forms of the Magisterium," 328.

180. William V. D'Antonio, James D. Davidson, Dean R. Hoge, and Mary L. Gautier, *American Catholics Today: New Realities of Their Faith and Their Church* (Lanham, MD: Rowman and Littlefield, 2007), 92–97.

181. Pope John Paul II, *Veritatis splendor*, no. 4–5, in *The Encyclicals of John Paul II*, ed. J. Michael Miller (Huntington, IN: Our Sunday Visitor, 2001), 586–87.

182. Pope John Paul II, *Apostolic Constitution: Sapientia Christiana on Ecclesiastical Faculties and Universities* (Washington, DC: US Catholic Conference, 1979); and John Paul II, *Ex corde ecclesiae*, *Origins* 20 (1990): 265–76.

183. Congregation for the Doctrine of the Faith, "Profession of Faith and an Oath of Fidelity," *Origins* 18 (1989): 661–63; see also Ladislas M. Örsy, *The Profession of Faith and the Oath of Fidelity: A Theological and Canonical Analysis* (Wilmington, DE: Glazier, 1990).

184. Congregation for the Doctrine of the Faith, "Instruction on the Ecclesial Vocation of the Theologian (*Donum veritatis*)," *Origins* 20 (1990): 117–26. For commentaries on this and other related documents see André Naud, *Un aggiormanento et son éclipse* (Anjou, Quebec: Fides, 1996), 73–175; and Boyle, *Church Teaching Authority*, 95–123 and 142–60.

185. Pope John Paul II, *Ad tuendam fidem*, *Origins* 28 (1998): 116–19.

186. Josef Ratzinger and Tarcisio Bertone, "Commentary on the Profession of Faith's Concluding Paragraph," *Origins* 28 (1998): 119.

187. Sullivan, *Magisterium*, 134.

188. Germain Grisez, *Way of the Lord Jesus*, vol. 1, *Christian Moral Principles* (Chicago: Franciscan Herald, 1983), 845–49.

189. Sullivan, *Magisterium*, 138–52. For the protracted discussion between Germain Grisez and Francis Sullivan on this issue, see Germain Grisez, "Infallibility and Specific Moral Norms: A Review Discussion," *Thomist* 49 (1985): 248–87; Francis A. Sullivan, "The 'Secondary Object' of Infallibility," *Theological Studies* 54 (1993): 536–50; Germain Grisez, "*Quaestio disputata*: The Ordinary Magisterium's Infallibility: A Reply to Some New Arguments," *Theological Studies* 55 (1994): 720–32, 737–38; and Francis A. Sullivan, "Reply to Germain Grisez," *Theological Studies* 55 (1994): 732–37. For a later discussion on the ordinary universal magisterium, see Richard Gaillardetz, "The Ordinary Universal Magisterium: Unresolved Questions," *Theological Studies* 63 (202): 447–71; Lawrence J. Welch, "*Quaestio disputata*: Reply to Richard Gaillardetz on the Ordinary Magisterium and to Francis Sullivan," *Theological Studies* 64 (2003): 598–609; and Francis A. Sullivan, "Reply to Lawrence J. Welch," *Theological Studies* 64 (2003): 610–15.

190. William Levada, "Infallible Church Magisterium and the Natural Moral Law," (STD diss., Pontifical Gregorian University, 1970).

191. Sullivan, *Magisterium*, 143–48.

192. For my further discussion of these issues, see Charles E. Curran, *The Catholic Moral Tradition Today* (Washington, DC: Georgetown University Press, 1999), 223–26.

CHAPTER 5

STRAND FIVE

Second Vatican Council

The SECOND VATICAN COUNCIL (1962–65) had a profound effect on the Catholic Church. However, in the fifty years since the Council there have surfaced discordant interpretations of what the Council actually did and how it fits into the life and the history of the Church. The controversy centers on whether one emphasizes the aspect of continuity or discontinuity of the Council with the previous Catholic tradition. In my judgment, there are aspects of both continuity and discontinuity. Vatican II in no way changed or even diminished one of the dogmas or core teachings of the Catholic Church. On the other hand, many other aspects did change. The existential experience of the average Catholic was discontinuity, especially in the celebration of the liturgy that after the Council used the vernacular and no longer used Latin. The debates within the Catholic Church about the significance and role of Vatican II continue and involve historians, theologians, and Church leaders, including Joseph Ratzinger—Pope Benedict XVI.[1]

Our concern here is on the more limited area of the effects of Vatican II on Catholic moral theology. The historical fact is that Vatican II changed the primary focus of moral theology from the manualistic concern of preparing confessors to the concern of living out the full Christian life. Thus, Vatican II had a very significant impact on Catholic moral theology.

On the other hand, it is also necessary to limit somewhat the causality of Vatican II with regard to the demise of the manuals of moral theology. Chapter 1 pointed out Bernard Häring's promising work in moral theology even before Vatican II. Even in regard to the effect of Vatican II on the Church in general, some caution is necessary. Vatican II did not come into existence out of the blue. There were stirrings and movements in the life of the Church in the decades before Vatican II that helped open the door to the reforms of Vatican II. Most significant were the developments with regard to the role and understanding of scripture in the Christian life. The liturgical movement began in monasteries but then spread to the call for a greater participation of all the faithful in the liturgical celebration of the Church. A catechetical movement called for a kerygmatic approach that aimed at nourishing and developing the faith and life of Catholics and recognized that catechetics could not be identified with memorizing the truths of faith. The twentieth century also witnessed in the Church the beginning of an ecumenical concern. In practice, Protestants and Catholics often found themselves in shared, common concerns and approaches. These developments were all below the radar of most Catholics. The papacy had opened the door a bit with regard to many of these developments, but they remained very much in the shadows of the life of the Church. In retrospect, however, there never could have been a Vatican II if it were not for the existence and contribution of these movements that emerged from the theological and pastoral life of the Church and not from the impetus of the hierarchical magisterium.[2]

Vatican II directly dealt with theology in general, and with moral theology only in *Optatam totius*—the Decree on Priestly Formation, in the section on the revision of ecclesiastical studies. The document briefly mentioned that theology in general should be taught in the light of faith and with the guidance of the Church's teaching authority and should strive to accurately draw Catholic doctrine from revelation so that students can profoundly understand that doctrine, nourish their spiritual lives with it, and be able to propose and defend it in their priestly ministry. In this short treatment just a few sentences are given to each of the theological and ecclesiastical disciplines. The section on moral theology was brief but to the point. "Special attention needs to be given to the development of moral theology. Its scientific exposition should be more thoroughly nourished by scriptural teaching. It should show the nobility of the Christian vocation of the faithful and their obligation to bring forth fruit and charity for the life of the world."[3] Bernard Häring originally drafted this section on moral theology.[4]

There can be no doubt, however, that Vatican II had a very significant impact on Catholic theology in general and moral theology in particular. In my judgment the Council exercised this influence in five distinct but overlapping ways—creating a new literary genre with content implications, shifting from classicism to historical consciousness, emphasizing the importance of scripture and the distinctively Christian aspects, replacing an older defensiveness with a greater openness, and emphasizing the importance of the person.

CREATING A NEW LITERARY GENRE WITH CONTENT IMPLICATIONS

The literary genre of Vatican II was quite different from that of previous Councils in the Catholic Church. According to Giuseppe Alberigo, the editor of the five-volume study of Vatican II, Pope John XXIII assigned the attribute "pastoral" to the Council.[5] In his famous opening address to the Council, "*Gaudet Mater Ecclesia*," on October 11, 1962, Pope John gave a strong indication of what he had in mind. In the past the Church has often condemned errors, sometimes with the greatest severity. But today the Church prefers to use the medicine of mercy rather than severity. She meets the needs of the present day by demonstrating the validity of her teachings rather than by condemnations. Yes, there are errors and dangerous concepts to be opposed. Some people totally deny God and others put all their trust in technological progress. But also there are many positive things happening in our world. Many are deeply convinced of the paramount dignity of the human person and often recognize the futility of violence and the right of arms. In this context the Catholic Church raising the torch of religious truth in this ecumenical Council desires to show herself to be the loving mother of all—benign, patient, full of mercy, and goodness to all. To human beings oppressed by many difficulties, like Peter she does not give them gold or silver but she opens to all the goods of divine grace which make people children of God and provide truly efficacious helps for a more human life. Through her children the Church tries to spread everywhere the fullness of Christian charity. There can be nothing more efficacious in eradicating seeds of discord and promoting concord, just peace, and the solidarity of all.[6]

One finds in this speech the basis for the famous opening lines of the Pastoral Constitution on the Church in the Modern World: "The joys and hopes, the griefs and the anxieties of the people of this age, especially those who are poor or in any way afflicted, these too are the joys and hopes, the griefs and anxieties of the followers of Christ. Indeed, nothing genuinely human fails to raise an echo in their hearts" (no. 1, pp. 199–200).

John XXIII here calls for a pastoral tone for the Council that tries to inspire and attract. How different such a tone is from the literary genre of previous ecumenical Councils. Previous Councils developed a very different approach and used a very different literary genre. They were either primarily juridical or legislative bodies. As juridical bodies, they heard cases and made judgments and established punishments for those who had done wrong. As legislative bodies, they produced specific norms and laws that were to govern the life of the Church. Councils from the very first Council of Nicea often employed the literary genre of "canons"—a short precise ordinance that often carried with it a punishment for violation. The Council of Trent, for example, issued about 135 such canons dealing with doctrinal matters following the same general formula: "If someone says (then gives an erroneous doctrine), let them be anathema." Even doctrines themselves were proposed in these very precise canons threatening anathema to those who denied them.[7] Thus, from the very beginning, John XXIII made it clear what the pastoral literary genre did not involve. There were to be no condemnations at Vatican II but attempts to expose the riches, the truth, and the attractiveness of Catholic teaching.

One of the startling developments of Vatican II was the rejection by the Council fathers of almost all the major documents proposed by the preparatory commissions under the leadership of the Roman Curia. Objections to these documents often coalesced under the criterion that they were not pastoral. They were often abstract, doctrinaire, and polemical.[8]

The term "pastoral" was then often understood as a criterion that could be more easily described in terms of opposition to the older approaches that had been used in previous Church documents in general. However, John O'Malley, a distinguished American Jesuit historian, has given a more positive description of the newer literary genre of the Council in his fascinating study of Vatican II.[9] O'Malley calls this literary genre "epideictic" from the technical name for panegyric in classical treatises on rhetoric. This literary genre was well known, described, and used by classical authors such as Aristotle, Cicero, and Quintilian. The fathers of the Church in the first seven centuries frequently employed this literary genre. O'Malley also found the same genre in the sermons preached in the Sistine Chapel in the Vatican during the Renaissance. The renewal of interest in the early sources of Christianity in the middle twentieth century in Catholicism put theologians and others in contact with this literary genre as found in these early Church writings.

The purpose of the epideictic genre is to heighten appreciation for a person, an event, or an institution and excite emulation of this ideal. Its goal is winning internal assent and not the imposition by conformity from the outside. Such an approach teaches by suggestion, insinuation, and example. By depicting the attractiveness of values and ideals, one hopes to invite and inspire the reader or hearer to accept and achieve these values.

O'Malley contrasts the epideictic genre with the genre of dialectic. Dialectic is the art of proving a point, of winning an argument, and of proving your opponent wrong. Dialectic expresses itself in the syllogism, in the debate, and in the disputation. Its language is abstract, impersonal, and ahistorical. From a positive perspective, the language is precise, technical, and always trying to propose unambiguous descriptions and definitions. By definition there is an "us versus them" character to this literary genre. The Scholastics in the Middle Ages used this genre and found it to be helpful and congenial.

Vatican II documents are not literary masterpieces by any stretch of the imagination, but they do adopt the epideictic approach. In general, Vatican II documents eschew the dialectics of winning an argument in favor of trying to find common ground. The opening speech by John XXIII well illustrates this literary genre. The major documents of Vatican II hold up ideals and invite others to appreciate and emulate them. The documents draw some practical conclusions from these ideals and values, but the style is soft compared to the hard-hitting style of canons and condemnations. O'Malley explicitly correlates the epideictic literary genre with the insistence that the Council be pastoral. By appealing to invitation and dialogue, the documents of Vatican II encourage conversion and interior change. This genre looks to persuasion and reconciliation and avoids commands and condemnations coming from on high. To be successful, persuaders need to establish an identity between themselves and their audience indicating that they share the same concerns, joys, and sorrows. In this context recall the opening sentence of *Gaudium et spes*. Obviously, the fathers of the Council did not set out to employ an epideictic literary genre, but what they did well illustrates an epideictic genre that in turn sheds light on what Vatican II did.

O'Malley maintains that the most concrete manifestation of this genre in Vatican II is the vocabulary adopted. First of all, note the absence of words frequently found in other councils and Church documents— exclusion, alienation, enmity, threat, intimidation, surveillance, and punishment. With regard to the positive new rhetoric, O'Malley points out a number of different categories. One category involves horizontal words or equality words, such as "sisters" and "brothers." Recall the description of the Church as the people of God. Another category includes words of reciprocity such as "cooperation," "partnership," and "collaboration." Recall how often the Council itself speaks of dialogue and conversation. In addition, humility words often occur. In an older approach the Church was a perfect society. Now it is a pilgrim Church. The final category is interiority words rather than an emphasis on externals. The understanding is that external actions and change will come from these interior dispositions such as holiness. Note here too the understanding of conscience found in the Pastoral Constitution on the Church in the Modern World—conscience is the most secret core and sanctuary of a person where one is alone with God whose voice echoes in these depths (no. 16, p. 213). O'Malley has made a persuasive case that the approach of Vatican II can best be understood in light of the epideictic literary genre.

O'Malley has called attention to the importance of form and literary genre. With this in mind, the different literary genres of the manuals of moral theology and Bernard Häring's *Law of Christ* are evident. The manuals were heavily legalistic in orientation. Law is the objective norm of morality. Moral theology was deeply associated with canon law. The moral theology of the sacraments for all practical purposes consisted of how to celebrate and receive the sacraments precisely in light of the requirements of canon law so that they would be both valid and licit. The purpose of the manuals was to point out which acts were sinful and how sinful they were. The Christian motivation for the Christian moral life was the implied fear of going to hell by committing a mortal sin.

It is not an exaggeration to say that the *Law of Christ*, which was originally written in 1954, fits into an epideictic literary genre. Häring presents the Christian life as the grateful and joyful participation in the love and live of the risen Lord brought about by the gift of the Holy Spirit. The moral life is based on the good news of the Gospel. The Christian moral life is our response to the gift and love that God has first showed to us. The Christian life is thus inspiring and attractive. It is not merely the external conformity to a set of norms but the internal conversion and the need for continuing growth in our love for God and neighbor. The sacraments are primarily seen as loving encounters with the God who comes to us through Jesus Christ in the loving gift of the Holy Spirit. Häring explains the living out of the Christian life in light of the cardinal Christian virtues. Virtue plays a very significant role for Häring, whereas it was practically forgotten in the manuals of moral theology. Yes, Häring also discusses the actions that go against the Christian life, but even here it is a much softer approach and not in the harsh tones of legalism and condemnation that characterized the manuals.[10] Some critics complained that at times Häring's approach verged on the homiletical; no one ever made that criticism of the manuals of moral theology.[11]

In light of Vatican II, moral theology itself needs to adapt a more epideictic literary genre that stresses the attractiveness and inspiring nature of the Christian moral life. The Christian moral life is a response to the loving invitation and gift of God. However, there will always be a secondary place for a careful and minute analysis of why particular actions are right or wrong. Casuistry will always have a place in moral theology, but it is never the only or the primary approach. In addition, the tendency in the United States is to write textbooks in moral theology for students, especially in colleges. As a result, the literary genre of the textbook at times plays a greater role than the epideictic literary genre, but the epideictic genre always needs to be present with its emphasis on a positive and attractive presentation of the Christian moral life.

SHIFTING FROM CLASSICISM TO HISTORICAL CONSCIOUSNESS

Catholic scholars have been discussing for years what happened at Vatican II and why it was so different from what went before. The Council changed no fundamental dogma or teachings. The Church continued to have the same scripture, the same tradition, and the same history. What changed? I agree with many scholars, such as Bernard Lonergan and John Courtney Murray, that what changed was the way in which Catholics tended to look at the world. Chapter 3 explains how historical consciousness affects the understanding of natural law. At Vatican II we moved from classicism to historical consciousness.[12] Many scholars have recognized this change, but the following paragraphs will show exactly how Vatican II exemplifies this shift.

Classicism and historical consciousness are two different ways of looking at the world. As explained in chapter 3, classicism sees reality in terms
of the static, the unchanging, and the eternal. Historical consciousness
sees reality in terms of historical change and puts more emphasis on
the particular and the individual, whereas classicism stresses the abstract
and the universal. Classicism understands objective truth through the
metaphor of seeing or looking at this objective truth. Truth remains
unchanged in the course of history, but it can be applied differently in
different situations. Historical consciousness wants to hold on to objective truth, but it recognizes the historicity of truth and the need for the
subject to grasp and understand it. Historical consciousness gives greater
importance to the subject seeking truth and to the historical reality itself.
Catholic proponents of historical consciousness are quick to point out
that historical consciousness is not the same as historical relativism. History involves both continuity and discontinuity. Historical consciousness
is a middle position between the extremes of classicism and existentialism.
The shift from classicism to historical consciousness describes what took
place at Vatican II as the Council moved away from the classicism of neo-
Scholasticism (not necessarily all Thomism) and embraced a historically
conscious worldview.

Three significant realities brought about this shift at the Council—
ressourcement, *aggiornamento*, and the change in the teaching on religious
liberty. Commentators on the Second Vatican Council generally agree
that the two approaches for reform in the Council were *ressourcement*—
the return to the sources—and *aggiornamento*—bringing the Church up
to date. Both of these approaches criticized the existing classicism of
neo-Scholasticism—one from the perspective of the past and the other
from the perspective of the present.[13] The following paragraphs discuss
these two prongs of the reform of Vatican II and then treat the specific
case of religious freedom as illustrating the acceptance of historical
consciousness.

Ressourcement as a return to the sources began in Catholic theology
even before Vatican II and served as a strong criticism of the existing
neo-Scholasticism. *Ressourcement* became intimately associated with the
movement called the *nouvelle théologie*, which began in the late 1930s.
Jürgen Mettpenningen describes four essential characteristics of the *nouvelle théologie*. The first is the French language, since the movement was
primarily found in France and Belgium. Second, the *nouvelle théologie*
wanted to accentuate the role of history rather than have history play a

very secondary role to the abstractions of neo-Scholastic Catholic theology. Theology must start with and give great importance to the sources, especially the biblical and patristic texts. In 1942, the Jesuits Jean Danielou, Claude Mondésert, and Henri de Lubac founded *Sources Chrétiennes*, a series of patristic texts. The Dominicans Marie-Dominique Chenu and Yves Congar made similar appeals to history. Third, this movement insisted on the importance of positive theology. With its emphasis on the basic building blocks of theology—scripture, the patristic testimony, and the liturgy—positive theology is most important, especially because existing Catholic speculative theology had lost contact with these basic sources of faith. The fourth and final characteristic of the *nouvelle théologie* was its critical attitude to neo-Scholasticism. In 1950, Pope Pius XII in the encyclical *Humani generis* condemned the *nouvelle théologie*, and many of its proponents were restricted by Church discipline.[14] However, *ressourcement* identified with the *nouvelle théologie* came to be one of the two reform approaches that guided Vatican II.

One finds the influence of *ressourcement* throughout the documents of Vatican II but especially in the emphasis on scripture and liturgy. John W. O'Malley maintains that *ressourcement* was the most pervasive of the strategies of reform in the work of the Council. Much of the Council's efforts involved an attempt to bring about a restoration. For example, one of the most significant developments in the understanding of ecclesiology was the insistence on collegiality. Proponents of collegiality with its emphasis on the role of the college of bishops and also the role of the local Church insisted on going back to the sources in the early centuries that emphasized these aspects.[15]

The second reform approach associated with Vatican II is *aggiornamento*—bringing the Church up to date. Pope John XXIII highlighted this aspect in his address at the opening of the Council. Through the Council the Church will become greater in spiritual energies and look to the future without fear. In fact, by bringing herself up to date where required, the Church will make individuals, families, and peoples really turn their minds to heavenly things. In that speech John insisted there should be no condemnations issued by the Church. The Church meets the needs of the present day by demonstrating the validity of her teaching rather than by condemnations.[16]

Giuseppe Alberigo points out how *aggiornamento* became a favorite word of Pope John XXIII, especially in his pastoral work in Venice. Even before his opening speech at Vatican II, he had referred on a number of different occasions to the Council as involving *aggiornamento*, which is a rather general term that has been understood somewhat differently by different people. Is it a summary for reform or a way to avoid the term "reform"? For Alberigo in his five-volume history of the Council, it means a readiness and a disposition to seek a renewed inculturation of the Christian message in new cultures. Alberigo quotes Marie-Dominique Chenu as saying that *aggiornamento* means to refashion the Church, its manner of speaking, and its structure into a Church that, within the unchanging truth received from Christ and safeguarded in it, seeks and finds the means of making this truth intelligible and communicable through dialogue.[17]

Pope Paul VI made his own John's insistence on *aggiornamento*:

> We cannot forget Pope John XXIII's word *aggiornamento*, which we have adopted as expressing the aim and object of our own pontificate. Besides ratifying it and confirming it as the guiding principle of the Ecumenical Council, we want to bring it to the notice of the whole Church. It should prove a stimulus to the Church to increase its ever growing vitality and its ability to take stock of itself and give careful consideration to the signs of the times, always and everywhere "proving all things and holding fast that which is good" with the enthusiasm of youth.[18]

One can find the theme of *aggiornamento* in practically every document of Vatican II. The very first paragraph of the very first document approved by the Council, the Constitution on the Sacred Liturgy, says one of its goals is to make more responsive to the requirements of our times those Church observances that are open to adaptation (no. 1, p. 137). The Constitution on the Church insists that through the action of the Holy Spirit the Church ceaselessly renews herself (no. 9, p. 26). The Decree on Ecumenism recognizes that the Church is on pilgrimage and is called by Christ to continual reformation that is necessary for an institution of people on earth. Church renewal thus has a notable ecumenical importance (no. 6, p. 350). The Church in the Modern World insists that the Church has the duty of scrutinizing the signs of the times and of interpreting them in the light of the Gospel. This is more significant today in light of the profoundly changed conditions in our world (no. 4–5, pp. 201–3). The second part of this document discusses five particular issues but begins each discussion with a reading of the signs of the times. More significant than individual passages in the documents of Vatican II is the fact that aggiornamento became the leitmotif of the entire Council.[19]

The two-pronged methodological focus of Vatican II—*ressourcement* and *aggiornamento*—together form a firm basis for justifying how the Council moved from classicism to historical consciousness. In addition, the Declaration on Religious Freedom, which changed the official teaching on religious freedom, also illustrates (with some further interpretation) the shift to historical consciousness. In dealing with the issue of religious freedom, Vatican II had to solve the question of how the hierarchical Church could deny religious freedom in the nineteenth century and accept it in the twentieth century. In the theory and explanation given in the discussions, the Council followed the approach first developed by American Jesuit John Courtney Murray. The older teaching annunciated again at the end of the nineteenth century by Pope Leo XIII condemned religious freedom because the state has an obligation to support the one true religion, which is the Catholic Church. Religious freedom can be tolerated only on the basis of the need to avoid a greater evil or to achieve a greater good, which can occur especially when Catholics are in the minority as in the United States. But the ideal situation calls for the union of church and state.

Murray started writing about religious freedom in the 1940s and developed his rationale in favor of religious freedom in a number of scholarly articles published in the early 1950s.[20] In arguing then for religious freedom, Murray also recognized that the bigger question was how to explain such a change in Church teaching. Murray proposed that the change involved a true development. He distinguished three aspects in the teaching of Pope Leo XIII—the doctrinal, the historical, and the polemical. In the historical circumstances of the nineteenth century, proponents of religious freedom called for a totalitarian monism in which the Church had no role to play in the public sphere. The Church's role was reduced to the private realm only. Such an approach was obviously unacceptable to Leo XIII and to the Catholic self-understanding. The whole thrust of the Church's teaching recognized the important public dimension calling for the Church to work for a better public human society.

However, according to Murray, Leo insisted on three transtemporal principles that are to be applied in all the changing historical circumstances. First, Leo explicitly recognized two distinct societies—the church and the state. The second principle is the freedom of the church, and the third is the harmony that should exist between the two societies. The two societies meet in the conscience of the individual person who is both a member of the church and a citizen. Leo was involved in a polemic with a totalitarian monism and a totally secular liberalism that allowed no public role for the church. Leo was also dealing with the phenomenon of a highly illiterate population. In these circumstances he strongly opposed religious liberty as it was understood, and he called for the confessional state.

In the twentieth century, historical circumstances were changing with an emphasis on the heightened personal and political consciousness, which resulted in a greater emphasis on the freedom of the individual and a limited constitutional government with a juridical rather than an ethical view of the state. In this understanding the state does not tell people what to do in religious matters but grants all the people, including the Catholic Church, the freedom to practice their religion and to have a role in working for a more just society. In applying these three transtemporal principles, one could come to a conclusion in defense of religious freedom as it was now understood. At Vatican II, Bishop Émile-Joseph de Smedt, in proposing the Declaration on Religious Liberty to the Council fathers, basically followed Murray's approach to development.[21]

What about Murray's theory of development? I doubt whether Leo XIII would see himself in the picture that Murray painted of him and his approach. Those who disagreed with Murray pointed out that Leo, in his apostolic letter *Longinqua oceani*, had expressly condemned the American understanding of church and state and called for the union of church and state in the United States.[22] However, there is no doubt that Murray's theory is ingenious in many ways or that it made it much easier for the Church at Vatican II to accept a new teaching on religious freedom. The Council could accept this teaching and at the same time not have to admit that the Church had been wrong in its previous teaching. The issue of a Church teaching on a specific issue being wrong would become a most contentious issue in the post–Vatican II Church, especially in the area of dissent on specific moral issues.

In my judgment there was more discontinuity in the case of religious freedom than Murray or Vatican II were explicitly willing to admit. At the very least there was some time between Leo XIII and Vatican II when the existing teaching was wrong and needed correction. The very word and concept of development downplays the reality of change. It does not sufficiently recognize the discontinuity that has occurred on this issue and on other issues where the Church has changed its moral teaching. Think, for example, of slavery, the role of women in society, the best form of civil government, human rights, usury, and the role of love and pleasure in human sexuality.[23]

In Murray's case, he became aware of the concept of historical consciousness from his reading of Bernard Lonergan, but this only occurred at the end of the Council itself. He had proposed his theory of development much earlier. It is true that after the Council Murray appealed in his writings to historical consciousness to explain the change that took place, but he still saw it primarily in terms of development.[24] However, in a talk in Toledo, Ohio, in April 1967, less than six months before he died, Murray discussed again at some length the shift from classicism to historical consciousness and described the teaching defending the condemnation of artificial contraception for spouses as an example of classicism.[25] Murray died before the publication of the encyclical *Humanae vitae* in 1968, which repeated the condemnation of artificial contraception. *Humanae vitae* raised as never before the possibility that a hierarchical Church teaching could be erroneous. Like Murray, the proponents of dissent from *Humanae vitae* recognized that the document itself was an example of classicism and argued that, in the light of historical consciousness, one could justify contraception if it was necessary for the good of the marriage.[26]

Chapter 3 has already pointed out how a historically conscious approach critiques the neo-Scholastic natural law methods. This section has tried to show that, in the light of the two primary focuses of the Council on *ressourcement* and *aggiornamento*, Vatican II marked the shift from classicism to historical consciousness. However, it is necessary to recognize the role of both *ressourcement* and *aggiornamento*, and even the tension between them. *Ressourcement* alone does not necessarily involve a shift to historical consciousness. *Ressourcement* tends to privilege and give very great importance to the sources or building blocks of faith and downplays the role of *aggiornamento*. This became evident soon after the Council, when the proponents of *ressourcement* expressed disagreement with the proponents of *aggiornamento*. These latter were associated with the international journal *Concilium* and included Karl Rahner, Yves Congar, Edward Schillebeeckx, and Hans Küng. The proponents of *ressourcement* started the international journal *Communio*. The theologians associated with *Communio* were Henri de Lubac, Hans Urs von Balthasar, Joseph Ratzinger, Jean Danielou, Louis Bouyer, and others. During the Council both approaches opposed neo-Scholasticism, but after the Council their differences became more apparent.[27]

EMPHASIZING THE IMPORTANCE OF SCRIPTURE AND THE DISTINCTIVELY CHRISTIAN ASPECTS

Another important methodological change for moral theology brought about by Vatican II concerns the important role of scripture and the uniquely Christian aspects. Recall that before Vatican II, the manuals of moral theology employed a natural law methodology, and the Catholic moral teaching of the papal encyclical tradition emphasized the philosophical approach of neo-Scholasticism in its dealing with social ethics. Thus, there was little or no room for scripture, Christology, and other distinctively Christian aspects in these approaches. But all this changed at Vatican II.

Vatican II insisted on the importance of scripture in the life of the Church and of the individual Christian. *Ressourcement* in Catholic theology even before Vatican II prepared the way for Vatican II's insistence on the importance of scripture. *Dei verbum*, the Dogmatic Constitution on Divine Revelation, stresses the primary importance of scripture. Many differences from the pre–Vatican II approach are obvious. The Church now works to provide easy access to scripture for all the faithful (no. 22, pp. 125–26). Scripture had not played a very significant role in the devotional life of Catholics in the pre–Vatican II Church. Vatican II also calls for scripture to play a much more important role in the liturgy. The Church venerates the scripture just as she venerates the body of the Lord, and she provides the bread of life for her members in the liturgy from the tables of the word of God and the Body of Christ (no. 21, p. 125). *Sacrosanctum concilium*, the Constitution on the Sacred Liturgy, develops the role of the liturgy in greater detail. The document calls for the treasure of the Bible to be opened more lavishly in the liturgy. The biblical readings are to be changed so that on Sundays Catholic people achieve a greater familiarity with all scripture. There are now three readings instead of two and there is an attempt to include all the Gospels in a three-year cycle, often with a continuous reading of a Gospel throughout the liturgical year. The homily is to be based on the scripture of the day. Catholics in light of Vatican II recognize two aspects of the "mass"—the liturgy of the Word and the liturgy of the Eucharist, each of which now has its own "table" (no. 24, 47–52, pp. 147, 154–55).

The Constitution on Revelation maintains that theology finds its primary and perpetual foundation in scripture. Theology is most powerfully strengthened and constantly rejuvenated by the word of God. The study of scripture is the soul of theology (no. 24, p. 127). As mentioned earlier, what *Dei verbum* applied to theology in general, *Optatam totius*, the Decree on Priestly Formation, applied to the role of scripture in moral theology. "Special attention needs to be given to the development of moral theology. Its scientific exposition should be more thoroughly nourished by Scriptural teaching" (no. 16, p. 452).

Scripture and liturgy both insist on the need to live out one's faith in daily life. *Gaudium et spes*, the Pastoral Constitution on the Church in the Modern World, makes explicit the need for Catholics to live out their faith in their daily lives. Catholics cannot shirk their earthly responsibilities. The Gospel calls for Christians to discharge their earthly duties conscientiously. "This split between the faith which many profess and their daily lives deserves to be counted among the more serious errors of our age." The prophets in the Hebrew Bible and Jesus himself struggled vehemently against this scandal and warned that the failure to live out the scriptural mandates in the world results in grave punishments (no. 43, p. 243). Thus, Vatican II recognizes the need to overcome the neo-Scholastic distinction and even the separation between the supernatural and the natural orders.

The Pastoral Constitution on the Church in the Modern World addresses the social mission of the Church and the activity of Christians in the world in light of the need to have faith, the Gospel, and Jesus have some direct effect on what the Christian does in the world. The document recognizes the need to use both distinctively Christian and common human sources of moral wisdom and knowledge. The doctrine of creation grounds the acceptance of human sources. The first part of this document discusses four topics—the human person, human community, human activity in the world, and the role of the Church in the modern world.

The first chapter on the human person begins with the fact that the human person is created in the image of God. A second paragraph discusses the reality of sin, indicating that what divine revelation makes known to us correlates with our own human experience. Sin affects our relationships not only with God but also with oneself, others, and all created things. This chapter then discusses the dignity of the mind, of conscience, and the importance of freedom. There is a long discourse on atheism. To its credit, the chapter includes a paragraph on death that shows the riddle of human existence. The chapter ends with a long paragraph on Christ as the new human being (no. 12–22, pp. 210–22). Chapter 2, on human community, follows somewhat the same methodological approach beginning with creation. There is a brief recognition of sin that diverts us from doing good and the social circumstances that spur us toward evil. But there is no separate paragraph on sin. The chapter emphasizes the common good, social justice, the need for more than an individualistic ethic, as well as the fundamental importance of responsibility and participation. The chapter ends with a final paragraph on the Incarnate Word and human solidarity (no. 23–32, pp. 222–31).

Chapter 3 discusses human activity in the world. The chapter treats the value and regulation of human activity and the rightful independence of human affairs. The chapter then ends with three substantial paragraphs on human activity as affected by sin, as finding perfection in the paschal mystery, and with the recognition that the new heaven and the new earth will only come about at the end of time (no. 33–39, pp. 231–38). A comparison of the third chapter with the first two chapters shows their failure to address the future aspect of eschatology. Also, they could have given somewhat greater importance to sin. Therefore, I agree with the criticism that at times this document is too optimistic because of its occasional failure to recognize the deep reality of sin in our world and the future aspect of eschatology. However, in keeping with the best of the Catholic tradition, I see sin as affecting the goodness of creation but in no way destroying it. In trying to overcome the separation between the supernatural and the natural, and in affecting human reality through faith, the Gospel, and Jesus Christ, the Pastoral Constitution tends to downplay somewhat the reality of sin and the future aspects of eschatology.

The second part of the Pastoral Constitution aims to discuss five particular issues at some depth in the light of the Gospel and human experience (no. 46, p. 428). However, in reality its treatment of these issues fails to give enough importance to the role of the Gospel. Perhaps this comes from the fact that for a long time the plan was to publish this second part as an appendix, so it did not receive the same attention as the first part of the document.[28] Despite some shortcomings, the Pastoral Constitution on the Church in the Modern World sets the example for moral theology by emphasizing the role of scripture and theology and by overcoming the distinction and even the separation between the natural and the supernatural orders.

REPLACING AN OLDER DEFENSIVENESS
WITH A GREATER OPENNESS

Another methodological change brought about by Vatican II and closely related to *aggiornamento* is the overcoming of the defensive attitude of the Catholic Church that pervaded the whole approach of Catholicism in the nineteenth and twentieth centuries before Vatican II. This defensiveness manifested itself first with regard to the world in general. This defensiveness also showed itself in the Church's relationship to other Christians and other religions. The very acceptance of *aggiornamento* and the opening speech of Pope John XXIII indicated the move away from such a defensive posture.

In December 1962, at the close of the first session of the Council, Cardinal Leo Suenens of Belgium, with the approval of Pope John himself, gave a very important speech that helped set the tone for all the Council subsequently did. Suenens said the Council should address the inner reality of the Church but also the Church *ad extra*, that is, in its relationship to the world outside the Church. The Council should proceed by engaging in three dialogues—a dialogue with its own membership, an ecumenical dialogue, and a dialogue with the modern world. The Council basically accepted this approach, which indicated the great shift from condemnations to dialogue.[29]

Suenens's speech gave the impetus for what became the Pastoral Constitution on the Church in the Modern World, with the Church sharing in the joys and sorrows, the griefs and anxieties of the modern world. In this document the Church addresses all of humanity. The Pastoral Constitution recognizes the triumphs and tragedies of the modern world, the possibilities and the problems. It proves its solidarity with the entire human family by engaging with it in conversation about these various problems (no. 103, pp. 199–201). The Pastoral Constitution goes on to speak about the mutual relationship between the Church and the world. The help that the Church strives to bring to individuals involves proposing a secure basis for the freedom, dignity, and rights of the human person. The Church also strives to give help to society and human activity in the world (no. 41–43, pp. 240–45). But the relationship is reciprocal. Just as it is in the world's interest to acknowledge the historical reality of the Church and its good intentions, "so the Church herself knows how richly she has profited by the history and development of humanity" (no. 44, pp. 245–46).

Vatican II thus overcomes the defensiveness that had marked the Church for well over a century before that time. As already noted, both the *ressourcement* approach and the *aggiornamento* approach strongly disagree with the existing neo-Scholasticism. The Catholic Church's dependence on neo-Scholasticism is now broken. A new openness to dialogue with contemporary culture also includes a willingness to dialogue with other philosophical approaches. For example, in his 1998 encyclical *Fides et ratio*, Pope John Paul II explicitly recognizes that "the Church has no philosophy of her own nor does she canonize one."[30] Theology, however, needs philosophy in carrying out its twofold methodological principles of hearing the faith and understanding it. Moral theology requires a sound philosophical and metaphysical vision of human nature and society as well as the general principles of ethical decision making.[31] From John Paul II's perception it is obvious that there is no one Catholic philosophy, but some philosophical approaches are better than others in the development of theology. One further point deserves mention. Vatican II breaks the relationship between Catholic theology and neo-Scholasticism, but, as chapter 2 has pointed out, in the period after Vatican II Thomism has had a renaissance even though it cannot claim to be *the* Catholic philosophy.

In this context a question arises about natural law. Recall the earlier distinction between the theological aspect and the philosophical aspect of natural law. The theological aspect refers to whether or not Christians recognize a source of moral wisdom and knowledge that is shared by all humankind. As noted, the Pastoral Constitution recognizes such a source but insists that it be integrated into an explicitly Christian framework. The philosophical aspect of natural law refers to what is meant by human nature and human reason. Logically it seems that if one claims there is no Catholic philosophy, then there is no one philosophical theory of natural law common to Catholics and all humankind. There is no doubt that the Pastoral Constitution, which deals with five specific issues in its second part, does not emphasize the use of natural law. In this long document, the term "natural law," *ius naturale* or *lex naturalis*, appears only three times, and those are in quite peripheral contexts. One reference is to "natural and evangelical law" (no. 74); a second to "divine and natural law" (no. 89); and a third use refers to the natural law of the nations: *iuris naturalis gentium* (no. 79).[32]

After Vatican II, papal teaching seems almost schizophrenic in its approach to natural law. Take, for example, the many official teachings of Pope John Paul II. His three social encyclicals—*Laborem exercens* (1981),

Sollicitudo rei socialis (1987), and *Centesimus annus* (1991)—never mention natural law as such, despite the fact that natural law served as the methodological basis for papal social teaching before Vatican II. One might expect the encyclical *Fides et ratio* (1998) to develop a concept of natural law since this encyclical deals with the relationship between faith and reason, and with theological and philosophical inquiry. However, the document never mentions natural law. On the other hand, *Veritatis splendor* (1993), which concerns moral theology and its approach to personal and especially sexual morality, makes natural law the basis of its teaching and employs the term "natural law" more than thirty times.[33] Natural law is used to explain and defend papal sexual teaching but is not used to explain and defend papal social teaching in the writings of John Paul II.

Defensiveness characterized pre–Vatican II Catholicism in its relationship to the world, and triumphalism characterized its relationship to other Christians and other religions. At Vatican II, Protestants went from being schismatics and heretics to separated brothers and sisters. *Unitatis redintegratio*, the Decree on Ecumenism of Vatican II, develops and expands ideas found in the Dogmatic Constitution on the Church. Both documents admit that the Body of Christ is larger than the Roman Catholic Church, that there are many elements of sanctification and truth outside the institutional Roman Catholic Church, and that Christian bodies outside the Church are recognized as "churches" and "ecclesial communities." The Catholic Church alone claims to have the fullness of the means of salvation, but other Christian churches and communities provide access to salvation in Christ Jesus. Jesus calls for the church to be one. Unfortunately, as time went on, divisions appeared among Christians, "developments for which, at times, men of both sides were to blame" (no. 3, p. 345).[34] Dialogue now characterizes the relationship of the Catholic Church to others. In addition to the Decree on Ecumenism, two other documents of Vatican II (*Orientalium ecclesiarum*, the Decree on Catholic Eastern Churches, and *Nostra aetate*, the Declaration on the Relation of the Church to Non-Christians) deal with ecumenical and interreligious dialogue. A most significant change thus occurred between the Catholic Church and the Jewish religion.[35]

In the years after Vatican II, the Vatican itself sanctioned international bilateral dialogues with more than ten denominational bodies, including the Orthodox Churches, the Anglican Communion, the Lutheran World Federation, the World Methodist Council, the Baptist World Alliance, the Disciples of Christ, and other evangelical and Pentecostal groups. On a national level in the United States, there have continued to be bilateral discussions occurring with most other religious communities. Very often these discussions have resulted in scholarly books that have contributed to ongoing ecumenical discussions.[36]

As a result, Catholic theology since Vatican II has been truly ecumenical. Catholic moral theology today is invariably done in an ecumenical context. A number of academic societies exist, especially in the first world, dedicated to the study of moral theology and Christian ethics. *Societas Ethica* began primarily as a German Protestant association but today includes Catholics and extends throughout Europe. In France and the French-speaking world, *l'ATEM* (*Association francophone et oecuménique de théologiens pour l'étude de la morale*) holds an annual meeting and publishes its scholarly papers in *Revue d'éthique et de théologie morale*. In Great Britain the Society of the Study of Christian Ethics has a similar function and structure.[37]

The oldest and probably the most vibrant of these associations is the Society of Christian Ethics, which exists in the United States and Canada. What is now called the Society of Christian Ethics officially came into existence in 1959 as a small group of professors of social ethics in Protestant seminaries. Catholics first joined the society in 1964; the first Catholic was elected president in 1971, and today one-third of the membership is Roman Catholic.[38]

A primary reason for the rapid development of the ecumenical dialogue in moral theology in the United States came from the openness of the leading Protestant Christian ethicists (Protestants generally refer to the discipline as "Christian ethics," whereas Catholics use the term "moral theology") to such dialogue and the fact that they were already familiar with the Catholic tradition. James M. Gustafson, a leading figure in Protestant Christian ethics, was very familiar with Aquinas as well as with recent European developments in moral theology before the Council, as illustrated in the work of Gérard Gilleman, Bernard Häring, and Dietrich von Hildebrand.[39] Paul Ramsey, another leading Protestant ethicist, in his 1961 book on war depended heavily on the Catholic theory of double effect.[40] Paul Lehmann, another well-respected Protestant ethicist, in his 1963 book showed an awareness of developments in pre–Vatican II European Catholic moral theology.[41] These leaders in Protestant thought welcomed a dialogue with Catholics as a result of Vatican II's encouragement.

An excellent illustration of the strength and depth of the ecumenical approach to moral theology and Christian ethics can be found in the writings and work of James M. Gustafson. At Yale, Chicago, and Emory Universities, Gustafson directed the doctoral dissertations of more than twenty Catholic moral theologians, almost all of whom have published extensively and made significant contributions to moral theology. No Catholic moral theologian in the United States in the latter part of the twentieth century even came close to directing that number of dissertations by future Catholic theologians who themselves have contributed important scholarly writings.[42] Thus, today, by its very nature, Catholic moral theology is ecumenical in its approach.

This emphasis on dialogue at Vatican II is in one sense new, but it is still in keeping with the best of the Catholic tradition. With regard to ecumenism and interreligious dialogue, there is recognized commonality with other Christians, with Jews, and other religions in general. There is no doubt that, in the polemics after the Protestant Reformation, exaggerations took place on both sides. The best example is the Catholic insistence on the sacraments and downplaying scripture and the word of God while Protestants stressed scripture alone. Today Catholics recognize the importance of the scripture, and many Protestants have Eucharistic liturgies on Sunday.[43] Concerning dialogue with the world, Catholic theology's acceptance of natural law recognized that Catholics share much even in the area of morality with all other people. A doctrine of creation constitutes the theological grounding for the acceptance of natural law. However, sin also affects the world. As a result, there is need for a dialogue in which at times the Church learns from the world and at other times the Church must criticize the world.

EMPHASIZING THE IMPORTANCE OF THE PERSON

Vatican II also insisted on a fifth methodological concern for moral theology, with its emphasis on the person, as contrasted with the manualistic moral theology, with its emphasis on actions. As mentioned, the Pastoral Constitution on the Church in the Modern World specifically deals with social ethics. The other three major documents—*Lumen gentium* (Dogmatic Constitution on the Church), *Dei verbum* (Dogmatic Constitution on Divine Revelation), and *Sacrosanctum concilium* (Constitution on the

Liturgy)—do not deal explicitly with moral theology. However, they put heavy emphasis on the importance of the Christian person, thus indirectly emphasizing the need for a more personalistic moral theology. The Dogmatic Constitution on Divine Revelation sees revelation not primarily as a list of truths to be believed. In goodness and wisdom God chose to reveal Godself to humankind. Through Christ the Word made flesh, human beings have access to the Father through the Holy Spirit and come to share in the divine nature. Out of the abundance of love, God spoke to us as friends who now enjoy friendship with God. Revelation is God's gift to us of new life in Christ Jesus through the power of the Spirit (no. 2, p. 112). This personalistic understanding of revelation as involving the relationship of God to the believer shows the importance of the person for moral theology.

The Dogmatic Constitution on the Church insists that the Church is primarily the people of God and not a hierarchical institution. The emphasis is on the people who are the Church. The very first paragraphs of the document develop a Trinitarian approach with a personalistic emphasis. The eternal Father's plan for the whole world was to dignify human beings with a participation in God's own life. Through Christ the Father chose us and predestined us to become adopted children. Through the Holy Spirit the Father gives life to human beings who are dead through sin. The Spirit dwells in the hearts of the faithful and in the Church. Thus, the Church is a people made one with the unity of the Father, the Son, and the Holy Spirit (no.1–4. pp. 14–17). The life in Christ is shared with us through the sacraments. Through baptism we have been united with Christ in the likeness of his death and his resurrection. We thus share in the paschal mystery of Jesus. Through the Eucharist we are taken up in communion with the risen Lord and with one another in the Body of Christ. In order that we might be unceasingly renewed in Christ, Christ has shared with us his Spirit who vivifies, unifies, and moves the whole body (no. 7, pp. 20–22).

The very first paragraph of the Constitution on the Liturgy maintains that the goal of fostering and renewing the liturgy is "to intensify the daily growth of Catholics in Christian living" (no. 1, p. 137). The second paragraph insists that "the liturgy is thus the outstanding means by which the faithful can express in their lives and manifest to others the mystery of Christ" (no. 2, p. 137). In the liturgy all who have been made children of God by faith and baptism come together to praise God and celebrate the Eucharist. The liturgy in turn inspires the faithful to become of one heart and love when they have tasted to their full of the paschal mystery. The renewal in the Eucharist of the covenant with the Lord draws the faithful into the compelling love of Christ and sets them afire (no. 10, p. 142). The document then goes on to insist on the full, conscious, and active participation of all the faithful in the liturgy (no. 14, p. 144).

There is an ironic aspect about this document and its relationship to moral theology. The Constitution goes on to point out that liturgy should be ranked among the compulsory and major subjects in seminaries. "It is to be taught under its theological, historical, spiritual, and juridical aspects" (no. 16, p. 144). No mention is made of the moral aspects. Recall that the Constitution on the Liturgy was the first document considered and approved at the Council. Unfortunately, it seems that in the mind of the Council fathers at that time, moral theology still dealt only with the sinfulness of particular acts and was therefore not that intimately connected with the liturgy. However, without doubt the Constitution itself strongly grounds a more personalistic approach to moral theology, insisting on the fact that through baptism we share in the life of Jesus the Christ.

The Dogmatic Constitution on the Church brought to the fore a most important aspect of the personalist approach to Vatican II. Chapter 5 is titled, "The Call of the Whole Church to Holiness." This chapter then develops the universal vocation of all Christians to holiness. All the faithful of Christ, of whatever rank or status, are called to the fullness of the Christian life and to the perfection of charity (no. 40, p. 67). This is a dramatic change from the pre–Vatican II neo-Scholastic approach. According to that understanding, ordinary Christians lived in the world and followed the Ten Commandments, whereas those who wanted to be perfect left the world and followed the evangelical counsels and religious life. Note that the Gospel was a counsel for some and not a gift for all to follow Jesus with their whole heart, mind, and soul. Without doubt, this emphasis on the call of Christians to holiness sharply contrasts with the previous neo-Scholastic approach, but there can be no doubt that such teaching is solidly grounded in the scriptural and patristic writings. This emphasis on the universal vocation of all Christians to perfection sounded the death knell for the manuals of moral theology with their focus on sinful acts and their degree of sinfulness. The moral life of the Christian could no longer be seen primarily in terms of its minimalistic requirements.

The emphasis on the person and the individual's call to perfection was also incompatible with the deontological and legalistic models of the manuals of moral theology. The manuals dealt with the morality of human acts. The objective norm of morality was law in all its different aspects, and the subjective aspect was conscience. Morality is an obedience of conscience to the law. Once the emphasis shifts from acts to persons, the legal model is no longer adequate. The emphasis on the person insists on the importance of the virtues that characterize the person. The moral person is both subject and agent. By our actions we make ourselves the kinds of persons we are. As agents, we are the ones who perform actions. The importance of the virtues for the person as agent reminds one of the biblical aspect that a good tree brings forth good fruit whereas a bad tree brings forth bad fruit. By their fruits you will know them. Thus, the good person tends to do good actions. More important than concern about particular individual actions is the concern about the person and the attitudes from which these actions come.

Vatican II avoids the danger of a narrow personalism, with the emphasis only on the individual person. In keeping with the best of the Catholic tradition, Vatican II sees the baptized Christian as belonging to the covenant community of the people of God and in solidarity with all others. However, Vatican II fails to appreciate the ecological reality of our relationship to all that God created.

The emphasis on the role of the person in the moral life does not mean there is no need to discuss the morality of particular acts. The second part of the Pastoral Constitution on the Church in the Modern World discusses many specific issues in five different areas. In its discussion of marriage and sexuality, the document proposes as a criterion for determining the morality of acts "the nature of the human person and his acts" (no. 51, p. 256). In this perspective, then, acts must always be considered in terms of their relationship to the person. There are many difficult and complex decisions that face both individuals and societies in our world today. Since they are often controversial issues, they will tend to attract quite a bit of attention and will need to be dealt with in some depth.

The emphasis on the person and on historical consciousness ground the importance that Vatican II gave to the role of human experience as a source of moral knowledge. The Pastoral Constitution on the Church in the Modern World well illustrates human experience as providing moral wisdom. The second part of the document discusses in some depth five urgent topics, "in the light of the Gospel and of human experience" (no.

46, p. 248). The five topics are marriage and family, culture, socioeconomic life, the political community, and peace. The treatment of each of these topics begins with considering the signs of the times. Such an inductive methodology contrasts with the older, deductive methodology that began with certain truths and deduced moral principles and conclusions from these truths.

The Declaration on Religious Freedom begins by recognizing the importance of human experience as a source of moral wisdom.

> A sense of the dignity of the human person has been impressing itself more and more deeply on the consciousness of contemporary persons. And the demand is increasingly made that human beings should act on their own judgment, enjoying and making use of a responsible freedom. . . . This demand for freedom . . . regards in the first place, the free exercise of religion in society. . . . This Vatican Synod takes careful note of these desires. . . . It proposes to declare them to be greatly in accord with truth and justice. (no. 1, pp. 675–76)

The Council fathers thus recognized that they learned the importance of religious freedom from the experience of people.

Vatican II also insisted on the faith experience of all the baptized. The Constitution on the Church affirms, "The Spirit dwells in the Church and in the hearts of the faithful. . . . He prays and bears witness to the fact that they are adopted sons" (no. 4, p. 17). Later the Constitution on the Church teaches that Christ's prophetic office is carried on "not only through the hierarchy that teach in His name and with His authority, but also through the laity" (no. 35, p. 60). The Constitution on Divine Revelation recognizes a growth in the understanding of the mysteries of faith. "This happens through the contemplation and study made by believers who treasure these things in their hearts (cf. Lk 2:19, 51), through the intimate understanding of spiritual things they experience," and through the preaching of the bishops (no. 8, p. 116). Through baptism all the faithful have this "*sensus fidei*," a sense or intuition of the faith.

There exists not only the *sensus fidei* of the individual baptized person but also the *sensus fidelium*—the sense of the faith of all believers. The Constitution on the Church asserts, "The body of the faithful as a whole, assisted as they are by the Holy One (cf. Jn 2:20, 27), cannot err in matters of belief. Thanks to a supernatural sense of the faith which characterizes the People as a whole, it manifests this unerring quality when, 'from the bishops down to the last member of the laity,' it shows universal agreement in matters of faith and morals" (no. 12, p. 29).

Since Vatican II, theologians have paid more attention to the *sensus fidei* and the *sensus fidelium*, but these concepts have a long history in the Church. As a consequence of recognizing the work of the Spirit in all the baptized, it follows that the teaching role in the church is broader than just that of the hierarchical magisterium.[44] Vatican II has made the contemporary Church more aware of the important role of experience in both the moral life and the life of the Church.

This chapter has explained five noteworthy methodological aspects from Vatican II that have important repercussions for moral theology. This chapter brings to a close the consideration of five major strands in the development of moral theology. The next chapter discusses where moral theology stands today in light of these strands.

NOTES

1. Massimo Faggioli, *Vatican II: The Battle for Meaning* (New York: Paulist, 2012).

2. For these and other developments, see John W. O'Malley, *What Happened at Vatican II* (Cambridge, MA: Belknap Press of Harvard University Press, 2008), 64–92.

3. Decree on Priestly Formation, no. 16 in *Documents of Vatican II*, ed. Walter M. Abbott (New York: Guild, 1966), 452. Subsequent references to Vatican documents in the text will give the paragraph number of the document (no.) and the page number (p.) from the Abbott edition of the documents. I will change the original to avoid exclusive language.

4. Bernard Häring, *Free and Faithful: An Autobiography: My Life in the Catholic Church* (Liguori, MO: Liguori, 1998), 103.

5. Giuseppe Alberigo, "Transition to a New Age," in *A History of Vatican II*, vol. 5, *The Council and the Transition: The Fourth Period and the End of the Council, September 1965–December 1965*, ed. Giuseppe Alberigo and Joseph A. Komonchak (Maryknoll, NY: Orbis, 2006), 580–84.

6. Pope John XXIII, "Opening Speech to the Council," in *Documents of Vatican II*, ed. Abbott, 716–17.

7. O'Malley, *What Happened at Vatican II*, 44–45.

8. Alberigo, "Transition to a New Age," in *History of Vatican II*, vol. 5, ed. Alberigo, 581.

9. The following paragraphs are based on O'Malley, *What Happened at Vatican II*, 43–52, and John W. O'Malley, "Vatican II: Did Anything Happen?" in *Vatican II: Did Anything Happen?* ed. David Schultenover (New York: Continuum, 2008), 72–83.

10. Bernard Häring, *The Law of Christ: Moral Theology for Priests and Laity*, 3 vols. (Westminster, MD: Newman, 1961–66); and James F. Keenan, "Bernard Häring's Influence," *Journal of Moral Theology* 1 (2012): 23–42.

11. Charles E. Curran, *Critical Concerns in Moral Theology* (Notre Dame, IN: University of Notre Dame Press, 1984), 21.

12. Bernard Lonergan, *Collection* (New York: Herder and Herder, 1967), 252–677; Lonergan, "A Transition from a Classicist World-View to Historical Mindedness," in *Law for Liberty*, ed. James E. Biechler (Baltimore: Helicon, 1967), 126–33; John Courtney Murray, "The Declaration on Religious Freedom: Its Deeper Significance," *America* 114 (April 23, 1966): 592–93; Murray, "The Declaration on Religious Freedom," *Concilium* 15 (May 1966): 11–16; and Murray, "Appendix: Toledo Talk," in *Bridging the Sacred and the Secular: Selected Writings of John Courtney Murray*, ed. J. Leon Hooper (Washington, DC: Georgetown University Press, 1994), 335–41. See also Joann Wolski Conn, "From Certitude to Understanding: Historical Consciousness in the American Catholic Theological Community in the 1960s," (PhD diss., Columbia University, 1974).

13. O'Malley, *What Happened at Vatican II*, 37–43.

14. Jürgen Mettepenningen, *Nouvelle Theologie—New Theology, Inheritor of Modernism, Precursor of Vatican II* (New York: T&T Clark, 2010), 4–13; see also Gabriel Flynn and Paul D. Murray, eds., *Ressourcement: A Movement for Renewal in Twentieth Century Catholic Theology* (New York: Oxford University Press, 2012).

15. O'Malley, *What Happened at Vatican II*, 301–5.

16. John XXIII, "Opening Speech," in *Documents of Vatican II*, ed. Abbott, 712 and 716.

17. Alberigo, "Transitions," in *History of Vatican II*, vol. 5, ed. Alberigo and Komonchak, 578–80.

18. Pope Paul VI, *Ecclesiam suam*, no. 50, Vatican website, www.vatican.va/holy_father/paul_vi/encyclicals/documents/hf_p-vi_ence06081964_ecclesiam_en.html.

19. O'Malley, *What Happened at Vatican II*, 37.

20. The five articles published by John Courtney Murray dealing with Pope Leo's approach to religious freedom are "The Church and Totalitarian Democracy," *Theological Studies* 13 (1952): 525–63; "Leo XIII on Church and State: The General Structure of the Controversy," *Theological Studies* 14 (1953): 1–30; "Leo XIII: Separation of Church and State," *Theological Studies* 14 (1953): 145–214; "Leo XIII: Two Concepts of Government," *Theological Studies* 14 (1953): 551–67; and "Leo XIII: Two Concepts of Government, II: Government and the Order of Culture," *Theological Studies* 15 (1954): 1–33. A sixth article that existed in galley proofs was not allowed to be published by Church authority but was published after Murray's death: Murray, "Leo XIII and Pius XII: Government and the Order of Religion," in John Courtney Murray, *Religious Liberty: Catholic Struggles with Pluralism*, ed. J. Leon Hooper (Louisville, KY: Westminster/John Knox, 1993), 49–125.

21. Émile-Joseph de Smedt, "Religious Freedom," in *Council Speeches of Vatican II*, ed. Yves Congar, Hans Küng, and Daniel O'Hanlon (London: Sheed & Ward, 1964), 157–68.

22. Francis J. Connell, "Reply to Fr. Murray," *American Ecclesiastical Review* 126 (1952): 56–57; and Joseph Clifford Fenton, "Principles Underlying Traditional Church–State Doctrine," *American Ecclesiastical Review* (1952): 453.

23. John T. Noonan Jr., *A Church That Can and Cannot Change: The Development of Catholic Moral Teaching* (Notre Dame, IN: University of Notre Dame Press, 2005);

and Charles E. Curran, ed. *Change in Official Catholic Moral Teaching: Readings in Moral Theology No. 13* (New York: Paulist, 2003).

24. Murray, "Declaration on Religious Freedom: Its Deeper Significance," *America* 114 (April 23, 1966): 592–93; and Murray, "Declaration on Religious Freedom," *Concilium* 15 (May 1966): 11–16.

25. Murray, "Appendix: Toledo Talk," 335–41.

26. Charles E. Curran and Robert E. Hunt, with John F. Hunt and Terrence R. Connelly, *Dissent In and For the Church: Theologians and Humanae Vitae* (New York: Sheed & Ward, 1970), 158–69.

27. Faggioli, *Vatican II: The Battle for Its Meaning*, 66–90.

28. Mark G. McGrath, "Note storiche sulla Costituzione," in *La Chiesa nel mondo di oggi*, ed. Guilherme Baraúna, 141–56 (Florence: Vallechi, 1966); and Charles Moeller, "History of the Constitution," in *Commentary on the Documents of Vatican II*, vol. 5, *Pastoral Constitution on the Church in the Modern World*, ed. Herbert Vorgrimler, 1–70 (New York: Herder and Herder, 1969).

29. O'Malley, *What Happened at Vatican II*, 157–59.

30. Pope John Paul II, *Fides et ratio*, no. 49, in *The Encyclicals of John Paul II*, ed. J. Michael Miller (Huntington, IN: Our Sunday Visitor, 2001), 879.

31. Ibid., no. 65–68, pp. 888–90.

32. In this case I am using the official Latin of *Gaudium et spes* as found at the Vatican website: www.vatican.va/archive/hist_councils/ii_vatican_council/documents /vat-ii_const_19651207_gaudium-et-spes_lt.html.

33. For my further development of this point, see Charles E. Curran, *The Moral Theology of Pope John Paul II* (Washington, DC: Georgetown University Press, 2005), 19–25.

34. Richard P. McBrien, *The Church: The Evolution of Catholicism* (New York: HarperOne, 2008), 234–44.

35. See, for example, Richard J. Sklba, "Catholic-Jewish Relations after Forty Years," *Origins* 35/31 (January 19, 2006): 509–14.

36. McBrien, *Church*, 237.

37. Further information about these societies can be found on their respective websites.

38. Edward LeRoy Long Jr., *Academic Binding and the Social Concern: The Society of Christian Ethics 1959–83* (N.P.: Religious Ethics, 1984).

39. James M. Gustafson, *Christ and the Moral Life* (New York: Harper & Row, 1968), 98–113.

40. Paul Ramsey, *War and the Christian Conscience: How Should Modern War Be Conducted Justly* (Durham, NC: Duke University Press, 1961), 66–90.

41. Paul Lehmann, *Ethics in a Christian Context* (New York: Harper & Row, 1963), 295–302.

42. See Lisa Sowle Cahill and James F. Childress, eds., *Christian Ethics: Problems and Prospects* (Cleveland, OH: Pilgrim, 1996). The twenty-two essays in this volume were written in honor of James M. Gustafson.

43. See three books by James F. White: *Protestant Worship: Traditions in Transition* (Louisville, KY: Westminster/John Knox, 1989); *Roman Catholic Worship: Trent to*

Today (New York: Paulist, 1995); and *Christian Worship in North America: A Retrospective, 1955–1995* (Collegeville, MN: Liturgical, 1997).

44. Daniel J. Finucane, *Sensus Fidelium: The Use of a Concept in the Post-Vatican II Era* (San Francisco: International Scholars Publications, 1996); and Ormond Rush, *The Eyes of Faith: The Sense of the Faithful and the Church's Reception of Revelation* (Washington, DC: Catholic University of America Press, 2009).

CONCLUSION

Where Do We Stand Today?

AFTER AN IN-DEPTH STUDY of the five strands in the historical development of moral theology, the question naturally arises: where do we stand today and in the immediate future?

This conclusion will first consider the historical development that has occurred in the first four strands. History shows that each of these four strands has been understood quite differently in the course of history. The point was explicitly made in the long discussion of natural law, but it applies to the other strands as well. The understanding of moral theology throughout history is not the understanding of moral theology that exists today. The term "moral theology" has been used to describe the *Secunda pars* of Thomas Aquinas, the *Summae confessorum*, the *Institutiones morales*, the seminary manuals of moral theology, and the contemporary post–Vatican II approaches. There is no monolithic moral theology that has existed throughout history.

Different understandings of Thomas Aquinas's role and work have occurred in the course of history. Some Catholic scholars throughout the time after Scholasticism have continued to follow the approach of John Duns Scotus rather than Aquinas in developing Catholic theology. Even with regard to Aquinas, various interpretations have appeared. The Second Thomism beginning in the sixteenth century differed considerably from the third Thomism championed by Pope Leo XIII. In the twentieth century some scholars charged that the neo-Scholasticism of the Third Thomism was not an adequate and accurate understanding of Aquinas. Other twentieth-century Thomists have developed a transcendental understanding of Aquinas. In the first part of the twentieth century, Aquinas was understood primarily as a philosopher, but more recent Thomists insist on the theological nature of his work.

Tremendous change has occurred in the understanding of the central teaching authority in the Church. The primacy of the papal role is a relatively recent development in history. The papacy played a comparatively insignificant role in moral teaching until the post-Tridentine period. The early interventions of the papal teaching office with regard to specific moral issues in the seventeenth century tended to condemn the extreme positions and leave the rest to theological discussion. By the late nineteenth and twentieth centuries, the papacy was frequently giving authoritative teaching on specific moral issues and claiming great certitude for such positions. The emphasis in contemporary times on papal centralization has reduced considerably the teaching role of bishops and theologians that existed in earlier historical periods.

The obvious conclusion from the historical analysis is that the meanings of moral theology, Thomism, natural law, and the primary teaching authority in the Church in moral matters are not monolithic concepts. Significantly different understandings of these have appeared in different historical circumstances. In addition, one must conclude on the basis of the historical evidence that development in these areas is not seamlessly progressive. There has been continuity but also considerable discontinuity in all these areas. What exists in any historical moment including the present is not necessarily something that is better than what went before. At any stage of the historical development there is a need to analyze and criticize the present reality. The remainder of this conclusion will attempt such an analysis and criticism with regard to the strands in the development of moral theology.

The first strand considered—the relationship of moral theology to sin and penance—has changed dramatically after Vatican II. The purpose of moral theology can no longer be to train priests for their role as confessors in the sacrament of penance with the primary responsibility of judging what is sinful and the degree of sinfulness. Moral theology must develop the whole of the Christian moral life including the call to holiness and perfection.

In practice today, the sacrament of penance no longer plays a notable role in the life of Catholics as it did in the pre–Vatican II Church. In the nineteenth and twentieth centuries, before Vatican II, the sacrament of penance, called confession, was a significant part of Catholic life. Today there has been a dramatic falloff in the number of Catholics going to confession. There is a crisis in the Church today concerning the sacrament of penance or reconciliation.[1] However, sin and reconciliation remain most important aspects of Christian life despite the fact that the sacrament of penance no longer has a place in the life of many Catholics.

Church authority continues to insist that the ordinary way of celebrating the sacrament of reconciliation involves the integral confession of sins according to number and species to the priest, who will then grant absolution. In the judgment of many commentators, a good part of the crisis comes from the official Church's insistence that this is the only ordinary ritual for the sacrament. There are two related problems with the contemporary ritual for the sacrament of reconciliation—its understanding of what is sin, and its understanding of what is reconciliation.[2]

The understanding of sin found in the ritual of the sacrament of reconciliation today is the same understanding of sin as found in the manuals of moral theology—an act against the law of God. Such an understanding of sin is inadequate. Even the pre–Vatican II manuals of moral theology recognized that grave sin involved three aspects—an act involving grave matter, full advertence of the intellect, and full consent of the will.[3] In other words, the external act itself cannot be the only basis for determining whether a mortal sin has occurred. One cannot fully reconcile this legitimate recognition of the role of the person in every act with the continued insistence on the need for the confession of acts of mortal sins in their species and number. On the basis of the act alone, one cannot know for sure if the person has really committed a mortal sin.

The approach developed in chapter 1 goes much further in its understanding of sin. I insist that sin is the breaking or lessening of our multiple relationships with God, neighbor, world, and self. One cannot determine on the basis of the act itself if there is a mortal sin that breaks these relationships. The sacramental ritual itself needs to be developed in such a way that this relational understanding of sin becomes more present.

To its credit, the contemporary legislation for the sacrament as found in Pope Paul VI's 1973 *Ordo paenitentiae* now calls the sacrament "reconciliation."[4] However, the primary reality in the rite itself is still confession. As already pointed out, the ritual of the sacrament of penance has taken different forms throughout history. But in the period after Trent in the whole Church and in the United States it was generally known as confession because confession was the primary act involved. A proper theological understanding of reconciliation gives much less importance to the role of confession. The aspect of reconciliation consequently must become most prominent in the ritual itself.[5] In keeping with the emphasis on mediation in the Catholic theological tradition, reconciliation with

God takes place in and through reconciliation with the Church. The Church community is the sacrament of the saving encounter with God and Christ Jesus through the Holy Spirit. The present rite is much too individualistic. The early Church especially recognized the role of the community. The sinner is reconciled to God in and through reconciliation with a Church community.

In the end, I opt for the acceptance of a number of different rituals for the sacrament of reconciliation. Chapter 1 points out the different formats and rituals for this sacrament that have existed in the course of history. No one ritual can ever fully express the reality of the sinner's reconciliation with God and the Church. Especially in the light of our previous practice, "confession" of sin can be a deep religious experience for some individuals, but the present format needs to be expanded to incorporate more community-centered rites of reconciliation. I worry that Catholics today have lost a true sense of sin and, hence, of reconciliation. Sin cannot be identified merely with actions against the Ten Commandments. In many ways, omissions are as important as negative actions that are done. In addition, we must become more conscious of social sin and the part of all individuals in that sin. The ritual of the sacrament of penance needs to be such that it makes the Church ever more conscious of all these dimensions of sin and reconciliation. Without doubt, a formidable catechesis will be necessary to make people more conscious of this reality of sin and reconciliation, but the ritual itself can incorporate many of these aspects. Moral theology itself can no longer have the primary focus of training confessors for their role as judges in the sacrament of penance, but moral theology can help to contribute to a better understanding of sin and reconciliation.

The second strand considered in the historical development of moral theology is the role of Thomistic philosophy and theology. In the period immediately before Vatican II, papal teaching and legislation made neo-Scholasticism the Catholic approach. Vatican II, however, with the shift from defensiveness to dialogue, opened the door for Catholic theology to dialogue with a variety of philosophies and theologies. There is no one Catholic philosophy or theology anymore. However, as noted, Thomistic thought has experienced a rejuvenation and revival after Vatican II. Thomists have emphasized the theological nature of Thomas as well as his openness to historicity. Many Thomists today are trying to do for our times what Thomas did for his times. But Thomism remains only one of a large number of possible approaches to Catholic theology and philosophy.

VATICAN II AND THE EMPHASIS
ON THE THEOLOGICAL

Vatican II exerted a very strong influence on moral theology since it called for an approach that recognized the fullness of the Christian moral life and that at the same time did away with the identification of moral theology with the manuals that had served as textbooks in seminaries. Above all, the Council insisted on the need to go back to the sources with a special emphasis on scripture. It is impossible in a comparatively short treatment to indicate all the ways that Vatican II has influenced moral theology. This section concentrates on the basic shape and structure of fundamental moral theology. One might summarize the change effected by Vatican II as an insistence that moral theology be truly theological.

In this context it is helpful to distinguish between unique and distinctive aspects of Christianity and the Christian approach. Love of enemies, for example, is not unique to Christians, as others also have called for such love and even try to practice it. But it is distinctive of the Christian approach. On the other hand, to love as Jesus loved is unique to Christians. Moral theology coming from the Vatican II perspective must focus on these unique and distinctive Christian aspects.

Moral theology itself is a thematic, systematic, and critical study of the Christian moral life. As a systematic approach, there are many different ways of putting together moral theology that can be legitimate expressions of a post–Vatican II moral theology. In the following pages I indicate briefly how my approach to moral theology is based on a Vatican II understanding. In my systematization, there are five steps involved in moral theology—stance, model, subject pole, object pole, and conscience and decision making, which brings the subject and object poles together.[6]

The stance is the fundamental perspective or horizon within which the Christian ethicist and all Christians envision the reality of our world. It is the perspective from which moral theology should view what is taking place in our existence. This stance or horizon involves the five-fold Christian mysteries of creation, sin, incarnation, redemption, and resurrection destiny. Creation reminds us that all that exists is good but is finite and affected by the second element in the stance, sin. However, sin does not destroy creation but definitely distorts it. The mystery of the incarnation underscores some continuing goodness of creation in humankind because Jesus himself, in his love for us, became human and accepted the human condition. The mysteries of redemption and resurrection destiny refer to the tension between the "already" aspect of redemption and the "not yet" aspect of the eschatological fullness. This tension between the "already" and the "not yet" calls for the Christian to grow and develop in the moral life and to try to transform the world in which we live toward its eschatological fulfillment but with the realization that we will always fall quite short.

The stance thus overcomes the pre–Vatican II separation or even dichotomy between the natural order and the supernatural order. There never was such a thing as the purely natural order. It is also obvious that this stance itself comes from the unique and distinctive Christian understandings. However, the Christian aspects of creation and incarnation ground the existence of human sources of moral wisdom and knowledge that Christians share with all humankind.

The second step in developing a systematic approach to moral theology involves the model of Christian ethics, which in my judgment is a relationality–responsibility model. Philosophical ethics and some religious ethics speak of deontology, teleology, relationality, or virtue ethics as normative theories. This norm talk, however, comes from a narrow perspective that sees ethics primarily as quandary ethics. "Model" is a much broader concept than normative theory, and it summarizes the basic understanding of how the Christian moral life develops. Distinctive and unique Christian sources coincide with some common human sources as the basis for seeing the moral life in terms of the person's multiple relationships with God, neighbor, world in history and in nature, and self—and the human responsibilities within these relationships. The Trinity reminds us that the divine image of personhood is relational. The basic love command in the New Testament involves God, neighbor, and self, and thus grounds and confirms the relationality model.

The relationship to God is core. Christian ethics differs from philosophical and human ethics precisely because it understands the moral life as a grateful response to the loving gift of God, who came so that we might have life and have it more abundantly. The relationship to our neighbor involves those we encounter in our daily lives, such as our relationships to those to whom we are committed, those with whom we work and play. But the Christian understanding calls for a broader and more universal love that embraces in a special way the poor, the marginalized, and the needy. In our complex world, relationships are not just interpersonal but involve the organizations, structures, and institutions that constitute a vital part of our global existence today. The relationship to self reminds us there is a proper love of self in the Christian understanding. God calls us to friendship, which is the basis for our true happiness and fulfillment. The relationship to the world and history reminds us of our own historicity and the need for historical consciousness. The relationship to the world of nature together with the creation element of the stance grounds the ecological aspect of the Christian life as dependent on nature and creation. However, one can never forget that sin touches all these relationships.

The third step in developing my systematic moral theology concerns the subject pole of morality—the person as both subject and agent. As a subject, the person makes herself who she is and grows in these multiple relationships; as agent, the person strives to act in the context of all these different relationships. Both the stance and the model contribute to the understanding of the subject in terms of theological anthropology. The human person is an image of God, finite, sinful, and graced who lives in these relationships. The emphasis on the person is not a narrow personalism that results in an unacceptable individualism. The social and relational understanding of the human person stands as a strong criticism of the prominent individualism in the American ethos today.

The subject pole involves both the fundamental commitment of the Christian person and the virtues that modify the person as subject and agent. The basic commitment is the most important reality in the formation of the Christian person. The New Testament, especially in the Gospels, puts special emphasis on discipleship as describing this fundamental commitment. In light of the model proposed earlier, I see this fundamental commitment in light of the four relationships. The basic or fundamental relationships cannot be taken for granted but need to develop and grow. The Christian person must become ever more conscious and explicit about the importance and role of this basic commitment and its influence on all our relationships. The Vatican II recognition that all are called to holiness emphasizes the fundamental importance of this basic commitment.

One would expect post–Vatican II moral theology to have developed this fundamental option or basic commitment in great detail, but that is not the case. Catholic theologians frequently wrote about the fundamental option, but invariably such writing has been in terms of explaining the reality of mortal sin. The manuals of moral theology tended to identify mortal sin with categorical actions involving grave matter, which meant that mortal sin was a frequent occurrence in Christian moral life. But mortal sin as the breaking of the fundamental option cannot be such a frequent occurrence and cannot be totally known just from external acts. This shows that even after Vatican II, the emphasis on what constitutes sin was still quite influential in moral theology.[7] Much more needs to be said about the positive role that this basic orientation or fundamental option should play in the lives of every Christian. The baptized must become ever more conscious of how the option and orientation influence all that we are and do. I choose to develop the basic orientation or fundamental option in terms of the multiple relationships, but obviously there can be other ways of understanding this basic orientation.

In addition to the fundamental option or basic orientation of the person, the subject pole of morality involves the virtues that should characterize the life of the Christian person in terms of both personal growth in the Christian life and influencing the actions done by a person. I understand the virtues in light of the fourfold relationships. Some virtues, such as the theological virtues of faith, hope, and love, as well as the virtues of creativity and fidelity, involve all four relationships.

There is not enough space here to develop the virtues with regard to all the four relationships, but a brief mention of the relationship to God will suffice. The two most important virtues in this relationship are openness to receive the gift of God's love and gratitude and thanksgiving for this gift. Such virtues correspond with the basic reality that the Christian life is our response to the life-giving gift of God through Jesus Christ in the Holy Spirit. Openness is the fundamental commitment to receive the gift of God and is rooted in the scriptural understanding of the poor in spirit. Gratitude for the gifts shows itself above all in thanksgiving, worship, and praise of God. The unique and distinctive Christian aspects have their greatest role to play with regard to the subject pole of ethics but with the realization that they do not deny our basic humanity but bring it to its fullness.

The basic orientation and virtues of the Christian person raise considerations that have often been treated under the heading of spiritual and ascetical theology. Vatican II reminded us that all Christians are called to the fullness of holiness, so all must strive for continual growth or conversion. Prayer and the spiritual and corporal works of mercy are important ways of growing in this orientation and in the panoply of Christian virtues. In addition, the liturgy has a fundamental role in nurturing and developing the Christian life. The liturgy celebrates the gift of God's love as well as the call to action in personal and social life. Just as we celebrate in the liturgy the risen Jesus's body that was broken and blood that was poured out for us, so too by active participation in the liturgy we commit ourselves to be persons whose body is broken and whose blood is poured out for others. The liturgy is the celebration of God's gift to us, and it reminds us of our special concern for all those who are hungry, poor, or needy. Even after Vatican II, moral theology has not given enough emphasis to these dimensions of the Christian life.

The object pole refers to the values, principles, and norms that guide life in the world. Principles are generally understood to be more general than norms, which are more specific or are determinations of broader principles. For example, the principle that life is to be respected is a basis for the norm that capital punishment is wrong. Since the object pole includes the world in which we live with all people of different or no religions, by its very nature it does not involve the unique or distinctive Christian aspects as much as the subject pole. Nevertheless, these aspects still have a significant place in a consideration of the object pole in Christian theological ethics. Think, for example, of the Christian values of love, mercy, forgiveness, justice, and concern for the poor. There are also principles such as the preferential option for the poor and the fact that the goods of creation exist to serve the needs of all God's people and respect for the person of others that have a significant role to play in the object pole. The area of norms remains a very significant and contentious issue in moral theology today and cannot be treated in any depth in this volume.

The fifth step in developing my systematic approach to moral theology involves conscience, which brings together the subject pole and the object pole in concrete decision making. Here the unique and distinctive Christian aspects have a more important place than is often recognized. The manuals of moral theology, for example, saw conscience as the subjective norm of morality in obedience to the objective norm of law, with a heavy emphasis on natural law. But scripture and the Christian tradition have developed what is often called the discernment of the spirit or discernment of spirits as a way to determine what is God's will. In the New

Testament the Holy Spirit is closely associated with determining the will of God for our life and actions. The New Testament also recognizes other spirits whose influence can be good or bad. Subsequent commentators on the Christian spiritual life such as Ignatius of Loyola and Francis de Sales have written much about the discernment of spirits. It is true that in earlier times people spoke much more about the role of these spirits (e.g., angels and demons), whereas today we would tend to see them primarily as natural causes, such as our inspirations and feelings. But what the early spiritual writers have said about the discernment of spirits and the discernment of the Holy Spirit can be applied to our understanding of conscience today.[8]

What are the criteria that spiritual writers have used to determine the discernment of spirits? An obvious criterion is the fact that by their fruits you will know them. Good spirits produce good fruits, whereas bad spirits result in bad fruits. Ignatius of Loyola and others also emphasize interior peace as a criterion for discerning spirits and the will of God. They recognize there is danger of a false peace, but in keeping with an old axiom, possible abuse does not take away legitimate use. The recognition of the role of interior peace in discerning the will of God coheres with what human experience as well as philosophy and psychology have taught us about the peace of a good conscience.[9] With regard to subsequent conscience (conscience after the act has been done), people often refer to the remorse of a bad conscience. The criterion of a good conscience decision, thus, is peace and joy. Such an approach does not in any way deny the importance of using all the moral means of determining what should be done. True peace and joy come only after one has assiduously used all means to determine what is a good decision.

In terms of the general development of moral theology as a whole, Vatican II's primary and quite inclusive contribution has been the attention to the sources of the discipline and the emphasis on the unique and distinctive aspects of moral theology. In this section I have briefly shown how my approach to fundamental moral theology illustrates the influence of Vatican II. However, there are many possible ways of structuring a post–Vatican II moral theology.

THE CRISIS OF DISSENT FROM OR
DISAGREEMENT WITH PAPAL TEACHING

Much can be said about the strands of natural law and papal moral teaching, but this conclusion focuses on how the strands of natural law and papal moral teaching come together to form what John Paul II called a genuine crisis. This crisis arises from "the *lack of harmony between the traditional response of the Church and certain theological positions*, encountered even in seminaries and in faculties of theology, *with regard to questions of the greatest importance* for the Church and for the life of faith of Christians, as well as for the life of society itself" (emphasis in the original).[10] John Paul II recognizes that the crisis is not only between theologians and hierarchical magisterium but also involves the life of the Christian people. Brief summaries and some conclusions from the strands of natural law and papal moral teaching will explain the reasons for the crisis.

The conclusions from the historical study of natural law that are applicable to the present crisis come first from the reality that the natural law as a coherent theory with an agreed upon body of ethical content existing throughout history has never existed even in the Catholic tradition. The approach of Thomas Aquinas to natural law differs from that of other Scholastics. Discussions about the theological character of natural law go back as far as Gratian in the twelfth century. Cardinal Ratzinger's understanding of the evidentiary nature of natural law differs remarkably from what is found in papal moral and social teaching in the nineteenth and twentieth centuries. In addition, within the ambit of papal teaching itself, there is a significant difference between the methodological approach found in papal sexual teaching and the methodological approach found in papal social teaching. Chapter 3 describes the three different approaches to natural law in the Catholic tradition today—the neo-Scholastic, the new natural law theory, and the revisionist. While the new natural law theory strongly supports the conclusions of papal moral teachings, it explicitly recognizes that its own method is neither neo-Scholastic nor Thomistic.

In addition, a number of ambiguities about natural law have surfaced in the study of its historical development. A broad discernment process has been more predominant than natural law theory in arriving at Catholic moral teachings. It is not just a one-way street from theory to practice. Natural law can refer either to a method or to conclusions, but papal moral teaching emphasizes the conclusion aspect of natural law. In theory, the Catholic tradition emphasizes that authority must conform itself to the truth. But *Humanae vitae* indicates that the teaching authority of the Church and not reason was the ultimate factor in Pope Paul VI's continued condemnation of artificial contraception. The Catholic tradition has recognized that the conclusions of natural law are not always certain and true, but the papal teaching office does not explicitly recognize this aspect of the tradition.

The strand of Vatican II developed historical consciousness and the emphasis on the person as two of the five important aspects emerging from the Council. As discussed earlier, a more historically conscious method together with the centrality of the person and the person's relationships would come to different conclusions from the existing papal teaching on some important sexual issues. The emphasis on the person argues against the physicalism that identifies the human, moral, and personal act with the physical structure of the act. The emphasis on the person also opposes an anthropology that maintains the rational and the personal cannot interfere with the inclinations that human beings share with all animals. Thus, for all these reasons, Catholic revisionist moral theologians have disagreed with some of the natural law–based papal teaching, especially the intrinsic evil of contraception, sterilization, masturbation, homosexual acts between committed persons, and artificial insemination.[11]

Papal moral teaching appeals not only to its natural law basis but also to the teaching authority that belongs to the papal teaching office. This section only deals with dissent, or the possibility of teaching being wrong, with regard to the general category of noninfallible moral teaching. Whether or not dissent is acceptable on specific issues requires an in-depth analysis of each particular issue.

Five reasons, most of which have been developed in earlier chapters, ground the possibility of error in noninfallible teaching and the possibility of dissent. The first reason is the language itself. Only in the nineteenth century, with the proclamation of papal infallibility, did the distinction become common between infallible and noninfallible teaching. One owed the assent of faith to infallible teaching, and a religious assent of intellect and will to noninfallible teaching. But noninfallible teaching by its very definition is fallible.

Second, the moral teaching of the Catholic Church including the papacy on specific moral issues has changed in the course of history. As often mentioned, change has occurred on a number of significant issues: religious freedom, democracy, human rights, slavery, taking interest on a loan, the right of defendants to silence, the role of pleasure in marital intercourse, the role of the intention of procreation in marital intercourse, the role of women in society. Thus, change has occurred on such teachings as a matter of fact.[12]

Third, the manuals of dogmatic theology in the time frame between Vatican I (1870) and Vatican II recognized that noninfallible teaching could be wrong according to the now-classic study of Joseph A. Komonchak. Vatican II itself referred to these authors and their positions. A question to the Doctrinal Commission of the Council invoked the case at least theoretically possible in which an educated person, confronted with a teaching proposed noninfallibly, cannot for solid reasons give internal assent to such a teaching. The answer from the Doctrinal Commission was short and simple: in this case, consult the approved authors. These authors, studied by Komonchak, recognize that one does not always have to give such internal assent but generally do not discuss the broader question of public dissent by theologians.[13]

Fourth, ecclesiological considerations, especially in the light of Vatican II, put the papal teaching office within a broader context. The pope has a special teaching office (often called authoritative from the Latin word *authenticum*) in the Church, but the papal teaching office is not the only teaching role in the Church. The primary teacher in the Church is the Holy Spirit. The Dogmatic Constitution on the Church insists that all who are baptized through the Spirit share in the threefold office of Jesus as priest, teacher, and ruler (no. 9–12, Abbott, pp. 24–30). In light of this, Catholic theology recognizes both the *sensus fidelium* and the role of reception in the Church. The *sensus fidelium* is the sense of the faith as found in all the members of the Church. "Reception" refers to the fact that authoritative Church teaching has to be received by the whole Church. These are two practical applications of the realization that all the baptized have some teaching role in the Church.[14]

The First Vatican Council dealt only with papal primacy and infallibility without having time to mention the role of bishops. Vatican II and the Constitution on the Church remedied this by having chapter 3 of the document deal with the episcopate. Bishops are not just vicars or agents of the pope. They are constituted as bishops by their sacramental consecration. This chapter especially emphasizes the role of the collegiality of bishops in the Church. The order of bishops is the successor to the college of Apostles in teaching authority and pastoral rule. Together with the head of the body (the Roman pontiff) and never without the head, the college of bishops is the subject of supreme and full power over the universal Church. In addition, each individual bishop also has a solicitude for the Church universal (no. 22–23, Abbott, pp. 42–46).

There is also the role of theologians, which has been discussed earlier, that has always had a place in the teaching function of the Church. There is no doubt that in earlier times theologians enjoyed a much more official teaching role, but Vatican II recognized the important role that theologians played. It is very fascinating that in retrospect more attention is given today to what theologians had to say about Vatican II than what individual bishops said. The bishops learned quite a bit from the theologians at the time of the Council. This recognition of the many different teaching roles in the Church underscores the need for the papal and hierarchical teaching offices to be in dialogue with the baptized, with theologians, and even with those outside the Church in its quest for moral truth. The failure to engage in such dialogue makes error in such teaching all the more possible.

As developed earlier, Vatican II moved away from a monarchical understanding of the Church to a recognition of the Church as the people of God and a "communion" ecclesiology.[15] Unfortunately, the Church still often operates in practice as a papal monarchy. The failure to live out the theory of Vatican II has created many tensions in the Church today, including the tensions between theologians and the hierarchical teaching office. In the last three decades or so, the Congregation for the Doctrine of the Faith has condemned in one form or another a good number of Catholic moral theologians throughout the world. Negative actions have also been taken against other Catholic theologians, but moral theology has received greater attention.[16] By the very nature of the two functions of the hierarchical teaching office and the theological role, one should expect that some tensions will always exist. Such tensions are a sign of life, but they should not cause a crisis.

John Paul II correctly recognized that the crisis of moral theology affects the life of people in the Church to a considerable degree. Ordinary Catholics face these moral issues in their daily lives. Many recent polls indicate that Catholics in theory and in practice disagree with specific Church moral teachings, especially in the area of sexuality. One example will suffice to show the extent of the problem. A team of well-respected Catholic sociologists have been conducting polls of Catholics in the United States from 1987 to 2011, raising the same questions each time. One basic question has been: who should have the final say about what is right or wrong—Church teaching, individuals, or both? There were five specific areas connected with this question—divorce and remarriage, abortion, sex outside of marriage, homosexuality, and contraception. The percentage of respondents saying that Church leaders should have the final decision in these matters has decreased since the poll was first taken in 1987. Today, the highest percentage of respondents who maintain that Church leaders should have the final say is 20 percent on the issue of divorce and remarriage. On three questions, more than 50 percent of the respondents maintain that the individual should have the final say.[17] From the perspective of the hierarchical teaching office, these attitudes and practices of Catholics in the United States certainly constitute a grave crisis.

Perhaps the best illustration of how the hierarchical magisterium should function in its search for moral truth comes from the procedures adopted by the US Catholic bishops in their two pastoral letters on peace and war in 1983 and on the economy in 1986. In the process of writing these documents, the bishops' committees engaged in a broad and in-depth dialogue with experts in the field, theoreticians and practitioners, and theologians. The documents themselves went through a number of drafts, and each draft was made public. As a result, there was much dialogue and discussion going on within the whole Church with regard to these documents, which were finally issued by the United States bishops. Unfortunately, at the present time papal documents are not developed in a similar manner. Obviously, there are people who draft these documents, but for the most part they are a small group whose identity is not known at the time of the writing. The papal teaching office would have greater credibility if it would engage in a more extensive and public dialogue than it has done up to the present. At the very least, popes should consult bishops throughout the world in a meaningful way.

Fifth, what is the nature of authoritative teaching? There is no doubt that, in the Catholic tradition, papal teaching has been very closely connected with the governing or ruling role, but there are very significant differences between the role of governing and the role of teaching.[18] Human teaching and governing are two very distinct functions. The teacher seeks the truth; the governor seeks the good order of society. A close connection between teaching and governing distorts the teaching role. Law comes from authority and is authoritatively imposed on members of society. But the function of teaching in the Church as described earlier recognizes different teaching roles in the Church. Obviously, someone in the role of Church authority makes the final decision but there must be a thoroughgoing dialogue before a final decision is made.[19]

Teaching, however, should not be restricted only to giving answers to questions. Today, we realize the good teacher is not necessarily the answer person but the one who raises questions and tries to make her students think and act with a broader and deeper horizon. Law, by its very nature, calls for obedience on the part of subjects. Those who do not obey are punished. Law thus has a degree of practical certitude; you may question it, but you have to obey it. But teaching aims at enlightening another. Teaching should not primarily follow the model of a command-and-obey approach. Without doubt, a governing model of teaching tends to claim too much certitude for what it proposes.

There is a problem with the very terminology of "authoritative teaching." At the very least, teaching in the Church is authoritative not because it comes from a particular power but because it proposes the truth. An earlier section insisted on the important aspect of intrinsic morality proposed by Thomas Aquinas. Something is commanded because it is good and never the other way around. The danger with the concept of authoritative teaching is that the authority claims to make something true or right. Recall that in *Humanae vitae* Pope Paul VI maintained that the ultimate reason why he could not change the teaching was because this would go against what the authoritative papal magisterium had taught.

Other Authority Problems

The exercise of papal teaching authority on moral matters is not the only manifestation of authority problems in the Church today. There is a growing dissatisfaction within the Catholic Church with regard to a number of issues involving Church authority. The child sex abuse scandal in the Church has caused many problems. One important part of the problem concerns the way that Church authority has dealt with the problem. The primary concern for the good name and reputation of the Church and not for the need to protect innocent children seemed to be the guiding principle. Pedophile priests were often moved from one parish to another without telling the people of the parish about the problem. Yet little or no disciplinary action was ever taken against bishops who tried to hide the existence of pedophile priests.

Many Catholic women (and males as well) are upset with the very subordinate role of women in the Catholic Church today. In practically every other area of social life, the contemporary world has recognized the equality and rights of women. The first world is experiencing a growing problem involving the shortage of priests. For this and other reasons, many voices are calling for a married priesthood. Many Catholics also insist on a greater voice in the appointment of bishops and in the way in which the Church itself is run. In connection with these particular issues, many different reform groups in the Church are calling for change.[20]

In this context a very notable development in the Western world has been groups of priests who have challenged their bishops and the pope to bring about change in the Church. In a true sense, priests are often caught in the middle. They are the ones who deal directly with God's people but often experience the conflict between the present official policies of the Church and what they believe to be the true needs of the people of God. On Trinity Sunday, June 19, 2011, a group of Austrian priests representing more than 10 percent of all Austrian diocesan clergy issued a very strong "priests' initiative," titled "Appeal to Disobedience." Long-needed reforms and inaction by bishops demand that priests act independently and follow their consciences even in disobedience of some existing Church regulations. The signers pledged that they would not deny communion to people of good will, especially divorced and remarried people and members of other churches. They would avoid as much as possible celebrating multiple times on Sundays, which the bishops think is required because of the shortage of priests. They would ignore the prohibition against preaching by competently trained laity, including women. They would advocate for a married clergy including women priests.[21] Theirs is a very strong statement by a significant number of Austrian priests, and no one at this time knows what its continuing and future effects will be.

The Irish Association of Catholic Priests was organized to provide an opportunity for Irish Catholic priests to engage proactively in the crucial debates taking place in the Church and Irish society. The association supports full implementation of the vision and teaching of Vatican II with special emphasis on the primacy of the individual conscience, the status and active participation of all the baptized, and the task of establishing a Church where all believers will be treated as equals. In particular, it supports a number of issues: redesigning the ministry of the Church to incorporate the gifts of all, both male and female; restructuring the governing system of a Church based on service and not on power; encouraging at every level a culture of consultation and transparency, especially for Church leaders; and reevaluating Catholic sexual teaching and practice

that recognizes the profound mystery of human sexuality and the experience and wisdom of God's people.[22]

The documents from these two priests' groups summarize the problems that many reform-minded Catholics have with the present policies
and structures of the Church. There can be no doubt that a significant
number of Catholics are involved in the reform movement in the Church,
but these groups involve only a comparatively small minority of the total
Church. However, they constitute a voice that wants to be listened to.
The existence of such groups, especially priests' groups, is an important
phenomenon in the life of the Catholic Church. For the purposes of this
book, problems with authority in the Church thus involve more than
moral issues, and these problems and issues play an important role in the
lives of some Catholics, especially those who minister on a local level.

Why Is There an Authority Problem?

What precisely is the nature of the authority problem in the Catholic
Church today and how did it arise? In my judgment, the problem comes
from the fact that Vatican II changed our understanding of the Church,
but the present Code of Canon Law and the existing practices in the
Church do not reflect in structure and policy the understanding of Vatican II. The present structures in the Church still insist on a centralization
of power in the papal office.

According to Richard McBrien, the changes in the understanding of
the Church at Vatican II were quite thorough. The Church is now considered a mystery or sacrament and not primarily an institution. Rather
than identifying the Church with the hierarchy, the Church is now the
people of God. The Church is understood as a communion and not as an
absolute monarchy.[23] Unfortunately, the Code of Canon Law promulgated in 1983 and other papal legislation does not adequately incorporate
the Vatican II understanding of the Church as a communion. In the
words of Eugenio Corecco, the Code of Canon Law does not give primacy to the ecclesiology of *communio* but still relies also on what Corecco
calls an ecclesiology of *societas*, that is, the Church as a society comparable
to human societies with powers given to office holders.[24] Ladislas Örsy is
even stronger in his criticism of the Code and contemporary policies for
not incorporating the centrality of the communion ecclesiology.[25] In my
judgment the Church and the practice of the Church today still stresses
the centralization of power and authority in the papal office.

As mentioned earlier, Vatican II overcame the one-sided emphasis on the papacy after Vatican I, which was cut short before any consideration of the role of bishops. Vatican II emphasized three points about the role of bishops—the role of the college of bishops with regard to governing the whole Church, the role of national and regional conferences of bishops throughout the world, and the role of the individual bishop who also has a solicitude for the universal Church. Unfortunately, the present laws and policies of the Catholic Church do not carry out the recognition of these conciliar approaches to the role of bishops.

In 1965, Pope Paul VI, with the *motu proprio, Apostolica sollicitudo*, established the institution of the Synod of Bishops. The new Code of Canon Law develops the structures of the synod in canons 342–48. There have been thirteen ordinary synods since Vatican II. There is a permanent general secretariat for the Synod of Bishops in Rome. However, according to the way it was set up by Pope Paul VI, the synod itself has only consultative power. The synod exists only to give counsel and advice to the pope.[26] But if the synod were truly an exercise of collegiality in the Church, it should have the power to share in the governing of the Church and not just give advice to the pope.

One of the developments after Vatican II was the role of national and regional conferences of bishops. These conferences had a great impact on the life of the local Church and also of the Church universal. In the United States the pastoral letters of the US bishops on peace (1983) and the economy (1986) had a great impact not only on the local and universal Church but also on public opinion in the United States. CELAM, the Latin American Episcopal Conference, issued a document in 1968 on liberation theology that exerted considerable influence in Latin America and throughout the Catholic world. These conferences were seen as limited participations on a national or regional level of the collegiality of bishops.[27]

There was some doubt in the Code of Canon Law about the exact nature and authority of these conferences. In 1988, the Vatican issued a draft document on the theological and canonical status of bishops' conferences that was criticized strongly by some bishops, theologians, and canonists for unnecessarily limiting the role of the conferences. But the final 1998 document, *Apostolicos suos*, continued in the same vein. A key provision of the document requires that doctrinal declarations of conferences must be unanimously approved by the bishops who are members of the conference, or they require approval by the Vatican if at least two-thirds of the bishops have approved. But absolute unanimity is practically impossible. Even in the election of a pope there is no such requirement of absolute unanimity. This legislation puts in doubt the role of bishops' conferences. On the other hand, such an approach is in accord with the already existing requirement at that time that canonical and liturgical decisions by episcopal conferences need Vatican approval. Thus, the Vatican, not the US bishops or English-speaking bishops, has had the final say about the translation of liturgical texts.[28] This is another illustration of the greater centralization that has occurred in the Catholic Church in the post–Vatican II period.

A third serious limitation with regard to the role of bishops in Church policy today comes from the way in which bishops are selected and those who are appointed as bishops. It is only since the nineteenth century that the pope has appointed practically all the bishops in the Church. The local clergy and laity played a significant role in the selection of bishops until the ninth century. After that time, their role decreased somewhat as secular rulers began to have primary power in the appointment of bishops. The Gregorian reform in the eleventh century fought against this lay investiture, which meant that secular rulers appointed bishops and other offices in the Church. After this period there was again an important role for local clergy in the appointment of bishops, but by the nineteenth century the pope made the appointment of most of the bishops in the world. Even in the first millennium, when the local clergy and laity played the primary role, the bishop of Rome received these candidates into communion with the universal Church.[29]

Especially since the papacy of John Paul II beginning in 1978, the bishops appointed by the popes have been of a very conservative bent. According to Richard McBrien, they are known for their readiness to do what they are told by the Vatican. Those who are appointed bishops have never said anything against existing Church policies and practices. McBrien sees this new breed of bishops as bringing about a crisis of leadership in the Catholic Church today as exemplified in the reaction of the bishops to pedophile priests. These bishops hold on to the status quo and are not responsive to the pastoral challenges raised by their own priests, religious, and laity. When a few individual bishops have spoken out, they have been forced to resign. As a result, the Church in the United States and in the world is not responding to the real pastoral needs of the present time.[30]

In light of the role of local bishops both individually and collegially in the Church, they should be the ones who respond to the practical needs of the Church on the basis of the contemporary understanding and experience, and should contribute this understanding for the whole college of bishops and the pope. However, today all policies and teachings in the Church come from the top down, and there is no room for the knowledge and experience that is happening in pastoral practice to come from the ground up. The inability of bishops to bring to the attention of the Church as a whole what is occurring in contemporary pastoral practice has contributed to the leadership problem (if one does not want to use the word "crisis") that exists in the Church today.

There is no doubt that the role of bishops, both individually and collectively, in the Church today contrasts unfavorably with the role in the immediate Vatican II time frame. For our purposes, a good illustration concerns the approach of two different bishops' conferences to the possibility of noninfallible papal teaching being wrong and the role of theological dissent. As mentioned earlier, in a letter on September 22, 1967, the German bishops in discussing noninfallible Church teaching explicitly recognized that "this teaching authority of the Church can, and on occasion actually does, fall into errors." Noninfallible teachings involve a certain element of the provisional even to the point of being capable of including error.[31] In their response to *Humanae vitae* and the theological dissent that occurred in this country, the US bishops in a pastoral letter in 1968 recognized a lawful freedom of inquiry and of thought and the legitimacy of theological dissent when three conditions are met—the reasons are well founded, the manner of dissent does not impugn the magisterium, and no scandal is given.[32] Neither individual bishops nor conferences of bishops have recently made similar statements about the possibility of error in noninfallible teaching and the legitimacy of theological dissent under certain conditions.

What about the role of the laity? As noted, according to Vatican II all the baptized share in the threefold office of Jesus as priest, teacher, and ruler. After Vatican II the laity have played a much greater role in the life of the Church. Laypersons have a very visible function in the liturgical life of the Church serving as readers and ministers of communion. Laypeople administer many Catholic organizations and structures, such as Catholic Charities and Catholic hospitals. Laypeople serve on boards and councils of the local Church, even though their role is only advisory.

However, the present Code of Canon Law stands in some contrast with this development. It excludes laypersons from significant decision-making processes where ecclesiastical jurisdiction is in play. The appropriate canon here is canon 129.

> Canon 129 no. 1. Those who have received sacred orders are qualified, according to the norm of the prescripts of the law, for the power of governance, which exists in the Church by divine institution and is also called the power of jurisdiction.
>
> no. 2. Lay members of the Christian faithful can cooperate in the exercise of this same power according to the norm of the law.[33]

This means that the power of governance in the Church belongs only to those who have received sacred orders, and no layperson is able to exercise this power. Laypeople can cooperate with the ordained but cannot participate in the power of governance.

Ladislas Örsy maintains that such a neat and radical exclusion of laypersons from participation in governance is truly an innovation and goes against an immemorial tradition of the Church. Structures that were once recognized as legitimate, such as laypersons voting in ecumenical councils and abbesses governing particular areas, are not acceptable according to this canon. This sharply draws the line between the ordained and the nonordained and excludes the laity from governance roles in the Church.[34]

The existing structure and policies in the Church today strongly support the centralization of the Church in the papacy. Laypersons cannot share in the power of governing. The power and role of bishops have been curtailed, emphasizing the all-embracing role of the papacy. Thus, in the current structures and policies of Church governance we see the papalization of the Church. Without doubt, this contributes to the problem and even crisis of authority in the Church today.

Responses to the Authority Problem

What are the options available for Catholics who disagree with authoritative moral teachings or with other policies or practices in the Church? With regard to moral teachings, there are three possibilities, and these three are not necessarily exclusive: decide in conscience that one can act against a teaching; try to bring about change in the Church; or decide to leave the Catholic Church.

Many Catholics do disagree with and act against official Church teaching but still consider themselves Catholic. The obvious example here concerns contraception. Statistics show that Catholic spouses use artificial contraception in just about the same numbers as non-Catholics in the United States.[35] These couples have solved the problem in the internal forum of conscience. They came to the judgment that one can practice artificial contraception and still be a loyal Roman Catholic. In my understanding, one should not appeal in this case simply to the primacy of conscience. Yes, in the Catholic tradition, one has to follow one's conscience, but conscience can be wrong. Society at large, for example, has not accepted the argument of those accused of war crimes who say they were following their conscience. In the particular case of contraception, there are reasons to justify the possibility of dissent that might not be present in other issues. Yes, a decision is made in the forum of conscience, but it should be an informed conscience. Divorced and remarried Catholics have often made similar judgments to fully participate in the Eucharistic life of the Church. Likewise, some gay and lesbian couples have made the same decision. In the area of controverted moral issues within the Church, a pastoral solution to the problem exists so that one can disagree with the teaching and still consider oneself to be a loyal Catholic.

Such a solution, however, does not exist in the area of structural issues such as clerical celibacy and the ordination of women. Here we are dealing not with the internal forum, as in the controverted moral issues, but with the external forum or the existing structures in the Church. Some people claim that they can disagree here in practice, but in the eyes of the hierarchical Church they no longer belong to the Catholic community. This is the difference between issues that in practice can be solved in the internal forum and those structural issues that cannot be. But there still exists some tension in the internal forum solutions to controversial moral issues. The difference between the practice of some Catholics and the hierarchical teaching creates problems of credibility for the Church and tends to weaken the credibility of the hierarchical Church across the board.

A third option is to leave the Catholic Church. In general, the Catholic Church in the United States faces a crisis in terms of the number of Catholics who have left the Church. The US Religious Landscape Survey by the Pew Research Center's Forum on Religion & Public Life reported that one out of three people who were brought up as Catholics in the United States are no longer Catholic. One out of every ten Americans is an ex-Catholic. However, the overall number of Catholics in the United States has stayed about the same because of the large influx of Hispanics.[36]

Why do Catholics leave the Church? In 1976, Andrew M. Greeley and other sociologists on the basis of research done by the National Opinion Research Center (NORC) concluded that *Humanae vitae* "seems to have been the occasion for massive apostasy and for a notable decline in religious devotion and belief." The sociological team did not begin its study with the intention of showing that *Humanae vitae* explained the deterioration of American Catholic belief and practice. In fact, Andrew Greeley, the principal investigator, had earlier invoked other reasons for the decline.[37]

In late fall 2011, in an informal inquiry, William J. Byron and Charles Zech surveyed nearly three hundred non-church-going Catholics in the diocese of Trenton, New Jersey, to understand why they no longer went to Mass on Sunday. They report many reasons given without ranking their importance. They include the exclusion of women from ordination, the perception that persons of homosexual orientation are unwelcome in the Church, the complexity of the annulment process, and the barring of divorced and remarried persons from the sacraments.[38]

The most recent scientifically based study was a follow-up study by the Pew Research Center in 2009 and revised in 2011. This study divided those Catholics who left the Church into two different groups of about the same number—those who are now unaffiliated religiously and those who joined Protestant churches. Two types of questions were asked of both groups. The first was a set of "yes" or "no" questions that asked about the factors that led them to leave the Catholic Church. Among the responses, 65 percent who are now unaffiliated checked "Stopped believing in the religion's teachings," and 43 percent checked "Spiritual needs not being met." And 71 percent of those who are now Protestant checked "Spiritual needs not being met," while 50 percent checked, "Stopped believing in the religion's teachings." The second question was an open-ended question asking them to explain in their own words the reasons why they left Catholicism. Half of the unaffiliated gave an explanation related to religious and moral beliefs. Four in ten of the now Protestant gave the same answer.[39]

There are many reasons why people leave the Catholic Church, and we will probably never know precisely why or what reasons are the most important, but moral teachings play a significant role. The studies mentioned here concern only the United States. There is a serious decline in Catholic membership in the Western world. Also in Latin America, Pentecostal churches are making serious inroads. However, the Church continues to grow and expand in Africa.

Reaction of the Hierarchical Church

How has the hierarchical Church reacted to the strong disagreements within the Church on moral and structural issues? The hierarchical Church has not made or even intimated any possible changes in its moral teachings and policies.

From the viewpoint of the authoritative nature of the teachings, significant differentiations exist among the issues mentioned. The law of clerical celibacy is a human-made law that therefore can change if there are appropriate reasons for doing so. Most of the moral issues are based on the natural law, which, according to Catholic understanding, is a participation in the eternal law of God. As mentioned, the ordination of women according to hierarchical teaching is a matter of divine law and according to some is an infallible teaching.

From such a perspective the easiest change is to the celibacy rule for priests. A primary reason for changing this rule is the shortage of priests, especially in the Western world. This obviously affects the Christian people as a whole but also puts a heavier burden on those who are now priests. However, the Vatican continues to assert the importance and need for priestly celibacy.[40] Among the moral issues, the condemnation of artificial contraception has affected the most people. The vast majority of Catholics spouses do not follow this teaching at the present time. However, there are no signs whatsoever that the hierarchical Church is anticipating a change in this teaching. It is safe to conclude that if the Church leadership will not change the teaching on artificial contraception, it will not change on any of the other controversial moral issues.

Not only does the hierarchical Church continue to support these moral teachings but it has insisted that law and public policy go along with such Catholic moral teaching on some specific issues. The Catholic approach to law and public policy in this area has called much more attention to these moral teachings. The Catholic Church in the United States and throughout the world has been the primary institution to oppose legalized abortion. Likewise, the Catholic Church has strongly opposed same-sex unions in this country and throughout the world. Even in the area of contraception in Catholic countries such as the Philippines, the

Church has vociferously opposed government-supported family-planning programs.[41] In the United States in 2012, the Catholic bishops strongly opposed a compromise solution proposed by President Obama that religious institutions (e.g., Catholic universities and hospitals) would be exempt from paying for contraception health care insurance benefits for employees, but women working in these institutions would not be denied contraceptive coverage.[42]

Catholic theology has recognized significant differences between the moral order and the legal order. Among other aspects, it might sometimes be necessary and even helpful for the common good to make some compromises.[43]

Why is the papal magisterium unwilling to admit that its moral teaching has been wrong? Why is the hierarchical magisterium so reluctant to admit the legitimacy of theological dissent from noninfallible teaching? There are no simple or easy answers to these questions. Without a doubt, control and power come into play here. However, in disagreeing with the position of another, I have always thought that one should try to recognize the strongest reason for the position with which you disagree. So, what is the best argument for not changing Church teaching on these issues and not explicitly acknowledging dissent?

An appropriate way into a response to this question is to try to fathom the mindset behind Pope Paul VI's position described earlier, that because of the teaching authority of the Church he could not change the teaching that condemns artificial contraception for spouses. The Catholic Church believes that the Holy Spirit assists the hierarchical teaching office. The whole purpose of the Holy Spirit is to help the Church in its various roles—in this case, its teaching role. Could the Holy Spirit ever allow the Church to teach something that was wrong? This would mean that instead of the Church trying to help people in their earthly lives, it was actually hurting people by its teaching. Would the Holy Spirit allow the Church to be wrong on such significant and important issues and thus be a source of harm to its members?

The above argument is forceful. Even the Second Vatican Council, as noted earlier, could not admit that the Church's teaching on religious liberty was wrong. The Council fathers ultimately followed the approach of John Courtney Murray, which was that historical circumstances had changed. In the light of the historical circumstances in the nineteenth century, the teaching of Pope Leo XIII opposing religious liberty was correct. However, in the changed circumstances of the twentieth century, the Church now can and should accept religious freedom.

In fact, as mentioned earlier, official Church teaching on a number of very significant specific moral issues has changed. This change was not simply a development but a true change whereby the previous teaching was recognized to be wrong. Part of the problem also comes from the fact that the hierarchical magisterium itself has claimed too great a certitude for its teaching. It should have pointed out that its teaching on these specific issues is a noninfallible teaching. The assistance of the Holy Spirit in no way substitutes for all the human ways of arriving at moral truth. The hierarchical magisterium must use human reason and experience and must consult as widely and deeply as possible. Since the traditional Catholic notion of mediation recognizes that the Holy Spirit works in and through the human, one cannot appeal to the assistance of the Holy Spirit to claim a greater certitude than the matter itself is capable of having. Yes, one can readily recognize the force of the reasoning that the Holy Spirit would not allow the hierarchical Church to be in error or to claim too great a certitude for its teaching, but part of the problem here comes from the way in which the hierarchical magisterium itself has functioned in this teaching role.

There would be strong negative effects if the hierarchical magisterium were willing to admit that some of its teachings had been erroneous or that it had claimed too great a certitude for them. Many people would be deeply hurt. Think, for example, of those who struggled in their marriage to be faithful to the teachings that condemn artificial contraception or divorce and remarriage. Those people obviously suffered and endured many difficulties in order to be faithful to the Church's teaching. I am sure that a good number of Catholics would be very angry with the Church if it were to admit error in some of these significant, specific moral issues. Such a change might easily be the occasion for many leaving the Church. To admit that papal teaching has been wrong on a number of issues also raises grave problems about the credibility of papal teaching on other issues.

There are no easy and simple responses to these possible effects coming from admitting that a papal teaching was wrong or claimed too great a certitude. At the very minimum, a concerted and sensitive pastoral ministry would have to be directed to those who were hurt or disillusioned by such a change. Such a ministry would have to appeal to the generosity, forgiveness, and large-heartedness of the people involved. I am reminded of a conversation I had with a married colleague on the faculty of Catholic University at the time of *Humanae vitae*. He said that he and his wife had faithfully lived out the teaching of the Church, but it was not easy. However, he hoped that the Church would change so that it would be much easier for his children when they were married. Perhaps an analogy of the relationship of children to their parents serves as a good illustration of the attitude that Catholics hurt by an admission of error in papal teaching should strive to adopt. Young children believe their parents are always right and can do no wrong. From the teenage period onward, there is almost the opposite reaction. However, as the children become adults, they are able to recognize and appreciate the good things that the parents did for them, their great love for them, and the advice they gave them, even though recognizing that at times they were wrong. One has to see a particular error or mistake in light of the broader and total picture.

To admit that a papal teaching was wrong certainly raises real problems for the credibility of the teaching office in the Church. It will be necessary to point out how this might help the credibility of the hierarchical magisterium in the long run since it would show that the teaching office tries to listen to the Holy Spirit wherever she speaks and is willing to adopt a teaching role that is more open and transparent.

In conclusion, the problems that would inevitably occur if papal teaching on specific moral issues were to change plus the continued insistence on these teachings even in the legal sphere show that there are no indications that the hierarchical magisterium is contemplating any changes now or in the near future in its moral teachings. In fact, the stronger and the louder that it repeats these teachings, the harder it becomes to change them in the future.

Reaction of the Church Leadership to Falling Numbers

How has the Church responded to the decline in Church attendance and the growing number of people leaving the Church, especially in the first world? In the United States, it is surprising that the US bishops have made no concerted effort to confront the fact that one out of every three people who were brought up Catholic in the United States are no longer Catholic today. One would expect any business, organization, or association that has lost one-third of its members to engage in a broad, ranging, and in-depth discussion of how to deal with the problem. But very little study or action has occurred in the United States.

On the universal level of the Church, Pope Benedict was aware of the problem and attempted to deal with the precipitous decline of Catholics in the first world and especially in Europe. In 2010, Pope Benedict announced the formation of a new dicastery (department) of the Roman Curia—the Pontifical Council for Promoting the New Evangelization. Its task is to promote a renewed evangelization in the countries where the first proclamation of the faith has occurred long ago but are now "experiencing a progressive secularization of society and a sort of 'eclipse of the sense of God' that poses a great challenge to finding appropriate ways to propose anew the perennial truth of the Gospel." The secularization process "has produced a serious crisis of the meaning of the Christian faith and of belonging to the Church."[44]

One year later, in 2011, the pope addressed the participants of the plenary assembly of the new pontifical council and repeated the same basic themes on the crisis in Christian life today in these countries that have long ago been evangelized. The vision of life proposed by secularization is in contrast with the life of faith. For Benedict the primary problem was secularization, but he also pointed out that the lifestyle of believers must be genuinely credible for this evangelization to succeed.[45] In these comparatively short addresses, the pope did not refer to any problems within the Church that might be addressed other than the need for all believers to live a truly Christian life.

In preparation for the thirteenth Ordinary Synod of Bishops in 2012 on the new evangelization, the Vatican sent out ahead of time a working document (*Instrumentum laboris*) for the synodal discussions.[46] As one would expect, this seventy-four-page document develops the basic concepts already mentioned by the pope. This document puts heavy but not total emphasis on the role of secularization with its denial of the transcendent. Unfortunately, secularization has also infiltrated the habitual behavior of many Christians and Church communities. But there are also positive aspects to secularization. It is in the *saeculum* (the world) where believers and nonbelievers interact and share a common humanity. This is a natural point for faith to enter through the evangelization, which shows how Jesus purifies and transforms the human. This very encounter can help Christians grow in their own faith (no. 52–54).

Most of the document deals with external challenges facing evangelization in various sectors of life, but one paragraph (no. 69) briefly mentions the internal problems that prevent the Church from meeting the challenge of the new evangelization. In addition to the weak faith and imperfect witness of Christians, mention is made of bureaucratic Church structures, routine liturgical celebrations, and the counterwitness of Christians as illustrated in unfaithfulness in one's vocation, scandals, and little sensitivity to everyday problems of others. However, there is no mention whatsoever of problems coming from existing Church structures, policies, or teachings.

At its conclusion in October 2012, the thirteenth Ordinary Synod of Bishops on the new evangelization issued a message to the people of God. Individual Christians and the Church are called to renewal and conversion to show to all the attractive force of the Christian life. The primary obstacle remains secularization in the many parts of the world. The situation of divorced and remarried people is painful. The Church loves them and welcomes them even if they cannot receive sacramental absolution and the Eucharist.[47]

These documents indicate no concern whatsoever for those who leave the Church because of their problems with specific moral teachings or the structures of the Church. This lack of concern is quite consistent with the hierarchical Church's understanding of the problem. The major obstacle that the Church faces today is secularization, and unfortunately this secularization has even found its way into the life of the Church itself. Dissent on specific moral issues is an indication of how secularization has affected the internal life of the Church. Cardinal Ratzinger explicitly made this point in his famous interview that became the basis for his book *The Ratzinger Report*.

> Looking at North America, we see a world where riches are the measure and where values and style of life proposed by Catholicism appear more than ever as a scandal. The moral teaching of the Church is seen as a remote and extraneous body which contrasts not only with the concrete practices of life but also with the basic way of thinking. It becomes difficult, if not impossible, to present the authentic Catholic ethics as reasonable since it is so far distant from what is considered normal and obvious. Consequently, many moralists (it is above all in the field of ethics that North Americans are involved, whereas in the fields of theology and exegesis they are dependent upon Europe) believe that they are forced to choose between dissent from the society or dissent from the magisterium. Many choose this latter dissent, adapting themselves to compromises with the secular ethics that ends up by denying men and women the most profound aspect of their nature, leading them to a new slavery while claiming to free them.[48]

Secularization constitutes a significant reality in Europe today. However, secularization is less prominent in the culture of the United States.

Sociological studies have shown that in the United States many have left the Catholic Church because of the existing moral teachings, practices, and structures of the Church. Even in Europe Catholic reform groups point to the same problems. In assessing why people leave, the Catholic Church must address both secularization and some existing Church moral teachings and policies.

How should people working for change react to the present situation? We should continue to work for change and in the process try to acquire all those attitudes that help to continue our struggle even if it does not seem to be successful. The Church, like individual Christians, will never be perfect. It is a sinful Church in need of conversion. The issues discussed here are quite serious, but they are by no means the most important realities in the life of the Church and in the life of believers. Above all, the Church gathers people together in the Eucharist to celebrate and give thanks for God's gift of love through Jesus in the Holy Spirit and challenges believers to live as Jesus lived in relationship with God, neighbor, and especially the poor and needy. The Church as the people of God has a unique role to play. God through Jesus made a covenant not with individuals but with a people. I belong to the Church not because I like the music or the people or the presbyter but because God has chosen to come to humankind through this community and we are to go to God through this pilgrim community, which will never be perfect. The theology of Church well illustrates the Catholic emphasis on mediation. God comes to us and we go to God in a human community with its sins, imperfections, and warts. As individuals, we too have our sins, imperfections, and warts.

Believers recognize the Holy Spirit as the primary power and force in the Church. History shows that reform has occurred in the Church in many different forms throughout the centuries. In the middle of the twentieth century there were very few signs that a substantial reform would occur, but the Second Vatican Council was about to commence. One never knows what history has in store. Above all, Christians are people who have hope. Recently, many have asked me if there are any signs of hope for the Church today. My answer is that Christian hope exists primarily when you do not see something. We can hope for light in the midst of darkness, joy in the midst of sorrow, and life in the midst of death. Hope is not easy. Paul reminds us that we are hoping against hope (Rom 4:18). We are called to be pilgrim people in a pilgrim Church as we strive to do the truth in love and work to reform in our own lives and in the life of the Church.

The Catholic Church by definition is inclusive and big. The challenge for all of us is to maintain the unity of the Church in the midst of all our differences. The moral issues discussed here are not core aspects of Catholic faith. We are called to love and respect others even in the midst of our disagreements. The Church community will always know the tensions of trying "to speak the truth in love" (Eph 4:15). As the people of God, we are called to live in accord with the ancient axiom—*in necessariis, unitas; in dubiis, libertas; in omnibus, caritas*—in necessary things, unity; in doubtful things, freedom; in all things, charity.[49]

The issue of dissent and disagreement with regard to some papal moral teaching is not the most important issue facing moral theology. The first part of this conclusion dealt with the most significant agenda for Catholic moral theology today—the need to develop a moral theology that is truly theological in light of Vatican II. However, the issue of disagreement with some papal moral teachings raises serious problems for the Church and for moral theology and will not go away very soon.

In conclusion, I have not tried to develop a full history of moral theology. Nor have I attempted to develop a full and complete moral theology for today. I have kept to the more limited role of discussing five distinctive strands in the development of Catholic moral theology and how these affect moral theology today.

NOTES

1. Fr. Gianfranco Girotti, "A Sacrament in Crisis," *Catholic Culture*, www .catholicculture.org/culture/library/view.cfm?id = 8904&repos = 1&subrepos = 0& searchid = 1046530.

2. John Cornwell, "Where Are the Penitents?" *Tablet* (August 18, 2012): 4–5; James Dallen, "Reconciliation and the Sacrament of Penance," *Worship* 64 (1990): 386–405; and Dallen, "Church Authority and the Sacrament of Penance: The Synod of Bishops," *Worship* 58 (1984): 194–214.

3. Marcellinus Zalba, *Theologiae moralis summa*, vol. 1, *Theologia moralis fundamentalis* (Madrid: Biblioteca de autores Cristianos, 1952–58), no. 628–30, pp. 618–23.

4. Committee on Divine Worship, US Conference of Catholic Bishops, "Celebrating the Sacrament of Penance: Questions and Answers," at nccbuscc.org/liturgy/penance.shtml.

5. David Coffey, *The Sacrament of Reconciliation* (Collegeville, MN: Liturgical, 2001).

6. For a more substantial development of my approach to moral theology without the specific references to Vatican II, see Charles E. Curran, *The Catholic Moral Tradition Today: A Synthesis* (Washington, DC: Georgetown University Press, 1999).

7. Timothy E. O'Connell, *Principles for a Catholic Morality*, rev. ed. (San Francisco: Harper & Row 1990), 92–97.

8. Richard M. Gula, *Moral Discernment* (New York: Paulist, 1997).

9. Timothy M. Gallagher, *Spiritual Consolation: An Ignatian Guide for the Greater Discernment of Spirits* (New York: Crossroad, 2007); and Jules J. Toner, *Discerning God's Will: Ignatius of Loyola's Teaching on Christian Decision Making* (St. Louis: Institute of Jesuit Sources, 1996).

10. Pope John Paul II, *Veritatis splendor*, no. 4, in *The Encyclicals of John Paul II*, ed. J. Michael Miller (Huntington, IN: Our Sunday Visitor, 2001), 586.

11. Charles E. Curran and Richard A. McCormick, eds., *Dialogue about Catholic Sexual Teaching: Readings in Moral Theology No. 8* (New York: Paulist, 1993).

12. John T. Noonan Jr., *A Church That Can and Cannot Change: The Development of Catholic Moral Teaching* (Notre Dame, IN: University of Notre Dame Press, 2005); and Charles E. Curran, ed., *Change in Official Church Teachings: Readings in Moral Theology No. 13* (New York: Paulist, 2003).

13. Joseph A. Komonchak, "Ordinary Papal Magisterium and Religious Assent," in *Contraception: Authority and Dissent*, ed. Charles E. Curran, 101–26 (New York: Herder and Herder, 1969).

14. Ormond Rush, *Eyes of Faith: The Sense of the Faithful and the Church's Reception of Revelation* (Washington, DC: Catholic University of America Press, 2009); and Rush, "The Prophetic Office in the Church: Pneumatological Perspectives on the *Sensus Fidelium*-Theology-Magisterium Relationship," in *When the Magisterium Intervenes: The Magisterium and Theologians in Today's Church*, ed. Richard R. Gaillardetz, 89–112 (Collegeville, MN: Liturgical, 2012).

15. Herman Pottmeyer, *Toward a Papacy in Communion: Perspectives from Vatican Councils I and II*, trans. Matthew J. O'Connell (New York: Crossroad, 1998); John R. Quinn, *The Reform of the Papacy: Costly Call to Christian Unity* (New York: Crossroad, 1999); Ladislas Örsy, "The Papacy for an Ecumenical Age: A Response to Avery Dulles," *America* 183, no. 12 (October 21, 2000): 9–15; and Richard P. McBrien, *The Church: The Evolution of Catholicism* (New York: HarperOne, 2008), 298–314.

16. Bradford Hinze, "A Decade of Disciplining Theologians," *Horizons* 37 (2010): 92–126; and Tobias Winright, "L'Affaire Farley and the Ongoing Chill Factor in Contemporary Moral Theology," *Catholic Moral Theology*, June 4, 2012, at http://catholicmoraltheology.com/laffaire-farley-and-the-ongoing-chill-factor-in-contemporary-moral-theology/.

17. Research Team, *Catholics in America*, table 17, "Trends in Sources of Moral Authority," at http://ncronline.org/news/catholics-america/right-and-wrong-who-has-final-say; nstable17.

18. Joachim Salaverri, *De Ecclesia Christi*, in *Sacrae theologiae summa*, vol. 1 (Madrid: Biblioteca de autores Cristianos, 1955), 964–87.

19. For the best one-volume study of teaching authority, see Richard R. Gaillardetz, *Teaching with Authority: A Theology of the Magisterium in the Church* (Collegeville, MN: Liturgical, 1997); see also McBrien, *Church*, 285–321. For a very insightful

recent article, see Francis A. Sullivan, "Developments in Teaching Authority since Vatican II," *Theological Studies* 73 (2012): 570–89. The following paragraphs depend heavily on these sources.

20. See, for example, International Movement We Are the Church (at www .imwac.net/413/) and Call to Action (at www.cta-usa.org/).

21. "Pfarrer-Initiative: Appeal to Disobedience," at www.pfarrer-initiative.at/ unge_en.pdf.

22. Association of Catholic Priests at www.associationofcatholicpriests.ie/.

23. McBrien, *Church*, 181.

24. Eugenio Corecco, "Aspects of the Reception of Vatican II in the Code of Canon Law," in *The Reception of Vatican II*, ed. Giuseppe Alberigo, Jean-Pierre Jossua, and Joseph A. Komonchak, 249–96 (Washington, DC: Catholic University of America Press, 1987).

25. Ladislas Örsy, *Receiving the Council: Theological and Canonical Insights and Debates* (Collegeville, MN: Liturgical, 2009).

26. John P. Beal, James A. Coriden, and Thomas J. Green, eds., *New Commentary on the Code of Canon Law* (New York: Paulist, 2000), canons 342–48, pp. 454–63.

27. Thomas J. Reese, ed., *Episcopal Conferences: Historical, Canonical, and Theological Studies* (Washington, DC: Georgetown University Press, 1989).

28. Editorial, "Future Doubtful for Bishops' Conferences," *America* 179, no. 3 (August 15, 1998): 3.

29. William W. Bassett, ed., *The Choosing of Bishops: Historical and Theological Studies* (Hartford, CT: Canon Law Society of America, 1971).

30. Richard P. McBrien, "More on the Leadership Crisis," *National Catholic Reporter*, June 1, 2009, http://ncronline.org/blogs/essays-theology/more-leadership-crisis .

31. The English translation of this document is found in Karl Rahner, "The Dispute concerning the Church's Teaching Office," in Rahner, *Theological Investigations*, vol. 14 (London: Darton, Longman, and Todd, 1976), 85–88.

32. US Catholic Bishops, *Human Life in Our Day* (Washington, DC: United States Catholic Conference, 1968), 18.

33. *New Commentary on Code of Canon Law*, 184.

34. Örsy, *Receiving the Council*, 35–45.

35. Joerg Dreweke, "Contraceptive Use Is the Norm among Religious Women," *Guttmacher Institute*, April 13, 2011, www.guttmacher.org/media/nr/2011/04/13/ index.html.

36. "Summary of Key Findings of the US Religious Landscape Survey," *Pew Forum on Religion & Public Life*, http://religions.pewforum.org/reports/.

37. Andrew M. Greeley, William C. McCready, and Kathleen McCourt, *Catholic Schools in a Declining Church* (Kansas City, MO: Sheed & Ward, 1976), 152–53.

38. William J. Byron and Charles Zech, "Why They Left," *America* 206, no. 14 (April 30, 2012): 17–23.

39. "Faith in Flux: Changes in Religious Affiliation in the US," April 2009, Pew Forum on Religion & Public Life, www.pewforum.org/newassets/images/reports/ flux/fullreport.pdf.

40. For arguments against the requirement of celibacy for all priests, see Donald B. Cozzens, *Freeing Celibacy* (Collegeville, MN: Liturgical, 2006); and Michael H. Crosby, *Rethinking Celibacy: Reclaiming the Church* (Eugene, OR: Wipf and Stock), 2003.

41. Sunshine Lichauco de Leon, "Philippines Birth Control Legislation Opposed by Church," *Guardian*, June 8, 2011, at www.guardian.co.uk/world/2011/jun/08/phil ippines-birth-control-legislation-church.

42. Editorial, "Policy, not Liberty," *America* 206, no. 7 (March 5, 2012): 5. The articles in this issue of *America* discuss religious liberty in the dispute over providing contraceptive health care insurance for employees in Catholic institutions such as hospitals and colleges.

43. David Hollenbach and Thomas A. Shannon, "A Balancing Act: Catholic Teaching on the Church's Rights—and the Rights of All," *America* 206, no. 7 (March 5, 2012): 23–26. For my approach, see Charles E. Curran, *The Social Mission of the US Catholic Church: A Theological Perspective* (Washington, DC: Georgetown University Press, 2011), 153–79.

44. Pope Benedict XVI, "Homily on the Solemnity of the Holy Apostles Peter and Paul," June 28, 2010, *Vatican*, www.vatican.va/holy_father/benedict_xvi/homi lies/2010/documents/hf_ben-xvi_hom_20100629_pallio_en.html.

45. Pope Benedict XVI, "Address to Participants in the Plenary of the Pontifical Council for Promoting the New Evangelization," May 30, 2011, *Vatican*, www.vati can.va/holy_father/benedict_xvi/speeches/2011/may/documents/hf_ben-xvi_spe_ 20110530_nuova-evangelizzazione_en.html.

46. "*Instrumentum laboris* for XIII Assembly of the Synod of Bishops," at www .vatican.va/roman_curia/synod/documents/rc_synod_doc_2 0120619_instrumentum-xiii_en.html. The pertinent paragraph numbers will be mentioned in the text.

47. "Message of the Synod of Bishops to the People of God," *Tablet*, www.the tablet.co.uk/page/evangelisation-synod.

48. Vittorio Messori, "Colloquio con Cardinale Josef Ratzinger," in *Jesus* (November 1984): 77. The translation is mine. For the somewhat altered version that appeared later in book form, see Josef Cardinal Ratzinger with Vittorio Messori, *The Ratzinger Report: An Exclusive Interview on the State of the Church* (San Francisco: Igna-tius, 1985), 86–87.

49. This axiom, often attributed to Augustine, is from Rupert Meldenius, a seventeenth-century Lutheran theologian. See Philip Schaff, *History of the Christian Church*, 2nd ed. (New York: Charles Scribner's Sons, 1911), 6:650–53.

INDEX